D0119388

6

EROS

EROS

An Anthology of Friendship

EDITED BY

ALISTAIR SUTHERLAND AND PATRICK ANDERSON

ANTHONY BLOND

First published 1961

Anthony Blond Ltd,
56 Doughty Street, London, W.C.1

This book has been set in Bembo type
face. It has been printed in Great Britain on
Antique Wove paper by Taylor Garnett
Evans & Co. Ltd, Watford, Herts, and
bound by them

ACKNOWLEDGEMENTS

Mr Patrick Anderson, Mr Alistair Sutherland and Anthony Blond Ltd wish to express their thanks to the following:

Macmillan & Co. Ltd, The Macmillan Company of Canada Ltd, St. Martin's Press Inc, N.Y. Homer, *The Iliad*, Bks 8, 9 and 11, tr. Lang, Leaf and Myers. J. M. Dent & Sons Ltd. *Greek Poetry for Everyman*, ed. and tr. F. L. Lucas. Plato, *Phaedrus*, tr. J. Wright. The Loeb Classical Library and Harvard University Press. Pindar, *Odes*, tr. Sir J. Sandys, Athenaeus, *Deipnosophists*, tr. C. B. Gulick, Nonnos, *Dionysiaca*, tr. W. H. D. Rouse, Strabo, *Geography*, tr. H. I. Jones, Theokritos, *Idyll XXIII*, tr. J. M. Edmonds, Antipater of Sidon, *On Anacreon*, tr. W. R. Paton, Philostratus, *Letters*, tr. Benner and Fobes, Cicero, *De Amicitia*, tr. W. A. Falconer, Virgil, *Eclogues II*, tr. H. Rushton Fairclough, Horace, *Odes* Bks II & IV, tr. J. Marshall, Tibullus, Bk I, 4, tr. J. P. Postgate. Mr James Michie for his translation of Horace's Ode *To Venus* (Bk II). The University of Chicago Press. Pindar, *The Sixth Pythian Ode*, tr. R. Lattimore. Mr Simon Raven for his translations from *The Greek Anthology*. Mr Richard Aldington, Chatto & Windus. *Medallions*, by R. Aldington. Chatto & Windus Ltd *Birds and Beasts of the Greek Anthology*, Strato XII, 221, tr. N. Douglas, Proust, *Remembrance of Things Past*, tr. K. Scott Moncrieff, *By Way of Sainte-Beuve*, tr. S. T. Warner, J. R. Ackerley, *Hindoo Holiday*. Thames & Hudson Ltd. Catullus, *Poems*, tr. H. Gregory. Faber & Faber Ltd, Harcourt Brace & World Inc., N.Y. Aristophanes, *Thesmophoriazusae*, tr. D. Fitts. Mr George Barker, *Selected Poems*, Mr Stephen Spender, *Collected Poems*, W. H. Auden, *Another Time*. New Directions N.Y., Mr D. Fitts, *From the Greek Anthology*, Rimbaud, *The Infernal Bridegroom*, tr. L. Varèse, C. Isherwood, *The Berlin Stories*. Jonathan Cape Ltd. *The Greek Anthology*, tr. R. A. Furness, W. Plomer, *Visiting The Caves*. The Society of Authors and Jonathan Cape. A. E. Housman, *Collected Poems*. The executors of the late T. E. Lawrence, Mr A. W. Lawrence, Jonathan Cape. T. E. Lawrence, *The Seven Pillars of Wisdom*. Laurence Pollinger Ltd, Jonathan Cape. Gontran de Poncins, *Kabloona*. Ernest Benn Ltd. *Greek Anthology*, tr. Sir S. Leslie. Curtis Brown Ltd, J. M. Dent & Sons Ltd. Plato, *Symposium*, tr. M. Joyce. George Allen & Unwin Ltd, Penguin Books Ltd. Aristotle, *Ethics*, tr. J. A. K. Thomson. George Allen & Unwin. E. Carpenter,

Towards Democracy. Roturman S.A., Penguin Books. Suetonius, *The Twelve Caesars*, tr. Robert Graves. The Cresset Press. Kai Ka'us Ibn Iskandar, *Mirror for Princes*, tr. R. Levy. John Murray Ltd. Hafiz of Shiraz, *Poems*, tr. Avery and Heath-Stubbs, F. Cauldwell, *The Firewalkers*. Cambridge University Press. *The Pennants*, tr. A. J. Arberry. Constable&Co. Ltd, *Mediaeval Latin Lyrics*, tr. H. Waddell. Mr D. S. Bailey, Longmans Green & Co. Ltd, *Homosexuality and the Western Christian Tradition*. Elek Books Ltd. Petronius, *Satyricon*, Paulinus of Nola *To Ausionius*, tr. J. Lindsay. Rupert Hart-Davis Ltd. B. Alexander, *Life at Fonthill*. Miss Enid Starkie, *Arthur Rimbaud*. Verlaine, *Forty Poems*, tr. R. Gant and C. Apcher (Falcon Press). Mr. Brian Hill, Rupert Hart-Davis. Verlaine, *The Sky Above the Roof*, tr. B. Hill, *No. 8 Great College Street Camden Town*, B. Hill. The Fortune Press Ltd. F. T. Prince, *Poems*, J. K. Huysmans, *Against the Grain*. Mr John Lehmann, *The Age of the Dragon*. Martin Secker & Warburg Ltd, Farrar Straus & Cudahy Inc., N.Y. Gide, *Corydon*, tr. P. B. Secker & Warburg, Alfred A. Knopf Inc., N.Y. Gide, *Journal*, tr. J. O'Brien. Secker & Warburg. R. Peyrefitte, *Special Friendships*, tr. E. Hyams, Gide, *If it Die* tr. for this anthology by P. Anderson. Mrs Sherwood Anderson, The Viking Press Inc., N.Y. Sherwood Anderson, *Hands*. The Liveright Publishing Corp., N.Y. Hart Crane, *Collected Poems*. Routledge & Kegan Paul Ltd. E. E. Bradford, *Poems*. Pantheon Books Inc., N.Y. Stefan George, *Poems*, tr. C. N. Valhope and E. Morwitz. Bowes & Bowes Ltd. E. K. Bennett, *Stefan George*. Verlag Helmut Küpper, Düsseldorf. Stefan George, *Mein Kind Kam Heim*. Macmillan & Co. Ltd, St Martin's Press Inc, Sir C. M. Bowra, *Heritage and Symbolism*. The Hogarth Press Ltd, Constantine Cavafy, *Poems*, tr. J. Mavrogordato. The executors of the late Lord Alfred Douglas, Rich & Cowan (The Hutchinson Publishing Group), Lord A. Douglas, *Lyrics*, and *Collected Poems*. Cassell & Co. Ltd, F. Rolfe, *The Desire and Pursuit of the Whole*. William Heinemann Ltd, the Estate of the late Mrs Frieda Lawrence, Laurence Pollinger Ltd. D. H. Lawrence, *The White Peacock*, and *Women in Love*. Mr W. S. Gilbert, Forrest Reid, *Apostate*, *Uncle Stephen*, *Private Road*. The executors of the late Denton Welch, David Higham Associates Ltd., Hamish Hamilton Ltd. D. Welch, *Journal*. Curtis Brown Ltd, William Collins Sons Ltd. *Public School Life*, by Alec Waugh. Peter Davies Ltd. G. F. Green, *In the Making*.

6

INTRODUCTION

A word of preliminary explanation: the idea of this book originated with the young scholar and writer whose name appears first on the title page. It was he who packed a tin trunk full of files and loose papers, together with check-lists of further references, a schedule for the arrangement of the material and more than one draft essay to explain his sense of its purpose and philosophy; even the title had been chosen, and the book advertised for publication, before my aid was sought. Indeed when I used to meet my future co-editor (if that appelation is quite fair to him) here and there about London, it was by no means always to hear of his long-projected work. He spoke shyly of it, if at all, with a degree of hesitation at its potential range and bulk; I had the impression of a remote and secret country over which his studies hovered, at once sensitive and scrupulous, often impeded by all sorts of difficult circumstance but, in any case, not eager to rush to the vulgarity of a quick conclusion. Once he hinted that I might care to collaborate, at a time when I didn't feel capable of doing so. And then later and rather quickly, his own circumstances worsening and the delivery of the manuscript being overdue, it became apparent that if somebody didn't put the thing into shape – define the hinterland, people the map, bluster about with bull-dozers and cement – the whole exploration would go by the board.

It was flattering to my scholarship to think that I could be at all efficient about this, but not, of course, pleasant to step into another man's shoes, inevitably alter his direction (for his general analytical plan had to be abandoned) and scurry where he had loitered and paused to think. Yet it was rewarding to plunge deep into libraries again, checking his references and adding now and then a discovery of my own; rewarding simply to know more –

about anything, I'd almost say – but in this case about a subject, not easily definable, which teased adolescence and now bore upon education and much else; and stimulating to find less of the smell of sulphur than one had imagined, less of the austere sweat-sour locker-room, and more that was lyrical and gay, more of jest and gesture – Alkibiades in search of Agathon, with the wreath slipping over his eyes, or the roses that must wear their even brighter recipient, or Ganymede being fanned by a feather from Hermes' wing – until one came to some of the noblest expressions of the greatest minds.

The subject, as I grew to see it, was any friendship between men strong enough to deserve one of the more serious senses of the world 'love'. ('. . . Sweet to me above all sweetness of this life' was St Augustine's cry in his old unreconstructed days, as he thought of the friend 'whom so passionately I had loved'. And St Anselm was to speak as strongly from his wealth of Christian fellowship: 'whatever I know about thee is sweet and joyous to my spirit . . . thy spirit and mine can never bear to be absent from each other, but unceasingly are intertwined'.) Thus amongst the Greeks Eros would include the heroic comradeship of Achilles and Patroklos, and also the noble example and manly training offered by Herakles to his page, Hylas, rough mythical prototypes of the educational relationship of *Inspirer* and *Listener*, and not dissimilar to that dependence of squire upon liege-lord we find in our own Old English poem, *The Wanderer:*

Þinceð him on mōde	Þœt hē his mondryhten
clyppe and cysse,	and on cneo lecge
honda and hēafod,	swā hē hwīlum ær
in geārdagum	giefstōles brēac . . .[1]

Plato's idealizing and sublimating attitude to manners he knew to be sensuous and often sensual would be an important part of it, propounding much to be found later in Persian *Sufism*, in aspects

---

[1] '. . . it seems to him in his mind that he clasps and kisses his lord and lays hands and head on his knee, as when erstwhile in past days he was near the gift-throne.'

of the Christian tradition and in the theory of the Renaissance and it would inevitably extend to extremes, to the dalliance of the Greek Anthology and the gross, if hilarious, amours of Rome.

This limiting extremism is far from most people's taste. Against the background of our society, whether conceived in terms of Christian ethics or of the 'natural' self-realization implicit in a scientific humanism, to accept it for oneself is pretty obviously to invite moral and psychological disaster. In the frank world of contemporary letters one hears enough in all conscience of restlessness, unhappy promiscuity, disillusion, guilt, cult attitudinizing, and the decay of feelings into sentimentality and self-pity, together with the alcoholism and even suicide so often brought in their train. I am enough of a Freudian to believe that strongly and narrowly erotic friendships are normal at stages of growing up but that there comes a time to put away childish things (which may be easier to do if one has had one's fill of them). A sense of history certainly militates against assuming that the Greek ideal – or, for that matter, the Greek licence – can be appealed to as condoning much that is prevalent today. Effeminacy was abhorrent to the Greeks and the family was of course essential to a vigorous *polis*. It is however an over-simplification to imagine that the placing of a supreme value upon the affinity of friends most often arose when the status of women was held to be inferior; this may have been true of Sparta and Athens but does not apply to some of the Greek communities in the East or in Southern Italy; it is certainly untrue of the Provence of the Troubadours, Medicean Florence or Elizabethan England. Aristocratic and militaristic societies often found the love of women distracting and enervating, beside which sexual infatuation was regarded as too unstable to provide a central value – it was, in fact, a madness. Thus Aristophanes argues in the *Symposium*: 'It is not immodesty that leads them to such pleasures, but daring, fortitude and masculinity . . . in after years they are the only men who show any real manliness in public life.' This sense of a high thinking and responsible élite extends down to the

Germany of Stefan George. There is an echo of it in the words of a twelfth-century Moor of Lisbon:

> Let me drink with lads of breed,
> Noble all of birth and deed.

Before the discovery of romantic love in marriage it was easy to think like Montaigne. This exceedingly clear-headed Frenchman put on record that he would have liked to have been friends with his wife, if this had been possible: to women men's feelings were 'a rash and wavering fire' which, at their strongest, became 'an ague' and 'mad'; such corporeal desires were quickly subject to satiety and could form no part of a friendship which was, by nature, spiritual; 'love' was thus inferior to friendship. Michelangelo makes the same point in one of his sonnets.

> The love of that whereof I speak ascends:
> Woman is different far; the love of her
> But ill befits a heart manly and wise.
> The one love soars, the other earthward tends;
> The soul lights this, while that the senses stir;
> And still lust's arrow at base quarry flies.

Nevertheless one could as little deny a fuller sense of Eros to Montaigne's relationship with de la Boëtie as to find Plato's idealism in the *Phaedrus* unpassionate, when a 'god-like face or form' echoes the heavenly vision and induces 'a shuddering chill' soon followed by 'a sweating and glow of unwonted heat' – or to accuse Michelangelo's or Shakespeare's sonnets of lack of feeling, or misunderstand the 'mystical union' of Sir Thomas Browne, Father Hopkins's 'To the Father through the features of men's faces' and the breezy democracy of Walt Whitman. This needs to be said because Eros is by no means generally 'erotic' and has intensities which may or may not involve sensuousness quite apart from carnality.

Nowadays we are more prepared to admit that there can be a graduated spectrum in these things, and that the Unconscious may have reasons and powers of its own which the individual releases in forms adjusted to his sense of reality, rejoicing in the richness of the impulse to live and praise and create but re-interpreting the hidden motive. A key figure here is Lawrence. Lawrence was a pioneer in the sexual revolution, a man who devoted a lifetime to the exploration of what really went on between men and women, but from *The White Peacock* to *The Plumed Serpent* he was also interested in 'mateship', the relationship between men: ' . . . we looked at each other with eyes of still laughter, and our love was perfect for a moment, more perfect than any love I have known since, either for man or woman'. That is from the early novel but it is echoed in the Gerald-Birkin scenes of *Women In Love*: 'I've gone after women – and been keen enough over some of them. But I've never felt *love*. I don't believe I've ever felt as much *love* for a woman, as I have for you . . .' Lawrence of course took life very seriously and was more than a bit of a puritan – his supporters in the recent Lady Chatterley case were no less humourless – and the male ritual of the Mexican novel may strike readers as nearing absurdity; the general truth of what he said, however, is not endangered by the dark and visceral nature of his treatment and must have been a commonplace of simple unanalytical people throughout history. Eros, after all, has woken the response of delight and praise, of the desire for possession whether materially or aesthetically, and the sense of consciousness heightened and exulting in its unity with the whole fabric of being, in relation to landscape, objects of nature, animals, children and their reflected presences in art. In our own period of a science and technology run wild, when the dominating images are of metal, plastic, smoke and fire, can we have enough of generalized Eros? I am reminded of the Theokritan poem: ' . . . and on the water floated the voice of a child saying "Rejoice ye that love, for he that did hate is slain; and love ye that hate, for the God knoweth how to judge".' A succeeding culture echoed this: *Cras amet qui numquam amavit quique amavit cras amet.*

To those who deny the shifting spectrum of human feelings, and the mystery of their source, it may seem heresy to place Tennyson's affection for Hallam alongside that of Wilde for Bosie or Proust's for his chauffeur: can Giton and Billy Budd,

'Posh' and Gide's Arab, Bathyllos and David Blaise exist in one
book? The question here may well be the nature of Eros – and,
as I have already explained, I have left this as I found it, imprecise:
veiled, if you will, in the radiance befitting a god[1]. I do not think
it is the job of an anthologist to be too firm about his categories,
at least when the collection is something of a pioneer. The grave
reader may object here and there to a passage which he feels quite
irrelevant; he may be surprised and shocked to find ardour in
unexpected places – in Sir Thomas Browne, for instance, or Gray
or Byron or Melville; he may turn back to his Aristotle or Cicero,
to common-sense and an equable tone, disturbed a little that even
the famous Abbot of Bec speaks of 'one soul in two bodies' which
echoes Peter Abelard on David and Jonathan. But although
Aristotle is schematic and measured, and Cicero charming and
cool, the god's wings flash behind the lines: 'It is only between
those who are good, and resemble one another in their goodness,
that friendship is perfect,' the voice from the Lyceum intones but
not without a reference shortly afterwards to physical beauty, and
beauty's waning, and the chance of a friendship lasting because
the two have learned to love each other's characters. And Cicero,
who may seem to some to go on and on, stands firmly for the ideal
friendship, the 'pure and faultless kind' whose entire profit, he
says, 'is in the love itself'. No wonder that Francis Bacon, thinking
of the classical past (and himself full of common-sensical points),
remarks 'they were princes that had wives, sons, nephews, and yet
all those could not supply the comfort of friendship'.

The net is widely cast, then, and its mesh is also irregular and
over-big. Experts will doubtless regret the absence of the literatures
of Russia, China and Japan and much else that might have gone
towards the making of a fuller book. What is here is mostly
western stuff, European and North American, with some influx
from the Moors and Persians: the expected passages, I imagine,
but with here and there a small surprise. Much is translation.

[1] Robert Graves says tartly in his *Greek Myths* (Penguin): 'Eros was never
considered a sufficiently responsible god to figure among the ruling Olympian
family of Twelve.'

Although the theme has been paramount – a theme for the most part expressed by writers of importance – I hope the passages read attractively on their own. A loose connective tissue has been provided. One imagines that people concerned professionally with education and the helping of youth may find the subject-matter of particular interest, for it is a youthful world that is presented; I hope that such readers will anyway be incapable of the brusque dismissal made by the favourite schoolmaster to whom I showed the copy of Petronius my father had given me at the age of fifteen or sixteen, 'A very wicked man!' thus blocking adolescent curiosity and creative drive. But to most *Eros* is likely to be, as I am sure my co-editor would wish, not a specialized garden to browse in or avoid, but one of the roads through the familiar but ever surprising public park of humanity.

★   ★   ★

Patrick Anderson

I

The
Great Originals

Generations of readers must have first learned the poetry of friendship from the Book of Samuel. Coming to the story as children, they may well have found it the ideal reflection of some affinity or twin-ship of their own in 'le paradis des amours enfantins'.

DAVID'S LAMENT

And David lamented with this lamentation over Saul and over Jonathan his son:

The beauty of Israel is slain upon thy high places: how are the mighty fallen!

Tell it not in Gath, publish it not in the streets of Askelon; lest the daughters of the Philistines rejoice, lest the daughters of the uncircumcised triumph.

Ye mountains of Gilboa, let there be no dew, neither let there be rain, upon you, nor fields of offerings: for there the shield of the mighty is vilely cast away, the shield of Saul, as though he had not been anointed with oil.

From the blood of the slain, from the fat of the mighty, the bow of Jonathan turned not back, and the sword of Saul returned not empty.

Saul and Jonathan were lovely and pleasant in their lives, and in their death they were not divided: they were swifter than eagles, they were stronger than lions.

Ye daughters of Israel, weep over Saul, who clothed you in scarlet, with other delights, who put on ornaments of gold upon your apparel.

How are the mighty fallen in the midst of the battle! O Jonathan, thou wast slain in thine high places.

I am distressed for thee, my brother Jonathan: very pleasant hast thou been unto me: thy love to me was wonderful, passing the love of women.

How are the mighty fallen, and the weapons of war perished!

(2 Samuel i, 17–27)

★　★　★

ACHILLES AND PATROKLOS

These two friends represented in Homeric legend, as the tyrant-slayers, Harmodios and Aristogeiton, were to do in Athenian history, the archetype of noble comradeship. In the first two extracts from the *Iliad* which follow, we see the friends' mutual establishment, withdrawn from the rest of the Greek army opposing Troy, at the moment when an embassy is attempting to win them back. The atmosphere is one of feudal simplicity and barbaric splendour: of fire, meat, wine, magnificently chased goblets and submissive captive girls. But the third passage concerns the grief of Achilles when he learns that his friend, to whom he has lent his armour, has been finally struck down fighting in his stead.

THEN ACHILLES fleet of foot greeted them and said: 'Welcome; verily ye are friends that are come – sore indeed is the need – even ye that are dearest of the Achaians to me even in my wrath.'

So spake noble Achilles and led them forward, and made them sit on settles and carpets of purple; and anon he spake to Patroklos being near: 'Bring forth a greater bowl, thou son of Menoitios; mingle stronger drink, and prepare each man a cup, for dearest of men are these that are under my roof.'

So said he, and Patroklos hearkened to his dear comrade. He cast down a great fleshing-block in the fire-light, and laid thereon a sheep's back and a fat goat's, and a great hog's chine rich with fat. And Automedon held them for him, while Achilles carved. Then he sliced well the meat and pierced it through with spits, and Menoitios' son, that godlike hero, made the fire burn high. Then when the fire was burned down and the flame waned, he scattered the embers and laid the spits thereover, resting them on the spit-racks, when he had sprinkled them with holy salt. Then when he had roasted the meat and apportioned it in the platters, Patroklos took bread and dealt it forth on the table in fair baskets, and Achilles dealt the meat. And he sate him over against godlike Odysseus by the other wall, and bade his comrade Patroklos do sacrifice to the gods; so he cast the first-fruits into the fire. Then put they forth their hands to the good cheer lying before them. And when they had put from them the desire of meat and drink, Aias nodded to Phoinix.

(Iliad, Book 9, tr. Lang, Leaf and Myers)

At the conclusion of speeches by Odysseus, the aged Phoinix and Aias, Achilles replies:

'...thou seemest to speak all this almost after mine own mind; but my heart swellest with wrath as oft as I bethink me of those things, how Atreides entreated me arrogantly among the Argives, as though I were some worthless sojourner. But go ye and declare my message; I will not take thought of bloody war until that wise Priam's son, noble Hector, come to the Myrmidons' huts and ships, slaying the Argives, and smirch the ships with fire. But about mine hut and black ship I ween that Hector, though he be very eager for battle, shall be refrained.'

So said he, and they took each man a two-handled cup, and made libation and went back along the line of ships; and Odysseus led the way. And Patroklos bade his fellows and handmaidens spread with all speed a thick couch for Phoinix; and they obeyed and spread a couch as he ordained, fleeces and rugs and fine flock of linen. Then the old man laid him down and tarried for bright Dawn. And Achilles slept in the corner of the morticed hut, and by his side lay a woman that he brought from Lesbos, even Phorbas' daughter fair-cheeked Diomede. And on the other side Patroklos lay, and by his side likewise fair-girdled Iphis, whom noble Achilles gave him at the taking of steep Skyros, the city of Enyous.

(Ibid.)

THE GRIEF OF ACHILLES

While thus he held debate in his heart and soul, there drew nigh unto him noble Nestor's son, shedding hot tears, and spake his grievous tidings: 'Ay me, wise Peleus' son, very bitter tidings must thou hear, such as I would had never been. Fallen is Patroklos, and they are fighting around his body, naked, for his armour is held by Hector of the glancing helm.'

Thus spake he, and a black cloud of grief enwrapped Achilles, and with both hands he took dark dust and poured it over his head and defiled his comely face, and on his fragrant doublet black ashes fell. And himself in the dust lay mighty and mightily fallen, and with his own hands tore and marred his hair. And the handmaidens, whom Achilles and Patroklos took captive, cried aloud in the grief of their hearts, and ran forth around valiant Achilles, and all beat on their breasts with their hands, and the knees of each of them were unstrung. And Antilochos on the other side wailed and shed tears, holding Achilles' hands while he groaned in his noble heart, for he feared lest he should cleave his throat with the sword. Then terribly moaned Achilles; and his lady mother heard him as she sate in the depths of the sea beside her ancient sire. And thereon she uttered a cry, and the goddesses flocked around her, all the daughters of Nereus that were in the deep of the sea . . . With these the bright cave was filled, and they all beat together on their breasts, and Thetis led the lament: 'Listen, sister Nereids, that ye all hear and know well what sorrows are in my heart. Ay me unhappy, ay me that bare to my sorrow the first of men! For after I had born a son noble and strong, the chief of heroes, and he shot up like a young branch, then when I had reared him as a plant in a very fruitful field I sent him in beaked ships to Ilios to fight against the men of Troy; but never again shall I welcome him back to his home, to the house of Peleus. And while he yet liveth in my sight and beholdeth the light of the sun, he sorroweth, neither can I help him any whit though I go unto him. But I will go, that I may look upon my dear child, and learn what sorrow hath come to him though he abide aloof from the war.'

[After her approach . . .] Then groaning heavily spake unto her Achilles fleet of foot: 'My mother, that prayer truly hath the Olympian accomplished for me. But what delight have I therein, since my dear comrade is dead, Patroklos, whom I honoured above all my comrades as it were my very self? Him have I lost, and Hector that slew him hath stripped from him the armour great and fair, a wonder to behold, that the gods gave to Peleus a splendid gift, on the day when they laid thee in the bed of a mortal man. Would thou hadst abode among the deathless daughters of the sea, and Peleus had wedded a mortal bride! But now, that thou mayest have sorrow a thousandfold in thy heart for a dead son, never shalt thou welcome him back home, since my soul biddeth me also live no longer nor abide among men, if Hector be not first smitten by my spear and yield his life, and pay for his slaughter of Patroklos, Menoitios' son.'

Then answered unto him Thetis shedding tears: 'Shortlived, I ween, must thou be then, my child, by what thou sayest, for straightway after Hector is death appointed unto thee.' Then mightily moved spake unto her Achilles fleet of foot: 'Straightway may I die, since I might not succour my comrade at his slaying. He hath fallen afar from his country and lacked my help in his sore need. Now therefore, since I go not back to my dear native land, neither have at all been succour to Patroklos nor to all my other comrades that have been slain by noble Hector, but I sit beside my ship a profitless burden of the earth, I that in war am such an one as is none else of the mail-clad Achaians, though in council are others better – may strife perish utterly among gods and men, and wrath that stirreth even a wise man to be vexed, wrath that far sweeter than trickling honey waxeth like smoke in the breasts of men, even as I was wroth even now against Agamemnon king of men. But bygones will we let be, for all our pain, curbing the heart in our breasts under necessity. Now go I forth, that I may light on the destroyer of him I loved, on Hector: then will I accept my death whensoever Zeus willeth to accomplish it and the other immortal gods.'

(Ibid, Book 18)

* * *

Alexander Pope's rendering of the passion of Achilles and of his first speech to his mother is as follows:

> A sudden horror shot through all the chief,
> And wrapp'd his senses in the cloud of grief;
> Cast on the ground, with furious hands he spread
> The scorching ashes o'er his graceful head;

His purple garments, and his golden hairs,
Those he deforms with dust, and these he tears;
On the hard soil his groaning breast he threw,
And roll'd and grovell'd, as to earth he grew.
The virgin captives, with disorder'd charms,
(Won by his own, or by Patroclus' arms,)
Rush'd from their tents with cries; and gathering round,
Beat their white breasts, and fainted on the ground:
While Nestor's son sustains a manlier part,
And mourns the warrior with a warrior's heart;
Hangs on his arms, amidst his frantic woe,
And oft prevents the meditated blow.

. . . . .

He, deeply groaning – 'To this cureless grief,
Not even the Thunderer's favour brings relief.
Patroclus – Ah! – say, goddess, can I boast
A pleasure now? revenge itself is lost;
Patroclus, loved of all my martial train,
Beyond mankind, beyond myself, is slain!
Lost are those arms the gods themselves bestow'd
On Peleus; Hector bears the glorious load.
Cursed by that day, when all the powers above
Thy charms submitted to a mortal love:
O hadst thou still, a sister of the main,
Pursued the pleasures of the watery reign:
And happier Peleus, less ambitious, led
A mortal beauty to his equal bed!
Ere the sad fruit of thy unhappy womb
Had caused such sorrows past, and woes to come.
For soon, alas! that wretched offspring slain,
New woes, new sorrows, shall create again.
'Tis not in fate the alternate now to give;
Patroclus dead, Achilles hates to live.
Let me revenge it on proud Hector's heart,
Let his last spirit smoke upon my dart;
On these conditions will I breathe: till then,
I blush to walk among the race of men.'

★   ★   ★

HERAKLES AND HYLAS

This friendship is archetypal, too, but is of the kind – so important
to the Greeks – which involves the love of an older man for a
younger, whom he seeks to train in virtue and manliness. Both
hero and lad were members of Jason's Argonauts who set sail in
search of the Golden Fleece.

Not, Nicias, as we dreamed once, for us alone was Love
Begotten – whoever his parent, among the powers above;
How lovely is life's loveliness, not first are we
To feel, whose mould is mortal, who no to-morrow see.
Long since that iron heart of the son of Amphitryon,
That braved the lion of the mountain, by the love of a lad was won –
By the young beauty of Hylas and the grace of his tossing hair.
He taught the boy those lessons, with a loving father's care,
That had made himself a hero, sung in the mouths of men;
Never an hour could part them – not the high noon, nor when
The white-maned steeds of Morning charged up the Heaven's steep,
Nor when the piping chickens were looking up to sleep
Where aloft on the sooty rafter their mother flapped her wings –
That the boy might grow to a manhood perfect in all things,
A yokefellow true and trusted, after the hero's heart.
  Then fell the days when Jason made ready to depart
In quest of the Golden Fleece; and now on every hand
Each warrior of valour, the flower of every land,
Flocked to the muster – among them, to rich Iolcus' shore,
That man of many labours, whom once Alcmena bore,
The heroine of Mideia; and in his company
Came Hylas, where fair-benched Argo lay beached beside the sea –
Argo, that like an eagle, soaring the watery waste,
Passed untouched through the Clashing Rocks, and onward raced
Towards the deep mouth of Phāsis – while rooted crags grew *they*.
But, at the Pleiads' rising, when Spring has gone her way,
And on the upland borders the young lambs flock to feed,
Then to the quest before them the heroes gave their heed;
The thwarts of hollow Argo they manned, and spreading sail
On the third day reached the Hellespont, before the south-west gale;
And moored her within Propontis, where the Kiānians' kine

Drive broad through the loam their furrow, till bright their plough-
    shares shine,
Then springing ashore her rowers made ready at evenfall,
Pair by pair, their supper – but a common couch for all;
For many bladed rushes, much galingale grew deep
There in the mead; and they mowed them, to make soft beds to sleep.
    But now for water Hylas, the golden-haired, was gone,
To cook the supper of Heracles and dauntless Telamon
(For ever they ate as comrades beside the selfsame board).
Brazen pitcher in hand, quickly he came where poured
A spring from a lowly hollow – thick grew the rushes there
Thick the dark celandine and pale-green maidenhair,
And parsley lush, and reed-grass that loves the marsh's cool.
And *there* lay the Nymphs' own dancing-place, within the midmost
    pool,
Those sleepless Nymphs, from whose dread power the peasant flies –
Euneica; Malis; Nycheia, with springtime in her eyes.
So, as the boy bent o'er the brink, in haste to dip
The wide mouth of his pitcher, all at once their grip
Closed on his wrist – for passion had thrilled their hearts to see
The Argive lad – and his body went shooting suddenly
Down the dark depths; as when, from Heaven, a star ablaze
Shoots on a sudden seaward, and sailor to sailor says:
'Quick lads, and lighten sail aloft – 'tis coming on to blow!'
The Nymphs on their knees took Hylas, there in the depths below,
With gentle words of comfort to charm away his tears;
But great Amphitryon's son, tormented now with fears,
Strode forth to seek his squire, with trusty club in hand
And curving bow, such as Scythians wield, beside Maeotis's strand.
Thrice he thundered 'Hylas!' with the strength of his stalwart frame,
And thrice the boy cried answer; but his voice so faintly came
From the pool's depth, that far he seemed, although so near.
Then, as a lion devouring, when falls upon his ear
In his lair high up the mountains the cry of some young fawn,
Rushes to seize his quarry; so through the pathless thorn
Heracles went searching, in anguish, far and wide.
Stubborn indeed are lovers – far o'er the countryside
He tramped, forgetting Jason, by thicket, hill, and dale,
While Argo, with all aboard her and ready-hoisted sail,

Waited. At last, near midnight, the heroes lowered once more
Her yard, to bide his coming. But onward still he tore,
Blindly and madly searching, by raging Love possest.
So was the lovely Hylas numbered with the Blest;
But bitterly the heroes called curses on the name
Of Heracles, 'the deserter', that quitted, to his shame,
The thirty thwarts of Argo; and so afoot came he
Unto the Colchian kingdom's inhospitality.

(Theokritos, *Idylls*, XIII, tr. F. L. Lucas)

*   *   *

ZEUS AND GANYMEDE

Amongst the many stories of gods who had youths as play-
fellows and lovers – Apollo and Hyacinthos, Poseidon and
Pelops, Dionysos and Ampelos – Zeus's capture of Ganymede is
important both because of the pre-eminence of the captor and the
fact that the boy achieved immortal life on Mount Olympos as
his cup-bearer. The suggestion is less of moral training than of
dalliance over the wine with the result that the story has tended to
embody the more sensual aspects of paedophilia. Ganymede's
presence is to be felt in the Rome of Catullus and Petronius, in the
orchards of medieval Persia and the arcades of the Spanish
Caliphate, in the plays of Marlowe, the gossip of Beckford and
perhaps the poetry of Byron: while not infrequently his name
recurs on the Fag List of a British Public School. The following
version of the tale is an early one, in which Zeus does not take on
the form of an eagle but makes use of a whirlwind to gain his ends.

So Zeus the all-devising for his beauty skyward bore
The fair-haired Ganymedes, to dwell there evermore,
Honoured among the Blessed, glorious to behold,
As he draws the deep-red nectar from the mixing-bowl of gold.
Fathomless was the sorrow that on Trōs his father lay,
Mourning the loss of his vanished son, long day by day,
Not knowing whither had whirled him the storm-blast from on high.

But the heart of Zeus was softened, hearing that father's cry,
And he bade to King Trōs in requital a team of steeds be given –
Such steeds as draw, high-prancing, the chariots of Heaven –
And sent the Argos-slayer, his messenger, before
To tell how Ganymedes god-like evermore
Should live – unaged, undying. That word came not in vain;
The Trojan ceased from weeping, glad grew his heart again,
As his steeds with the feet of the tempest swept down the Trojan Plain.
(Homeric Hymn to Aphrodite, tr. F. L. Lucas)

And here is the boy's ascent when the eagle is Zeus's messenger but not the god himself.

> Soar, eagle, soar, to holy heaven convey
> The boy upon the pinions twain away:
> Soar with soft Ganymede, nor let him fall,
> Page of Jove's sweetest nectared carnival.
> And, lest the god be grieved, do thou take heed
> That thy bent claws make not the young lad bleed.
> (Strato: Greek Anthology, tr. Norman Douglas)

The allusion was always popular amongst Greek and Roman lyricists.

> Hate him O Zeus if he hates me –
> Theokritos, my Theokritos, deliciously bronzed –
> Hate the boy four times as much as he hates me!
>
> Heavenly Zeus, by Ganymede I swear,
> The golden haired,
> You in your time have loved.
> I say no more.
> (Kallimachos, Greek Anthology, tr. Dudley Fitts)

Christopher Marlowe gives what is a characteristically rich and also a shrewd and amusing description of infatuate god and cajoling coquettish ephebe.

Jupiter dandling Ganymede upon his knee, and Hermes lying asleep.

JUP.:
What is't, sweet wag, I should deny thy youth?
Whose face reflects such pleasure to mine eyes,
As I, exhal'd with thy fire-darting beams,
Have oft driven back the horses of the Night,
Whence they would have hal'd thee from my sight.
Sit on my knee, and call for thy content,
Control proud Fate, and cut the thread of Time:
Why, are not all the gods at thy command,
And heaven and earth the bounds of thy delight?
Vulcan shall dance to make thee laughing sport,
And my nine daughters sing when thou art sad;
From Juno's bird I'll pluck her spotted pride,
To make thee fans wherewith to cool thy face;
And Venus' swans shall shed their silver down,
To sweeten out the slumbers of thy bed;
Hermes no more shall show the world his wings,
If that thy fancy in his feathers dwell,
But, as this one, I'll tear them all from him.

Plucks feather from Hermes' wings.

Do thou but say, 'their colour pleaseth me.'
Hold here, my little love; these linked gems.

Gives jewels.

My Juno ware upon her marriage day,
Put thou about thy neck, my own sweet heart,
And trick thy arms and shoulders with my theft.

GAN.:
I would have a jewel for mine ear,
And a fine brooch to put in my hat,
And then I'll hug with you an hundred times.

JUP.:
And shalt have, Ganymede, if thou wilt be my love.

Enter Venus (very angry)

VEN.:

Ay, this is it: you can sit toying there,
And playing with that female wanton boy,
While my Aeneas wanders on the seas,
And rests a prey to every billow's pride . . .

*   *   *

MORE THAN TWO THOUSAND YEARS after the great originals,
the twin themes of noble comradeship and of an older man's
influence on a younger were still being given expression. In 1571,
the age of classical values idealized by a militant Protestantism,
that of Spenser, Sidney and their circle, a curious doggerel play
about Damon and Pythias was written, with this instructive
conclusion:

What force, what mighty power true friendship may possess,
To all the world Dionysius' court now plainly doth express . . .
Purged is the court of vice, since friendship ent'red in;
One loveth another now for virtue, not for gain;
Where virtue does not knit the knot, there friendship cannot reign;
Without the which no house, no land, no kingdom can endure,
As necessary for man's life as water, air, and fire . . .
Unhonest things friendship ne craveth, ne yet consents thereto.
In wealth a double joy, in woe a present stay,
A sweet companion in each state true friendship is alway.
A sure defence for kings, a perfect trusty band,
A force to assail, a shield to defend the enemies' cruel hand;
A rare and yet the greatest gift that God can give to man.
A gift so strange and of such price, I wish all kings to have;
But chiefly yet, as duty bindeth, I humbly crave,
True friendship and true friends, full fraught with constant faith,
The giver of all friends, the Lord, grant her, most noble Queen
   Elizabeth.

(Richard Edwards)

Equally quaint but more charming is this comment of Burton:

For the nature of true friendship is to combine, to be like affected, of one mind . . . as the poet saith, still to continue one and the same. And where this love takes place there is peace and quietness, a true correspondence, perfect amity, a diapason of vows and wishes, the same opinions, as between David and Jonathan, Damon and Pythias, Pylades and Orestes, Nisus and Euryalus, Theseus and Pirithous, they will live and die together, and persecute one another with good turns – *nam vinci in amore turpissimum putant*, for they think it the greatest reproach to be surpassed in the display of affection – not only living, but when their friends are dead, with tombs and monuments, *naenias* (funeral songs), epitaphs, elegies, inscriptions, pyramids, obelisks, statues, images, pictures, histories, poems, annals, feasts, anniversaries, many ages after (as Plato's scholars did) they will *parentare* still, omit no good office that may tend to the preservation of their names, honours, and eternal memory.

(*Anatomy of Melancholy*)

★　　★　　★

IN MODERN TIMES Oscar Wilde provides a moving, if not in all respects a personally appropriate, defence of the Socratic relationship.

Mr. C. F. Gill (cross-examining): Is it not clear that the love described [in Lord Alfred Douglas's poem] relates to natural love and unnatural love?

Wilde: No.

Mr. Gill: What is the 'Love that dare not speak its name'?

Wilde: 'The love that dare not speak its name' in this century is such a great affection of an elder for a younger man as there was between David and Jonathan, such as Plato made the very basis of his philosophy, and such as you find in the sonnets of Michelangelo and Shakespeare. It is that deep, spiritual affection that is as pure as it is perfect. It dictates and pervades great works of art like those of Shakespeare and Michelangelo, and those two letters of mine, such as they are. It is in this century misunderstood, so much misunderstood it may be described as the 'Love that dare not speak its name,' and on that account of it I am placed where I am now. It is beautiful, it is fine, it is the noblest form of affection. There is nothing unnatural about it. It is intellectual, and it repeatedly exists between an elder and a younger man, when the elder man has intellect, and the younger man has all the joy, hope and glamour of life before him. That it should be so the world does not understand. The world mocks at it and sometimes puts one in the pillory for it.

(*The Trials of Oscar Wilde*, edited by H. Montgomery Hyde)

2

The Greeks

INTRODUCTION

In *The Greek Experience* Sir Maurice Bowra puts the case with telling succinctness. 'The Greeks gave to friendship the attachment and the loyalty which elsewhere accompany the love of women. Of this Homer presents a classic example, when he makes the friendship of Achilles and Patroclus a pivot in his story and tells how grief and anger at Patroclus's death send Achilles back to battle that he may take his vengeance on Hector. The essence of such a relation was for a friend to share another's fortunes, both good and bad, to support him with complete truth and faithfulness in his loves and his enmities, his pleasures and his sorrows, to be scrupulously candid, and to fail in no call made upon him. This is the burden of much literature from convivial songs of the sixth century to Aristotle's schematic analysis of friendship in the *Nicomachean Ethics*. Attic tragedy presented it dramatically through devoted couples like Ajax and Teucer, or Orestes and Pylades; Zenophon reports as a commonplace that "a clear and good friend is the best of all possessions". Friendship of this kind was easy in a society where men partook of common interests and relaxed in each other's company.'

Sir Maurice goes on to suggest that such friendships had, for all their nobility, elements of masculine harshness, restraint and decorum, and also of self-interest, which are less likely to be associated with the love of women. He then approaches the rather shadowy problem of how these loves were expressed. 'The affection which Greek men felt for each other had its physical side. Of this there is no trace in Homer, who implicitly denies it for Achilles and Patroclus. But from the eighth century onwards it plays a marked part in Greek life. If tradition ascribed its introduction to the Dorians, it seems to have been prevalent and accepted in most parts of Greece, and usually to have taken the form of an older man's love for a younger. Its origins may be variously explained, by the relative seclusion and scarcity of women, by the isolation and emotional tensions of military life, by the cult of the naked body in games, by the natural tendency of the sexual impulse to assert itself where the affections are engaged. That it had its crude side we cannot doubt. Archaic inscriptions of the seventh century from the Dorian island of Thera suggest a forcible rite of initiation, and many vases depict a courtship which is quite unconcealed.'

Other authorities have commented on points such as these. That early German romantic, Johann Gottfried von Herder, spoke enthusiastically of games, comradeship and comradely education and thus became a standard-bearer of all those Nordics who have admired the classical sunlight: Winkelemann, Goethe, Count Platen, Hölderlin, Wagner, Nietzsche and so on down to Thomas Mann's fatally infatuated von Aschenbach. 'Thus the various public games gave a peculiar turn to education in Greece, as they made bodily exercises its principal object, and the excellencies acquired by them the aim of the whole nation.' They formed, he continued, a youth that was handsome, healthy and gay, and that sought fame through public and patriotic living, but, above all, they 'rooted in their hearts that taste for manly intercourse, and manly friendship, for which the Greeks were peculiarly distinguished. In Greece woman was not the supreme object of contest . . . The female sex, notwithstanding the fine patterns of every virtue it produced in Greece, remained a subordinate object: the thoughts of nobler youths were bent on something higher; the bands of friendship, which they formed with each other, or with more experienced men, trained them for a school, which no Aspasia could easily supply.' Having paid tribute to the training of gymnasia and military organizations, von Herder made this admission: 'I am far from defending the depravity of manners, which in time sprang from the abuse of these institutions, particularly where youth exercised naked; but alas! this abuse flowed from the character of the people, whose warm imagination, and love almost to madness of everything beautiful, in which they placed the supreme enjoyment of the gods, rendered such disorders inevitable.' The climate was partly to blame, he concluded – at least such affairs were not secret but capable of being utilized by the state, which gave 'vent to the flame that raged within'.

In his famous *Paideia* Werner Jaeger emphasized the moral and educational aspects of erotic friendship – 'the love of a man for a youth or a boy was an essential part of the aristocratic society of early Greece, and was inextricably bound up with its moral and social ideals' – but also made it clear that, precisely because of its historical and political implications, it was by no means universally accepted. 'From this point of view it is much easier for us to understand why large sections of the nation despised and punished it, while in other social strata it had developed until, for men at least, it was part of the highest conceptions of moral nobility and spiritual perfection.' Its educational significance was pre-eminent. 'The relation of the lover to his beloved had an educational authority similar to that of the parent to the child; in fact, it was in many respects superior to parental authority at the age when youths began to ripen into manhood and to cast off the bonds of domestic authority and family tradition. It is impossible to doubt the numerous affirmations of the educational power of Eros, which reach their culmination in Plato's *Symposium*.'

This accords with the opinion of Lowes Dickinson: 'It was the prerogative of this form of love, in its finer manifestations, that it passed beyond persons to objective ends, linking emotion to action in a life of common danger and toil.' (*The Greek View of Life*.) And with that of Hans Licht: 'Everything that made Greece great, everything that created for the Greeks a civilisation that will be admired as long as the world exists, has its roots in the unexampled ethical valuation of the masculine character in public and private life.' (*Sexual Life in Ancient Greece.*) But, of course, it must not be forgotten that Plato's attitude to Eros changed from the beautiful idealism of the *Symposium* and the *Phaedrus*; in the *Republic* it is merely tolerated while in the *Laws* it is condemned.

Certainly we must not suppose that the Greeks were indifferent to women. It is usual to regard their status as secluded, regimented and in consequence lowly, although Professor Kitto has persuasive arguments to question this view. Can the creators of an Antigone or Lysistrata have thought their women of no account? What of the loyalty of Penelope, the beauty of Nausikaa, the wisdom of the bright-eyed goddess, Athena? There is, of course, a great body of erotic legend and literature which celebrates feminine attractiveness: many of the Idylls of Theokritos, to give but one example. There is also much sculpture. And then again we must recognize how different from ours was the context of Greek life, with its passion for the family on one side and for political organization on the other. If the Greeks are to be narrowed down to a modern concept of 'homosexuality', then how did these friends succeed in marrying and bearing children and why was effeminacy always the butt of jokes and contempt? If we are to categorize, the Greek was often a bi-sexual, who tended to leave the young family to his womenfolk while building his structure of political, military and athletic interests, and of philosophical and scientific speculation, upon his friends.

★   ★   ★

PINDAR AND THE ARISTOCRATIC TRADITION

Of Pindar's work only the odes to victors in the Olympic and other Games, together with one or two fragments, have survived. This is a world of 'bright-limbed youth', 'the flame of excellence', 'Divine Youth lying on the eyelids of young girls, and of boys', and of a morality acquired by nature and family tradition rather than by learning. The Odes do not usually devote much space to the beauty, skill and nobility of the victor (a brief reference is enough) because they pass beyond him to the doings of his family both in athletics and history, and to those associated legends and myths which bring elegant piety and sober moralizing in their train. Since Pindar has often been described as magnificent but untranslatable, his atmosphere can perhaps best be sensed in conjunction with the sculptures of the fifth century B.C. and particularly those youths, like the Kritios Boy or the so-called Strangford Apollo in the British Museum, whose air of sweetness combined with severity, and of a candour as modest as it is complete, achieves an absolute efficiency which cannot help but seem religious.

THE AMBITIONS of youths, if constantly exercised with toil, win glory; and, in time, their deeds are bathed in light, when lifted aloft to the air of heaven.

(Fragment, tr. Sir John Sandys)

Pindar is said to have died in the arms of the youth he eulogizes here:

ON THEOXENUS OF TENEDOS

Right it were, to cull love's blossom in due season, in life's prime; but whosoever, when once he hath seen the rays flashing from the eyes of Theoxenus, doth not swell with desire, his black heart, with his frozen flame, hath been forged of adamant or of iron; and, unhonoured of brightly glancing Aphrodite, he either toileth over hoarded wealth, or, with a woman's courage, is borne along enslaved to a path that is utterly cold.

But I, for the sake of that Queen of love, like the wax of the holy bees that is melted beneath the heat of the sun, waste away when I look at the young limbs of blooming boys. Thus I ween that even in Tenedos Suasion and Charm dwelt in the soul of the son of Hagesilas.

(Tr. Sir John Sandys)

The following Ode was written for Xenokrates of Akragas in Sicily, the brother of the 'tyrant' Theron, whom Pindar much

33

admired, and also for the actual charioteer, Thrasyboulos, who was his son and a close friend of the poet. The chariot race was at Delphi in 490 B.C. Delphi was one of the shrines of Apollo, also called Pytho; the 'centrestone' referred to is the great *omphalos*, supposedly the centre or navel of the earth.

THE SIXTH PYTHIAN

Listen! It is the field of Aphrodite
with the fluttering eyes of the Graces
we labour now. We approach the templed
centrestone of the thunderous earth.
There stands builded for the glory of Emmenos's children
and Akragas of the river, and for Xenokrates,
a treasure house of song
for victory at Pytho in Apollo's
glen, with its burden of gold.

Neither rain driven from afar on the storm,
nor the merciless armies
of the crying cloud, no wind shall sweep it, caught
and stricken with the blown debris into the corners
of the sea. The front shines in the clear air,
Thrasyboulos, on your father announcing
for you and yours the pride
of a chariot victory in the folds of Krisa—
a tale to run on the lips of men.

You, keeping Victory erect beside your right hand,
bring home the meaning
of the things men say once on the mountain Chiron,
Philyra's son, urged on strong Peleiades
left in his care: *First of all gods, honour*
the deep-voiced lord of the lightning and thunderstroke,
Zeus Kronides;
next, through all their destiny never deprive
your parents of such reverence even as this.
In the old days mighty Antilochos proved one
who lived in that word.

He died for his father, standing up
to the murderous onset of the Aithiop champion,
Memnon; for Nestor's horse, smitten by the shaft of Paris,
had fouled the chariot, and Memnon attacked
with his tremendous spear.
And the old Messenian was shaken
at heart and cried aloud on his son's name.

And the word he flung faltered not to the ground; in that place
standing, the young man
in his splendour bought by his own death his father's rescue.
And of those who lived long ago men judged him
pre-eminent among the youth for devotion
to those who begot them, for that terrible deed.
All that is past.
Of men living now, Thrasyboulos
comes beyond others to the mark in his father's eyes,
and visits his father's brother with fame complete.
He carries wealth with discretion.
The blossom of youth he gathers is nothing violent,
but wise in the devious ways of the Muses.
To you, Poseidon, shaker of the earth, lord
of the mastering of horses, he comes, with mind to please you.
Also his heart, that is gentle
in the mixing of friends,
passes for sweetness the riddled work of the bees.

(Tr. Richmond Lattimore)

*   *   *

AT LEAST THREE GENERATIONS before Pindar, Theognis of
Megara had been equally conservative and far more bitter – the
landed gentleman who, unlike his Athenian contemporary Solon,
thoroughly disapproved of the spread of wealth and the growth
of a commercial democracy. In poems to his squire, Cyrnus, he
bewails the way of the world, and his favourite's behaviour.

THE BELOVED

To thee, my love, for ever I have given wings to raise thee
　To fly the wide world over, to cross the infinite sea,
Swift as a thought: laid lightly on the lips of men that praise thee
　At every feast and revel in the midst thou too shalt be.
And youths in the flower of their beauty, to the flute's clear voice
　　replying
　With voices as clear and lovely, in order due shall sing
Of thee; and when thou goest to that place of bitter crying,
　Deep in earth's abysses, where Hades sits as king,
Not even in death shall thy glory fade, thy memory wither,
　Thou shalt not lie forgotten, not even in the grave;
Through Greece, through the Isles, my Cyrnus, thou shalt wander,
　　hither, thither,
　Journeying for ever o'er the tireless, teeming wave;
Riding, but not upon horses. Not steeds, but the glorious guerdon
　Of the Muses shall bear thee onward, the Violet-garlanded;
All that love *them* hereafter, shall make *thy* name the burden
　Of a song that sounds for ever, till earth and sun be dead.
And yet for all this, my Cyrnus, I am nothing in thine eyes!
　Shameless, thou hast deceived me, like a little child, with lies.
　　　　　　　　　(Tr. F. L. Lucas, *Greek Poetry For Everyman*)

BETRAYAL

Now at his hour Love rises, while all the earth is springing,
　Springing into blossom with all the flowers of May.
Out of lovely Cyprus, Love comes and wanders flinging
　His seed in hearts of menfolk through all the world away.
Alas! Love came and whispered to thee of me, and bade
　That thou shouldest turn elsewhither and leave my love betrayed.
　　　　　　　　　　　　　　　　　　(*Ibid.*)

REJECTION

I love the lad no longer; I have spurned my bitter sadness;
　I am escaped rejoicing from the toils of misery.
The fair-crowned Cytherea has delivered me from madness;
　Boy, thou art fair no longer, no longer fair to me.
　　　　　　　　　　　　　　　　　　(*Ibid.*)

★　　★　　★

MODESTY AND DECORUM

The following two passages emphasize the ideal of decorum, both early and late.

THE OLD-FASHIONED WAY

. . . in his days, when justice flourished and self-control was held in honour, a boy's voice was never heard. He walked in order with his comrades of the same quarter, lightly clad even in winter, down to the school of the harp-player. There he learned old-fashioned hymns to the gods, and patriotic songs. While he sat, he took care to cover his person decently; and when he rose, he never forgot to rub out the marks which he might have left upon the dust lest any man should view them after he was gone. At meals he ate what was put before him, and refrained from idle chattering. Walking through the streets, he never tried to catch a passer's eye or to attract a lover. He avoided the shops, the baths, the Agora, the house of Hetairai. He reverenced old age and formed within his soul the image of modesty. In the gymnasium he indulged in fair and noble exercise, or ran races with his comrades among the olive-trees of the Academy.
(Aristophanes, *The Clouds*, adapted by J. A. Symonds, *A Problem in Greek Ethics*)

★   ★   ★

How different is a boy! In the morning he rises from his chaste couch, washes the sleep from his eyes with cold water, puts on his chlamys, and takes his way to the school of the musician or gymnast. His tutors and guardians attend him, and his eyes are bent upon the ground. He spends the morning in studying the poets and philosophers, in riding, or in military drill. Then he betakes himself to the wrestling-ground, and hardens his body with noontide heat and sweat and dust. The bath follows and a modest meal. After this he returns for awhile to study the lives of heroes and great men. After a frugal supper sleep at last is shed upon his eyelids.

Truly he is worthy to be loved. Who would not love Hermes in the palaestra or Phoebus at the lyre, or Castor on the racing-ground? Who would not wish to sit face to face with such a youth, to hear him talk, to share his toils, to walk with him, to nurse him in sickness, to

attend him on the sea, to suffer chains and darkness with him if need
be? He who hated him should be my foe, and whoso loved him should
be loved by me. At his death I would die; one grave should cover us
both; one cruel hand cut short our lives!

(Lucian, *Dialogue On Love*, quoted by J. A. Symonds, *op. cit.*)

★　★　★

SOME OF THE TRADITIONAL IDEAS as to friendship are summed
up in that curious rag-bag of literary pickings and cooking
recipes which Athenaeus composed about the end of the second
century A.D. The story, however, soon becomes diffuse and
gossipy:

HIERONYMUS THE PERIPATETIC declares these love affairs with boys
became widespread because it often happened that the vigour of the
young men, joined to the mutual sympathy of their companionship,
brought many tyrannical governments to an end. For if their favourites
were present, lovers would choose to suffer anything rather than incur
a reputation for cowardice in the mind of their favourites. This was
proved, at any rate, by the Sacred Band organized at Thebes by
Epameinondas, and by the murderous attempt made on the Peisistra-
tidae by Harmodius and Aristogeiton; and again in Sicily at Agrigen-
tum, by the love of Chariton and Melanippus. The latter was Chariton's
favourite, according to Heracleides of Pontus in his work *On Love
Affairs* . . . Apollo gave forth an oracle concerning Chariton and his
followers:

Happy the twain, Chariton and Melanippus his friend,
For that to creatures of clay they were patterns of god-like loving.

. . . Because of these love affairs, then, tyrants, to whom such friendships are inimical, tried to abolish entirely relations between males,
extirpating them everywhere. Some even went so far as to set fire to
the wrestling-schools, regarding them as counter-walls to their own
citadels, and so demolished them: this was done by Polycrates, the
tyrant of Samos.

. . . Among the barbarians the Celts also, though they have very
beautiful women, enjoy boys more; so that some of them often have

two lovers to sleep with on their beds of animal skins. As for the Persians, Herodotus says they learned the use of boys from the Greeks . . .

. . . King Alexander also was madly devoted to boys. Dicaearchus, at any rate in his book *On the Sacrifice at Ilium*, says that he was so overcome with love for the eunuch Bagoas that, in full view of the entire theatre, he, bending over, caressed Bagoas fondly, and when the audience clapped and shouted in applause, he, nothing loath, again bent over and kissed him. But Carystius in *Historical Notes* says: 'Charon of Chalcis had a beautiful boy who was dear to him. But when Alexander, at a drinking-party in the house of Craterus, praised the boy, Charon bade him kiss Alexander; and Alexander said, "Not so! For that will not delight me so much as it will pain you." For passionate as the king was, he was in like measure self-controlled when it came to observance of decency and the best form.'

(Athenaeus, *Savants at Dinner*, tr. C. B. Gulick)

★   ★   ★

DIONYSOS WAS PARTIALLY an oriental god and brought with him an orgiastic element seemingly at odds with the Apollonian concepts of 'Nothing in excess' and the 'Golden Mean', although he came to share the shrine of Delphi with Apollo. A god of wine and holy frenzy, he and his satyrs presided over the rituals that led to the Greek drama. The following passage is admittedly very late, from the fifth century A.D., but it seems best to follow the essentially Homeric and aristocratic note with this account of a god's activities before embarking on the mass of lyrics, so short, brilliant and teasing and yet sometimes so monotonously restricted in scope, about mortals and their loves. (Dionysos is sometimes called Bacchos, Lyaios, Bromios or Euios.)

A GOD AND HIS PLAYFELLOW

Once while hunting in the shady lurking wood Dionysos was delighted by the rosy form of a young comrade. Ampelos was a merry boy who had grown up already on the Phrygian hills, a new sprout of the Loves. No dainty bloom was yet on his reddening chin, no down yet marked the snowy circles of his cheeks, the golden flower of youth. Spring itself shone from his limbs; where his silvery foot stept the meadow blushed with roses.

The god took him as playmate in his sports. Then in admiration of his beauty he spoke to him as a man, artfully concealing his divine nature, and asked him:

'What father begat you? What immortal womb brought you forth? Which of the Graces gave you birth? What handsome Apollo made you? Tell me, my friend, do not hide your kin. If you come another Eros, unwinged, without arrows, without quiver, which of the Blessed slept with Aphrodite and bred you? How is it you wear your hair uncut falling down your neck? Can you be Phoibos himself come to me without harp, without bow, Phoibos shaking the locks of his unshorn hair unbound! If Cronides begat me, and you are from a mortal stock, if you have the short-living blood of the horned Satyrs, be king at my side, a mortal with a god; for your looks will not disgrace the heavenly blood of Lyaios.'

So he spoke, and the youth was delighted with his words, and proud that he surpassed the beauty of his young agemates by a more brilliant display. And in the mountain coppice if the boy made melody Bacchos listened with pleasure; and no smile was on his face if the boy was not there. If ever he lingered by the flowery stream of Pactolos, that he might bring himself sweeter water for the supper of his king, Bacchos was lashed with trouble so long as the boy stayed away. If carried away by wild passion for high capers, he skipt with dancing paces and joined hands with a sporting satyr in the round, Bacchos looked on shaken with envious feeling. If he ever conversed with the Satyrs, if he joined with a yearsmate hunter to follow chase, Dionysos jealous held him back, lest another be struck like himself with a heartbewitching shaft, and now enslaved by love should seduce the fickle boy's fancy and estrange the lovely youth from Lyaios, as a freshblooming boy might well charm a comrade of his own age.

When Bacchos lifted his thyrsus against a maddened bear, or cast his stout fennel javelin-like at a lioness, he looked aside watchfully towards the west; for fear the deathbringing breath of Zephyros might blow again, as it did once before when the bitter blast killed a young man while it turned the hurtling quoit against Hyacinthos. He feared Cronides might suddenly appear over Tmolos as a love-bird on amorous wing unapproachable, carrying off the boy with harmless talons into the air, as once he did the Trojan boy to serve his cups. He feared also the lovestricken ruler of the sea, that as once he took up Tantalides in his golden car, so now he might drive a winged wagon coursing through the air and ravish Ampelos – the Earthshaker mad with love!

And so Euios, pierced by the sting of the young man's sweetness, cried out to Cronides his father, another unhappy lover:

'Grant one grace to me the lover, O Phrygian Zeus! I do not ask the heavenly fire of your lightning, nor the cloud, nor the thunderclap. If it please you, give fiery Hephaistos the spark of your thunderbolt; let Ares have a corselet of your clouds to cover his chest with; give the pouring rainshower of Zeus as largesse to Hermaon; let Apollo, if you will, wield his father's lightning. My Satyr's beauty is dearer to me than Olympos. Tell me, father, do not hide it, swear by your own young friend – when you were an Eagle, when you picked up the boy on the slopes of Teucrian Ida with greedy gentle claws, and brought him to heaven, had the clown such beauty as this, when you made him one of the heavenly table still smelling of the byre? Forgive me, Father Longwing! Don't talk to me of your Trojan winepourer, the servant of your cups. Lovely Ampelos outshines Ganymedes, he has a brilliancy in his countenance more radiant – the Tmolian beats the Idalian! There are plenty more beautiful lads in troops – court them all if you like, and leave one boy to Lyaios!'

Not Apollo in the thick Magnesian woods, when he was herdsman to Admetos and tended his cattle, was pierced by the sweet sting of love for a winsome boy, as Bacchos rejoiced in heart sporting with the youth. Both played in the woods together, now throwing the thyrsus to travel through the air, now on some unshaded flat, or again they tramped the rocks hunting the hillbred lion's cubs. Sometimes alone on a deserted bank, they played on the sands of a pebbly river and had a wrestling-bout in friendly sport; no tripod was their prize, no flower-graven cauldron lay ready for the victory, no horses from the grass, but a double pipe of love with clear-sounding notes. It was a delightsome strife for both, for mad Love stood between them, a winged Hermes in the Ring, wreathing a lovegarland of daffodil and iris.

Both stood forward as love's athletes. They joined their palms garlandwise over each other's back, packed at the waist with a knot of the hands, squeezed the ribs tight with the muscles of their two forearms, lifted each other from the ground alternately. Bacchos was in heaven amid this honeysweet wrestling, and love gave him a double joy, lifting and being lifted. Ampelos enclosed the wrist of Bromios in his palm, then joining hands and tightening that intruding grip interlaced his fingers and brought them together in a double knot, squeezing the right hand of willing Dionysos. Next Bacchos ran his two hands round the young man's waist squeezing his body with a loving grip, and lifted Ampelos high; but the other kicked Bromios neatly behind the knee; and Euios laughing merrily at the blow from his young comrade's tender foot, let himself fall on his back in the dust. Thus while Bacchos lay willingly on the ground the boy sat across his naked belly, and Bacchos in delight lay stretched at full length on the ground sustaining the sweet burden on his paunch . . . Then both rolled in the dust, and the sweat poured out to tell that they were tired.

Thus Dionysos was conquered with his own consent, like his father as an athlete, who was conquered at last though invincible: for mighty Zeus himself, wrestling with Herakles beside the Alpheios, bent willing knees and fell of his own accord.

So ended the playful bout: the young man held out a happy hand and lifted his prize, the double pipes. He cleansed the sweat from his limbs in the river and washed off the damp dust; as he bathed, a pleasant brightness shone from the sweating skin . . .

. . . The lovely lad, exulting in his victory, threw his arm about Dionysos; and when Iobacchos saw him jumping about so proud, he said to him affectionately:

'Hurry now – try another match, swim against your comrade Bacchos and see if you can beat him! You had the best of it, Ampelos, in wrestling with me on the sands; now show yourself more agile than Dionysos in the rivers!

'This lovely stream suits you, suits the beauty of your limbs alone, that there may be a double Ampelos cutting the goldgleaming flood with golden palm; while you stretch naked limbs for victory, all the Pactolian water shall adorn your beauty. Phaëton himself shoots his rosy beams on Oceanos; grant an equal Olympian glory to this river: you too give your brightness to Pactolos, that Ampelos may be seen riding like Phosphoros. Both are radiant, this river with its red metal and you with your limbs; in the deep riches of his flood let him receive this youth also with the same colour on his skin; let him mix beauty with beauty, that I may cry to the Satyrs – "How came rose to rose? How is ruddy flesh and sparkling water mingled into one radiant light?"

'Let the other Satyrs see to wide-flowing Hermos, for he has no golden springs. But you are the only golden boy, and you shall have the golden water.'

Thus speaking, he plunged into the water; Ampelos joined him, and a jolly course the two had, zigzag from point to point of the opulent river . . . Now his boy-comrade's course ran beside the god's own, now he shot past him carefully, just so much as to leave Ampelos still a near neighbour to Bacchos in the way; sometimes he let his hands go round and round as if tired by the water, and willingly yielded the victory to the other swimmer.

Leaving the river stream, Ampelos repaired to the shelter of the woods, lifting a proud neck for his victory in the river. When he saw Iobacchos in a car driving panthers about the hills, he showed off exultantly his gambols with rockloving beasts; now mounting the shaggy back of a woodland bear, he pulled back the ruff of the grim hurrying beast; now he drove an unbridled tiger with delight.

(Nonnos, *Dionysiaca*, tr. W. H. D. Rouse)

This gay story has a mournful end. Heedless of his friend's warning the exuberant satyr-boy is gored by a bull. Dionysos is inconsolable – until Ampelos is re-born as a vine, the original in fact of all viticulture and wine-bibbing.

★　★　★

THE RAPE OF BOYS IN CRETE

There is evidence of forcible initiations in early times, especially amongst the Dorians. But Strabo, basing his account on Ephorus of Cyme, suggests there was a preponderant element of polite ceremonial to what happened in Crete, although in primitive times the 'rape' must have been violent. (Minos, the legendary king and lawgiver, was a rival abductor of Ganymede.) Notice here that the ephebe's character is more important than his looks.

THEY HAVE a peculiar custom in regard to love affairs, for they win the objects of their love, not by persuasion, but by abduction. The lover tells the friends of the boy three or four days beforehand that he is going to make the abduction; but for the friends to conceal the boy, or not to let him go forth by the appointed road, would be a most disgraceful thing, a confession, as it were, that the boy is unworthy to obtain such a lover. When they meet, if the abductor is the boy's equal, or superior in rank or other respects, the friends pursue him and lay hold of him, though only in a very gentle way, so as to satisfy the custom; after that they cheerfully turn the boy over to him to lead away. If, however, the abductor is unworthy, they take the boy away from him. The pursuit is at an end when the abductor takes the boy to his 'Andreion' (youths' mess or house). They regard as a worthy object of love, not the boy who is exceptionally handsome, but the boy who is exceptionally manly and decorous.

After giving the boy presents, his lover takes him away to any place in the country he wishes; and those who were present at the abduction follow them, and after feasting and hunting with them for two months (for it is not permitted to detain the boy a longer time), they return to the city. The boy is released after receiving as presents a military outfit, an ox, and a drinking-cup (these are the gifts required by law), and other things so costly and numerous that the friends, on account of all these expenses, make contributions thereto. Now the boy sacrifices the ox to Zeus and feasts those who returned with him; and then he makes known the facts about his intimacy with his lover, whether, perchance, it has pleased him or not, the law allowing him this privilege in order that, if any force was applied to him at the time of the abduction, he might be able at this feast to avenge himself and be rid of the lover. For those who are handsome in appearance or descendants of illustrious ancestors, it is a disgrace to fail to obtain lovers, the presumption being that it is the boy's character that is responsible. The boys who are given preference by the rape are specially honoured; so in the dances and in the races they have the best positions and they are allowed to dress better than the rest, namely, in the outfit given them by their lovers; and not then only, but even after they have grown to manhood, they wear a distinctive dress, so that anyone who has become 'kleinos' can be immediately recognised, they call the loved one 'kleinos' (the famous, the celebrated), and the lover 'philetor'.

(Strabo, *Geography*, tr. H. I. Jones)

★ ★ ★

'LOVE-SONGS by Ibycus and Anacreon express feelings which might in different circumstances have been given to girls,' Sir

Maurice Bowra writes, but the sad fact is that these lyricists of soft Asiatic Ionia and of nearby Lesbos – the first love-poets of Greece, in the seventh and sixth centuries – are known mostly to us through a few fragments. Not all, however, devote themselves to male affections. In the later seventh century Alcman of Sparta (probably a Lydian by birth) wrote choral songs for maidens. His contemporary, Mimnermus of Colophon, sang the praises of a flute-girl, Nanno. Semonides of Amorgos had, as we might expect in so male a society, many harsh things to say about women but concluded that a good woman, albeit rare, was a priceless gift.

AGAINST VARIOUS WOMEN

God from the first created diversely
The minds of women. One from a bristly sow
He made, within whose house the goods and chattels
Lie filthy, tumbling higgledy, piggledy,
While she, the slattern, dressed in dirty clothes
Sits in her muck and fattens.
    Another kind, God made from a vicious vixen –
Omniscient. There's nothing, good or bad,
Escapes *her* comprehension.
Evil she'll twist to good, and good to evil,
Just as, from day to day, the whimsy takes her.
    Another has a dog's soul – nimble mongrel,
That needs must know all, hear all, everywhere
Nosing, and scurrying, and giving tongue,
Though none be there to bark at. Nothing stops her,
Not threats, not gentleness – not though in rage
One lifted up a stone and dashed her teeth out.
Even as guest, sitting at others' tables,
Still, unabashed, she plies her futile yapping.
    Then there's another sort the Olympians made
From simple clay – a half-wit, knowing nothing –
Nor good, nor bad – all that *she* understands
Is eating – *that* apart, she has not sense,

In the depth of the worst winter God can send,
Although she's shivering, to pull near the fire.

.   .   .   .   .

Another's born of a dainty, long-maned filly,
Shying away from trouble and drudgery –
Never ask *her* to grind flour, or to finger
Dishes, or empty slops.
As for an oven – lest a smut fall on her,
She'll not go near it. *Her* love's tyranny.
Never a day but twice or thrice she washes,
And daubs herself with perfume; and her hair,
Flows deep, smooth combed, all shaded o'er with flowers.
A lovely thing to look at, such a woman,
For other men; but a curse to him that has her –
Unless he be a king or a dictator,
To glorify his fancy with such toys.

.   .   .   .   .

A man can gain no prize on earth that's better
Than a good woman, nor grislier than a bad.
(Quoted in F. L. Lucas, *Greek Poetry for Everyman*)

★   ★   ★

IF WE WANT a detailed picture of the beloved, we find Anacreon's Bathyllus, but not in the poet's own words, for it is the
Alexandrian Anacreontea that have survived.

PORTRAIT OF BATHYLLUS

Paint for me Bathyllus, the lover, as I tell you. Make his hair bright;
black at the roots, yet golden at the ends; and let the free tendrils of his
hair lie lawless as they choose.

Let his eyebrow, which is darker than a serpent, garland his dew-
soft brow. Let his fierce dark eye be tempered with grace – the fierce-
ness of Ares, the grace of Aphrodite – so that any one who flees from
the one surrenders to the other.

Make his downy cheek like a rose-tinted apple. Make the flush of his skin like that of Modesty if you had to paint him. And I know not in what fashion you should make his lips – soft and full like Persuasion; yet the wax keeps all his speech in silence.

After his face set down his ivory throat, surpassing Adonis. Paint his chest and two hands like Hermes, his thighs like Polydeuces, and his belly like Dionysus; and above his soft thighs, make his smooth sex, the fire near his thighs, already desirous of the Paphian.

Yours is a poor art since you cannot show his back as well. And what shall I say to you of his feet?

Take your money, take whatever you ask. Depose Apollo himself and make Bathyllus, and if ever you come to Samos set up Bathyllus instead of Phoebus.

(Anacreontea, tr. Richard Aldington)

ON ANACREON

This is Anacreon's tomb; here sleeps the Teian swan and the untempered madness of his passion for lads. Still singeth he some song of longing to the lyre about Bathyllus, and the white marble is perfumed with ivy. Not even death has quenched thy loves, and in the house of Acheron thou sufferest all through thee the pangs of the fever of Cypris.

(Antipater of Sidon, Gk. Anth., tr. W. R. Paton)

ON THE SAME

Now sleepest thou, Anacreon,
Among the dead, thy work well done.
Now sleeps the harp that would repeat
Night after night its chatter sweet.
Sleeps too the Springtime of Desire,
Smerdis, for whom the poet's lyre
Would pour from quivering strings its own
Nectar of harmonious tone.
Created as thou wert to be
The target of Boy's-love, for thee
He kept his bow, for thee alone
The long slant shots, Anacreon.

(Ibid., tr. R. A. Furness)

★　　★　　★

FONDNESS OVER WINE

Here is the *sunposeion* or symposium, the wine-party that lasts long into the night. The men's club, the *hetaereia*, have arrived and put on their garlands. They recline upon the *triclinia* of wood and ivory and bronze. A flute-girl plays perhaps amongst the apparatus of the resinated drink from Rhodes or Kerkyra, Samos or the Attic plain: the amphorae with their incredibly slender bases, the wine-cooler and the great mixing-bowl.

NUNC EST BIBENDUM

Come bathe in the scented waters,
  And weave for us garlands bright;
For boys and wine won't stay for ever,
  And the grave offers no delight:

So drink your fill, Damocrates;
  There's a long, grey sleep ahead;
Let the wine flow into my living body –
  And the sea can flow over it dead.
      (Strato, *Greek Anthology*, tr. Simon Raven)

DRINK, SAD LOVER!

Drink, Asklepiades. Why are you crying?
What troubles you? You are not the only prisoner
Of Kypris, not for you alone has cruel Eros sharpened his arrows.
Why lie there in the dust when you are still alive?
Drink Bacchos' wine – unmixed with water. The day is short.
Shall we wait to see again the lamp that lights us to bed?
Drink, sad lover. That long night is not far off
Wherein we shall find sleep.
(Asklepiades of Samos, *Gk. Anth.*, after translation by Forrest Reid)

AN ARGUMENT WITH HIMSELF

'Let the die be cast! Light the torch. I will go.'
'Hey, there! What boozy daring – in your state, pissed with wine ..'.

'What's wrong, why pick on me? I will go roistering to my pleasure.'
'Roistering indeed! What's your bird-brain up to now?'
'Do you think love is to be reasoned with? Light up, I say, light up!'
'And where is all your precious study of philosophy now, eh?'
'To hell with that old bore! I only know one thing. Zeus himself was nailed by Eros.'

(Meleager, *Greek Anthology*)

A KISS

When parched with the heat of summer
    I drank at a fair youth's kiss,
And my thirst was quenched at a moment,
    And I called out in my bliss:

'O father Zeus, your Ganymede
    Never brought wine like this;
For I have drunk the sweet soul's honey
    Of the loveliest lad there is.'

(Meleager, *Greek Anthology*, tr. Simon Raven)

ALCIBIADES AND AGATHON

Well, it wasn't long before they could hear Alcibiades shouting in the courtyard, evidently drunk, and demanding where Agathon was, because he *must* see Agathon at once. So the flute-girl and some of his other followers helped him stagger in, and there he stood in the doorway, with a mass of ribbons and an enormous wreath of ivy and violets sprouting on his head, and addressed the company.

'Good evening, gentlemen,' he said; 'I'm pretty well screwed already, so if you'd rather I didn't join the party, only say the word and I'll go away, as soon as I've hung this wreath on Agathon's head – which is what I really came for. I couldn't get along yesterday, so here I am tonight, with a bunch of ribbons on my head, all ready to take them off and put them on the head of the cleverest, the most attractive, and, I may say – well, anyway, I'm going to crown him. And now I suppose you're laughing at me, just because I'm drunk. Go on, have your laugh out, don't mind me; I'm not so drunk that I don't know what I'm saying, and you can't deny it's true. Well,

what do you say, gentlemen? Can I come in on that footing? And shall
we all have a drink together or shan't we?'

At that they all cheered and told him to come in and make himself
at home, while Agathon gave him a more formal invitation. And while
his people helped him in he started pulling off the ribbons, so that he
could transfer them to Agathon's head as soon as he was near enough.
As it happened, the wreath slipped over his eyes and he didn't notice
Socrates, although he sat down on the same couch, between him and
Agathon – for Socrates had made room for him as soon as he came in.
So down he sat, with a 'how d'you do!' to Agathon, and began to tie
the ribbons round his head.

(Plato, *Symposium*, tr. Michael Joyce)

SOPHOCLES AND THE WINE-WAITER

Sophocles was fond of young lads, as Euripides was of women. The
poet Ion, at any rate, in the work entitled *Sojournings*, writes as follows:

I met Sophocles the poet at Chios when I was sailing as general to
Lesbos. He was playful at wine, and clever. A Chian friend of mine,
Hermesilaus, who was the proxenus of Athens, entertained him, when
there appeared, standing beside the fire, the wine-pourer, a handsome,
blushing boy; Sophocles was plainly stirred and said: 'Do you want
me to drink with pleasure?' And when the boy said 'Yes', he said, 'Then
don't be too rapid in handing me the cup and taking it away.' When
the boy blushed still more violently he said to the man who shared his
couch: 'That was a good thing Phrynicus said when he wrote: "There
shines upon his crimson cheek the light of love".' To this the man from
Eretria, who was a schoolmaster, made answer: 'Wise you are, to be
sure, Sophocles, in the art of poetry; nevertheless Phrynicus did not
express himself happily when he described the handsome boy's cheeks
as crimson. For if a painter should brush a crimson colour on this
boy's cheeks he would no longer look handsome. Surely one must not
compare the beautiful with what is obviously not beautiful.' Laughing
loudly at the Eretrian Sophocles said: 'So then, stranger, you don't
like that line of Simonides, either, though the Greeks think it very well
expressed: "From her crimson lips the maiden uttered speech"; nor
again the poet who speaks of "golden-haired Apollo"; for if a painter
had made the god's locks golden instead of black, the picture would
not be so good. And so for the poet who said "rosy-fingered": for if

one should dip his fingers into a rose-dye, he would produce then hands of a purple-dyer and not those of a lovely woman.'

There was a laugh at this, and while the Eretrian was squelched by the rebuke, Sophocles returned to his conversation with the boy. He asked him, as he was trying to pick off a straw from the cup with his little finger, whether he could see the straw clearly. When the boy declared he could see it Sophocles said, 'Then blow it away, for I shouldn't want you to get your finger wet.' As the boy brought his face up to the cup, Sophocles drew the cup nearer to his own lips, that the two heads might come closer together. When he was very near the lad, he drew him close with his arm and kissed him. They all applauded, amid laughter and shouting, because he had put it over the boy so neatly; and Sophocles said, 'I am practising strategy, gentlemen, since Pericles told me that whereas I could write poetry, I didn't know how to be a general. Don't you think my strategy has turned out happily for me?' Many things of this sort he was wont to say and do cleverly when he drank or when he did anything. In civic matters, however, he was neither wise nor efficient, but like any other individual among the better class of Athenians.

(Athenaeus, *Savants At Dinner*, tr. C. B. Gulick)

DRUNK

Boy, hold my wreath for me.
The night is black,
   the path is long,
And I am completely and beautifully drunk.
Nevertheless I will go
To Themison's house and sing beneath his window.
You need not come with me:
   though I may stumble,
He is a steady lamp for the feet of love.

(Anon., *Gk. Anth.*, tr. Dudley Fitts)

* * *

BOY-FLOWERS

As in love poetry of all kinds, the charm of ephebes was often compared to the ephemeral beauty of flowers. 'How with this rage shall beauty hold a plea, Whose action is no stronger than a flower?' (Shakespeare, Sonnet 65.) One is reminded of the ambiguous and sinister M. de Trèves in Peyrefitte's *Les Amitiés Particulières* who was wont to wake the boys in the dormitory sometimes with a stern command that they fall on their knees and pray, and at others by waving a rose before their faces, as he recited a line of Musset: 'Les lèvres des enfants s'ouvrent comme des roses'.

THE GARLAND

For you, Kypris, Eros gathered with his own hands this garland of boy-flowers, a wreath of many blossoms.

He wove into it the lily of Diodorus and the sweet white violet of Asclepiades, and Heraclitus, like a thorny rose.

The vine of Dion blooms in it, and he bound into it Theron, a yellow-haired crocus, and Ouliades, a sprig of white thyme.

And also he added soft-haired Myiscus, an ever-green olive shoot, and the lovely bough of Aretos.

O happiest of islands, sacred Tyre, to you belongs this fragrant grove of boys bearing the flowers of Kypris.

(Meleager, *Gk. Anth.*, translation after Forrest Reid)

THE IMPORTANCE OF ROSES

The roses, borne on their leaves as on wings, have made haste to come to you. Receive them kindly, either as mementos of Adonis or as tinct of Aphrodite or as eyes of the earth. Yes, a wreath of wild olives becomes an athlete, a tiara worn upright the Great King, and a helmet crest a soldier; but roses become a beautiful boy, both because of affinity of fragrance and because of their distinctive hue. You will not wear the roses: they will wear you.

(Philostratos, *Letter 1*, tr. A. R. Benner and F. H. Fobes)

WHO WEARS WHICH?

The Lacedaemonians used to attire themselves in crimson-coloured corselets, either to shock their enemies by the fearsome hue, or, by having the colour the same as that of blood, to prevent their noticing blood stains; and you handsome boys must equip yourselves with naught but roses – this the panoply that you accept from your lovers. Now a larkspur suits a boy who has a light complexion, a narcissus a boy who is dark; but a rose suits all, inasmuch as it has long since existed both as a boy and as a flower, as a drug and as a perfume. 'Twas roses that won the heart of Anchises, 'twas they that stripped Ares of his armour, they that prompted Adonis to come; they are spring's tresses, they earth's lightning flashes, they the torches of love.

(*Ibid., Letter 4*)

PHILOSTRATOS, who seems really to have been three writers in very late Hellenistic times, wrote a parallel series of prose letters to boys and women, all equally characterized by voluptuous hyperboles and ingenious conceits. Although their effect is of continuous cooing in a hot-house, they are not without charm. The following is another example.

A BED OF ROSES

You have done well to use the roses for a bed also; for pleasure in gifts received is a clear indication of regard for the sender. So through their agency I also touched you, for roses are amorous and artful and know how to make use of beauty. But I fear that they may actually have been restless and oppressed you in your sleep, even as the gold oppressed Danae. If you wish to do a favour for a lover, send back what is left of them, since they now breathe a fragrance, not of roses only, but also of you.

(*Ibid., Letter 46*)

THE PRECARIOUS GARLAND

Your lips are sweeter in the evening hours
    Than spices from distant lands:
Awake, and I will give you a garland of fresh flowers
    Into your cherished hands.

Then, coming close, I'll whisper in your ear
    That the minutes cannot be stayed;
And as you see this garland droop at dawn, my dear,
    So your own youth will fade.

(Marcus Argentarius, *Greek Anthology*, tr. Simon Raven)

THE GARLANDS OF TEARS

My garlands, rest festooned upon these doors,
And be not quick to shed your petals.
I have watered you with my tears, for lovers' eyes know
    much of weeping.

But when the door opens and you see him,
Let fall this dew upon his head
That his fair hair at least may drink my tears.

                     (Asklepiades, *Gk. Anth.*)

          ★   ★   ★

EYES OF FIRE AND VIRTUE

There is a fragment of Aristotle's which reads 'Lovers look at
none of the bodily charms of their favourites more than at their
eyes, wherein dwells the secret of boyish virtues'. Such windows
of the soul are a frequent inspiration.

ALEXIS

In summer season, when they shear
The harvest-tresses of the year,
Walking abroad at full noon-tide
Alexis in the lane I spied.

A double brightness burned me: rays
There were which travelled in the gaze
Of that boy's eyes, the beams of Love;
And others from the Sun above.

These, of the Sun, fell to repose
When Night came on; but in dreams those,
Fed by his phantom shape so fair,
Flamed up still fiercer than they were.

So Sleep, who gives to others peace,
To me gave pain without release,

Fashioning for my soul's desire
A beauty that is living fire.
(Meleager, *Gk. Anth*. tr. R. N. Furness)

THE VIGIL

Now blithely breaks the dawn; but Damis lies
In the porch, sleepless, gasping out his soul;
Wrecked by a glimpse of Heraclite, whose eyes
Made him as wax thrown on a burning coal.
Come, poor Damis, get up! I too have bled
For love, and tears over your tears I shed.
(*Ibid.*, tr. R. N. Furness)

THE HUNTER SNARED

How many times, do you think, have I unclosed my eyes to release
you, even as hunters open their nets to give their quarry a chance to
escape? And you sit fast, like those vexatious squatters who, when
once they have seized on other people's land, will not hear of moving
off again. Lo, once more, as so often in the past, I raise my eyelids; now
at long last, I pray you, fly away, and raise the siege, and become a
guest of other eyes. You are not listening, not you! You are pressing
ever farther on, into my very soul! And what is this new fiery heat?
In my perilous plight I cry for water; but no one assuages the heat,
for the means of quenching this flame is very hard to find, whether
one brings water from a spring or from a stream; yes, for love's fire
sets even the water ablaze.
(Philostratos, *Letter 2*, tr. A. R. Benner and F. H. Fobes)

THE NESTED BOY

Nests are hosts to birds, rocks to fish, eyes to handsome boys; birds and
fish migrate, moving from one place to another and shifting their
abodes, for they wander as the seasons lead them; but when beauty
has once made its way into eyes it never departs again from the lodging
it there finds. Even so have I become your host and carry you everywhere in the snare of my eyes: if I go forth a wayfarer as it were, you
appear to me in the guise of a shepherd, of one who sits and by his
beauty charms the very rocks; and if I go to the sea, out from the sea
you rise, as Aphrodite rose from the depths; and if to a meadow, above

the very flowers you stand out – yet no such thing as you grows there, for verily, though the flowers are in other ways fair and lovely, yet they last but a single day. Yes truly, if I come near a river, the river, I know not how, vanishes suddenly from my sight, and in its place, methinks, I see you flowing fair and great and greater far than is the sea. If I look up into heaven, I think that the sun has fallen and is making his way afoot somewhere below, and that in his place my heart's desire shines. And if night comes, I see but two stars, Hesperus and you.

(*Ibid.*)

★　　★　　★

SIGNIFICANCE ATTACHED TO HAIR

As later amongst the Moors of Spain, there is a good deal of discussion as to the propriety of down on a boy's cheek, and the advantages – or more likely disadvantages – of the first appearance of veritable beard. The ever complaisant and tolerant Philostratos can argue the matter both ways. Here is Strato on the 'shades of night'.

THEUDIS

I caught aflame when Theudis first
　　Among the boys outshone
As though upon the stars there burst
　　The newly risen sun.

I burnt, and I am burning yet,
　　While shades of night creep on
Over his cheeks; for though he set
　　He still remains the sun.

(Strato, *Gk. Anth.*)

★　　★　　★

THE VARIETY OF LOVES – AND OF LOVE

CATHOLICITY

Oh here's to the boy that is pale as the snow,
　　And to those with the colour of honey:

I dote on 'em dark and I'll have 'em when tow
And I love them when open and sunny.

I covet them fair and I don't mind 'em thin,
I adore them as brown as a pebble:
But the best of the bunch have a rich olive skin
And flashing black eyes like the devil.

(Strato, *Gk. Anth.*, tr. Simon Raven)

AN INTENSITY

Soul, did I not cry aloud to you, 'By Kypris, unhappy lover, if you fly too near the limed twigs you will be caught!'

Did I not cry a warning? See, now you are snared! Why flutter vainly in your bonds? Eros himself has bound your wings.

He has set you on fire, and poured perfumes on your fainting body, and given you hot tears to drink.

(Meleager, *Gk. Anth.*, tr. Forrest Reid)

ANOTHER

When Menecharmus, the son of Anticles, won at boxing, I crowned him with ten pliant wreaths and thrice I embraced him saturated with blood that was sweeter to me than myrrh.

(Strato, *Gk. Anth.*, tr. Shane Leslie)

AND ANOTHER

My soul, when I kissed Agathôn, crept up to my lips
As though it wished (poor thing!) to cross over to him.

(Plato, *Gk. Anth.*, tr. Dudley Fitts)

AND YET ANOTHER

Last night when we came to say goodbye – whether really or in a dream I simply don't know – Moeris kissed me.

I can recall everything else quite clearly, what he said and the questions he asked, but whether he really kissed me remains utterly mysterious.

C*—E

For if he did, how is it that I – thus made divine – am still wandering on earth?

(Strato, Gk. Anth.)

A SECRET INTENSITY

Our guest has a secret wound. Saw ye the pain with which he drew breath through his body when he drank the third cup? And all the roses upon the fellow's garland lost petal and fell to the ground. Something burns him fiercely. By the gods, I do not guess haphazardly. A thief myself, I know the signs of a thief.

(Kallimachos, Gk. Anth., tr. Shane Leslie)

FAILED OATHS

We called on Holy Night
    To bind us both together,
And we bade the Lamp to heed us,
    That our love should be forever:

But like the passing stream
    Are vows to a lover;
When Night comes now, the Lamp
    Shows him to another.

(Meleager, Gk. Anth., tr. Simon Raven)

THE BLACKBIRD

A blackbird Dexionicus grasps which he
Had limed and taken in a green plane-tree,
Making the holy bird shrill wail and piercing cry.
    Ye Graces fair and Eros, would that I
    Within his hands a thrush or blackbird were,
    To ease with tearful voice my longing there.

(Rhianus, Gk. Anth., tr. Norman Douglas)

TWO LOVES –

Zeus, to steal boy Ganymede,
    An eagle's form put on;
And when he wanted the lady Leda
    He turned into a swan.

Now some like girls, and some like boys;
 But the moral's plain to see:
If both are good enough for Zeus,
 They're both good enough for me.
     (Anon., *Gk. Anth.*, tr. Simon Raven)

— OR ONE

For woman's love nought care I,
But brands for the burning within me lie:
Man than woman stronger is,
The power to kindle these brands, his.
     (*Ibid.*, tr. Simon Raven)

ELEGIAC

They told me, Heraclitus, they told me you were dead;
They brought me bitter news to hear and bitter tears to shed.
I wept, as I remembered, how often you and I
Had tired the sun with talking and sent him down the sky.

And now that thou art lying, my dear old Carian guest,
A handful of grey ashes, long, long ago at rest,
Still are thy pleasant voices, thy nightingales, awake,
For Death, he taketh all away, but them he cannot take.
     (Kallimachos, *Gk. Anth.*, William Cory)

MORAL

By the very fact that we breathe our love into handsome boys we
keep them from avarice, increase their enjoyment in work, trouble
and dangers, and develop their modesty and self-control.
     (Xenophon)

IMMORAL

Let Aphrodite herself,
   let all the company of love
Curse me, shrivel my sick heart with their hate, if ever
I turn to the love of boys.
   O Goddess,
From sliding error and perversion guard me!

> To sin with girls is sin enough:
> Pittalkos may have the rest.
>
> (Agathias, *Gk. Anth.*, tr. Dudley Fitts)[1]

★   ★   ★

PLATO AND LOVE AS MORALITY

Plato is one of the greatest writers on male affections, although his attitude was perforce to harden later as logic and abstraction grew extreme, and the intellectual reformer usurped the urbane and charming conversationalist. Both Socrates and Plato knew this love 'from inside' but, for all their poetry, all their sensuous delight in beautiful faces and bodies, the pleasures of the wine-party and the witty dialectics of colonnade and grove, they had finally, as idealists, to deny the flesh and the world about them. By the side of shadow-boys, crowned with wreaths of meta-physical imperfection, they came to drink a spectral wine. In this sense they seem to many less characteristically Greek than their contemporaries – closer to Christianity and St Paul, to the dualisms of the Middle Ages and to the strain and fervour of public-school Victorianism; it was not Socrates but Isocrates and the schools of rhetoric who handed Hellas to Rome and Egypt.

The first of the following quotations from the *Symposium* concerns the speech of Aristophanes. It is early in the party that the comic poet argues his delicious theory that the human race started off with three sexes, male, female and combined, who were of globular shape and had each four arms and four legs, not to mention 'one head, with one face one side and one the other, and four ears, and two lots of privates, and all the other parts to match'. These creatures, who were very strong and could roll at a prodigious speed, soon committed the sin of *hubris* – they tried to take over the privileges of the gods – and so Zeus punished them by cutting them in two and having Apollo move their half-heads round to the internal and wounded side, which was sewn

---

[1] Agathias Scholasticus was a Byzantine Greek of the Sixth Century A.D. His scholarship provided one of the sources of the *Anthology*.

up and (but only later, when Zeus took pity on them) had the genitalia repositioned. After this everybody began wildly to seek his twin.

. . . while men who are slices of the male are followers of the male, and show their masculinity throughout their boyhood by the way they make friends with men, and the delight they take in lying beside them and being taken in their arms. And these are the most hopeful of the nation's youth, for theirs is the most virile constitution.

I know there are some people who call them shameless; but they are wrong. It is not immodesty that leads them to such pleasures, but daring, fortitude, and masculinity; the very virtues that they recognise and welcome in their lovers – which is proved by the fact that in after years they are the only men who show any real manliness in public life. And so, when they themselves have come to manhood, their love in turn is lavished upon boys: they have no natural inclination to marry and beget children. Indeed, they only do so in deference to the usage of society, for they would just as soon renounce marriage altogether and spend their lives with one another.

Such a man, then, gentlemen, is of an amorous disposition, and gives his love to boys, always clinging to his like. And so, when this boy-lover – or any lover, for that matter – is fortunate enough to meet his other half, they are both so intoxicated with affection, with friendship, and with love, that they cannot bear to let each other out of sight for a single instant. It is such reunions as these that impel men to spend their lives together, although they may be hard put to it to say what they really want with one another; and indeed, the purely sexual pleasures of their friendship could hardly account for the huge delight they take in one another's company. The fact is that both their souls are longing for a something else – a something to which they can neither of them put a name, and which they can only give an inkling of in cryptic sayings and prophetic riddles.

Now supposing Hephaestus were to come and stand over them with his tool-bag as they lay there side by side; and suppose he were to ask:

'Tell me, my dear creatures; what do you really want with one another?'

And suppose they didn't know what to say, and he went on:

'How would you like to be rolled into one, so that you could always be together, day and night, and never be parted again? Because if that's what you want, I can easily weld you together; and then you can live your two lives in one, and when the time comes, you can die a common death and still be two-in-one in the lower world. Now, what do you say? Is that what you'd like me to do? And would you be happy if I did?'

We may be sure, gentlemen, that no lover on earth would dream of refusing such an offer, for not one of them could imagine a happier fate. Indeed, they would be convinced that this was just what they'd been waiting for – to be merged, that is, into an utter one-ness with the beloved.

(Plato, Symposium, tr. Michael Joyce)

Shortly afterwards Socrates presents his own opinion under the guise of instruction given to him by a wise woman called Diotima.

THE LADDER OF PERFECTION

'Well then,' she began, 'the candidate for this initiation cannot, if his efforts are to be rewarded, begin too early to devote himself to the beauties of the body. First of all, if his preceptor instructs him as he should, he will fall in love with the beauty of one individual body, so that his passion may give life to noble discourse. Next he must consider how nearly related the beauty of any one body is to the beauty of any other, when he will see that if he is to devote himself to loveliness of form it will be absurd to deny that the beauty of each and every body is the same. Having reached this point, he must set himself to be the lover of every lovely body, and bring his passion for the one into due proportion by deeming it of little or of no importance.

'Next he must grasp that the beauties of the body are as nothing to the beauties of the soul; so that wherever he meets with spiritual loveliness, even in the husk of an unlovely body, he will find it beautiful enough to fall in love with and to cherish: and beautiful enough to quicken in his heart a longing for such discourse as tends towards the building of a noble nature. And from this he will be led to contemplate the beauty of laws and institutions; and when he discovers how nearly every kind of beauty is akin to every other he will conclude that the beauty of the body is not, after all, of so great moment.

'And next, his attention should be diverted from institutions to the sciences, so that he may know the beauty of every kind of knowledge;

and thus, by scanning beauty's wide horizon, he will be saved from a slavish and illiberal devotion to the individual loveliness of a single boy, a single man, or a single institution; and, turning his eyes towards the open sea of beauty, he will find in such contemplation the seed of the most fruitful discourse and the loftiest thought, and reap a golden harvest of philosophy; until, confirmed and strengthened, he will come upon one single form of knowledge, the knowledge of the beauty I am about to speak of. And here,' she said, 'you must follow me as closely as you can.

'Whoever has been initiated so far in the mysteries of Love and has viewed all these aspects of the beautiful in due succession, is at last drawing near the final revelation. And now, Socrates, there bursts upon him that wondrous vision which is the very soul of the beauty he has toiled so long for. It is an everlasting loveliness which neither comes nor goes, which neither flowers nor fades; for such beauty is the same on every hand, the same then as now, here as there, this way as that way, the same to every worshipper as it is to every other.

'Nor will his vision of the beautiful take the form of a face, or of hands, or of anything that is of the flesh; it will be neither words, nor knowledge, nor a something that exists in something else such as a living creature, or the earth, or the heavens, or anything that is, but subsisting of itself and by itself in an eternal one-ness; while every lovely thing partakes of it in such sort that, however much the parts may wax and wane, it will be neither more nor less, but still the same inviolable whole.

'And so, when his prescribed devotion to boyish beauties has carried our candidate so far that the universal beauty dawns upon his inward sight, he is almost within reach of the final revelation. And this is the way, the only way, he must approach, or be led towards, the sanctuary of Love; starting from individual beauties, the quest for the universal beauty must find him ever mounting the heavenly ladder, stepping from rung to rung, that is, from one to two, and from two to *every* lovely body; from bodily beauty to the beauty of institutions; from institutions to learning, and from learning in general to the special lore that pertains to nothing but the beautiful itself; until at last he comes to know what beauty is.

'And if, my dear Socrates,' Diotima went on, 'man's life is ever worth the living, it is when he has attained this vision of the very soul of beauty. And once you have seen it, you will never be seduced again by the charm of gold, of dress, of comely boys or lads just ripening to manhood; you will care nothing for the beauties that used to take your breath away and kindle such a longing in you, and many others like you, Socrates, to be always at the side of the beloved and feasting your eyes upon him; so that you would be content, if it were possible, to deny yourself the grosser necessities of meat and drink, so long as you were with him.

'But if it were given to man to gaze on beauty's very self – unsullied, unalloyed, and freed from the mortal taint that haunts the frailer loveliness of flesh and blood – if, I say, it were given to man to see the heavenly beauty face to face, would you call *his*,' she asked me, 'an unenviable life, whose eyes had been opened to the vision, and who had gazed upon it in true contemplation until it had become his own for-ever? And remember,' she said, 'that it is when he looks upon beauty's visible presentment, and only then, that a man will be quickened with the true, and not the seeming, virtue – for it is virtue's self that quickens him, not virtue's semblance. And when he has brought forth and reared this perfect virtue, he shall be called the friend of god: and if ever it is given to man to put on immortality, it shall be given to him.'

*   *   *

In the *Phaedrus* Socrates and his young friend walk down the streamlet of the Illysos (now, alas, an Athenian drain) with their feet in the water to keep them cool. Coming upon a plane-tree which rises from the bank, they sink into its grassy shade to discourse on love.

Eventually Socrates reveals the heart of his vision on this matter, which is a beautiful and complex series of metaphors or analogies concerning the feathery-winged soul, the soul as charioteer of a two-horsed chariot and the procession of the charioted gods and souls about heaven. His idea is that the great procession of gods (who handle their chariots perfectly) and of godly souls (who have the disadvantage of one unruly bestial horse) ascends to the summit of heaven for the time of feasting and revelry. There the gods ride their chariots on to the outside of heaven's revolving sphere quite easily, and contemplate, as they are carried round, the various Absolutes. But the souls of even the godliest men only succeed by fits and starts in breaking through on to the outer edge and hence miss most of the beauties to be seen, while the average common-or-garden soul does not get there at all but is whirled in the lower element, bumping, plunging, and hence losing its feathers. The soul that has lost its plumage returns to earth, is reincarnated and takes ten thousand years to recover its buoyancy *unless it has belonged to a guileless lover of philosophy, or a philosophic lover of boys*, when the time is much shorter.

In the following passage Socrates refers to the experience of beauty as a reflection of the Heavenly Vision once glimpsed by the soul, for beauty makes the feathers begin to grow again.

THE MAN, it is true, whose initiation is of ancient date, or who has lost his purity here, is slow in being carried hence to the essential beauty of the upper world, when he sees that which bears its name in this. Accordingly, he feels no reverence as he gazes on the beautiful object, but, abandoning himself to lust, attempts like a brute beast to gratify his appetite, and in his wanton approaches knows nor fear nor shame at this unnatural pursuit of pleasure. But whenever one who is fresh from those mysteries, who saw much of that heavenly vision, beholds in any god-like face or form a successful copy of original beauty, he first of all feels a shuddering chill, and there creep over him some of those terrors that assailed him in that dire struggle; then, as he continues to gaze, he is inspired with a reverential awe, and did he not fear the repute of exceeding madness, he would offer sacrifice to his beloved as to the image of a god. Afterwards follow the natural results of his chill, a sudden change, a sweating and glow of unwonted heat. For he has received through his eyes the emanation of beauty, and has been warmed thereby, and his native plumage is watered. And by the warmth the parts where the feathers sprout are softened, after having been long so closed up by their hardness as to hinder the feathers from growing. But as soon as this nourishing shower pours in, the quill of the feather begins to swell, and struggles to start up from the root, and spread beneath the whole surface of the soul; for in old time the soul was entirely feathered.

(Plato, *Phaedrus*, tr. J. Wright)

Shortly afterwards the subject of ideal and carnal love is discussed:

THE SOUL AS CHARIOTEER

So beautiful is the desire of those who truly love, and if they accomplish their desire, so beautiful is the initiation, as I call it, into their holy mystery, and so fraught with blessing at the hand of a friend, whom love has maddened, to the object of the friendship, if he be but won. Now he who is won, is won in the following manner.

As at the commencement of this account I divided every soul into three parts, two of them resembling horses, the third a charioteer, so let us here still keep to that division. Now of the horses one, if you remember, we said, was good, and the other bad; but wherein consists the goodness of the one, and the badness of the other, is a point which, not distinguished then, must be stated now. That horse of the two which occupies the nobler rank, is in form erect and firmly knit, high-necked, hook-nosed, white-coloured, black-eyed; he loves honour with temperance and modesty, and, a votary of genuine glory, he is driven without stroke of the whip by voice and reason alone. The bad horse, on the other hand, is crooked, bulky, clumsily put together, with thick neck, short throat, flat face, black coat, grey and bloodshot eyes, a friend to all riot and insolence, shaggy about the ears, dull of hearing, scarcely yielding to lash and goad united. Whenever therefore the driver sees the sight which inspires love, and his whole soul, being thoroughly heated by sense, is surcharged with irritation and the stings of desire, the obedient horse, yielding then as ever to the check of shame, restrains himself from springing on the loved one; but the other pays heed no longer to his driver's goad or lash, but struggles on with unruly bounds, and doing all violence to his yoke-fellow and master, forces them to approach the beautiful youth, and bethink themselves of the joys of dalliance.

And though at first they resist him with indignation at the lawless and fearful crime he is urging, yet at last when there is no end to the evil, they move onward as he leads them, having yielded him submission and agreed to do his bidding. So they all come up to the beautiful boy, and see his countenance gleaming with beauty. But as the driver looks, his memory is carried back to the essence of beauty, and again he sees her by the side of Continence standing on a holy pedestal. And at the sight he shudders, and with a holy awe falls backward to the ground, and falling cannot help pulling back the reins so violently that he brings both the horses on their haunches, the one indeed willingly, because he is not resisting, but the rebel in spite of struggling. And when they are withdrawn to some distance, the former in his shame and ravishment drenches all the soul with sweat, but the other when he is recovered from the pain which the bit and the fall inflicted, and has with difficulty regained his breath, breaks out into passionate revilings, vehemently railing at his master and his comrade for their treacherous cowardice in deserting their ranks and agreement. And again he urges them, again refusing, to approach, and barely yields a reluctant consent when they beg to defer the attempt to another time. But soon as the covenanted time is come, though they affect forgetfulness, he reminds them of their engagement, and plunging and neighing and dragging, he again obliges them to approach the beautiful youth to make the same proposals. And when they are near, he stoops his head and gets the bit between his teeth, and drags them on incontinently.

But the driver experiences, though still more strongly, the same sensation as at first; backward he falls like racers at the barrier, and with a wrench still more violent than before pulls back the bit from between the teeth of the riotous horse, thereby drenching his jaws and railing tongue with blood; and bruising against the ground his legs and haunches, consigns him to anguish. But as soon as by this treatment oft repeated, the evil horse is recovered from his vice, he follows with humbled steps the guidance of his driver, and at sight of the fair one is consumed with terror. So that then, and not till then, does it happen that the soul of the lover follows his beloved with reverence and awe. And the consequence is, that the youth being now worshipped with all the worship of a god, by a lover who does not feign the passion, but feels it in his soul, and being himself by nature fondly inclined to his worshipper, even though haply in time past he may have been set against lovers by the remarks of his school-fellows or others on the scandal of allowing their approaches, and is therefore disposed to reject his present wooer, yet now that the latter is thus changed he is led in course of time, by the instinct of his years, and the law of destiny, to admit him to familiarity. For surely it was never destined for the bad to be friends of the bad, or the good aught but friendly to the good.

But when the advances have been accepted and speech and intercourse allowed, the affection of the lover being brought into near connection with the loved one, strikes him with wonder, as it compels him to feel that the friendship shown him by all the rest of his friends and relations put together, is as nothing beside the love of his god-inspired friend. And if he continues long thus to indulge him, and allows him the closest contact both in gymnastic schools and other places of meeting, then it is that the stream of that effluence, to which Zeus when enamoured of Ganymedes gave the name of desire, pours upon the lover in a plenteous flood, and partly sinks within him, partly flows off him when he is full; and just as a wind or a noise rebounds from smooth and hard substances and is carried back again to the place from which it came; so the tide of beauty passes back into the beautiful boy through his eyes, the natural channel into his soul; and when it has come there and has fledged it anew, it waters the outlets of the feathers, and forcing them to shoot up afresh fills the soul of the loved one as well as that of his lover with love. He is in love therefore, but with whom he cannot say; nay, what it is that has come over him he knows not, neither can he tell, but like one who has caught a disease in the eye from the diseased gaze of another, he can assign no reason for the affection, but sees himself in his lover, as in a glass, without knowing who it is that he sees. And when they are together, he enjoys the same respite that his lover does from his anguish; but when they are parted, he yearns for him as he himself is yearned for, since he holds in his bosom love's reflected image, love returned. He calls it, however, and believes it to be not love but friendship, albeit, he feels the same desire as the other does, though in a feebler degree, for the sight, the touch, the kiss, the embrace. And consequently, as might be expected, his conduct thenceforward is as follows. When they are lying side by side, the lover's unbridled horse has much to say to its driver, and claims as the recompense of many labours a short enjoyment; but the vicious horse of the other has nothing to say, but burning and restless clasps the lover and kisses him as he would kiss a dear friend, and when they are folded in each other's embrace, is just of such a temper as not for his part to refuse indulging the lover in any pleasure he might request to enjoy; but his yoke-fellow, on the other hand, joins the driver in struggling against him with chastity and reason. Should it appear then that the better part of their nature has led both the lover and loved into a life of order and philosophy, and established its own ascendancy, in bliss and harmony they live out their existence here, being masters of themselves and decorous before the world, having enslaved that portion of the soul wherein vice is contained, and liberated that where virtue dwells; and at last when they come to die, being winged and lightened, they have in one of their three truly Olympic combats achieved the prize, than which no greater good can either human prudence or godly madness bestow on man. But if they have given in to a coarser habit of life, and one unfriendly to wisdom, though not to honour, it may well happen that in a moment of drunkenness or like abandonment, those two unruly beasts will surprise the souls off their guard, and bringing them together into one place will choose and consummate that practice which the world deems happy, and once consummated will for the future indulge in it, though sparingly, as doing what is not approved by all their mind. Dear, therefore, to each other, though not so dear as the former two, do these continue both while their love is burning and when it is extinct; for they conceive themselves to have given and received the strongest pledges, which it were impious at any time to violate by becoming alienated. And in the end, without their wings it is true, but not without having started feathers, they go forth from the body, so that they carry off no paltry prize for their impassioned madness; for there is a law that the paths of darkness beneath the earth shall never again be trodden by those who have so much as set their foot on the heavenward road, but that walking hand in hand they shall live a bright and blessed life, and when they recover their wings, recover them together for their love's sake.

(*Ibid.*)

★ ★ ★

JOKES ABOUT EFFEMINACY

IT seems clear that the Ancient Greeks disliked effeminate people and were not likely to be won over by behaviour that was sissy. In the *Symposium* Aristophanes qualifies his use of the term 'hermaphrodite' for the original combined-sex he posits by adding that it 'is only used nowadays as a term of contempt'. It was only later that a statue of Hermaphroditos became a popular decorative addendum to gymnasia and baths. The following piece is from Aristophanes' *Thesmophoriazusae* and concerns the minor poet Agathon (who also appears in the *Symposium*). Euripides hopes to persuade the maidenly Agathon to insinuate himself, dressed as a woman, into the Ladies Ritual and there to defend his reputation. Mnesilochos, Euripides' father-in-law, is trying to help.

                        – Young man
whoever you are, permit me to address you
in the style of Aischylos:
   'What woman, or what man, or both
   Combinéd, with cosmetic art
   Bewrays the stigma of his youth
   I' th' costume of a virile tart?'
I understand the lyre, of course; but what
are you doing with a hair-net? A bottle
of gymnasium oil, yes; but why the girdle?
Why a hand-mirror and a sword at the same time?
What are you, you recumbent paradox? A man?
Show me; or, if that makes you blush,
where are your Spartan boots, your cavalry cloak?
Or are you a woman? If so, where are your breasts?
No answer. Bashful. If I want to find out,
I suppose I'll have to read your *Collected Poems*.

  Agathon:
Greybeard, greybeard, your malicious envy
bombards my ears, but I heed it not at all.
However, if you must know,
I wear this particular costume by design.
A dramatist embarked upon his art
should prepare for the voyage; and since my best plays
are female, my manner suggests the Heroine.
Do you follow me?

  Mnesilochos:
               More or less. I take it
You're barearse when you go to work on a *Phaidra*.

  Agathon:
Again, a male role calls for male properties.
Thus art makes up for natural defect.

Mnesilochos:
Remember me when you write a satyr play:
I've a fundamental art that will enchant you.

Agathon:
Furthermore, who wants a hairy poet?
Bah, these rugged artists!
                    No, let me have
Ibykos, – there's a writer for you! – or Anakreon
or Alkaïos, all of them simply a-swim with music.
Those boys liked pretty hats and pretty manners,
and that's the reason their songs are pretty, too,
Or take Phrynichos – you've heard of him, surely:
He was a fancy poet with a fancy taste,
and his fancy poems go fancying down the ages.
It's a law of nature:
Art is the perfect mirror of character.
              (Aristophanes, *Thesmophoriazusae*, tr. Dudley Fitts)

★　　★　　★

FINALLY THIS ROMANTIC but melancholy tale which has been
attributed, probably in error, to Theokritos:

THE HEARTLESS LOVER

There was once a heart-sick swain had a cruel fere, the face of the fere
goodly but his ways not like to it; for he hated him that loved him,
and had for him never a whit of kindness, and as for Love, what
manner of God he might be or what manner of bow and arrows carry,
or how keen and bitter were the shafts he shot for his delectation, these
things wist he not at all, but both in his talk and conversation knew no
yielding. And he gave no comfort against those burning fires, not a
twist of his lip, not a flash of his eye, not the gift of a hip from the hedge-
row, not a word, not a kiss, to lighten the load of desire. But he eyed
every man even as a beast of the field that suspects the hunter, and
his lips were hard and cruel and his eyes looked the dread look of fate.
Indeed his angry humour made change of his face, and the colour of his
cheeks fled away because he was a prey to wrathful imaginings. But

even so he was fair to view; his wrath served only to prick his lover
the more.

At last the poor man would bear no more so fierce a flame of the
Cytherean, but went and wept before that sullen house, and kissed the
doorpost of it, and lifted up his voice saying 'O cruel, O sullen child,
that wast nursed of an evil she-lion; O boy of stone which art all unworthy to be loved; lo! here am I come with the last of my gifts,
even this my halter. No longer will I vex you with the sight of me; but
here go I whither you have condemned me, where they say the path
lies all lovers must travel, where is the sweet physic of oblivion. Yet if
so be I take and drink that physic up, every drop, yet shall I not
quench the fever of my desire.

'And lo! now I bid this thy door farewell or ever I go. I know what
is to be. The rose is fair and Time withers it, the violet is fair in the
year's spring and it quickly groweth old; the lily is white, – it fades
when it's flowering's done; and white the snow, – it melts all away
when the wind blows warm; and even so, the beauty of a child is
beautiful indeed, but it liveth not for long. The day will come when
you shall love like me, when your heart shall burn like mine, and your
eyes weep brinish tears. So I pray you, child, do me this one last courtesy: when you shall come and find a poor man hanging at your door,
pass him not by; but stay you first and weep awhile for a libation upon
him, and then loosening him from the rope, put about him some
covering from your own shoulders; and give him one last kiss, for your
lips will be welcome even to the dead. And never fear me; I cannot do
thee any mischief; thou shalt kiss and there an end. Then pray thee
make a hole in some earthy bank for to hide all my love of thee; and
ere thou turn thee to go thy ways, cry over me three times "Rest, my
friend," and if it seems thee good cry also "My fair companion's dead."
And for epitaph write the words I here inscribe upon thy wall:

> Here's one that died of love; good wayfarer,
> Stay thee and say: 'his was a cruel fere.'

This said, he took a stone and set it up, that dreadful stone, against
the wall in the midst of the doorway; then tied that slender string into
the porch above, put the noose about his neck, rolled that footing
from beneath his feet, and lo! he hung a corpse.

Soon that other, he opened the door and espied the dead hanging to his own doorway; and his stubborn heart was not bended. The new-done murder moved him not unto tears, nor would he be defiling all his young lad's garments with a dead corpse; but went his ways to the wrestling-bouts and betook himself light of heart to his beloved bath. And so came he unto the God he had slighted. For there stood an image of him upon the margin looking towards the water. And lo! even the graven image leapt down upon him and slew that wicked lad; and the water went all red, and on the water floated the voice of a child saying 'Rejoice ye that love, for he that did hate is slain; and love ye that hate, for the God knoweth how to judge.'

(Theocritus, XXIII, tr. J. M. Edmonds)[1]

---

[1] The reader may wish to be reminded of the love between Hippotheos and Hyperanthes in Xenophon of Ephesus' *An Ephesian Tale*. Here the lover actually murders his beloved's rich abductor. The date is the Third Century A.D.

3

The Romans

In the troubled years 45 and 44 B.C., not long before his murder, Cicero poured himself out in a number of philosophic works, of which his dialogue *De Amicitia* is one. This dialogue consists of the opinions of one Laelius, praetor, consul, philosopher and scholar (186 – 88 B.C.) who had in fact learned them from his bosom-friend, Scipio Africanus the Younger, and which Cicero received at second-hand when he was a law-student. The Scipionic circle was a group of illustrious and virtuous friends. Since the dialogue goes back to Aristotle's *Ethics*, and indeed to the *Lysis* of Plato, it has been thought best to preface it with some of Aristotle's points.

Less high-flying than Plato, Aristotle begins his argument with the remark. 'No one would choose a friendless existence on condition of having all the other good things in the world'. But friendship can have three different objects: it can be good, pleasant or useful. Of these, utility and pleasure are accidental qualities which do not promote a love of the friend in himself: a business relationship for mutual profit, for instance, or simply liking somebody because he is witty. The relation of the pleasant to the good is shown in the following passages:

RESTLESS AND SLOW-RIPENING FRIENDS

But when it is young people who form a friendship, the object of it, we all think, is the pleasure they get from it. This seems natural, when we reflect that the life of the young is one emotion after another, their grand object being to amuse themselves and catch the moments as they fly. And as they grow older the things that please them change too, so that they both make and drop friends quickly. (Their affections change with the source of their pleasures, and their tastes change rapidly.) Also the young are much subject to the passion of love, which for the most part is a longing for delight working upon the emotions. And so it comes about that they fall in and out of love quickly, often passing from one stage to the other before the day is out. But of course the young desire to pass the hours in the society of their friends. For that is what friendship means to them, and that is what they get.

But it is only between those who are good, and resemble one another in their goodness, that friendship is perfect. Such friends are both good in themselves and, so far as they are good, desire the good of one another. But it is those who desire the good of their friends for their friends' sake who are most completely friends, since each loves the other for what the other is in himself and not for something he has about him which he need not have. Accordingly, the friendship of such men lasts as long as they keep their goodness – and goodness is a lasting quality. And when two such men are friends, each is good not only absolutely but in relation to the other, the good being both good in themselves and profitable to one another. So this kind of friendship *includes* the utilitarian kind. But it also includes the kind which has pleasure for its motive. For each of these friends is pleasant in both ways, since the good are pleasant both in themselves and to each other. For every man is pleased with his own behaviour and, as a consequence, with behaviour that resembles his own. But all good men behave in the same or much the same way. That friendships of this quality should be rare is only what was to be expected, for men of that quality are rare. And besides goodness they need time and intimacy to establish perfect friendship. As the proverb has it, you cannot learn to know a man until you have eaten a peck of salt with him. Just so, before one man can be admitted to the friendship of another and be his friend, he must prove to the other that he is deserving of his friendship and can be trusted. Those who 'make friends' quickly have the desire to be friends; but they cannot really be friends unless they are worthy to be such and both parties know it. Wishing to be friends is quick work, but friendship is a slow-ripening fruit.

(*Ethics*, Book 8, tr. J. A. K. Thomson)

THE LESSER TYPES OF FRIENDSHIP

The kind of friendship that is sought for the sake of the pleasure it
affords has a resemblance to the perfect friendship between good men,
for such find pleasure in each other's society. But we can say the same
of utilitarian friendship, for good men are useful to one another. We
may add that the friendship between them lasts longer when each friend
receives from the other the same good gift – pleasure for example –
and moreover receives it from the same source, as happens when there
is a friendship between two witty people, and as does not happen when
the friends are lovers, because these do not have their delight in the
same things. The lover finds his pleasure in looking on the beloved, and
the beloved in the attentions of his lover. And sometimes when the
lad's beauty wanes the friendship wanes also. For the lover is no longer
delighted by the sight of the loved one, who for his part is no longer
gratified by the attentions of his friend. Yet many do remain friends if,
being alike in character, their intimacy has taught them to love each
other's character. But when it is not pleasure that passes between lovers
but material gain, then the affection between them is less deep and
lasting. If all they seek is some mutual advantage, they part as soon as
the profit goes. They were not friends for friendship's sake, but to get
something out of it.

(*Ibid.*)

PLURALITY IS DIFFICULT

But to have many friends in the way of perfect friendship is no more
possible than to be in love with many at the same time. It is not even
easy for a man to have at the same time a large circle of agreeable
acquaintances, and indeed it may be doubted if good men are so
common. When you do find such a man you must become intimate
with him and learn to know him before you make him your friend,
and nothing is harder than that. On the other hand it is perfectly
possible to have a *liking* for quite a number of people at the same time
for the pleasure and profit one gets out of them. There are plenty of
people capable of providing us with either, and it does not take long to
furnish ourselves with the advantages they offer.

(*Ibid.*)

POLITICAL IMPLICATIONS

The affection between husband and wife is the same as that which exists between the government and the governed in an aristocracy. For the degree of it is measured by the relative merits of husband and wife, the husband, who is superior in merit, receiving the larger share of affection, and either party receiving what is appropriate to it. And the claims of justice in this relationship are satisfied in the same way. As for the friendliness between brothers, it is like what we get between the members of some club or association. You have equality of rank and age, and where you have that you have as a rule a similarity of sentiments and habits. This is the kind of sympathy one finds between the citizens of a timocracy. For the timocratic ideal is that all shall be equal as well as good. Hence political power is shared among the citizens equally and in turn, and the result is that the friendship between them is friendship upon terms of equality.

But in the perverted constitutions friendship, like justice, goes but a little way, and least in the worst; for under a tyranny there can be little or no kindness between ruler and ruled. They have nothing in common, so there can be no friendliness between them, just as there can be no justice. The relations between them are those of the skilled workman to his tool or of the soul to the body. No doubt the instrument is in every case all the better for the manipulation it receives from the user, but there can be no friendship or justice in our dealings with inanimate things. We cannot even have it towards a horse or cow, nay, towards a slave in his character of slave. . . . There can therefore be no friendship of a master for his slave as such, though there may be for him as a man. For clearly there must be some form of justice involved in the relations between one man and another who is capable of acting legally or being a party to a contract. Similarly, friendship is possible with any man so far as he is a human being. We cannot then maintain that there is much room for friendship and justice between rulers and ruled under a tyranny. They are most adequately realized in democracies, the citizens of a democracy being equal and having many things in common.

(*Ibid.*)

In Book 9 Aristotle makes the very interesting point that 'The characteristic element in our friendship for our neighbours, and the points which distinguish and delimit the various forms of friendship, seem to have their origin in the sympathetic feelings with which we regard ourselves'. This leads to:

THE PSYCHOPATH'S INABILITY TO LOVE

. . . Possessing no lovable quality, they have no love for themselves. Consequently such men have no sympathetic consciousness of their own joys and sorrows. For the soul of them is divided against itself. One part of it, being depraved, feels pain in denying itself certain things, while another part has a sense of gratification – one part pulling this way and the other that – and they are like to be torn in pieces. If it is impossible to feel pain and pleasure at the same time, at any rate a feeling of pleasure is followed after a little by a sense of remorse in a man of this type, who can only wish that he had never indulged in such gratifications. For a bad man is always full of regrets. From this we may see that a bad man is never on good terms with himself, because he is devoid of any lovable quality. If then a state of mind like this is wretched to a degree, one ought to strain every nerve to avoid wicked-ness and attain to virtue. Only then will one be at peace with oneself and become dear to another.

(Book 9, *Ibid.*)

*　　*　　*

CICERO'S VIEW that only good men can be friends, etc.:

This, however, I do feel first of all – that friendship cannot exist except among good men; nor do I go into that too deeply, as is done by those who, in discussing this point with more than usual accuracy, and it may be correctly, but with too little view to practical results, say that no one is good unless he is wise . . .

For it seems clear to me that we were so created that between us all there exists a certain tie which strengthens with our proximity to each other. Therefore, fellow countrymen are preferred to foreigners and relatives to strangers, for with them Nature herself engenders friendship, but it is one that is lacking in constancy. For friendship excels relationship in this, that goodwill may be eliminated from relationship while from friendship it cannot; since, if you remove goodwill from friendship the very name of friendship is gone; if you remove it from relationship, the name of relationship still remains. Moreover, how great the power of friendship is may most clearly be recognised from the fact that, in comparison with the infinite ties uniting the human race and fashioned by Nature herself, this thing called friendship has been so narrowed that the bonds of affection always unite two persons only, or, at most, a few.

For friendship is nothing else than an accord in all things, human and divine, conjoined with mutual goodwill and affection, and I am inclined to think that, with the exception of wisdom, no better thing has been given to man by the immortal gods. Some prefer riches, some good health, some power, some public honours, and many even prefer sensual pleasures. This last is the highest aim of brutes; the others are fleeting and unstable things and dependent less upon human foresight than upon the fickleness of fortune. Again, there are those who place the 'chief good' in virtue and that is really a noble view; but this very virtue is the parent and preserver of friendship and without virtue friendship cannot exist at all. To proceed then, let us interpret the word 'virtue' by the familiar usage of our everyday life and speech, and not in pompous phrase apply to it the precise standards which certain philosophers use; and let us include in the number of good men those who are so considered – men like Paulus, Cato, Gallus, Scipio, and Philus – who satisfy the ordinary standard of life; but let us pass by such men as are nowhere to be found at all.

Therefore, among men like those just mentioned, friendship offers advantages almost beyond my power to describe. In the first place, how can life be what Ennius calls 'the life worth living', if it does not repose on the mutual goodwill of a friend? What is sweeter than to have someone with whom you may dare discuss anything as if you were communing with yourself? How could your enjoyment in times of prosperity be so great if you did not have someone whose joy in them would be equal to your own? Adversity would indeed be hard to bear, without him to whom the burden would be heavier even than to yourself. In short, all other objects of desire are each, for the most part, adapted to a single end – riches for spending; influence, for honour; public office, for reputation; pleasures, for sensual enjoyment; and health, for freedom from pain and full use of the bodily functions; but friendship embraces innumerable ends; turn where you will it is ever at your side; no barrier shuts it out; it is never untimely, and never in the way. Therefore, we do not use the proverbial 'fire and water' on more occasions than we use friendship. I am not now speaking of the ordinary and commonplace friendship – delightful and profitable as it is – but of that pure and faultless kind, such as was that of the few whose friendships are known to fame. For friendship adds a brighter radiance to prosperity and lessens the burden of adversity by dividing and sharing it.

Seeing that friendship includes very many and very great advantages, it undoubtedly excels all other things in this respect, that it projects the bright ray of hope into the future, and does not suffer the spirit to grow faint or to fall. Again, he who looks upon a true friend, looks, as it were, upon a sort of image of himself. Wherefore friends, though absent, are at hand; though in need, yet abound; though weak, are strong; and – harder saying still – though dead, are yet alive; so great is the esteem on the part of their friends, the tender recollection and the deep longing that still attends them. These things make the death of the departed seem fortunate and the life of the survivors worthy of praise. But if you should take the bond of goodwill out of the universe no house or city could stand, nor would even the tillage of the fields survive. If that statement is not clear, then you may understand how great is the power of friendship and of concord from a consideration of the results of enmity and disagreement. For what house is so strong, or what state so enduring that it cannot be utterly overthrown by animosities and division?

From this it may be judged how great good there is in friendship.
(Cicero, *De Amicitia*, tr. W. A. Falconer)

NOT FROM NEED BUT NATURE

If people think that friendship springs from weakness and from a purpose to secure someone through whom we may obtain that which we lack, they assign her, if I may so express it, a lowly pedigree indeed, and an origin far from noble, and they would make her the daughter of poverty and want. If this were so, then just in proportion as any man judged his resources to be small, would he be fitted for friendship; whereas the truth is far otherwise. For to the extent that a man relies upon himself and is so fortified by virtue and wisdom that he is dependent on no one and considers all his possessions to be within himself, in that degree is he most conspicuous for seeking out and cherishing friendships. Now what need did Africanus have of me? By Hercules! none at all. And I, assuredly, had no need of him either, but I loved him because of a certain admiration for his virtue, and he, in turn, loved me, because, it may be, of the fairly good opinion which he had of my character; and close association added to our mutual affection. Although many and great advantages did ensue from our friendship, still the beginnings of our love did not spring from the hope of gain. For as men of our class are generous and liberal, not for the purpose of demanding repayment – for we do not put our favours out at interest, but are by nature given to acts of kindness – so we believe that friendship is desirable, not because we are influenced by hope of gain, but because its entire profit is in the love itself.

(Ibid.)

FORMATION OF FRIENDSHIPS

As a rule decisions about friendships should be formed after strength and stability have been reached in mind and age; nor should men who in boyhood were devoted to hunting and games of ball, keep as their intimates those whom they loved at that period simply because they were fond of the same pursuits. For on that principle nurses and the slaves who attended us to and from school, will, by right of priority of acquaintance, claim the largest share of our good will. I admit that they are not to be neglected, but they are to be regarded in an entirely different way; under no other conditions can friendship remain secure. For difference of character is attended by difference of taste and it is this diversity of taste that severs friendships; nor is there any other cause why good men cannot be friends to wicked men, or wicked men to good men, except that there is the greatest possible distance between them in character and taste.

(Ibid.)

REVERENCE

. . . For he who takes reverence from friendship, takes away its brightest jewel. Therefore, a fatal mistake is made by those who think that friendship opens wide the door to every passion and to every sin. Friendship was given to us by nature as the handmaid of virtue, not as a comrade of vice; because virtue cannot attain her highest aims unattended, but only in union and fellowship with another. Such a partnership as this, whether it is, or was, or is yet to be, should be considered the best and happiest comradeship along the road to nature's highest good. In such a partnership, I say, abide all things that men deem worthy of pursuit – honour and fame and delightful tranquillity of mind; so that when these blessings are at hand life is happy, and without them, it cannot be happy.

(Ibid.)

INTEGRITY

As, therefore, it is characteristic of true friendship both to give and to receive advice and, on the one hand, to give it with all freedom of speech, but without harshness, and on the other hand, to receive it patiently, but without resentment, so nothing is to be considered a greater bane of friendship than fawning, cajolery, or flattery; for give it as many names as you choose, it deserves to be branded as a vice peculiar to fickle and falsehearted men who say everything with a view to pleasure and nothing with a view to truth. Moreover, hypocrisy is not only wicked under all circumstances, because it pollutes truth and takes away the power to discern it, but it is also especially inimical to friendship, since it utterly destroys sincerity, without which the word friendship can have no meaning. And since the effect of friendship is to make, as it were, one soul out of many, how will that be possible if not even in one man taken by himself shall there be a soul always one and the same, but fickle, changeable, and manifold? For what can be as pliant and erratic as the soul of the man who changes not only to suit another's humour and desire, but even his expression and his nod?

(Ibid.)

★   ★   ★

VIRGIL'S ECLOGUE about Corydon and Alexis achieved notoriety at the time of the Renaissance; one of the charges very dubiously laid against Marlowe was that he had blasphemously described St John as the Alexis of Christ. But Virgil was, of course, very different to the 'new poets' like Catullus, Ovid,

Tibullus and Propertius. Byron recognizes this in an amusing passage:

> Ovid's a rake, as half his verses show him,
>   Anacreon's morals are a still worse sample,
> Catullus scarcely has a decent poem,
>   I don't think Sappho's Ode a good example,
> Although Longinus tells us there is no hymn
>   Where the sublime soars forth on wings more ample;
> But Virgil's songs are pure, except that horrid one
> Beginning with 'Formosum Pastor Corydon.'
>   (*Don Juan*, Canto I)

THE ALEXIS ECLOGUE

Corydon, the shepherd, was aflame for the fair Alexis, his master's pet, nor knew what to hope. So his one solace, he would day by day come among the thick beeches with their shady summits, and there alone in fruitless passion fling these artless strains to the hills and woods:

'O cruel Alexis, care you naught for my songs? Have you no pity for me? You will drive me at last to death. Now even the cattle court the cool shade; now even the green lizards hide in the brakes, and Thestylis pounds for the reapers, spent with the scorching heat, her savoury herbs of garlic and thyme. But as I scan your footprints, the copses under the burning sun ring with the shrill cicalas's voice along with mine. Was it not better to brook Amaryllis' sullen rage and scornful disdain? or Menalcas, though he was swart and you are fair? Ah, lovely boy, trust not too much to your bloom! The white privets fall, the dark hyacinths are culled!

'You scorn me, Alexis, and ask not what I am – how rich in cattle, how wealthy in snow-white milk! A thousand lambs of mine roam over the Sicilian hills; new milk fails me not, summer or winter. I sing as Amphion of Dirce used to sing, when calling home the herds on Attic Aracynthus. Nor am I so unsightly; on the shore the other day I looked at myself, when, by grace of the winds, the sea was at peace and still. With you for judge, I should fear not Daphnis, if the mirror never lies!

'O if you would but live with me in our rude fields and lowly cots, shooting the deer and driving the flock of kids to the green mallows! With me in the woods you shall rival Pan in song. Pan it was who first taught man to make many reeds one with wax; Pan cares for the sheep and the shepherds of the sheep. Nor would you be sorry to have chafed your lip with a reed; to learn the same art, what did not Amyntas do? I have a pipe formed of seven uneven hemlock-stalks, a gift Damoetas once gave me, and said on his death-bed, "Now it claims thee as second master." So said Damoetas; Amyntas, foolish one, felt envious. Nay more, two roes – I found them in a dangerous valley – their hides still sprinkled with white, drain a ewe's udders twice a day. These I keep for you. Thestylis has long been begging to get them from me – and so she shall, as in your eyes my gifts are mean.

'Come hither, lovely boy! See, for you the Nymphs bring lilies in heaped-up baskets; for you the fair Naiad, plucking pale violets and poppy heads, blends narcissus and sweet-scented fennel-flower; then, twining them with cassia and other sweet herbs, sets off the delicate hyacinth with the golden marigold. My own hands will gather quinces, pale with tender down, and chestnuts, which my Amaryllis loved. Waxen plums I will add – this fruit, too, shall have its honour. You too, O laurels, I will pluck, and you, their sweet neighbour myrtle, for so placed you blend sweet fragrance.

'Corydon, you are a clown! Alexis cares naught for gifts, nor if with gifts you were to vie, would Iollas yield. Alas, alas! what wish, poor wretch, has been mine? Madman, I have let in the south wind to my flowers, and boars to my crystal springs! Ah, fool, whom do you flee? Even the gods have dwelt in the woods, and Dardan Paris. Let Pallas dwell by herself in the cities she has built; but let my chief delight be the woods! The grim lioness follows the wolf, the wolf himself the goat, the wanton goat the flowering clover, and Corydon follows you, Alexis. Each is led by his liking. See, the bullocks drag home by the yoke the hanging plough, and the retiring sun doubles the lengthening shadows. Yet my love still burns; for what bound can be set to love? Ah, Corydon, Corydon, what madness has gripped you? Your vine is but half-pruned on the leafy elm. Nay, why not at least set about plaiting some thing your need calls for, with twigs and pliant rushes? You will find another Alexis, if this one scorns you!'

(Virgil, *Eclogue II*, tr. H. Rushton Fairclough)

*   *   *

'HORACE WROTE GRAVELY of the moral degeneration of the family; yet he himself never married, and his gayest poems were addressed to pretty conscienceless girls and pretty, soft boys,' Gilbert Highett explains in his *Poets in a Landscape*. In the *Latin Love-Elegy* Georg Luck has this comment: 'Horace addressed one of his most beautiful odes to Valgius, urging him to cease the laments over the death of the handsome boy Mystes and to celebrate Augustus' victories instead. He calls these laments *flebiles modi*, perhaps because they were in the elegiac metre. The theme – love to a handsome boy – reminds one of Phanocles' *Erotes* or Tibullus' group of Marathus-poems.' Yet Horace was far from extreme. 'Horace's wildest dissipations tinkle like the teacups at Strawberry Hill . . .' (Helen Waddell, *The Wandering Scholars*.)

TO VALGIUS

Not always from black clouds the rainstorm pours
Upon the sodden fields; the gusty sleet
   Doth not for aye the Caspian beat,
     Nor on Armenian shores

Stands, Valgius, through all months the ice as hard.
Gargan's great oaks do not for ever toss,
   Nor ash-tree mourn of leaves the loss,
     By storms continuous scarred!

But thou dost never cease thy dreary wails,
Harping on Mystes dead; nor do thy sighs
   End when the Evening Star doth rise,
     Nor when at dawn he pales.

Not so did the thrice-aged Nestor keep
Mourning for aye his dear Archilochus;
   Not so did for young Troilus
     His sire and sisters weep.

O cease at length to bruit thus thy woe
In womanish plaints! Better for us to sing
   Augustus Caesar's triumphing;
    How with less boastful flow

Wintery Niphates and the Meiian tide,
Ranked with the conquered now, go slinking past;
   How the Gelonians cooped at last
    In narrower limits ride.
                (Horace, *Odes*, Book II, tr. John Marshall)

TO LIGURINUS

Though hard thou art still, thyself on the dear gift of beauty pluming,
Yet when the unlooked-for change shall come to check thy pride's
   presuming;
When clipt the locks that now about thy neck in curls repose,
When thy complexion's radiance, now more bright than any rose,
Fading hath changed thy daintiness to gloom of year's decays –
'Alas!' thou'lt cry, as on an altered self in glass thou'lt gaze,
'Why to my youth was not the wisdom given which now I share?
Or with my old desires why come not back youth's cheeks as fair?'
                                 (*Ibid.*)

TO VENUS

   Must it be war again
After so long a truce? Venus, be kind, refrain,
   I beg you. The time's over
When Cinara was my gracious queen and I her lover.
   Fifty years, pitiless
Mother of the sweet Loves, weigh hard. You must not press
   This old tough-jointed horse
To run to your cajoling order round the course.
   Leave me. Go back to where
The young men call for you with a persuasive prayer.
   To Paulus Maximus' house
Pilot your lustrous swans, in proper style carouse,
   And, seeing you desire

A hot and likely heart, choose his to set on fire.
 Handsome, blue-blooded, young,
He for his nervous clients wields a ready tongue,
 And knows a hundred arts
To spread your army's banners to remotest parts.
 And when some rival, free
With lavish presents, fails, grateful and jubilant he
 Shall by the Alban lake
Beneath a cedar roof yourself in marble make.
 Thick incense you'll inhale,
Sweet to your nostrils, there, and music shall regale
 Your ears – concerted lute
And curly Berecynthian pipe and shepherd's flute.
 With the sun's earliest rays
And last, young boys and girls shall give your godhead praise,
 Flashing their snow-white feet,
Dancing the Salian dance, treading the triple beat.
 Yet I here take no joy
In the naïve hope of mutual love with woman or boy,
 Or drinking bouts with men,
Or garlanding my temples with fresh flowers. Why then,
 My Ligurinus, why
Should the reluctant-flowing tears surprise these dry
 Cheeks, and my fluent tongue
Stumble in unbecoming silences among
 Syllables? In dreams at night
I hold you in my arms, or toil behind your flight
 Across the Martian Field,
Or chase through yielding waves the boy who will not yield.

   (*Ibid.*, Book IV, tr. James Michie)

   ★ ★ ★

IN THE MARATHUS POEMS Tibullus forgets his Delia and considers the love of ephebes.

PRIAPUS' ADVICE TO THE LOVELORN

'Priapus, tell me,—so may the sheltering shade be thine, nor thy head be harmed by sun or snows – what cunning of thine captures the handsome lads? Sure thou hast no glossy beard nor well-kept hair. Naked thou art all through the cold of stormy winter, naked through the parching season of the Dog-star's heats.'

Thus I; and thus to me replied the country child of Bacchus, the god armed with the curving billhook:

'O beware of trusting thyself to the gentle band of boys; for they furnish always some valid ground for love. One pleases, for he keeps a tight hand on his horse's rein; another drives the calm water before a breast of snow. This one has taken you with his brave assurance, that one by the maiden shame that guards his young cheeks.

'Perchance at first he will refuse thee; but let not this dishearten thee. Little by little his neck will pass beneath the yoke. Length of time has taught lions to submit to man; with length of time weak water has eaten through rock. The year's flight ripens the grapes on the sunny hillside; the year's flight carries the radiant signs along their unvarying round.

'Be not afraid to swear. Null and void are the perjuries of love; the winds bear them ineffective over land and the face of the sea. Great thanks to Jove! The Sire himself has decreed no oath should stand that love has taken in the folly of desire. Dictynna lets thee without harm assever by her arrows, Minerva by her hair.

'But if thou art slow, thou wilt be lost. Youth is gone how quickly! Time stands not idle, nor returns. How quickly does the earth lose its purple hues! How quickly the tall poplar its beauteous leaves! How neglected is the horse, when the lot of weak age overtakes him, that once shot free from the barriers of Elis! I have seen a young man on whom later years were closing round mourning for his folly in the day that had fled. Cruel gods! The snake sheds his years, and is young: but the Fates grant no respite to beauty. Only Bacchus and Phoebus have youth everlasting; of either god are unshorn tresses the glory.

'Do thou yield to thy lad in aught that he is minded to attempt: love wins most by compliance. Nor refuse to go with him, though far be his purposed journey and the Dog-star bake the land with parching drought, though, threatening the coming storm, the rain-charged bow fringes the sky with hues of purple. Should he wish to fly over the blue waves in a boat, take the oar thyself and drive the light bark through the sea. Nor grieve to undergo rough labour or if thy hands are chafed by tasks to which they are strange. If round the deep glen he would place the ambush, then, so thou canst pleasure him, let thy shoulders not refuse to bear the hunting nets. If he would fence, thou wilt try thy light hand at the sport, and often leave thy side unguarded, that he may win.

'Then will he be gentle with thee; then thou mayest snatch the precious kiss: he will struggle, but let thee snatch it. He will let thee snatch at first; but later will he bring it for the asking, and presently even he will be fain to hang upon thy neck.

'But now, alas! our perverse age plies wretched crafts. Now gentle lads have learned to look for gifts. Whoever thou art that first didst teach the sale of love, may an unhallowed stone weigh heavy on thy bones.

'Love the Pierid maidens, lads, and gifted poets; to no golden presents let the Pierian maids succumb. Verse keeps the lock of Nisus purple. Were verses not, no ivory would have shone on Pelops' shoulder. He whom the Muses tell of shall live, while earth bears oaks, sky stars, and rivers water. But he who has no ear for the Muses, who sells his love – let him follow the car of Ops of Ida and traverse, a vagabond, three hundred towns and slash the parts he slights to Phrygian measures. Venus herself allows love's blandishments their play. She sides with piteous weeping and suppliant complaints.'

These things did the god's voice utter for me to sing to Titius; but them doth Titius' wife forbid him to remember. So let *him* listen to his dear; but do ye throng to my school whom some crafty lad with many wiles treats ill. Each of us has his proper glory. Let slighted lovers seek advice from me; to all my doors are open. A time shall come when round the master of the lore of Venus shall crowd the attentive young and take the old man home.

Alas! what lingering torture is this love for Marathus: helpless is my skill, and helpless all my cunning. Spare me, I pray thee, boy, lest I become a byword, when folk shall laugh at my useless teaching.

(Tibullus, Book I, 4, tr. J. P. Postgate)

★　　★　　★

WHAT SHOULD I HAVE DONE hadst thou not thyself been in love with a maid? May she be fickle – fickle, I pray, taking pattern by thee. Oh, how oft in the late night, that none should be privy to thy wooing, did I myself attend thee with the light in my hand! Often, when thou didst not hope for her, she came through my good offices, and stood hid, a veiled figure, behind the fast shut door. Then, poor wretch, was my undoing: I fondly trusted to Love: I might have been warier of thy snares. Nay, in my craze of mind I made verses in thy honour; but now I am ashamed for myself and the Muses. May the Fire-god shrivel those verses with devouring flame, or the river wash them out in its running waters. Go thou far hence whose aim is to sell thy beauty and to return with a great wage filling thy hand.

And thou who durst corrupt the boy with thy gifts, may thy wife unpunished make a constant jest of thee by her intrigues; and when the gallant is spent with her furtive dalliance, let her lie by thee lax with the coverlet between. Let there be always stranger tracks upon thy bed, and thy house be always free and open to the amorous. Nor let it be said that her wanton sister can drain more cups or exhaust more gallants. She, folk say, often prolongs her wine-bibbing revels until the wheels of the Light-bringer rise to summon forth the day. Than she could none lay out the night hours better, or arrange the different modes of love.

But thy spouse has learned it all, and yet thou, poor fool, dost notice naught when she moves her limbs with an unaccustomed art. Dost thou think that it is for thee that she arranges her hair and through her fine tresses passes the close-toothed comb? Is it *thy* beauty prompts her to clasp gold on her arms and come forth arrayed in Tyrian drapery? Not thee, but a certain youth would she have find her charming. For him she would consign to ruin thee and all thy house. Nor does she this out of depravity; but the dainty girl shrinks from limbs that gout disfigures and an old man's arms.

Yet by him has my own lad lain. I could believe that he would mate with a savage beast. Didst thou dare, mad youth, to sell caresses that belonged to me and to take to others the kisses that were mine? Thou wilt weep, then, when another lad has made me his captive and shall proudly reign in thy realm.

In that hour of thy punishment I shall rejoice, and a golden palm-branch shall be put up to Venus for her goodness, with this record of my fortunes:

TIBULLUS WHOM FROM TREACHEROUS LOVE, GODDESS, THOU DIDST
UNBIND

OFFERS THEE THIS AND BEGS THEE KEEP FOR HIM A THANKFUL MIND.

(*Ibid.*, Book I, 9)

* * *

CATULLUS, TOO, can at times leave his celebrated *vituperatio* and his excruciated passion for the whorish Clodia-Lesbia in order to celebrate a friend.

TO JUVENTIUS

O if you would let me, fair Juventius,
I would be kissing your honeyed eyes forever.
Three hundred thousand times I would kiss you
with new rapture,
nor could find enough of this blissful pastime
promised in my dreams. Even if our kisses
grew to such profusion
they outnumbered sheaves
ripening in the wheat field.

(Catullus, tr. Horace Gregory)

* * *

PETRONIUS' SATYRICON

This is a great realistic novel about spivs on the move, unique in ancient times, and also a splendid satire on life during the early empire, as in the portraits of the upstart tycoon, Trimalchio, and of the decadent aristocrats at Croton. It contains, too, a good deal of pungent literary criticism. Yet it seems to be only a small part of a much longer book, a life-work like that of Proust, whose Madame Verdurin and Baron de Charlus would feel at home in its pages. Its author is supposed to be the Petronius referred to by Tacitus, a courtier and dandy of the time of Nero, an *arbiter elegantiae* who 'passed the day in sleepe, and the night in delight-full sports, or other affaires of life' although capable of sterner things – 'being Proconsull of Bithynia, and anon after Consull, he shewed himselfe quicke and stout, and able to wade thorow great matters'.

Middle-class Encolpius is the hero and is accompanied by the handsome, and perhaps more aristocratic, Ascyltos, and later by the old poet Eumolpus, both of whom are inclined to make passes at Gito, the fifteen- or sixteen-year-old boy whom Encolpius protects. Jack Lindsay has this to say about their muddled flirtations: 'The parts of the book that deal with homosexual relations have perhaps to some extent got in the way of a correct evaluation of the book's importance . . . But we cannot wish that Petronius had excluded them. For without them he would not be telling the truth, the whole truth and nothing but the truth about the men of his world . . .' Of Giton and his like C. K. Scott Moncrieff comments, in his edition in the Abbey Classics: '. . . The latter and his companions are still only emerging from a long period of oblivion in literature and obscurity in life. Like the pagan deities who have shrunk in peasant mythology to be elves and pooks and suchlike mannikins, these creatures, banished from the polite reading of the Victorians, reappeared instantly in that grotesque microcosm of life which the Victorians invented as an outlet for one of their tightest repressions, the School Story. I shall not press the analogy between Lycas and Steerforth, but merely remind you how, years before you ever heard the name (unless it is mentioned there) of Petronius Arbiter, you welcomed Gito's acquaintance in the pages of *Eric, or Little by Little*, where he is known as Wildney, and painted in the most attractive colours, and were rather bored whenever old Eumolpus walked into the School Library as Mr Rose. Dear old Eumolpus, with his boring culture and shameless chuckle, no school is complete without him . . .' Miss Helen Waddell, who has translated some of the thirty poems of Petronius scattered through the medieval anthologies, emphasizes that aspect of his spirit which lay farthest from the *Satyricon*, not only Tacitus's scholar and artist of exquisite living but the possessor of a clean casualness, an incorruptibility resulting from 'a curious *simplicitas*'.

A LAYABOUT AFFAIR

I had almost traverst the City round, when through the dusk I saw

Gito on the Beggars-Bench of our Inn; I made up to him, and going in, ask'd him, what Ascyltos had got us for Dinner? The Boy sitting down on the Bed, began to wipe the Tears that stood in his Eyes; I was much concern'd at it, and ask'd him the occasion; he was slow in his answer, and seem'd unwilling; but mixing Threats with my Intreaties; ''Twas that Brother or Comrogue of yours,' said he, 'that coming ere while into our Lodging, wou'd have been at me, and put hard for it. When I cry'd out, he drew his Sword, and "if thou art a Lucreece," said he, "thou hast met a Tarquin."''

I heard him, and shaking my Fist at Ascyltos; 'What saist thou,' said I, 'thou Catamite, whose very Breath is tainted?'

He dissembled at first a great trembling, but presently throwing my Arms aside, in a higher Voice cry'd out: 'Must you be prating, thou ribaldrous Cut-throat whom, condemn'd for murdering thine Host, nothing but the fall of the Stage could have sav'd? You make a noise, thou Night-Pad, who when at thy best hadst never to do with any Woman but a Bawd? On what account, think ye, was I the same to you in the Aviary, that the Boy here, now is?'

'And who but you,' interrupted I, 'gave me that slip in the Portico?' 'Why what, my Man of Gotham,' continu'd he, 'must I have done, when I was dying for hunger? Hear Sentence forsooth, that is, the ratling of broken Glasses, and the expounding of Dreams? So help me Hercules, as thou art the greater Rogue of the two, who to get a meal's Meat wert not asham'd to commend an insipid Rhimer.' When at last, having turn'd the humour from Scolding to Laughing, we began to talk soberly.

But the late Injury still sticking in my Stomach, 'Ascyltos,' said I, 'I find we shall never agree together, therefore let's divide the common Stock, and each of us set up for himself: Thou'rt a piece of a Scholar, and I'll be no hindrance to thee, but think of some other way; for otherwise we shall run into a thousand mischiefs, and become Town-talk.'

Ascyltos was not against it; and 'since we have promis'd,' said he, 'as Scholars, to sup together, let's husband the Night too; and to-morrow I'll get me a new Lodging, and some Comrade or other.'

' 'Tis irksome,' said I, 'to defer what we like,' (the itch of the Flesh occasion'd this hasty parting, tho' I had been a long time willing to shake off so troublesome an observer of my Actions, that I might renew my old Intrigue with my Gito).

Ascyltos taking it as an Affront, without answering, went off in a heat: I was too well acquainted with his subtle Nature, and the violence of his Love, not to fear the effects of so suddain a breach, and therefore made after him, both to observe his Designs and prevent them; but losing sight of him, was a long time in pursuit to no purpose.

When I had search'd the whole Town, I return'd to my Lodging, where, the Ceremony of Kisses ended, I got my Boy to a closer hug, and, enjoying my wishes, thought myself happy even to Envy: Nor had I done when Ascyltos stole to the Door, and springing the Bolt, found us at leap-Frog; upon which, clapping his Hands, he fell a laughing, and turning me out of the Saddle; 'What,' said he, 'most reverend Gentleman, what were you doing, my Brother Sterling?' Not content with Words only, but untying the Thong that bound his Wallet, he gave me a warning, and with other reproaches, 'As you like this, so be for parting again.'

The unexpectedness of the thing made me take no notice of it, but politickly turn it off with a laugh, for otherwise I must have been at Loggarheads with my Rival: Whereas sweetening him with a counterfeit Mirth, I brought him also to laugh for company: 'And you, Encolpius?' began he, 'are so wrapt in Pleasures, you little consider how short our Money grows, and what we have left will turn to no account: There's nothing to be got in Town this Summertime, we shall have better luck in the Country; let's visit our Friends.'

Necessity made me approve his Advice, as well as conceal the smart of his Lash; so loading Gito with our Baggage, we left the City, and went to the House of one Lycurgus, a Roman Knight; who, because Ascyltos had formerly been his Pathick, entertain'd us handsomly; and the Company, we met there, made our Diversions the pleasanter: For, first there was Tryphoena, a very beautiful Woman, that had come with one Lycas, the owner of a ship, and of a small seat, that lay next the Sea.

The Delight we receiv'd in this place was more than can be exprest, tho' Lycurgus's Table was thrifty enough: The first thing was every one to chuse his Play-Mate: The fair Tryphoena pleas'd me, and readily inclin'd to me; but I had scarce given her the Courtesie of the House. when Lycas storming to have his old Amour slockt from him, accus'd me at first of under-dealing; but soon from a Rival addressing himself as a Lover, he pleasantly told me, I must repair his Damages, and plyed me hotly: But Tryphoena having my Heart, I could not lend him an

Ear. The refusal set him the sharper; he follow'd me where-ever I went, and getting into my Chamber at night, when Entreaty did no good, he fell to downright Violence; but I rais'd such an out-cry that I wak'd the whole House, and, by the help of Lycurgus, got rid of him for that bout.

(Petronius, *The Satyricon*, Made English by Mr Burnaby of the
Middle-Temple, and another hand. 1694)

THE PRIZE IS LOST

After we enter'd the Bed-Chamber, having plentifully feasted; prest by impatient Nature, I took my Gito aside; and wrapt in Pleasures, spent the Night.

> Who can the Charms of that blest Night declare,
> How soft ye Gods! our warm Embraces were?
> We hugg'd, we cling'd, and thro' each other's Lips,
> Our Souls, like meeting Streams, together mixt;
> Farewell the World, and all its Pageantry!
> When I, a Mortal! so begin to Dye.

'Tis without Reason I hug myself; Ascyltos, [that cause of all my woe, carried my friend off during the night and transferred him to his own section of the room. His act was against all the etiquette of mateship; and whether or not Giton realized what was happening, he went on peacefully sleeping, forgetful of every human right. I awoke to all the anguish of a despoiled bed. Doubting if there was any faith in lovers, I debated whether to draw a sword and turn the repose of sleep into that of death. More prudent counsels, however, prevailed. I roused Giton with some whacks][1] and looking sternly as I cou'd upon Ascyltos, thus address'd my self: 'Since you've play'd the Villain by your Treachery, and breaking the Common Laws of Friendship, pack up your Matters quickly, and find another Comrade to abuse.'

Ascyltos consented; and, after we had made an exact division of our Booty; 'Now,' says he, 'Let's share the Boy too:' I believ'd it a jest at parting, but, he with a Murderous resolution, drew his Sword; 'nor shall you,' added he, 'think to ingross this prize, which should, like the

[1] The preceding few lines are from Jack Lindsay's version.

rest, be common to us both. I must have my share, or with this Sword will be content to take it.' Upon which, on the other side, having twisted my gown under my arm, I made advances to Ingage.

The unhappy Boy rush'd between, and kissing both our knees, with tears, entreated that we would not expose our selves in a pitiful Alehouse, nor with our blood pollute the Rites of so dear a Friendship: but, raising his voice, says he, 'if there must be Murder, behold my naked bosom, hither direct your fury: 'Tis I deserve death, who violated the sacred Laws of Friendship.'

Upon which we sheath'd our Swords; and first Ascyltos, 'I'll,' says he, 'end the difference: Let the Boy himself follow the man he likes, that, in chusing a Friend, at least, he may have an unquestion'd liberty.'

I, that presum'd so long an acquaintance, had made no slight impressions on his Nature, was so far from fearing, that with an eager haste I accepted the proffer, and to the Judge committed the dispute: Gito, that he might not seem to consider, at my consent jump'd up, and Chose Ascyltos.

I, like one thunderstruck, at the sentence, void of defence, fell upon the bed, and had not surviv'd the loss, if envy of my Rival had not stopp'd my Sword.

Ascyltos, proud of the conquest, goes off with the Prize, leaving me expos'd in a strange place, that before he caress'd as a Friend and sharer of his Fortune:

> 'Tis in the World, as in a Game of Chess;
> We serve our Friends but where our profit is.
> When Fortune smiles, we're yours, and yours alone;
> But when she frowns, the servile Herd are gone.
> So, in a Play, they Act with mimick Art,
> Father, or Son, or griping Miser's part;
> But when at least the Comic Scenes are o'er,
> They quit the Visards they assum'd before.

Nor did I there very long complain, for fearing one Menalaus, an Usher of a School, might, among other Misfortunes, find me alone in the Inn, I made up my Wallet, and, very pensive, took me a Lodging in a private place near the Sea; there, after I had been mewed up for three days, reflecting afresh on my despis'd and abject condition, I beat my breast, as sick as it was; and, when my deep sighs would suffer me, often cry'd out: 'Why has not the Earth burst open, and swallow'd me? Why has not the Sea o'er whelm'd me that respects not even the Innocent themselves? Have I been a Murderer? when I had violated Lycas's Wife, have I fled Justice? have I escap'd even when I was condemn'd to Dye, to live in a strange place, to have my name recorded only among Beggars and Vagabonds? and who condemn'd me to this solitude? – A Boy! One who is a prostitute to all manner of Lust; and by his own confession deserves to dye; whom vice has enobl'd from a Slave; who was publickly contracted with as a Girl, by one that knew he was of the other Sex; and what a wretch is that other, ye Gods! whom, when he might have writ Man, his Mother perswaded even out of his Sex, and putting on Petty-coats, was condemn'd to a Maids Office in a Prison: who, after he had spent what he had, and chang'd the scene of his Lust; having contracted an old Friendship, basely left it; and, frontless impudence like a hot Whore, for one night's pleasure, sold his Friend. Now the Lovers lye whole nights lockt in each other's arms, and who knows but in those intervals they recruit their weary Strength, may laugh at me: but they shan't go off so, for if I'm a man, or a freeborn one at least, I'll make their blood compensate the injury.'

(*Ibid.*)

THE BOY RETURNS

And there whom did I spy but a hangdog Giton, drooping with towels and scrapers in his hands, and doing his best to disappear through the wall. You could see at a glance he was unhappy at his work. As though to let me catch his eye, he turned round, and with pleasure softening through the sullen mask of his face, he said to me, 'Please forgive me, brother. As there's no horrid swords here, I can speak freely. Take me away, do, from this awful man, he's cruel and you can do anything you want to punish me if you want to. Once I could have chosen you and I didn't and so I'd be glad enough to be dead now, if it was you that wanted me to die.'

I bade him stop his whimpering or someone would overhear what we meant to do. Then, abandoning Eumolpus, who was reciting a poem in the bathroom, I smuggled Giton off down a gloomy and smelly passage, and dragged him along at all speed to my lodgings. Once there, with the door fast behind me, I pressed my face against his tear-wet cheek. For a while neither of us could get a word out.

One sob after another jerked itself up through his slender body.

'It's all wrong,' I said. 'I'm a fool to care for you after the way you left me – and the scar I thought branded here over my heart washed out so easily with a few tears. Have you any excuses to make for throwing yourself at a stranger's head? Did I deserve quite that?'

As soon as he felt that I couldn't help treating him well, he began to look coyly into my face.

'I submitted our case to no other judge,' I continued, 'but I've got no complaint now to make. I'll put the whole thing out of my mind if you're really sorry and show no signs of relapse.'

I stammered all this out broken with tears and groans; but Giton wiped his face on his cloak and said, 'Oh but, Encolpius, truly try and remember what happened. Did I desert you or did you let me down? All I know, and I confess it, I don't deny it, is that there were two men waving swords and things about, and I ran to get behind the bigger one.'

I put my arms round his neck and kissed the brow that hid such precocious wit; and I did my best to let him see that we were friends again, without any reservations, and that I had complete confidence in him.

By now it was pitch dark and the woman had our supper prepared when Eumolpus knocked on the door. I called out, 'How many of you are there?' And as I spoke, I managed to get a good squint through a crack in the door to see if he had Ascyltos with him. Finding that he was alone, I at once admitted him. He threw himself on the pallet-bed; and when he saw Giton before him waiting at table, he nodded to me.

'I admire your Ganymede,' he observed. 'A good day today.'

I wasn't at all pleased at this prying preamble, and feared that I'd taken in a second Ascyltos. And Eumolpus got worse. When Giton brought him a drink, he said, 'I like you better than the whole bathfull.' He thirstily drained the cup and remarked that he'd never tasted anything with a sharper tang.

(Tr. Jack Lindsay)

*   *   *

THE EMPEROR AS PRIMA DONNA

Returning to Italy, Nero disembarked at Naples, where he had made his debut as a singer, and ordered part of the city wall to be razed – which is the Greek custom whenever the victor in any of the Sacred Games comes home. He repeated the same performance at Antium, at Alba Longa, and finally at Rome. For his processional entry into Rome he chose the chariot which Augustus had used in his triumph nearly a hundred years previously; and wore a Greek mantle spangled with gold stars over a purple robe. The Olympic wreath was on his head, the Pythian wreath in his right hand, the others were carried before him, with placards explaining where and against whom he had won them, what songs he had sung, and in what plays he had acted. Nero's chariot was followed by his regular claque, who shouted that they were Augustus's men celebrating Augustus's triumph. The procession passed through the Circus (he had the entrance arch pulled down to allow more room), then by way of the Velabrum and the Forum to the Palatine Hill and the Temple of Apollo. Victims were sacrificed in his honour all along the route, which was sprinkled with perfume, and the commons showered him with song-birds, ribbons, and sweetmeats as compliments on his voice. He hung the wreaths above the couches in his sleeping quarters, and set up several statues of himself playing the lyre. He also had a coin struck with the same device. After this, it never occurred to him that he ought to refrain from singing, or even sing a little less; but he saved his voice by addressing the troops only in written orders, or in speeches delivered by someone else; and would attend no entertainment or official business unless he had a voice-trainer standing by, telling him when to spare his vocal chords, and when to protect his mouth with a handkerchief. Whether he offered people his friendship or plainly indicated his dislike for them, often depended on how generously or how feebly they had applauded.

· · · · ·

Not satisfied with seducing free-born boys and married women, Nero raped the Vestal Virgin Rubria. He nearly contrived to marry the freedwoman Acte, by persuading some friends of consular rank to swear falsely that she came of royal stock. Having tried to turn the boy Sporus into a girl by castration, he went through a wedding ceremony with him – dowry, bridal veil and all – which the whole Court attended; then brought him home, and treated him as a wife.

99

He dressed Sporus in the fine clothes normally worn by an Empress and took him in his own litter not only to every Greek assize and fair, but actually through the Street of Images at Rome, kissing him amorously now and then. A rather amusing joke is still going the rounds: the world would have been a happier place had Nero's father Domitius married that sort of wife.

(Suetonius, *The Twelve Caesars*, tr. Robert Graves)

★   ★   ★

VICES OF ROME

Yea, Rome shall see you, lewdlier clad, erewhile
(For none becomes at once completely vile)
In some opprobrious den of shame, combined
With that vile herd, the horror of their kind,
Who twine gay fillets round the forehead, deck
With strings of orient pearls the breast and neck,
Soothe the Good Goddess with large bowls of wine
And the soft belly of a pregnant swine.
No female (foul perversion) dares appear,
For males, and males alone, officiate here.
'Far hence,' they cry, 'unholy sex retire:
Our purer rites no lowering horn require.'
At Athens thus, involved in thickest gloom,
Cotytto's priests her secret torch illume,
And to such orgies give the lustful night
That e'en Cotytto sickens at the sight.
With tiring-pins one spreads the sooty dye,
Lengthens the eyebrow, tints the trembling eye.
One binds his flowing locks in cauls of gold.
One swills a goblet of immodest mould:
Chekes of sky-blue or smooth-faced green he wears,
And by his Juno, hark! the attendant swears.

.   .   .   .   .

No reverence for the tables here is found,
But brutal mirth and jests obscene go round:
They lisp, they squeal, and the rank language use

Of Cybele's lewd votaries or the stews.
Some wild enthusiast, silvered o'er with age,
Yet fired by gluttony's insatiate rage,
Fit guide of hungry youth, is named the priest
And sits as umpire of the unhallowed feast.

. . . . .

   Gracchus, fantastic as the story sounds,
Has dowered a bugler with ten thousand pounds.
The contract signed, the wonted bliss implored,
A costly supper decks the nuptial board;
And the new 'bride' amid the wondering room
Lies in the bosom of the accursed 'groom'.
Nobles, pray do we now a censor need
Or a soothsayer? Do not these exceed
Those portents (all that Nature disavows)
Of calving women and of lambing cows?
Gracchus the priest, whose limbs dissolved with heat
What time he danced beneath the great shield's weight,
Now flings the ensigns of his god aside
And takes the stole and *flammea* of a bride!

. . . . .

   'Tomorrow with the dawn I must attend
In yonder vale'. 'What for?' 'Why ask? A friend
Takes him a husband there and bids a few
Be present.' Wait awhile and we shall view
Such contracts formed without shame or fear,
And entered on the records of the year.
Meanwhile one pang these passive monsters find,
One ceaseless pang that preys upon the mind:
They cannot shift their sex and pregnant prove
With the dear pledges of a husband's love;
For in this case Dame Nature's careful plan
Lets not the will direct the flesh of man.
For them fat Lyde's pills no powers retain,
And the Luperci strike their palms in vain.
           (Juvenal, *Satires II*, tr. William Gifford)

4

The Dark and Middle Ages

INTRODUCTION

Pagan faded into Christian. As well as developments and reinterpretations and stern anathemas there were lingerings and afterthoughts. 'Pan is dead!' was a voice over the waters but the novice in Cassian's *Dialogues* cries plaintively: 'How shall I be rid of these things? At mass, in the very act of contrition, the old stories flaunt before my mind, the shameless loves, the sight of the old heroes going into battle.' In the ninth century a grammarian, Ermenrich of Ellwagen, apologizes for quoting Virgil too much; 'the sight of him terrifies me', he says, and the poems under his pillow give him evil dreams, so that he must sign the cross and hurl the book far from his bed; doubtless Virgil lies, with Apollo and the Muses, 'in the foulest swamp of the Styx'. Nevertheless he can be studied for technical reasons. 'Since even as dung spread upon the field enriches it to good harvest, so the filthy writings of the pagan poets are a mighty aid to divine eloquence.' Jerome found this practice dangerous. 'The very priests of God are reading comedies, singing the love songs of the Bucholics, turning over Virgil: and that which was a necessity in boyhood, they make the guilty pleasure of their maturity.' Nevertheless Christendom was a cosmopolitan Greek and Roman world; the last three centuries of the Empire were those of Augustine, Jerome and Ambrose, of the *De Civitate Dei* and the Vulgate and the order of St Benedict; Hadrian the negro helped organize the British church; Geoffrey of Monmouth, like so many others, was later to trace a meticulous family tree from Troy, for to be Trojan (unlike Greek, except in the East) signified respectability on a heroic scale. (See Helen Waddell, *The Wandering Scholars*, Constable, from whom these quotations come.) As for Plato, he reappears in unexpected places; perhaps amongst the troubadours of Provence, whose idealizing love turns out to have been more of the Friend and Lord than of the Lady and Rose; in Hafiz of Shiraz and the other Sufi singers who saw the love of youths as mystical; and in the heretics who were *bougres*.

Although there was less of the hair-shirt to these long centuries than was once thought, we cannot expect pious Christians to come anywhere near Persians and Moors. Yet the life of church and monastery could breathe an affection as sweet as any – in the letters of St Anselm, for example, or the poet-scholars that Charlemagne grouped around him. Did not such things begin with the young Augustine's friendship, and the letters exchanged between Ausonius and Paulinus of Nola? That the physical expression of Eros occurred in the monasteries from time to time we can guess from the penitentials: in that of Cummean boys under twenty who kiss must keep six special fasts, and if they do so licentiously eight, and if with embraces ten. But there seems no reason to suppose, as some have done, that vice was prevalent in the monasteries. Extreme practices were the fashion in the court of the very knightly William Rufus, who was either a pagan or a witch, and probably in that circle of courtiers who perished with Prince William in the *Blanche-Nef*; they were also known amongst the lesser ranks of the Cathars, whose heresy regarded the procreation of children as a particular sin.

THE GROWTH OF PENALTIES

Only five passages in the Old Testament, and three in the New, deal specifically with physical relations between men. Thus Leviticus, xvii, 22: 'Thou shalt not lie with mankind, as with womankind: it is abomination [tō'ēbhāh].' Yet so powerful was the story of Sodom that it provided sanction for the severely punitive measures established, if not necessarily carried out, by the Christian Church. It seems possible, however, that the Sodom story was misinterpreted. When God sent two angels in the form of men to report on the city's reputation for wickedness, they lodged with Lot who was himself not a citizen but a sojourner. The populace gathered round Lot's house and cried: 'Bring them out unto us, that we may know them' – and the crux of the story rests in the meaning of the word 'know', *yadha'*, which could mean coitus but more frequently did not. 'The story does not in the least demand the assumption that the sin of Sodom was sexual, let alone homosexual – indeed, there is no evidence to show that vice of the latter kind was prevalent there.' (D. S. Bailey, *Homosexuality and the Western Christian Tradition*, Longmans, Green, to whom we are indebted for most of this section.)

The licentiousness of Rome under the Empire was in any case provoking measures, whether effective or not. Except for the obscure Scantinian Law nothing much seems to have been done until the Emperor Philip abolished the *exsoleti* (mercenary catamites) in about 249. In the third century, too, the *Lex Julia de adulteriis* appears to have been reinterpreted and extended to cover male activities. In 390 the Theodosian Code declared (IX vii. 6): 'All persons who have the shameful custom of condemning a man's body, acting the part of a woman's, to the sufferance of an alien sex (for they appear not to be different from women), shall expiate a crime of this kind in avenging flames in the sight of the people.' In 538, Justinian's *novellae* were as anxious for repentance and reform as for strictness. To these edicts may be added John Chrysostom's stern pronouncement against those who came to church to look with lustful curiosity upon handsome youths, the eleventh-century *Liber Gomorrhianus* of Peter Damiani, the twelfth-century Council of Naplouse and, of course, the numerous penitentials.

Curious superstitions also played their part in the universal condemnation. Moses was thought to have pronounced the hare unclean because it acquired an additional anus each year and this multiplicity of orifices accounted for its prolific birthrate; it rebuked, said Novatian, men '*deformates in feminam*'. Similarly the weasel, thought to conceive via the mouth, and condemned by Leviticus, was seen to militate against *fellatio*.

There follows a number of key condemnatory passages, the first of which is obviously out of context and included here for convenience only.

MIDDLE ASSYRIAN LAWS (TWELFTH CENTURY B.C.)

TABLET A, 19   If a seignior [arvēlum] started a rumour against his neighbour [tappau] in private saying, "People have lain repeatedly with him", or he said to him in a brawl in the presence of [other] people, "People have lain repeatedly with you; I will prosecute you", since he is not able to prosecute [him and] did not prosecute [him], they shall flog that seignior fifty [times] with staves [and] he shall do the work of the king for one full month; they shall castrate him and he shall also pay one talent of lead.

TABLET A, 20   If a seignior lay with his neighbour, when they have prosecuted him [and] convicted him, they shall lie with him [and] turn him into a eunuch.

(D. S. Bailey, op. cit.)

★   ★   ★

NEW TESTAMENT REFERENCES

ROMANS i, 27 . . . the men, leaving the natural use of the women, burned in their lust one toward another, men with men working unseemliness, and receiving in themselves that recompense of their error which was due.

I CORINTHIANS vi, 9–10 . . . Be not deceived: neither fornicators, nor idolaters, nor adulterers, nor effeminate [malakoi – Vulg., molles], nor abusers of themselves with men [arsenokoitai – Vulg., masculorum concubitores], nor thieves, nor covetous, nor drunkards, nor revilers, nor extortioners, shall inherit the kingdom of God.

1 TIMOTHY i, 9–10 . . . law is not made for a righteous man, but for the lawless and unruly . . . for abusers of themselves with men [arseno-koitai – Vulg., masculorum concubitores] . . .

(*Ibid.*)

★ ★ ★

THE RABBINICAL VIEW

Briefly, it may be said that the Jewish Halakah exonerates from the penalty of the law against male homosexual practices only the passive minor, and the active minor if the passive partner is under the age of nine – or three, according to the more severe view. All others committing male homosexual acts actively or passively incur the sentence of death imposed by Leviticus xx, 13, which is to be carried out by stoning. As already noted, there is no evidence that this punishment was ever actually inflicted, and the discussions in the Mishnah and the Talmud concerning the application of this law are doubtless mainly theoretical in character.

(*Ibid.*)

★ ★ ★

THE NOVELLAE OF JUSTINIAN

Nov. 77 . . . since certain men, seized by diabolical incitement, practise among themselves the most disgraceful lusts, and act contrary to nature: we enjoin them to take to heart the fear of God and the judgement to come, and to abstain from suchlike diabolical and unlawful lusts, so that they may not be visited by the just wrath of God on account of these impious acts, with the result that cities perish with all their inhabitants. For we are taught by the Holy Scriptures that because of like impious conduct cities have indeed perished, together with the men in them. 1. For because of such crimes there are famines, earthquakes, and pestilences; wherefore we admonish men to abstain from the aforesaid unlawful acts, that they may not lose their souls. But if, after this our admonition, any are found persisting in such offences, first, they render themselves unworthy of the mercy of God, and then they are subjected to the punishment enjoined by the law. 2. For we order the most illustrious prefect of the Capital to arrest those who persist in the aforesaid lawless and impious acts after they have been warned by us, and to inflict on them the extreme punishments, so that the city and the state may not come to harm by reason of such wicked deeds. And if, after this our warning, any be found who have concealed their crime, they shall likewise be condemned by the Lord God. And if the most illustrious prefect find any who have committed any such offence, and shall omit to punish them according to our laws, first, he will be liable to the judgement of God, and he will also incur our indignation.

Nov. 141   Preamble: Though we stand always in need of the kindness and goodness of God, yet is this specially the case at this time, when in various ways we have provoked him to anger on account of the multitude of our sins. And although he has warned us, and has shown us clearly what we deserve because of our offences, yet he has acted mercifully towards us and, awaiting our penitence, has reserved his wrath for other times – for he has "no pleasure in the death of the wicked; but that the wicked turn from his way and live". Wherefore it is not right that we should all despise God's abundant goodness, forbearance, and longsuffering kindness and, hardening our hearts and turning away from penitence, should heap upon ourselves wrath in the day of wrath. Rather, we ought to abstain from all base concerns and acts – and especially does this apply to such as have gone to decay through that abominable and impious conduct deservedly hated by God. We speak of the defilement of males [de stupro masculorum] which some men sacrilegiously and impiously dare to attempt, perpetrating vile acts with other men.

I. For, instructed by the Holy Scriptures, we know that God brought a just judgement upon those who lived in Sodom, on account of this very madness of intercourse, so that to this very day that land burns with inextinguishable fire. By this God teaches us, in order that by means of legislation we may avert such an untoward fate. Again, we know what the blessed Apostle says about such things, and what laws our state enacts. Wherefore it behoves all who desire to fear God to abstain from conduct so base and criminal that we do not find it committed even by brute beasts. Let those who have not taken part in such doings continue to refrain in the future. But as for those who have been consumed by this kind of disease, let them not only cease to sin in the future, but let them also duly do penance, and fall down before God and renounce their plague [in confession] to the blessed Patriarch; let them understand the reason for this charge and, as it is written, bring forth the fruits of repentance. So may God the merciful, in the abundance of his pity, deem us worthy of his blessing, that we may all give thanks to him for the salvation of the penitents, whom we have now bidden [to submit themselves] in order that the magistrates too may follow up our action, [thus] reconciling to themselves God who is justly angry with us. And we also, wisely and prudently having in reverence the sacred season, entreat God the merciful that those who have been contaminated by the filth of this impious conduct may strive for penitence, that we may not have to prosecute this crime on another occasion. Next, we proclaim to all who are conscious that they have committed any such sin, that unless they desist and, renouncing it [in confession] before the blessed Patriarch, take care for their salvation, placating God during the holy season for such impious acts, they will bring upon themselves severer penalties, even though on other counts they are held guilty of no fault. For there will be no relaxation of enquiry and correction so far as this matter is concerned, nor will they be dealt with carelessly who do not submit themselves during the time of the holy season, or who persist in such impious conduct, lest if we are negligent we arouse God's anger against us. If, with eyes as it were blinded, we overlook such impious and forbidden conduct, we may provoke the good God to anger and bring ruin upon all – a fate which would be but deserved.'

(*Ibid.*)

MONASTIC ADVICE

'If thou art young in either body or mind, shun the companionship of other young men and avoid them as thou wouldest a flame. For through them the enemy has kindled the desires of many and then handed them over to eternal fire, hurling them into the vile pit of the five cities under the pretence of spiritual love . . . At meals take a seat far from other young men. In lying down to sleep let not their clothes be near thine, but rather have an old man between you. When a young man converses with thee, or sings psalms facing thee, answer him with eyes cast down, lest perhaps by gazing at his face thou receive a seed of desire sown by the enemy and reap sheaves of corruption and ruin. Whether in the house or in a place where there is no one to see your

actions, be not found in his company under the pretence either of studying the divine oracles or of any other business whatever, however
necessary.'

(Basil, *De renuntiatione reculi*, quoted Bailey, *op. cit.*)

★　　★　　★

AUSONIUS was the last of the old Romans, rhetorician and poet,
who died before the Sack of Rome in 410. His friend and pupil,
Paulinus, was converted, sold his estates and repaired to a chapel
in Spain. 'Cry not to Apollo and the Muses to bring me back;
you call to deaf things and vain, *sine numine nomina* . . . No more
do I seek the word from woods and hill-tops, but from the
Word . . .' After many unanswered letters from Ausonius he at
last replied:

TO AUSONIUS

Through all the fates of earth, through every spell
　　that works on man its spleen,
while I am bolted in the body's cell,
　　though worlds should come between,
I hold you mine, entwined in every part –
　　not dim, with distant face.
Clasping you close, I see you in my heart,
　　here and in every place;
and when, set free, I go another quest
　　and pay no more earth's toll,
wherever God, our Father, bids me rest,
　　still you shall share my soul.
O there's no end of love, we'll safely find,
　　when there's an end of earth.
The mind survives the wreck of flesh, the mind
　　from heaven had its birth.
The sense is quick, the emotion prospers yet,
　　eternal in the sky.
The soul would die if it could once forget,
　　and, friend, it cannot die.

　　　　(Paulinus of Nola, *c.* 393, tr. Jack Lindsay)

★　　★　　★

ST. AUGUSTINE OF HIPPO (354–430). In *The Confessions*, a book addressed personally to God, Augustine tells of an early friendship when he was still a Manichee, disbelieving in baptism and God as creator of matter and Father of an incarnate Son. (The Manichees held that a Perfect God could not possibly take on the forms of this world.)

ON THE LOSS of his friend, and reflections on the limitation of human friendship, save that it be through the Divine; and on the necessary transience of all that comes into being.

(IV *He relates the sickness and baptism of his Friend, whom himself had affected with Heresy: he grievously laments his death*) In those years when I first of all began to teach rhetoric in the town where I was born [Thagaste], I had gained a very dear friend, upon the occasion of the nearness of our studies; one who was about mine own age [twenty-one], now springing up with me in the flower of youth. He had grown up of a child with me, and both school-fellows and play-fellows we had been. But yet was he not so truly my friend, no not at that later time even, as true friendship should be indeed: for true it cannot be, unless thou solderest it betwixt such parties as cleave together, by that love which is shed abroad in our hearts by the Holy Ghost, which is given unto us. But yet a very sweet friendship it was, being ripened by the heat of like studies. For, from the true faith (which he being a youth was not soundly and thoroughly grounded in) I had rapt him, even towards those selfsame superstitious and pernicious fables, for which my mother bewailed my condition. With me now that man was wandering in error, nor could my soul be without him. But behold thou, ever at the back of thy runaways, the God of revenge, and fountain of mercies, both at the same time, who turnest us to thyself by most wonderful means, tookest that man out of this life, when he had scarce continued one whole year in my friendship, sweet to me above all sweetness of this life.

What one man is able to recount all thy praises which he hath felt in himself alone? What was it thou then didst, my God, and how unsearchable is the bottomless depth of thy judgements? For whenas one day, sore sick of his fever, he lay senseless in a deadly sweat, and all despairing of his recovery, he was baptised, unwitting to himself;

myself meanwhile little regarding, and presuming that his soul would have retained rather what it had learnt of me, and not what was now wrought in the body of him that knew nothing of it. But it fell out far otherwise; for he became refreshed, and recovered his health upon it. And as soon as ever I could come to speak with him (and I could, so soon as he could: for I had never yet gone from him, and we very nearly depended one upon another), I offered to scoff, as if he also would have scoffed with me for company, at that baptism, which he, being most absent both in understanding and feeling, had lately received, and had now understood that he had received it. But he looked with a great indignation upon me, as I had been his mortal enemy; and with an admirable and sudden freedom of language, advised me, that if I purposed to continue his friend, I should forbear such talk to him. But I, all astonished and amazed, put off the disclosing of my private commotions, till he should grow well again, and had recovered so much strength of health, that he were fit for me to deal with as I would. But he was taken away from my folly, that with thee he might be preserved for my future comfort; falling in my absence a few days after into a relapse of his fever, he died.

At the grief of this, my heart was utterly over clouded; and whatsoever I cast mine eyes upon, looked like death unto me. Mine own country was a very prison to me, and my father's house a wonderful unhappiness; and whatsoever I had communicated in with him, wanting him turned to my most cruel torture. Mine eyes roved about everywhere for him, but they met not with him; and I hated all places for that they had not him; nor could they now tell me, Behold, he will come shortly, as when he was alive they did whenever he was absent. I became a great riddle to myself, and I often asked over my soul, why she was so sad, and why she afflicted me so sorely: but she knew not what to answer me. And if I said, 'Put thy trust in God,' very justly she did not obey me; because that most dear man whom she had lost, was both truer and better than that fantastical god she was bid to trust in. Only tears were sweet to me, for they had now succeeded in my friend's place, in the dearest of my affections.

(v ⸲ *Of Tears in our Prayers for, and Bewailing of, the Thing Beloved*)
And now Lord, are these things well passed over, and time hath assuaged the anguish of my wound. May I learn this from thee who art Truth, and may I apply the ear of my heart unto thy mouth, that

thou mayest tell me the reason, why weeping should be so sweet to people in misery? Hast thou (notwithstanding thou art present everywhere) cast away our misery far from thee? And thou remainest constant in thyself, but we are tumbled up and down in divers trials: and yet unless we should bewail ourselves in thine ears, there should no hope remain for us. How comes it then to pass, that such sweet fruit is gathered from the bitterness of life, namely to mourn, and weep, and sigh, and complain? Is it this that sweetens it, that we are in hope thou hearest us? This may rightly be thought of our prayers, because they have a desire to approach unto thee. But may it be so said too concerning that grief and mourning for the thing lost, with which I was then wholly overwhelmed? For I did not hope he should revive again, nor did I pray for this with all my tears; but bemoan him only I did, and weep for him: seeing a wretch I was, and had utterly lost all my joy. Or is weeping a truly bitter thing, pleasing to us only from a distaste for the things we once enjoyed and only while the distaste remains keen?

(VI   *He tells with what great Affection he loved his Friend*) But why speak I of these things? For 'tis no time to ask questions, but to confess unto thee. Wretched I was; and wretched is every soul that is bound fast in the friendship of mortal beings; who becomes all to pieces when he forgoes them, and then first he becomes sensible of his misery, by which he is already miserable even before he forgoes them. This was my case at that time, I wept full bitterly, and yet was best at quiet in that bitterness. Thus was I wretched enough, and that wretched life I accounted more dear than my friend himself. For though I would gladly have changed it, yet more unwilling I was to lose that, than I had been to lose him; yea I know not whether I would have forgone that, even to have enjoyed him. Like as the tradition (if it be not a fiction) goes of Pylades and Orestes, who would gladly have died one for another, both together, it being to them worse than death not to live together. But a strange kind of affection prevailed with me which was clean contrary to theirs, for both grievously tedious to me it was to live, and yet fearful was I to die. I suppose that how much the more affectionately I loved him, so much the more did I both hate and fear (as my cruellest enemy) death, which had bereaved me of him: and I imagined it would speedily make an end of all other men, because it had the power to do of him. Even thus, I remember, stood I then affected. Behold my heart, O my God, yea, search it thoroughly; search it because I remember it well, O my Hope, who cleanest me from the impurity of such affections, directing mine eyes towards thee, and plucking my feet out of the snare. For I much marvelled that other mortals did live, since he whom I so loved, as if he never should have died, was now dead: yea, I more marvelled that myself who was to him a second self, should be able to live after him. Rightly has a friend been called, 'thou half of my soul': for I still thought my soul and his soul to have been but one soul in two bodies: and therefore was my life a very horror to me, because I would not live by halves. And even therefore perchance I was afraid to die, lest he should die, whom so passionately I had loved.

(VII *The impatientness of grief constrains us to shift our dwellings*) O Madness, which knowest not how to love men, as men should be loved! O foolish man, which so impatiently endurest the chances Mortality is subject unto! Thus mad and foolish was I at that time. Therefore I stormed, and puffed, and cried, and chafed, being capable neither of rest nor counsel. For I was fain to carry my shattered and bleeding soul, which yet had not patience enough to be carried by me; yet a place where to dispose of it, I could not light upon. Not in the delightful groves, not where mirth and music was, nor in the odoriferous gardens, nor in curious banquetings, nor in the pleasures of the bed and chambering; nor, finally, in reading over either verse or prose, took it any contentment. Everything was offensive, yea, the very light itself; and whatsoever were not he, was alike painful and hateful to me, except groaning and weeping. For only in those found I a little refreshment. But so soon as I had retired my soul from these, a huge misery overloaded me, which thou only could ease and lighten, O Lord. I knew thus much, and yet indeed I would not, nor was I able; the more so, for that thou wert not any solid or substantial thing unto me, when in those days I thought upon thee. For not thou thyself, but mine own idle fantasy and error were then my God. If I offered to discharge my burden upon that, to give it some easement, it fell as it were through the empty air, and came tumbling again upon me: whereupon I remained so unfortunate a place to myself, as there I could neither stay, nor get away from it. For whither should my heart fly from my heart? Whither was it possible to fly from mine own self? Whither should I not have followed myself? And yet after all this, out of my country

I fled: for so should mine eyes less look for him there, where they were not wont to see him. And thus I left the town of Thagaste, and came to Carthage.

(VIII *Time cures Sorrow*) Time takes no holiday. Time loses no time: nor does it idly go by and return about these senses of ours; but through them it causes strange operations in our minds. Behold, it came and went day by day, and by going and coming to and again, they brought into my mind other notions, and other remembrances, and by little and little pieced me up again with my old kind of delights, unto which my present sorrow gave some way. And to that again there succeeded, though not other griefs, yet the causes of other griefs. For how came that former grief so easily and so deeply to make impression in me, but even from hence, that I had spilt my soul upon the sand, in loving a man that must die, as if he never had been to die? For the comfortings of other friends did mostly impair and refresh me, with whom I did love, what afterwards I did love [the things of earth, in place of thee]: and this was a great fable, and a long lie; by the impure tickling whereof, my soul, which lay itching in my ears, was wholly corrupted.

But that fable would not die with me, so oft as any of my friends died. They were other things which in their company did more fully take my mind; namely, to discourse, and to laugh with them, and to do obsequious offices of courtesy one to another; to read pretty books together; sometimes to be in jest, and other whiles seriously earnest to one another; sometimes so to dissent without discontent, as a man would do with his own self, and even with the seldomness of those dissentings, season our more frequent consentings; sometimes would we teach, and sometimes learn one of another; wish for the company of the absent with impatience, and welcome home the newcomers with joyfulness. With these and the like expressions, proceeding out of the hearts of those that loved and repaired one another's affections, by the countenance, by the tongue, by the eyes, and by a thousand other most pleasing motions, did we set our souls ablaze, and make but one out of many.

(IX *The comparing of Human Friendship with Divine*) This it is which a man loves in his friends; and so loves it, that he must in conscience confess himself guilty if he should not love him that loves him again, or not love that man again that loves him first, expecting no other thing from him besides the pure demonstration of his love. Hence is that mourning whenever a friend dies, yea, those overcastings of sorrows, that steeping of the heart in tears, all sweetness utterly turned into bitterness: hence too upon the loss of the life of the dying, comes the death of the living. But blessed is the man that loves thee, and his friend in thee, and his enemy for thee. For he alone loses none that is dear unto him, to whom all are dear, in him that can never be lost. And who is this but our God, the God that made heaven and earth, and who filleth them, because in filling them he created them? Thee, no man loses, but he that lets thee go. And he that lets thee go, whither goes he, or whither runs he, but from thee well pleased, back to thee offended? For where shall not such a one find thy Law fulfilled in his own punishment? And thy Law is truth, and Truth is thyself.

(x   *All Beauty is from God, who is to be prayed for all*) Turn us, O God of Hosts, show us the light of thy countenance and we shall be whole. For which way soever the soul of man turns itself, unless towards thee, it is even riveted into dolours: yea, though it settles itself upon beautiful objects without thee, and without itself: which beauties were no beauties at all, unless they were from thee. They rise, and set; and by rising, they begin to have being: they grow up, that they may attain perfection; which having attained, they wax old and wither: though all grow not old, yet all must wither. Therefore when they spring up and tend towards a being, look how much more haste they make to be, so much the more they make not to be. This is the law of them. Thus much hast thou given to them, because they are portions of things which are not extant all at one time, but which by going and coming do altogether make up the whole universe, whereof they are the portions. Lo, even thus is our speech delivered by sounds significant: for it will never be a perfect sentence, unless one word give way when it hath sounded his part, that another may succeed it. And by them let my soul praise thee, O God, Creator of all things; but yet let not my soul be fastened unto these things with the glue of love through the senses of my body. For these things go whither they were to go, that they might no longer be; and they cleave the soul in sunder with most pestilent desires: even because the soul earnestly desires to be one with them, and loves finally to rest in these things which she loves. But in those things she finds not settlement, which are still fleeing, because they stand not: they flee away; and who is he that can follow them with the senses of his flesh; yea, who is able to overtake them, when they are hard by him?

For the sense of our flesh is slow, even because it is the sense of our flesh: and itself is its own measure. Sufficient enough it is for the end it is made for; but it is not sufficient for this, namely, to hold at a stay things running their course from their appointed starting place to their appointed end. For in thy word by which they are created, they hear this signal: 'Hence, and thus far.'

(*The Confessions*, tr. William Watts [1631], Book IV, iv–x)

★　　★　　★

THIS MAY BE from the seventh century or the ninth; it is sent by an older man to a younger.

★　　★　　★

WRITTEN BY COLMAN THE IRISHMAN
TO COLMAN RETURNING
TO HIS OWN LAND

So, since your heart is set on those sweet fields
　　And you must leave me here,
Swift be your going, heed not any prayers,
　　Although the voice be dear.

Vanquished art thou by love of thine own land,
　　And who shall hinder love?
Why should I blame thee for thy weariness,
　　And try thy heart to move?

Since, if but Christ would give me back the past,
　　And that first strength of days,
And this white head of mine were dark again,
　　I too might go your ways.

Do but indulge an idle fond old man
　　Whose years deny his heart.

The years take all away, the blood runs slow,
  No leaping pulses start.

All those far seas and shores that must be crossed,
  They terrify me: yet
Go thou, my son, swift be thy cleaving prow,
  And do not quite forget.

Hear me, my son; little have I to say.
  Let the world's pomp go by.
Swift is it as a wind, an idle dream,
  Smoke in an empty sky.
                                    (Tr. Helen Waddell)

*   *   *

THERE WAS a tradition that these verses were written by
Charlemagne himself. They date from before 795.

WRITTEN TO PAUL THE DEACON
AT MONTE CASSINO

Across the hills and in the valley's shade,
  Alone the small script goes,
Seeking for Benedict's beloved roof,
  Where waits its sure repose.
They come and find, the tired travellers,
  Green herbs and ample bread,
Quiet and brothers' love and humbleness,
  Christ's peace on every head.
              (*MS. of Monte Cassino*, tr. Helen Waddell)

*   *   *

HRABANUS MAURUS (so nicknamed by Alcuin), abbot of Fuld,
scholar-hermit and finally the formidable archbishop of Mainz
(776–856):

TO GRIMOLD, ABBOT OF ST GALL

Then live, my strength, anchor of weary ships,
   Safe shore and land at last, thou, for my wreck,
My honour, thou, and my abiding rest,
   My city safe for a bewildered heart.
What though the plains and mountains and the sea
   Between us are, that which no earth can hold
Still follows thee, and love's own singing follows,
   Longing that all things may be well with thee.
Christ who first gave thee for a friend to me,
Christ keep thee well, where'er thou art, for me.
   Earth's self shall go and the swift wheel of heaven
Perish and pass, before our love shall cease.
   Do but remember me, as I do thee,
And God, who brought us on this earth together,
   Bring us together in His house of heaven.

                     (Tr. Helen Waddell)

⋆   ⋆   ⋆

WALAFRID STRABO, abbot of Reichenau and consummate scholar (809–849):

TO HIS FRIEND IN ABSENCE

When the moon's splendour shines in naked heaven,
   Stand thou and gaze beneath the open sky.
See how that radiance from her lamp is riven,
   And in one splendour foldeth gloriously
Two that have loved, and now divided far,
Bound by love's bond, in heart together are.

What though thy lover's eyes in vain desire thee,
   Seek for love's face, and find that face denied?
Let that light be between us for a token;
   Take this poor verse that love and faith inscribe.
Love, art thou true? and fast love's chain about thee?
Then for all time, O love, God give thee joy!

                     (Tr. Helen Waddell)

PETER ABELARD (1079–1142): one of a set of six biblical laments.

DAVID'S LAMENT FOR JONATHAN

Low in thy grave with thee
    Happy to lie,
Since there's no greater thing left Love to do;
    And to live after thee
      Is but to die,
For with but half a soul what can Life do?

So share thy victory,
    Or else thy grave,
Either to rescue thee, or with thee lie:
    Ending that life for thee,
      That thou didst save,
So Death that sundereth might bring more nigh.

Peace, O my stricken lute!
    Thy strings are sleeping.
Would that my heart could still
    Its bitter weeping!

                    (Tr. Helen Waddell)

    ★   ★   ★

LETTERS OF ST ANSELM (1033–1109)

TO GONDULPH:

Greeting from brother Anselm to his honoured master, best beloved brother and most attached friend, Master Gondulph.

Though I desire to write to thee, soul most beloved of my soul, though I intend to write to thee, I know not how best to begin my address. For whatever I know about thee is sweet and joyous to my spirit: whatever I desire for thee is the best which my mind can conceive. For I saw thee such that I loved thee as thou knowest; I hear thee to be such that I yearn after thee, God knoweth how much: whence it cometh that whithersoever thou goest, my love follows thee; and wherever I remain, my longing embraces thee. And since thou dost eagerly ask me by thy messengers, exhort me by thy letters, and urge me by thy gifts, to have thee in remembrance: 'Let my tongue cleave to the roof of my mouth' if I have not held Gondulph first among my friends. I do not here mean Gondulph the layman, my father,[1] but my friend, Gondulph the monk. Now how could I forget thee? How could he fade from my memory who is impressed upon my heart as is a seal upon wax? Also, why dost thou, as I hear, complain with so much sadness that thou never receivest a letter of mine, and why dost thou ask so affectionately to have one frequently, when in the spirit thou has me always with thee? When therefore thou art silent, I know thou carest for me; and when I make no sign, 'thou knowest that I love thee.' Thou art a sharer in my existence, for I have no doubts of thee; and I am witness to thee that thou art sure of me. Since therefore we are mutually sharers in each other's consciousness, it only remains that we should tell each the other what concerns us, that we may alike either rejoice or be anxious for each other. But as to my affairs, and the reasons why I would have thee rejoice or be anxious with me, thou wilt better learn from the bearer of this missive than from the writer of the letter. . . .

Salute Master Osbern who is with you for my dear dead Osbern; for I would impress on thee and on all my friends in as few words as I know how, and with the greatest earnestness I can, that wherever Osbern is, his soul is my soul. I therefore while alive would receive for him whatever if dead I might hope from your friendship, lest you be negligent when I am dead.

Farewell, farewell, my beloved (*mi charissime*); and, to repay thee according to thine importunity, I pray and pray and pray, remember me, and forget not the soul of Osbern my beloved. If I seem to burden thee too heavily, forget me, and remember him.

(*St Anselm: Letter*, tr. R.C. [written while a monk])

TO GONDULPH:

His own to his own, friend to friend, Anselm to Gondulph, wishes through love of bliss perseverance in holiness, and for the reward of holiness an eternity of blessedness.

And now, this Gondulph and Anselm is witness that I and thou are never so in want of each other as that we must needs prove our mutual

---

[1] His natural father by kinship.

affection by letters. For since thy spirit and mine can never bear to be absent from each other, but unceasingly are intertwined; we mutually need nothing from each other, save that we are not together in bodily presence. But why should I depict to thee on paper my affection, since thou dost carefully keep its exact image in the cell of thy heart? For what is thy love for me but the image of mine for thee? Therefore thy known wish induces me to write somewhat to thee on account of our bodily separation; but since we are known to each other by the presence together of our spirits, I know not what to say to thee, save – may God do with thee as He knoweth shall please him, and be profitable to thee. Farewell.

(Ibid. [written while a monk])

TO WILLIAM:

BROTHER ANSELM, *called Abbot of Bec, to his loved and longed-for* (*would it were loving and longing*) WILLIAM: despise dangerous and miserable vanities, and seek the secure and blessed verity.

So completely, oh my beloved whom I yearn after, has Almighty God filled my soul (by His grace, not through my own merits) with love of thee, that, agitated between the longing for thy salvation and the fear of thy peril, being excited day and night by anxiety for thee, it cannot rest; blessed be God for His gifts, and would that He might take away from thee thy hatred for thine own soul even as He has given unto me the yearning for thy salvation. Bear with me, dear friend, and endure him who loveth thee, should I appear to thee importunate, and speak to thee more sternly than thou wouldst wish. For the love of thy soul compelleth mine, nor alloweth it to suffer that thou shouldst hate that which it loveth with an ever-present love. Receive, therefore, most dear one, with a love which I pray God to impart to thee, the sayings of him who loveth thee. Thou, dearly beloved, art what love sayeth with pain, and grief sayeth lovingly, who (which may God put away from thee) hast hated that soul of thine beloved of mine; for 'whoso loveth iniquity hateth his own soul' (Ps. xi, 6). Iniquity of a truth, and many iniquities are they with which thou dost so eagerly make thyself happy, oh my beloved. Iniquity, and many iniquities are they whither the force of worldly things, rushing to ruin, impels thee, my loved one. For the bloody confusion of war is iniquity. The ambition of worldly vanity is iniquity. The insatiable desire for false advantages and false riches is iniquity. Towards these, alas! I see him whom I so long to keep back by loving him, drawn by the subtle enemy deceiving his heart. Oh God, friend and deliverer of man, let not the enemy draw Thy servant away!

Thou tellest me, beloved brother: 'I do not love these things, but I love my brother who is entangled in them: and therefore I hasten to be involved therein with him, that I may help and guard him.' Alas! wretched grief from the miserable error of the sons of Adam! . . . Answer me, brother: who shall help and guard thee helping and guarding him? God, whom thou carest less to follow than that brother of thine! Christ, who calleth thee, thou scornest to follow in peace and in thine own country and among thy relations and friends that as 'heir of God' and 'joint-heir with Him' thou mayest possess the kingdom of heaven; and by such and so many difficult rugged ways, through rough seas and stormy tempests thou hastenest to thy brother amid the confusion of war, that thou mayest see him (to suppose something great) bearing rule over the Greeks . . . God is wroth if He seeth anyone loved by any other more than that other loveth Him.

But perchance thou sayest: 'If I begin to follow Christ, I fear lest on account of my weakness I should fall away.' How over and over again one must grieve and weep at the error of the sons of men! They fear not failure in following after those things which always do fail; rather they run after them with all their heart; and they venture not to follow after God who never fails them and promises them His aid, fearing lest they fail. They rejoice in falling away that they may fail, and fear to advance lest they fall away. Believe, I exhort thee, in the counsel of God, and thou shalt experience no failure in His service. Last, beloved and longed-for, and dear friend, 'Cast thy burden upon the Lord,' and be assured, since the Holy Spirit so promises, that 'He shalt nourish thee.'

Delay not thy so great good, and fulfil my yearning for thee, that I may have thee for my companion in following Christ; and that we may strive together so that as thou seest me, so I may see thee a companion in Christ's inheritance, which He gives. Be not ashamed of breaking the chains of vain intentions; since it is no shame, but an honour, to pass into the liberty of the truth . . . Blush not to confess thyself one of Christ's poor, for thine will be the kingdom of heaven. Fear not to become the soldier of so great a King, for the King

Himself will be beside thee in every danger. Delay no longer to enter in this life on the road which thou hast chosen . . . I advise, counsel, pray, adjure, enjoin thee as one most dear to abandon that Jerusalem which now is no vision of peace, but of tribulation, where with bloody hands men contend for the treasures of Constantinople and Babylon: and to enter upon the road to the heavenly Jerusalem, which is the vision of peace, where thou shalt find a treasure only to be received by those who despise the others.

I end this long letter unwillingly, since out of the abundance of the heart my mouth desireth to speak much to thee. May Almighty God, who in that other one whom I spoke of just now, in whom I desired to rejoice with a like but lesser longing, since with less hope than I have in thee, worked more than my heart hoped, not disappoint my greater hope of thee and my greater longing for thee. And if God should inspire thy heart before my return: God is at Bec with our brethren when I am absent as when I am there. God direct thy heart according to His will, and gratify my desire of thee according to His mercy. Amen.

(Ibid.)

★   ★   ★

Certain poems of a conventionally erotic nature are quoted by E. R. Curtius in his *European Literature And The Latin Middle Ages* (Routledge). A bishop of Rennes (c. 1035–1123) proclaims his reformation with the words, 'Displicit amplexus utriusque quidem mihi sexus' (Unpleasing to me now the embrace of either sex) for he is no longer 'fervore libidinis amens'. In the same period a future archbishop of Dol in Brittany declares 'Virginibus scripsi nec minus et pueris' (To maids I wrote and wrote to boys no less). A wandering scholar named Hilary, who attended Peter Abelard's lectures about 1125, carried on epistolary flirtations with both nuns and ephebes. He makes the pagan past reappear, and with it Ganymede.

> Crede mihi, si redirent prisca Jovis secula,
> Ganimedes iam non foret ipsius vernacula,
> Sed tu, raptus in supernis, grata luce pocula,
> Gratiora quidem nocte Jovi dares oscula.

(Believe me, if the Golden Age were to come again, Ganymede wouldn't be the butler of Jove but thou, caught up into heaven, would give him sweet cups by day, and by night even sweeter kisses.)

It was earlier, probably in the ninth century, that a Veronese *clericus* produced the amusing verses that follow.

> O admirable Veneris ydolum
> Cuius materiae nichil est frivolum:
> Archos te protegat, qui stellas et polum
> Fecit et maria condidit et solum.
> Furis ingenio non sentias dolum:
> Cloto te diligat, quae baiulat colum. Etc.

.   .   .   .   .

> O thou eidolon of Venus admirable,
> Perfect thy body and nowhere deplorable!
> The sun and the stars and the sea and the firmament,
> These are like thee, and the Lord made them permanent.
> Treacherous death shall not injure one hair of thee,
> Clotho the thread-spinner, she shall take care of thee.
>
> Heartily, lad, I implore her and prayerfully
> Ask that Lachesis shall treasure thee carefully,
> Sister of Atropos – let her love cover thee,
> Neptune companion, and Thetis watch over thee,
> When on the river thou sailest forgetting me!
> How canst thou fly without ever regretting me,
> Me that for sight of my lover am fretting me?
>
> Stones from the substance of hard earth maternal, he
> Threw o'er his shoulder who made men supernally;
> One of these stones is that boy who disdainfully
> Scorns the entreaties I utter, ah, painfully!
> Joy that was mine is my rival's tomorrow,
> While I for my fawn like a stricken deer sorrow!
> (Tr. H. M. Jones in P. S. Allen, *The Romanesque Lyric*,
> quoted Curtius, *op. cit.*)

THE PERSIANS

We turn now to the world of Islam, presenting first a letter of fatherly advice from a medieval Lord Chesterfield.

ON TAKING ONE'S PLEASURE

Let it be clear to you, my son, that if you fall in love with a person, you should not indiscriminately and whether drunk or sober indulge in sexual congress. It is well known that the seed which issues from you is the germ of a soul and of a person, so that when you have congress it should not be while you are in a state of intoxication, for in that condition it has detrimental effects. More properly and preferably it should come in the condition after intoxication. Yet do not indulge each time the thought occurs to you; that is the behaviour of beasts, which know not the season for any action but act as they find occasion. A man, for his part, should select the proper season and thus preserve the distinction between him and the beasts.

As between women and youths, do not confine your inclinations to either sex; thus you may find enjoyment from both kinds without either of the two becoming inimical to you. Furthermore, if, as I have said, excessive copulation is harmful, [complete] abstention also has its dangers. When you do it, let it be in accordance with appetite and not as a matter of course, so that it may have as little effect as possible. But, whether indulged in with appetite or not, have a care during the height of the hot weather or the depth of the cold; at these two seasons sexual congress has the most malign effect, particularly upon elderly men. Of the seasons, the spring is the most suitable, the air being then temperate, springs of water most abundant and the world endowed with a pleasing countenance. Then, when the greater world renews its youth, and the strength of our body, which is the world in little, similarly behaves and the humours which are in conflict with it become temperate, the blood in the veins increases together with the semen in the loins. Irrespective of his own volition the need for intercourse and relief becomes urgent in every man and it is then, when the natural desires are genuine, that least harm is done.

In this respect also you should refuse as far as possible to have blood let from your veins either during the height of the warm season or in the depth of the cold. If you experience an excess of blood, still it by means of cold draughts.

During the summer let your desires incline towards youths and during the winter towards women. But on this topic it is requisite that one's discourse should be brief, lest it engender appetite.

(*The Qabus Nama* by Kai Ka'us Ibn Iskandar, tr. Reuben Levy)

★   ★   ★

HAFIZ OF SHIRAZ: Shams Ud-Din Mahammad, who is known as Hafiz, was an almost exact contemporary of Chaucer. He died in 1389. His poetry is influenced by the Shi'a sect of Islam, then a subtle minority of initiates with a background of Mithraism and Greek and Manichaean ideas, and also by the Sufism that influenced so many Persian poets in the Middle Ages, with its probable debt to Greek Neo-Platonism and its heterodoxy in the adoration of alcohol (forbidden to Muslims), together with the Wine-Seller (or Magian) and the Wine-Shop. The poems can be simultaneously urbane and elegant, erotic and sexual, and yet mystical quests for Divine Unity and absorption in the Absolute – an erotic mysticism such as is also to be found in Spain, notably in St John of the Cross. Two recent translators explain this as follows: 'Though, as has been said, Sufi sources outside Islam are extremely debatable, it is not improbable that it was from the Neo-Platonist tradition that the Sufis adopted the conception of the Divine as Absolute Beauty, of which all images of beauty to be discerned in the natural world are partial and fleeting representations. This led to the formulation of a conception of romantic love, the germ of which is to be found in Diotima's speech to Socrates in Plato's *Symposium*. It is highly probable that Arabic love-poetry, which belongs to the same tradition as the Persian, strongly influenced the romantic love-poetry of the Provençal and early Italian lyrists. At any rate, there are many parallels, both in form and imagery, between Medieval European and Islamic (including Persian) lyrical poetry. For the Persians, however, as for the Greeks, the earthly expression of that Divine

Beauty which the lover contemplates is embodied primarily in the form of a beautiful youth. The Beloved celebrated by Hafiz and the other Sufi poets is a conventionalized and not an individual figure. His beauty is described in terms of a number of stock images: thus the rose always represents his face, the moon his cheeks or brow, the narcissus his eyes, the hyacinth his curling locks, the cypress his graceful form, and so on. A similar conventional symbolism marks all the use of natural imagery, as employed by the later Persian poets. The nightingale, hopelessly enamoured of the rose, represents the lover, as does the violet, with its humble growth and mournful hue. The morning breeze is the messenger of Love, bearing the scent of musk out of the beloved's tresses. The beloved is sometimes the seller of sweetmeats, and the poet an eloquent, sugar-loving parrot. However stylized this imagery may seem, it belongs to the universal symbolic language of poetry. We find a similar symbolism in Chinese poetry, and there are many parallels in European Medieval lyrics and in later folk song, in which the old tradition survives. Much of the poet's art consists in the ingenious re-combination and re-application of these traditional symbols. The degree to which they become, in the hands of Hafiz, vivid, natural, and personal, is no small token of his genius.' (Hafiz of Shiraz, *Thirty Poems*, tr. Peter Avery and John Heath-Stubbs, Murray)

At dawn's first breath the nightingale said to the opening rose:
'Less of the jilt, please; plenty like you have bloomed in this garden.'

Laughing, the rose replied: 'The truth won't vex me.'
But no lover says harsh things to the one he loves.

'Tears, tears like pearls, must thread your eyelashes
Before you drink the wine from this jewelled cup;

'Nor love's perfume visit your longing sense
Till you've swept the tavern's threshold with your cheek.'

Last night, when in the gardens of Iram
The gentle dawn-wind ruffled the hyacinth's tresses,

I said: 'O throne of Jamshid, where now is his all-seeing cup?'
And came reply: 'Alas, that vivid splendour sleeps.'

The words of love fall short upon the tongue:
Boy, bring the wine; we'll speak of this no more.

Since Hafiz's tears swept prudence to the sea
What shall he do? He cannot hide love's pain.

(*Ibid.*)

    .   .   .   .   .

With locks dishevelled, flushed in a sweat of drunkenness,
His shirt torn open, a song on his lips and wine-cup in hand—

With eyes looking for trouble, lips softly complaining—
So at midnight last night he came and sat at my pillow.

He bent his head down to my ear, and in a voice full of sadness
He said: 'Oh my old lover, are you asleep?'

What lover, being given such wine at midnight,
Would prove love's heretic, not worshipping wine?

Don't scold us, you puritan, for drinking down to the dregs:
This fate was dealt us in God's prime Covenant.

Whatever He poured into our tankard we'll swallow:
If it's liquor of Paradise, or the wine that poisons.

A laughing wine cup, a tangle of knotted hair—
And let good resolutions, like those of Hafiz, be shattered!

(*Ibid.*)

    .   .   .   .   .

No-one has seen your face and there are a thousand watchers:
O rose, you are only a bud, and there are a hundred nightingales.

Small wonder if I, a stranger, have sought your country:
In this terrain there are legions of such as I.

Though I am far from you, (and yet may no-one be far!)
I live in the hope of an instant union with you.

Love knows no difference between monastery and drinking-booth,
For the light of the Friend's face irradiates all.

Where the business of the hermit's cell is transacted meetly,
Is the clapper of the Christians' sanctuary, and the name of the Cross.

Is there any lover whose state the Friend does not notice?
Sirs, there is no pain; if there were, we have a physician.

Not useless, after all, was this outcry of Hafiz,
But a most strange history, and a tale of marvels.

(Ibid.)

. . . . .

The rose has come into the garden, from Nothingness into Being,
And the violet bends down low at its feet in adoration.

Take your morning draft to the notes of the harp and the tambourine,
To the sound of the flute and the mandoline kissing the cup-bearer's
throat.

Don't sit round the rose without wine, a beautiful youth and a harp,
For the days of our life are measured to a brief season.

Now the earth with its zodiac of herbs is as bright as the sky,
The star of good omen rising in favourable ascendant.

In the garden the tulip is kindled with Nimrod's furnace,
And we will renew that ancient cult of fire.

Take wine from the hand of the smooth-cheeked boy, miraculous-
breathed as Jesus,
And retail me no more legends of the doom of infidel tribes.

The world grows like Paradise ever-during, for the lily and rose come
round:
But to what purpose do they? – nothing is permanent.

When the rose mounts up on the wind which Solomon rode,
There is a bird that rises with David's lament.

Call for a morning cup to the health of our modern Asaph—
King Solomon's minister, Imad ud-Din Mahmud—

So that Hafiz' companions may gain from his patronage—
And may he be prosperous in all that he undertakes!

(Ibid.)

. . . . .

When the one I love takes a cup of wine in his hand
His beauty creates a slump in the market of idols.

Everyone who has seen the look in his eye is saying,
'Where's the police to put this drunkard in custody?'

I have tumbled like a fish into the ocean of love,
That he might come with a hook to haul me out.

I have fallen down at his feet in my deep affliction:
Will he be the one that will raise me up by the hand?

His heart is unburdened, who, like Hafiz, takes
A cup of wine as his covenanted destiny.

(Ibid.)

. . . . .

At dawn I came into the garden to catch a breath of the roses,
To cool my head for a little, like the nightingale sick with love.

I gazed upon the red rose in its glory,
Shining like a lamp that irradiates the darkness of night.

So proud it was of its beauty and its youth,
It could show all colours of disdain to the poor nightingale.

The narcissus lets fall a sorrowful tear from its eye:
Black-souled with grief, the heart of the tulip is marked with a thousand
   brands.

The iris shoots out its tongue, the sword of a rebel, against it:
The anemone gapes its mouth wide like a scandalmonger.

Here is a flower that lifts up a cup, like those whose worship is wine:
And one with a jug, like the youth who pours out for the drunkards.

Take your fill, like the rose, of revelry and all the lusts of youth:
Hafiz – the messenger needs only deliver his message.

(Ibid.)

. . . . .

Though a thousand enemies are making plans for my death,
So long as you are my friend I have no fear.

Hope of being one with you keeps me alive,
Or every moment apart would be filled with the fear of death.

Breath! breath! If I get no breath of him on the wind,
O time, O time! like the bursting rose I'll rip the collar from my throat.

Let my eyes never sleep till they gain the sight of you:
God's ban on the heart's patience while you are absent.

The wound that you give is better than another's salve:
If you give poison it is better than another's balm.

To die by the stroke of your blade is life eternal,
For my spirit is glad if it is your holocaust.

Don't swerve your horse aside; if you strike with your sword
I will give my head to dangle at your saddle-bow.

How can each eye behold you as you are?
Each comprehends according to his knowledge.

In the eyes of others Hafiz is the word's darling,
Because his face is hidden in the dust before your dwelling.

(Ibid.)

.　　.　　.　　.　　.

The lips of the one I love are my perpetual pleasure:
The Lord be praised, for my heart's desire is attained.

O Fate, cherish my darling close to your breast:
Present now the golden wine-cup, now the rubies of those lips.

They talk scandal about us, and say we are drunks—
The silly old men, the elders lost in their error.

But we have done penance on the pious man's behalf,
And ask God's pardon for what the religious do.

O my dear, how can I speak of being apart from you?
The eyes know a hundred tears, and the soul has a hundred sighs.

I'd not have even an infidel suffer the torment your beauty has caused
To the cypress which envies your body, and the moon that's outshone
　　by your face.

Desire for your lips has stolen from Hafiz' thought
His evening lectionary, and reciting the Book at dawn.

(Ibid.)

★   ★   ★

THE MOORS

In A.D. 1243 a Spanish Moor, Ibn Sa'id Al-Andelusi, compiled
an anthology which he divided into geographical regions and
subdivided as to the social status of the authors. This was *The
Pennants of the Champions and the Standards of the Distinguished*,
an arabesque of words and meanings, with endless play upon the
comparison of the saki's blushing cheeks with the glowing red
wine. All the translations are from A. J. Arberry, *The Pennants*,
Cambridge University Press.

THE WINE-BEARER

And when you passed, for all to seek,
The winecup of your blushing cheek,
Assuredly I was not slow
To quaff that wine aglow.

The tender grape is pressed below
Men's feet, to loose its precious flow;
The wine that in your soft cheek lies
Is quickened by men's eyes.

(Habib, Seville)

GOLDEN GLOW

See, his slender fingers shine
In the sunlight of the wine,
As the wild narcissus tips
With its gold the oxen's lips.

(Abul Hasan. Seville)

SAKI

Slender bough a-swing.
On a swelling dune,
Fruit of flame a-swoon
My heart gathering.

Curling tresses slide
O'er his cheeks: behold
Over silver, gold
Streaming liquefied.

Perfect loveliness
Dwells upon his brow;
Lovely is the bough
In his leafy dress.

Aureate the cup
In his fingers gleams;
Over dawn meseems
Day is mounting up.

Wine, the sun, swings high
Westward to his lips,
And his finger-tips
Frame its eastern sky.

Down his throat it flows
To the sleep it seeks,
Leaving in his cheeks
Sunset's flaming rose.

(Al-Taliq, Cordova)

THE ARMY

O wielder of the lance,
Be satisfied: refrain!
Has not your shining glance
Inflicted ample pain?

Although but one you are,
Do you not realise
You carry into war
An army in your eyes?

(Abu Zaid, Africa)

THE SWIMMER

Once (O wonderful)
In a shining pool
I saw a negro swim;
The waters did not dim
The gleaming pebbles spread
On its stony bed.

Now as I observed,
The little pool was curved
Like an eye, and blue
As an eye too;
Who was the negro? Why,
The pupil of that eye!

(Ibn Khafaja, Alcira)

DAWN

Dawn is rising bright and clear,
Yonder see its shine appear:
Pour me wine, and quickly, ere
Sounds the solemn call to prayer.

As the wine is mixing now
Pearly bubbles wreathe its brow,
Sprinkled jewels, glittering
As they float, a liquid ring.

Let me drink with lads of breed,
Noble all of birth and deed,
Interchanging as they sit
Merry tales of spicy wit.

Other wine they quaff as well
From the cheeks of a gazelle
Blushing sweetly, and therein
Blooming rose and jessamin.

Miracles his beauties seem
All unclouded as they gleam,
Locks of jet, sublime, to see
On that brow of ivory.

Lissom bough (oh what amaze!)
On a rounded hillock sways,
Night of loveliness divine
Overshadows morning's shine.

The soft pinion of the air,
As we pass the winecup there
Hand to hand, bedews the lawn
With the rose-water of dawn.

See, the white narcissus sips
The sweet fragrance as it drips
Flowing gently from the skies,
Teardrops spilled by lovers' eyes.

As the sun mounts up the sky
Dazzling the beholder's eye,
There ascends thy aureole,
Prince of every faithful soul!

(Ibn Muqlana, Lisbon)

★　　★　　★

The preoccupation of the following with a youth's beard and hair is reminiscent of Philostratos and the *Greek Anthology*.

BEARDLESS YOUTH

A lustrous face,
My lovely gipsy's,
Whose sun no trace
Of moss eclipses.

(Ibn Iyad, Cordova)

FAVOURITES

O you, who on your cheek
Have drawn two lines of down
That wild disorder wreak
And panic all the town:

I never knew your glance
Was such a cutting blade,
Till you appeared by chance
In your down-thongs arrayed.

(Ibn Abd Rabbihi, Cordova)

[NOTE: The Arab poets were fond of comparing the favourites
affected by a handsome youth with the shoulder-belt on which the
sword would be suspended – the sword being in this case the sharp
and wounding glances of the beloved's eyes. – A.J.A.]

THE YOUTH

See, his beard is sprouting yet,
Beauty's fringes delicate;
Delicately through my heart
Passion's thrilling raptures dart.

It is not that, so to speak,
Blackness covers up his cheek,
But his eyes have sprinkled there
Of their blackness on its fair.

(Ibn Sara, Santarem)

THE SPROUTING BEARD

Your cheeks were oh how fair,
How full of glowing grace
Until that sprouted there,
Your beauty to deface.

And then your cheeks became
A candle that, alack
Extinguishing its flame,
Reveals its wick is black.

(Al-Isra'ili, Seville)

THE SHAVEN BEAUTY

They have shaved his head
In ugliness to dress him;
They were full of dread,
And jealous to possess him.

Black as night, and bright
As dawn, until his shaving,
Now he's lost his night,
Thank God his dawn still saving!

(Al-Ramadi, Cordova)

★　　★　　★

SOLITUDE

To unfrequented worlds I soaring fly,
Sad is the town without thy cheering eye.
Since thou art gone I've no affection known,
And tho' midst crowds, I seem to stray alone.
No dread of solitude my soul assails,
Where'er I go thy image never fails.
Bound with Love's fetters, a distracted swain,
I seek thee thro' the world, and wear thy chain.
Whether on silk or roses of the mead

I tread; all paths to aught but thee that lead,
O'ergrown with thorns, and set with briars rude,
Retard my love, and all my hopes delude.
I said, alas! my life I freely give;
Depriv'd of thee I've no desire to live,.
Some spirit whisper'd patience to my heart,
That e'en to-day for aye I might depart.

(Jami, 817–92, tr. by Stephen Weston, 1747–1830)

5

The Renaissance

MICHELANGELO BUONARROTI (1474–1564) This great Renaissance artist described himself as follows: 'You must know that I am, of all men who were ever born, the most inclined to love persons. Whenever I behold someone who possesses any talent or displays any dexterity of mind, who can do or say something more appropriately than the rest of the world, I am compelled to fall in love with him; and then I give myself up to him so entirely that I am no longer my own property, but wholly his.' He thus excused himself from attending a particularly attractive dinner-party. 'If I were to do so, as of all of you are adorned with talents and agreeable graces, each of you would take from me a portion of myself, and so would the dancer, and so would the lute-player, if men with distinguished gifts in those arts were present. Each person would filch away a part of me, and instead of being restored to health and gladness, as you said, I should be utterly bewildered and distraught, in such wise that for many days to come I should not know in what world I was moving.'

This extreme sensitivity was occasioned by personal grace and beauty as well as by talent. The atmosphere of extravagant compliment and Platonic devotion, such as is to be found between Hubert Languet and Sir Philip Sidney, or Shakespeare and Mr. W. H., pervades the letters and poems Michelangelo wrote to Urbino, his servant, to Tommaso Cavalieri and to Febo di Poggio, and the interest he took in his friend Luigi del Riccio's affection for Cecchino dei Bracci, a youth who attracted much brilliant attention – the sculptor referred to him in a letter as 'our idol' and wrote no fewer than forty-two epigrams on his untimely death. Such affections were accepted at the time but became suspect later, especially after the Council of Trent. Michelangelo's grand-nephew was worried by the tone of some of the sonnets when he was preparing them for the press, and other commentators and editors have sought to interpret the affections expressed as disguised tributes to his greatest woman friend, Vittoria Colonna. *Donna* has had a way of becoming substituted for *Signore* ... Faced by pre-Freudian psychiatrists, John Addington Symonds approached what was still a 'delicate topic' in his *Life*, to the extent of adding an appendix in which he concluded that Michelangelo was 'one of those exceptional, but not uncommon men, who are born with sensibilities abnormally deflected from the ordinary channel. He showed no partiality for women, and a notable enthusiasm for the beauty of young men.' He went on, however, to emphasize that there was no reason to doubt the artist's moral probity: '. . . he was a man of physically frigid temperament . . . who habitually philosophized his emotions, and contemplated the living objects of his admiration as amiable not only for their personal qualities, but also for their aesthetical attractiveness.'

Cavalieri was indeed fortunate. His friend drew for him a Ganymede and eagle, a Tityos with the vulture at his heart, a fall of Phaeton and a Bacchanal of children, as well as a rare (or even perhaps unique) cartoon portrait.

TO TOMMASO CAVALIERI:

January 1, 1533

Without due consideration, Messer Tomao, my very dear lord, I was moved to write to your lordship, not by way of answer to any letter received from you, but being myself the first to make advances, as though I felt bound to cross a little stream with dry feet, or a ford made manifest by paucity of water. But now that I have left the shore, instead of the trifling water I expected, the ocean with its towering waves appears before me, so that, if it were possible, in order to avoid drowning, I would gladly retrace my steps to the dry land whence I started. Still, as I am here, I will e'en make of my heart a rock, and proceed further; and if I shall not display the art of sailing on the sea of your powerful genius, that genius itself will excuse me, nor will be disdainful of my inferiority in parts, nor desire from me that which I do not possess, inasmuch as he who is unique in all things can have peers in none. Therefore your lordship, the light of our century without paragon upon this world, is unable to be satisfied with the productions of other men, having no match or equal to yourself. And if, peradventure, something of mine, such as I hope and promise to perform, give pleasure to your mind, I shall esteem it more fortunate than excellent; and should I ever be sure of pleasing your lordship, as is said, in any particular, I will devote the present time and all my future to your service; indeed, it will grieve me much that I cannot regain the past, in order to devote a longer space to you than the future only will allow, seeing I am now too old. I have no more to say. Read the heart, and not the letter, because 'the pen toils after man's good-will in vain.'

I have to make excuses for expressing in my first letter a marvellous astonishment at your rare genius; and thus I do so, having recognised the error I was in; for it is much the same to wonder at God's working miracles as to wonder at Rome producing divine men. Of this the universe confirms us in our faith.

(Quoted in J. A. Symonds, *The Life of Michelangelo Buonarroti*, Macmillan)

TO THE SAME:

July 28, 1533

'My dear Lord, – Had I not believed that I had made you certain of the very great, nay, measureless love I bear you, it would not have seemed strange to me nor have roused astonishment to observe the great uneasiness you show in your last letter, lest, through my not having written, I should have forgotten you. Still it is nothing new or marvellous when so many other things go counter, that this also should be topsy-turvy. For what your lordship says to me, I could say to yourself: nevertheless, you do this perhaps to try me, or to light a new and stronger flame, if that indeed were possible: but be it as it wills: I know well that, at this hour, I could as easily forget your name as the food by which I live; nay, it were easier to forget the food, which only nourishes my body miserably, than your name, which nourishes both body and soul, filling the one and the other with such sweetness that neither weariness nor fear of death is felt by me while memory preserves you to my mind. Think, if the eyes could also enjoy their portion, in what condition I should find myself.'

(Ibid.)

★   ★   ★

In a letter to another friend, Bartolommeo Angelini, these passionate phrases occur:

'And so, if I yearn day and night without intermission to be in Rome, it is only in order to return again to life, which I cannot enjoy without the soul . . . My dear Bartolommeo, although you may think that I am joking with you, this is not the case. I am talking sober sense, for I have grown twenty years older and twenty pounds lighter since I have been here . . .

'I beg you, if you see Messer T. Cavalieri, to recommend me to him infinitely; and when you write, tell me something about him to keep him in my memory; for if I were to lose him from my mind, I believe that I should fall down dead straightway.'

(Ibid.)

★   ★   ★

SONNETS TO CAVALIERI

Why should I seem to ease intense desire
    With still more tears and windy words of grief,
    When heaven, or late or soon, sends no relief
    To souls whom love hath robed around with fire?
Why need my aching heart to death aspire,
    When all must die? Nay, death beyond belief
    Unto these eyes would be both sweet and brief,
    Since in my sum of woes all joys expire!
Therefore, because I cannot shun the blow
    I rather seek, say who must rule my breast,
    Gliding between her gladness and her woe?
If only chains and bands can make me blest,
    No marvel if alone and bare I go,
    An armed KNIGHT's captive and slave confessed.

(Sonnet XXI, Ibid.)

With your fair eyes a charming light I see,
  For which my own blind eyes would peer in vain;
  Stayed by your feet, the burden I sustain
  Which my lame feet find all too strong for me;
Wingless upon your pinions forth I fly;
  Heavenward your spirit stirreth me to strain;
  E'en as you will, I blush and blanch again,
  Freeze in the sun, burn 'neath a frosty sky.
Your will includes and is the lord of mine;
  Life to my thoughts within your heart is given;
  My words begin to breathe upon your breath:
Like to the moon am I, that cannot shine
  Alone; for, lo! our eyes see naught in heaven
  Save what the living sun illumineth.

(Sonnet xxx, Ibid.)

*   *   *

There seems to have been some difficulty with a certain Febo di Poggio, to whom the following letter and accompanying verse were addressed, although Febo replied the next month, in an illiterate hand, but signing himself 'Vostro da Figliuolo', yours like a son.

December, 1533

'FEBO, – albeit you bear the greatest hatred toward my person – I know not why – I scarcely believe, because of the love I cherish for you, but probably through the words of others, to which you ought to give no credence, having proved me – yet I cannot do otherwise than write to you this letter. I am leaving Florence tomorrow, and am going to Pescia to meet the Cardinal di Cesis and Messer Baldassare. I shall journey with them to Pisa, and thence to Rome, and I shall never return again to Florence. I wish you to understand that, so long as I live, wherever I may be, I shall always remain at your service with loyalty and love, in a measure unequalled by any other friend whom you may have upon this world.

'I pray God to open your eyes from some other quarter, in order that you may come to comprehend that he who desires your good more than his own welfare, is able to love, not to hate like an enemy.'

143

Naught comforts you, I see, unless I die:
   Earth weeps, the heavens for me are moved to woe;
   You feel of grief the less, the more grieve I.
O sun that warms the world where'er you go,
   O Febo, light eterne for mortal eyes!
   Why dark to me alone, elsewhere not so?

(Ibid.)

★   ★   ★

SONNET TO CONSOLE DEL RICCIO ON CECCHINO'S DEATH

Scarce had I seen for the first time his eyes,
   Which to your living eyes were life and light,
   When, closed at last in death's injurious night,
   He opened them on God in Paradise.
I know it, and I weep – too late made wise:
   Yet was the fault not mine; for death's fell spite
   Robbed my desire of that supreme delight
   Which in your better memory never dies.
Therefore, Luigi, if the task be mine
   To make unique Cecchino smile in stone
   For ever, now that earth hath made him dim,
If the beloved within the lover shine,
   Since art without him cannot work alone,
   You must I carve to tell the world of him.

(Sonnet VIII, Ibid.)

★   ★   ★

PLATONIC POEMS

Life in Renaissance Italy was by no means pure. Savonarola attacked homosexual practices and a British traveller, Lithgow, reported from Padua: '. . . for beastly Sodomy, it is rife here as in Rome, Naples, Florence, Bullogna, Venice, Ferrara, Genoa, Parma not being excepted, nor yet the smallest Village of Italy: A monstrous Filthinesse, and yet to them a pleasant pastime, making songs and singing Sonets of the beauty and pleasure of their Bardassi, or buggerd boyes.' Yet these poems by Michelangelo are reminiscent of Father Gerard Hopkins – 'To the Father through the features of men's faces'.

As one who will re-seek her home of light,
   Thy form immortal to this prison-house
   Descended, like an angel piteous,
   To heal all hearts and make the whole world bright.
'Tis this that thralls my soul in love's delight,
   Not thy clear face of beauty glorious;
   For he who harbours virtue still will choose
   To love what neither years nor death can blight.
So fares it ever with things high and rare
   Wrought in the sweat of nature; heaven above
   Showers on their birth the blessings of her prime:
Nor hath God deigned to show Himself elsewhere
   More clearly than in human forms sublime,
   Which, since they image Him, alone I love.

                            (Sonnet LVI, *Ibid.*)

★   ★   ★

From thy fair face I learn, O my loved lord,
   That which no mortal tongue can rightly say;
   The soul imprisoned in her house of clay,
Holpen by thee, to God hath often soared.
And though the vulgar, vain, malignant horde
   Attribute what their grosser wills obey,
   Yet shall this fervent homage that I pay,
   This love, this faith, pure joys for us afford.
Lo, all the lovely things we find on earth,
   Resemble for the soul that rightly sees
   That source of bliss divine which gave us birth:
Nor have we first-fruits or remembrances
   Of heaven elsewhere. Thus, loving loyally,
   I rise to God, and make death sweet by thee.

                            (Sonnet LIV, *Ibid.*)

★   ★   ★

Love is not always harsh and deadly sin,
   When love for boundless beauty makes us pine;
   The heart, by love left soft and infantine,
   Will let the shafts of God's grace enter in.
Love wings and wakes the soul, stirs her to win
   Her flight aloft, nor e'er to earth decline;

'Tis the first step that leads her to the shrine
Of Him who slakes the thirst that burns within.
The love of that whereof I speak ascends:
Woman is different far; the love of her
But ill befits a heart manly and wise.
The one love soars, the other earthward tends;
The soul lights this, while that the senses stir;
And still lust's arrow at base quarry flies.

(Sonnet LII, *Ibid.*)

*   *   *

Finally, here is a contemporary's view of Michelangelo as artist and Platonist:

He has loved the beauty of the human body with particular devotion, as is natural with one who knows that beauty so completely; and has loved it in such wise that certain carnally minded men, who do not comprehend the love of beauty, except it be lascivious and indecorous, have been led thereby to think and to speak evil of him: just as though Alcibiades, that comeliest young man, had not been loved in all purity by Socrates, from whose side, when they reposed together, he was wont to say that he arose not otherwise than from the side of his own father. Oftentimes have I heard Michelangelo discoursing and expounding on the theme of love, and have afterwards gathered from those who were present upon these occasions that he spoke precisely as Plato wrote, and as we may read in Plato's works upon this subject. I, for myself, do not know what Plato says; but I know full well that, having so long and so intimately conversed with Michelangelo, I never once heard issue from that mouth words that were not of the truest honesty, and such as had virtue to extinguish in the heart of youth any disordered and uncurbed desire which might assail it. I am sure, too, that no vile thoughts were born in him, by this token, that he loved not only the beauty of human beings, but in general all fair things, as a beautiful horse, a beautiful dog, a beautiful piece of country, a beautiful plant, a beautiful mountain, a beautiful wood, and every site or thing in its kind fair and rare, admiring them with marvellous affection. This was his way; to choose what is beautiful from nature, as bees collect the honey from flowers, and use it for their purpose in their workings which indeed was always the method of those masters who have acquired any fame in painting. That old Greek artist, when he wanted to depict a Venus, was not satisfied with the sight of one maiden only. On the contrary, he sought to study many; and culling from each the particular in which she was most perfect, to make use of these details in his Venus. Of a truth, he who imagines to arrive at any excellence without following this system (which is the source of a true theory in the arts), shoots very wide indeed of his mark.

(Condivi, LXIV: pp. 79–81. Quoted *ibid.*)

★   ★   ★

MICHEL DE MONTAIGNE (1533–92) As is proclaimed by the extract from the essay on Friendship given below, this great Renaissance figure thought perfect sympathy between men to be the greatest happiness when he retired dur ing the last nine years o his life to the library of his tower, with its 'farre-extending, rich and unresisted prospect' of the Bordeaux countryside, there to dally with 'the learned maidens', 'by peece-meales to turne over and ransacke one booke and now another', to reflect that 'the greatest thing of the world is for a man to know how to be his owne' and, above all, to remember the happy days with his friend Estienne de la Boëtie.

In a chapter entitled 'L'Amitié Pure' the author of *L'Amour Qui N'Ose Pas Dire Son Nom* describes the four-year association of the two noblemen who both had a lively enjoyment of women but who banished them from their friendship. Montaigne, M. François Porché says, 'had lost his virginity so early (doubtless with one of his mother's maids) that he could not recall at what age. The joys of bed, the leafy intimacies of the countryside, seemed to him as natural, simple and honest as the pleasures of the table. But, once his doublet was buttoned again, he resumed a distrustful and contemptuous attitude towards women. Not that he considered, in principle, that physical passion and the union of souls should never be confused. On the contrary, such an alliance seemed to him ideally desirable . . . unfortunately, friendship with a woman was an unrealisable dream.' In this connexion M. Porché explains that Montaigne not only had a

Greek way of mingling the concepts of love and friendship, but that to him friendship was the deeper term: 'l'amitié etant la chose essentielle, l'amour la chose surajoutée'.

When la Boëtie fell mortally ill, his wife effaced herself, the priest came and departed; it was the friend who stayed by the bedside. From time to time he answered 'I am here' – '. . . dans l'instant ou l'âme s'échappe, un nom, un seul, toujours le même prononcé deux fois, comme un adieu à la terre, comme une affirmation solennelle de la vie devant l'inconu de la mort: "Michel! Michel!" '

In the following translations by the Tudor scholar John Florio, we have edited and cut the text to form two sections: the first dealing with la Boëtie, the second comparing Montaigne's concept of friendship with marriage and with Greek ideas.

ONE SOULE IN TWO BODIES

If a man urge me to tell wherefore I loved him, I feele it cannot be expressed, but by answering; Because it was he, because it was my selfe. There is beyond all my discourse, and besides what I can particularly report of it, I know not what inexplicable and fatall power, a meane and Mediatrix of this indissoluble union. Wee sought one another, before we had seene one another, and by the reports we heard one of another; which wrought a greater violence in us, than the reason of reports may well beare; I thinke by some secret ordinance of the heavens, we embraced one another by our names. And at our first meeting, which was by chance at a great feast, and solemne meeting of a whole towneship, we found our selves so surprized, so knowne, so acquainted, and so combinedly bound together, that from thence forward, nothing was so neere unto us, as one unto another. He writ an excellent Latyne Satyre; since published; by which he excuseth and expoundeth the precipitation of our acquaintance, so suddenly come to her perfection; Sithence it must continue so short a time, and begun so late, (for we were both growne men, and he some yeares older than my selfe) there was no time to be lost. And it was not to bee modelled or directed by the paterne of regular and remisse friendship, wherein so many precautions of a long and preallable conversation are required.

This hath no other *Idea* than of it selfe, and can have no reference but to it selfe. It is not one especiall consideration, nor two, nor three, nor foure, nor a thousand: It is I wot not what kinde of quintessence, of all this commixture, which having seized all my will, induced the same to plunge and lose it selfe in his, which likewise having seized all his will, brought it to lose and plunge it selfe in mine, with a mutuall greedinesse, and with a semblable concurrance. I may truly say, lose, reserving nothing unto us, that might properly be called our owne, nor that was either his, or mine . . .

Our mindes have jumped so unitedly together, they have with so fervent an affection considered of each other, and with like affection so discovered and sounded, even to the very bottome of each others heart and entrails, that I did not only know his, as well as mine owne, but I would (verily) rather have trusted him concerning any matter of mine, than my selfe. Let no man compare any of the other common friendships to this. I have as much knowledge of them as another, yea of the perfectest of their kinde: yet will I not perswade any man to confound their rules, for so a man might be deceived. In these other strict friendships a man must march with the bridle of wisdome and precaution in his hand; the bond is not so strictly tied, but a man may in some sort distrust the same. *Love him* (said Chilon) *as if you should one day hate him againe. Hate him as if you should love him againe.* This precept, so abhominable in this soveraigne and mistris Amitie, is necessarie and wholesome in the use of vulgar and customarie friendships: toward which a man must employ the saying *Aristotle* was wont so often to repeat, *Oh you my friends, there is no perfect friend* . . .

Common friendship may bee divided; a man may love beauty in one, facility of behaviour in another, liberality in one, and wisdome in another, paternity in this, fraternity in that man, and so forth: but this amitie which possesseth the soule, and swaies it in all soveraigntie, it is impossible it should be double. If two at one instant should require helpe, to which would you run? Should they crave contrary offices of you, what order would you follow? Should one commit a matter to your silence, which if the other knew would greatly profit him, what course would you take? Or how would you discharge yourselfe? A singular and principall friendship dissolveth all other duties, and freeth all other obligations. The secret I have sworne not to reveale to another, I may without perjurie impart it unto him, who is no other but my selfe. It is a great and strange wonder for a man to double himselfe; and those that talke of tripling, know not, nor cannot reach unto the height of it . . .

Ancient *Menander* accounted him happy, that had but met the shadow of a true friend: verily he had reason to say so, especially if he had tasted of any: for truly, if I compare all the rest of my forepassed life, which although I have by the meere mercy of God, past at rest and ease, and except the losse of so deare a friend, free from all grievous affliction, with an ever-quietnesse of minde, as one that have taken my naturall and originall commodities in good payment, without searching any others: if, as I say, I compare it all unto the foure yeares, I so happily enjoied the sweet company, and deare-deare society of that worthy man, it is nought but a vapour, nought but a darke and yrksome [night]. Since the time I lost him . . . I doe but languish, I doe but sorrow: and even those pleasures, all things present me with, in stead of yeelding me comfort, doe but redouble the griefe of his losse. We were co-partners in all things. All things were with us at halfe; me thinkes I have stolne his part from him . . . I was so accustomed to be ever two, and so enured to be never single, that me thinks I am but halfe myselfe . . .

There was never a better Citizen, nor more affected to the welfare and quietnesse of his countrie, nor a sharper enemie of the changes, innovations, new-fangles, and hurly-burlies of his time: He would more willingly have imployed the utmost of his endevours to extinguish and suppresse, than to favour or furthen them: His minde was modelled to the patterne of other best ages.

WAVERING FIRES

To compare the affection toward women unto it, although it proceed from our owne free choise, a man cannot, nor may it be placed in this ranke: Her fire, I confesse it to be more active, more fervent, and more sharpe. But it is a rash and wavering fire, waving and divers: the fire of an ague subject to fits and stints, and that hath but slender hold-fast of us. In true friendship, it is a generall and universall heat, and equally tempered, a constant and setled heat, all pleasure and smoothness, that hath no pricking or stinging in it, which the more it is in lustfull love, the more is it but a ranging and mad desire in following that which flies us . . .

As soone as it creepeth into the termes of friendship, that is to say, in the agreement of wils. it languisheth and vanisheth away: enjoying doth lose it, as having a corporall end, and subject to sacietie. On the other side, friendship is enjoyed according as it is desired, it is neither bred, nor nourished, nor increaseth but in jovissance, as being spirituall, and the minde being refined by use and custome. Under this chiefe amitie, these fading affections have sometimes found place in me, lest I should speake of him, who in his verses speakes but too much of it. So are these two passions entred into me in knowledge one of another, but in comparison never: the first flying a high, and keeping a proud pitch, disdainfully beholding the other to passe her points farre under it. Concerning marriage, besides that it is a covenant which hath nothing free but the entrance, the continuance being forced and constrained, depending else-where than from our will, and a match ordinarily concluded to other ends: A thousand strange knots are therein commonly to be unknit, able to break the web, and trouble the whole course of a lively affection; whereas in friendship, there is no commerce or business depending on the same, but itselfe. Seeing (to speake truly) that the ordinary sufficiency of women, cannot answer this conference and communication, the nurse of this sacred bond: nor seeme their mindes strong enough to endure the pulling of a knot so hard, so fast, and durable. And truly, if without that, such a genuine and voluntarie acquaintance might be contracted, where not only mindes had this entire jovissance, but also bodies, a share of the alliance, and where a man might wholy be engaged: It is certaine, that friendship would thereby be more compleat and full: But this sex could never yet by any example attaine unto it, and is by ancient schooles rejected thence. And this other Greeke licence is justly abhorred by our customes, which notwithstanding, because according to use it had so necessarie a disparitie of ages, and difference of offices betweene lovers, did no more sufficiently answer the perfect union and agreement, which here we require: *Quis est enim iste amor amicitiae? cur neque deformem adolescentem quisquam amat, neque formosum senem?* (CIC, Tusc. Que. iv). *For, what love is this of friendship? why doth no man love either a deformed young man, or a beautifull old man?* For even the picture the *Academie* makes of it, will not (as I suppose) disavowe mee, to say thus in her behalfe: That the first furie, enspired by the son of *Venus* in the lovers hart, upon the object of tender youths-flower, to which they allow all insolent and passionate violences, an immoderate heat may produce, was simply grounded upon an externall beauty; a false image of corporeall generation: for in the spirit it had no power, the sight whereof was yet concealed, which was but in his infancie, and before the age of budding. For, if this furie did seize upon a base minded courage, the meanes of it's pursuit [were] riches, gifts, favour to the advancement of dignities, and such like vile merchandise, which they reprove. If it fell into a most generous minde, the interpositions were likewise generous: Philosophicall instructions, documents to reverence religion, to obey the lawes, to die for the good of his countrie: examples of valor, wisdome and justice. The lover endevouring and studying to make himselfe acceptable by the good grace and beauty of his minde (that of his body being long since decayed) hoping by this mentall societie to establish a more firme and permanent bargaine. When this pursuit attained the effect in due season, (for by not requiring in a lover, he should bring leasure and discretion in his enter-prise, they require it exactly in the beloved; forasmuch as he was to judge of an internall beauty, of a difficile knowledge, and abstruse discovery) [then] by the interposition of a spiritual beauty was the desire of a spiritual conception engendered in the beloved. The latter was here chiefest; the corporall, accidentall and second, altogether contrarie to the lover. And therefore doe they preferre the beloved, and verifie that the gods likewise preferre the same . . .

To conclude, all can be alleaged in favour of the Academy, is to say, that it was a love ending in friendship, a thing which hath no bad reference unto the Stoical definition of love: *Amorem conatum esse amicitiae faciendae ex pulchritudinis specie* (CIC. *ibid.*). That love is an endevour of making friendship, by the shew of beautie.

(Essays, Book I, Chapter 27)

★ ★ ★

THE FLOWER OF ENGLAND No more perfect model of physical grace, scholarly training and literary talents – a Christian gentle-man to outdo Castiglione's *Il Cortegiano* – can be found than Sir Philip Sidney who, as a boy of seventeen, charmed the scholars of Europe. Thus one of them, Theophile de Banos: 'I remembered, that day when I first saw you, and wondered at your excellent gifts both of body and mind – I remembered, I say, old Pope Gregory, who declared that the English whom he

saw coming to Rome were angels: non Angli, sed Angeli.' And
thus Lipsius: 'Anglia est flors regionum, et tu flos Angliae.'

Sidney's European studies were guided by Hubert Languet,
one of the most distinguished of Protestant scholars, and Languet's
feelings towards his pupil (now fatherly, now fussy) were clearly
tinged with the idealizing Eros of the age. He shared the feelings,
for instance, of the scholar-printer, Henri Estienne, who dedicated
an edition of the Greek Testament to Sidney: 'For somehow or
other every time I see you and enjoy your company I feel
more and more affection towards you . . . at Strasburg the love
which I felt for you at Heidelburg greatly increased, and at
Vienna the love I felt for you at Strasburg grew still more.'
Languet had a way of doting upon Sidney's likeness when the
youth was absent, in Vienna or travelling through Italy: ' . . .
and then immediately I pay the penalty for it, because it only
renews the pain I felt when you went away'. And then again,
over the portrait by Veronese: 'I kept it with me some hours
to feast my eyes on it, but my appetite was rather increased than
diminished by the sight.'

Sidney paid tribute to his mentor in Philisides' song in the
Arcadia.

> The song I sang old Lanquet had me taught,
> Lanquet, the shepherds best swift Ister knew,
>   For clerkly read, and hating what is naught,
> For faithful heart, clean hands, and mouth as true:
> With sweet skill my skilless youth he drew,
>   To have a feeling taste of him that fits
>   Beyond the heaven, far more beyond your wits.
>
> He said the music best thilk power pleased
> Was jump concord between our wit and will;
>   Where highest notes to godliness are raised,
> And lowest sink not down to jot of ill:
> With old true tales he wont mine ears to fill.
>   How shepherds did of yore, how now they thrive,
>   Spoiling their flock, or while 'twixt them they strive.

> He liked me, but pitied lustful youth:
> His good strong staff my flipp'ry years upbore:
> He still hop'd well because I loved truth:
> Till forc'd to part with heart and eyes e'en sore,
> To worthy Corydon he gave me o'er,
>> But thus in oaks true shade recounted be,
>> Which now in night's deep shade sheep heard of me.

Many were the laments on Sidney's chivalrous but untimely death. 'An Elegie, or Friend's Passion, for his Astrophel', 'A Pastorall Aeglogue', 'The Mourning Muse of Thestylis', 'The Dolefull Lay of Clorinda', 'Astrophel' and so on, all to be found in Edmund Spenser's collected works although not all by him. He, of course, mourned the paragon,

> That all mens hearts with secret ravishment
> He stole away, and weetingly beguyled.

Of the two passages following, the first is said to be by Matthew Roydon, the second's author is unknown.

> You knew, who knew not Astrophill?
> (That I should live to say I knew,
> And have not in possession still!)
> Things knowne permit me to renew;
>> Of him you know his merit such,
>> I cannot say, you heare, too much.

> Within these woods of Arcadie
> He chiefe delight and pleasure tooke,
> And on the mountaine Parthenie,
> Upon the chrystall liquid brooke,
>> The Muses met him ev'ry day
>> That taught him sing, to write, and say.

> When he descended downe to the mount,
> His personage seemed most divine,
> A thousand graces one might count

Upon his lovely cheerfull eine;
    To heare him speake and sweetly smile,
    You were in Paradise the while.

A sweet attractive kinde of grace,
A full assurance given by lookes,
Continuall comfort in a face,
The lineaments of Gospell bookes;
    I trowe that countenance cannot lie
    Whose thoughts are legible in the eie.

Was never eie did see that face,
Was never eare did heare that tong,
Was never minde did minde his grace,
That ever thought the travell long;
    But eies, and eares, and ev'ry thought,
    Were with his sweete perfections caught.

O God, that such a worthy man,
    In whom so rare desarts did raigne,
Desired thus, must leave us than,
And we to wish for him in vaine!
    O could the stars that bred that wit,
    In force no longer fixed sit!

.   .   .   .   .

England doth hold thy lims that bred the same,
Flaunders thy valure where it last was tried,
The Campe thy sorrow where thy bodie died;
Thy friends, thy want; the world, thy vertues fame.

Nations thy wit, our mindes lay up thy love;
Letters thy learning, thy losse, yeeres long to come;
In worthy harts sorrow hath made thy tombe;
Thy soule and spright enrich the heavens above.

Thy liberall hart imbalmed in gratefull teares,
Yoong sighes, sweet sighes, sage sighes, bewaile thy fall:
Envie her sting, and spite hath left her gall;
Malice her selfe a mourning garment weares

That day their Hanniball died, our Scipio fell;
Scipio, Cicero, and Petrarch of our time!
Whose vertues, wounded by my worthlesse rime,
Let Angels speake, and heaven thy praises tell.

★   ★   ★

SHAKESPEARE'S SONNETS

THE PRECEDING WRITERS, from three countries fired by the Renaissance, form an admirable background to the genius of Shakespeare whose 'sugred sonnets among his private friends' (the reference is from 1598) represent in fact the most considerable description of erotic friendship in our literature. Such friendship, of course, is felt in many of his works: in the *Merchant of Venice* and *Julius Caesar*, in the sexual ambiguities of Viola and Rosalind, and also in the poems. Mr. Wilson Knight bears this out. '*A Lover's Complaint*, which was published with them (the Sonnets), turns on what looks like a rather bitter study of the same young man; *Venus and Adonis* and *The Rape of Lucrece*, taken together, balance love for a young man against lust for a lady, as do the Sonnets; and *The Phoenix and the Turtle* condenses the central statement of spiritual union in a series of tight paradoxes. All Shakespeare's poems inter-relate.' (*The Mutual Flame*, p. 53.)

Before proceeding to the Sonnets we may recall Hamlet's declaration of friendship to Horatio:

> *Horatio:*
> Here, sweet lord, at your service.

> *Hamlet:*
> Horatio, thou art e'en as just a man
> As e'er my conversation coped withal.

> *Horatio:*
> O my dear lord.

Hamlet:
　　Nay, do not think I flatter,
For what advancement may I hope from thee
That no revenue hast but thy good spirits
To feed and clothe thee? Why should the poor be flattered?
No, let the candied tongue lick absurd pomp,
And crook the pregnant hinges of the knee
Where thrift may follow fawning. Dost thou hear—
Since my dear soul was mistress of her choice,
And could of men distinguish, her election
Hath sealed thee for herself, for thou hast been
As one in suffering all that suffers nothing,
A man that fortune's buffets and rewards
Hast ta'en with equal thanks; and blessed are those
Whose blood and judgement are so well comedled,
That they are not a pipe for Fortune's finger
· To sound what stop she please. Give me that man
That is not passion's slave, and I will wear him
In my heart's core, ay in my heart of heart
As I do thee.

★　　★　　★

There has been much speculation as to who the 'lovely boy' of
the Sonnets was. Assuming that the *Master W. H.* of the Dedica-
tion was the same person, the most popular candidate has been
Henry Wriothesley, Earl of Southampton (with the initials
reversed, as was often the custom), while William Herbert,
Earl of Pembroke, has also been considered, despite the chrono-
logical difficulties involved (Pembroke was born in 1580).
However, towards the close of the last century both Oscar Wilde
and Samuel Butler argued in favour of a less socially elevated
subject, Wilde suggesting that W.H. might be a Will Hughes
who played the female parts in Shakespeare's plays, a theory
accepted by James Joyce and André Gide, and made fairly plausible
by the various references to 'shadows' and to wigs and paintings.
Whoever the subject, eyebrows have been raised. Thus A.E.
saw the Dark Lady shocked:

> I grew sick,
> Seeing the dawn of an unnatural love,
> The kind that marred the Grecian genius . . .

while, to quote Mr. Wilson Knight again, Butler merely thought Shakespeare's love 'more Greek than English'. Wyndham Lewis went so far as to find the poet one whose 'wits and senses had been sharpened and specialized in the school of Sodom'.

In the selection below, Sonnet 20 has been taken out of context and placed first, since it expressly denies a physical consummation. For the rest the sequence is followed over the more than three years that fall within its scope: the boy is urged to marry, his beauty and qualities are praised, certain shadows fall upon the scene (now the boy is gently blamed, and now the poet) and these shadows introduce the woman with whom he becomes sensually involved and a poetic rival who praises him. Towards the end Sonnet 144 provides a summation.

20 (THE MASTER – MISTRESS)

> A woman's face, with Nature's own hand painted,
> Hast thou, the master-mistress of my passion;
> A woman's gentle heart, but not acquainted
> With shifting change, as is false women's fashion;
> An eye more bright than theirs, less false in rolling,
> Gilding the object whereupon it gazeth;
> A man in hue all hues in his controlling,
> Which steals men's eyes and women's souls amazeth.
> And for a woman wert thou first created,
> Till Nature as she wrought thee fell a-doting,
> And by addition me of thee defeated,
> By adding one thing to my purpose nothing.
>   But since she prick'd thee out for women's pleasure,
>   Mine be thy love, and thy love's use their treasure.

12

> When I do count the clock that tells the time,
> And see the brave day sunk in hideous night;

When I behold the violet past prime,
And sable curls all silver'd o'er with white;
When lofty trees I see barren of leaves,
Which erst from heat did canopy the herd,
And summer's green, all girded up in sheaves,
Borne on the bier with white and bristly beard;
Then of thy beauty do I question make,
That thou among the wastes of time must go,
Since sweets and beauties do themselves forsake,
And die as fast as they see others grow;
    And nothing 'gainst Time's scythe can make defence
    Save breed, to brave him when he takes thee hence.

13

O that you were yourself! but, love, you are
No longer yours than you yourself here live:
Against this coming end you should prepare,
And your sweet semblance to some other give.
So should that beauty which you hold in lease
Find no determination; then you were
Yourself again, after yourself's decease,
When your sweet issue your sweet form should bear.
Who lets so fair a house fall to decay,
Which husbandry in honour might uphold
Against the stormy gusts of winter's day
And barren rage of death's eternal cold?
    O, none but unthrifts: dear my love, you know
    You had a father; let your son say so.

17

Who will believe my verse in time to come,
If it were fill'd with your most high deserts?
Though yet, heaven knows, it is but as a tomb
Which hides your life, and shows not half your parts.
If I could write the beauty of your eyes,
And in fresh numbers number all your graces,
The age to come would say, 'This poet lies,
Such heavenly touches ne'er toucht earthly faces.'
So should my papers, yellow'd with their age,

Be scorned, like old men of less truth than tongue;
And your true rights be term'd a poet's rage,
And stretched metre of an antique song:
    But were some child of yours alive that time,
    You should live twice, in it and in my rime.

18

Shall I compare thee to a summer's day?
Thou art more lovely and more temperate:
Rough winds do shake the darling buds of May,
And summer's lease hath all too short a date:
Sometime too hot the eye of heaven shines,
And often is his gold complexion dimm'd;
And every fair from fair sometime declines,
By chance, or nature's changing course, untrimm'd;
But thy eternal summer shall not fade,
Nor lose possession of that fair thou ow'st;
Nor shall Death brag thou wander'st in his shade,
When in eternal lines to time thou grow'st:
    So long as men can breathe, or eyes can see,
    So long lives this, and this gives life to thee.

19

Devouring Time, blunt thou the lion's paws,
And make the earth devour her own sweet brood;
Pluck the keen teeth from the fierce tiger's jaws,
And burn the long-lived phoenix in her blood;
Make glad and sorry seasons as thou fleets,
And do whate'er thou wilt, swift-footed Time,
To the wide world and all her fading sweets;
But I forbid thee one most heinous crime:
O, carve not with thy hours my love's fair brow,
Nor draw no lines there with thine antique pen;
Him in thy course untainted do allow
For beauty's pattern to succeeding men.
    Yet, do thy worst, old Time: despite thy wrong,
    My love shall in my verse ever live young.

22

My glass shall not persuade me I am old,
So long as youth and thou are of one date;
But when in thee time's furrows I behold,
Then look I death my days should expiate.
For all that beauty that doth cover thee
Is but the seemly raiment of my heart,
Which in my breast doth live, as thine in me:
How can I, then, be elder than thou art?
O, therefore, love, be of thyself so wary
As I, not for myself, but for thee will;
Bearing thy heart, which I will keep so chary
As tender nurse her babe from faring ill.
Presume not on thy heart when mine is slain;
Thou gavest me thine, not to give back again.

27

Weary with toil, I haste me to my bed,
The dear repose for limbs with travel tired;
But then begins a journey in my head,
To work my mind, when body's work's expired:
For then my thoughts, from far where I abide,
Intend a zealous pilgrimage to thee,
And keep my drooping eyelids open wide,
Looking on darkness which the blind do see:
Save that my soul's imaginary sight
Presents thy shadow to my sightless view,
Which, like a jewel hung in ghastly night,
Makes black night beauteous, and her old face new.
Lo, thus, by day my limbs, by night my mind,
For thee and for myself no quiet find.

29

When, in disgrace with fortune and men's eyes,
I all alone beweep my outcast state,
And trouble deaf heaven with my bootless cries,
And look upon myself, and curse my fate,
Wishing me like to one more rich in hope,
Featured like him, like him with friends possest,

Desiring this man's art, and that man's scope,
With what I most enjoy contented least;
Yet in these thoughts myself almost despising,
Haply I think on thee,—and then my state,
Like to the lark at break of day arising
From sullen earth, sings hymns at heaven's gate;
 For thy sweet love remember'd such wealth brings,
 That then I scorn to change my state with kings.

41

Those pretty wrongs that liberty commits,
When I am sometime absent from thy heart,
Thy beauty and thy years full well befits,
For still temptation follows where thou art.
Gentle thou art, and therefore to be won,
Beauteous thou art, therefore to be assailed;
And when a woman woos, what woman's son
Will sourly leave her till she have prevailed?
Ay me! but yet thou mightst my seat forbear,
And chide thy beauty and thy straying youth,
Who lead thee in their riot even there
Where thou art forced to break a twofold truth, –
 Hers, by thy beauty tempting her to thee,
 Thine, by thy beauty being false to me.

42

That thou hast her, it is not all my grief,
And yet it may be said I loved her dearly;
That she hath thee, is of my wailing chief,
A loss in love that touches me more nearly.
Loving offenders, thus I will excuse ye:—
Thou dost love her, because thou know'st I love her;
And for my sake even so doth she abuse me,
Suff'ring my friend for my sake to approve her.
If I lose thee, my loss is my love's gain,
And losing her, my friend hath found that loss;
Both find each other, and I lose both twain,
And both for my sake lay on me this cross:

But here's the joy; my friend and I are one;
Sweet flattery! then she loves but me alone.

53

What is your substance, whereof are you made,
That millions of strange shadows on you tend?
Since every one hath, every one, one shade,
And you, but one, can every shadow lend.
Describe Adonis, and the counterfeit
Is poorly imitated after you;
On Helen's cheek all art of beauty set,
And you in Grecian tires are painted new:
Speak of the spring, and foison of the year;
The one doth shadow of your beauty show,
The other as your bounty doth appear;
And you in every blessed shape we know.
   In all external grace you have some part,
    But you like none, none you, for constant heart.

54

O, how much more doth beauty beauteous seem
By that sweet ornament which truth doth give!
The rose looks fair, but fairer we it deem
For that sweet odour which doth in it live.
The canker-blooms have full as deep a dye
As the perfumed tincture of the roses,
Hang on such thorns, and play as wantonly
When summer's breath their masked buds discloses:
But, for their virtue only is their show,
They live unwoo'd, and unrespected fade;
Die to themselves. Sweet roses do not so;
Of their sweet deaths are sweetest odours made:
   And so of you, beauteous and lovely youth,
    When that shall vade, my verse distils your truth.

62

Sin of self-love possesseth all mine eye,
And all my soul, and all my every part;
And for this sin there is no remedy,

It is so grounded inward in my heart.
Methinks no face so gracious is as mine,
No shape so true, no truth of such account;
And for myself mine own worth do define,
As I all other in all worths surmount.
But when my glass shows me myself indeed,
Beated and chopt with tann'd antiquity,
Mine own self-love quite contrary I read;
Self so self-loving were iniquity.
   'Tis thee, myself, that for myself I praise,
   Painting my age with beauty of thy days.

67

Ah, wherefore with infection should he live,
And with his presence grace impiety,
That sin by him advantage should achieve,
And lace itself with his society?
Why should false painting imitate his cheek,
And steal dead seeing of his living hue?
Why should poor beauty indirectly seek
Roses of shadow, since his rose is true?
Why should he live, now Nature bankrout is,
Beggar'd of blood to blush through lively veins?
For she hath no exchequer now but his,
And, proud of many, lives upon his gains.
   O, him she stores, to show what wealth she had
   In days long since, before these last so bad.

73

That time of year thou mayst in me behold
When yellow leaves, or none, or few, do hang
Upon those boughs which shake against the cold,
Bare ruin'd choirs, where late the sweet birds sang.
In me thou see'st the twilight of such day
As after sunset fadeth in the west;
Which by and by black night doth take away,
Death's second self, that seals up all in rest.
In me thou see'st the glowing of such fire,
That on the ashes of his youth doth lie,
As the death-bed whereon it must expire,

Consumed with that which it was nourisht by.
   This thou perceivest, which makes thy love more strong,
   To love that well which thou must leave ere long.

79

Whilst I alone did call upon thy aid,
My verse alone had all thy gentle grace;
But now my gracious numbers are decay'd,
And my sick Muse doth give another place.
I grant, sweet love, thy lovely argument
Deserves the travail of a worthier pen;
Yet what of thee thy poet doth invent
He robs thee of, and pays it thee again.
He lends thee virtue, and he stole that word
From thy behaviour; beauty doth he give,
And found it in thy cheek; he can afford
No praise to thee but what in thee doth live.
   Then thank him not for that which he doth say,
   Since what he owes thee thou thyself dost pay.

80

O, how I faint when I of you do write,
Knowing a better spirit doth use your name,
And in the praise thereof spends all his might,
To make me tongue-tied, speaking of your fame!
But since your worth, wide as the ocean is,
The humble as the proudest sail doth bear,
My saucy bark, inferior far to his,
On your broad main doth wilfully appear.
Your shallowest help will hold me up afloat,
While he upon your soundless deep doth ride;
Or, being wrackt, I am a worthless boat,
He of tall building and of goodly pride:
   Then if he thrive, and I be cast away,
   The worst was this; my love was my decay.

98

From you have I been absent in the spring,
When proud-pied April, drest in all his trim,

Hath put a spirit of youth in every thing,
That heavy Saturn laught and leapt with him.
Yet nor the lays of birds, nor the sweet smell
Of different flowers in odour and in hue,
Could make me any summer's story tell,
Or from their proud lap pluck them where they grew:
Nor did I wonder at the lily's white,
Nor praise the deep vermilion in the rose;
They were but sweet, but figures of delight,
Drawn after you, – you pattern of all those.
   Yet seem'd it winter still, and, you away,
   As with your shadow I with these did play.

99

The forward violet thus did I chide:
Sweet thief, whence didst thou steal thy sweet that smells,
If not from my love's breath! The purple pride
Which on thy soft cheek for complexion dwells
In my love's veins thou hast too grossly dyed.
The lily I condemned for thy hand;
And buds of marjoram had stoln thy hair:
The roses fearfully on thorns did stand,
One blushing shame, another white despair;
A third, nor red nor white, had stoln of both,
And to his robbery had annext thy breath;
But, for his theft, in pride of all his growth
A vengeful canker eat him up to death.
   More flowers I noted, yet I none could see
   But sweet or colour it had stoln from thee.

104

To me, fair friend, you never can be old,
For as you were when first your eye I eyed,
Such seems your beauty still. Three winters' cold
Have from the forests shook three summers' pride;
Three beauteous springs to yellow autumn turn'd
In process of the seasons have I seen,
Three April perfumes in three hot Junes burn'd,
Since first I saw you fresh, which yet are green.

Ah, yet doth beauty, like a dial-hand,
Steal from his figure, and no pace perceived;
So your sweet hue, which methinks still doth stand,
Hath motion, and mine eye may be deceived:
  For fear of which, hear this, thou age unbred, –
  Ere you were born was beauty's summer dead.

106

When in the chronicle of wasted time
I see descriptions of the fairest wights,
And beauty making beautiful old rime
In praise of ladies dead and lovely knights,
Then, in the blazon of sweet beauty's best,
Of hand, of foot, of lip, of eye, of brow,
I see their antique pen would have exprest
Even such a beauty as you master now.
So all their praises are but prophecies
Of this our time, all you prefiguring;
And, for they lookt but with divining eyes,
They had not skill enough your worth to sing:
  For we, which now behold these present days,
  Have eyes to wonder, but lack tongues to praise.

110

Alas, 'tis true I have gone here and there,
And made myself a motley to the view,
Gored mine own thoughts, sold cheap what is most dear,
Made old offences of affections new;
Most true it is that I have lookt on truth
Askance and strangely: but, by all above,
These blenches gave my heart another youth,
And worse essays proved thee my best of love.
Now all is done, have what shall have no end:
Mine appetite I never more will grind
On newer proof, to try an older friend,
A god in love, to whom I am confined.
  Then give me welcome, next my heaven the best,
  Even to thy pure and most most loving breast.

116

Let me not to the marriage of true minds
Admit impediments. Love is not love
Which alters when it alteration finds,
Or bends with the remover to remove:
O, no! it is an ever-fixed mark,
That looks on tempests, and is never shaken,
It is the star to every wandering bark,
Whose worth's unknown, although his height be taken.
Love's not Time's fool, though rosy lips and cheeks
Within his bending sickle's compass come;
Love alters not with his brief hours and weeks,
But bears it out even to the edge of doom.
    If this be error, and upon me proved,
    I never writ, nor no man ever loved.

135

Whoever hath her wish, thou hast thy *Will*,
And *Will* to boot, and *Will* in overplus;
More than enough am I that vext thee still,
To thy sweet will making addition thus.
Wilt thou, whose will is large and spacious,
Not once vouchsafe to hide my will in thine?
Shall will in others seem right gracious,
And in my will no fair acceptance shine?
The sea, all water, yet receives rain still,
And in abundance addeth to his store;
So thou, being rich in *Will*, add to thy *Will*
One will of mine, to make thy large *Will* more.
    Let no unkind, no fair beseechers kill;
    Think all but one, and me in that one *Will*.

144 (THE TWO LOVES)

Two loves I have of comfort and despair,
Which like two spirits do suggest me still;
The better angel is a man right fair,
The worser spirit a woman colour'd ill.
To win me soon to hell, my female evil
Tempteth my better angel from my side,

And would corrupt my saint to be a devil,
Wooing his purity with her foul pride.
And whether that my angel be turn'd fiend,
Suspect I may, yet not directly tell;
But being both from me, both to each friend,
I guess one angel in another's hell.
    Yet this shall I ne'er know, but live in doubt,
    Till my bad angel fire my good one out.

★   ★   ★

In conclusion we print some stanzas of *The Lover's Complaint* for, although it is a 'maid' who speaks, she pictures a beautiful but tricky boy who may be relevant to Shakespeare's experience.

But woe is me, too early I attended
A youthful suit – it was to gain my grace –
Of one by nature's outwards so commended,
That maidens' eyes stuck over all his face.
Love lack'd a dwelling and made him her place;
And when in his fair parts she did abide,
She was new lodg'd and newly deified.

His browny locks did hang in crooked curls,
And every light occasion of the wind
Upon his lips their silken parcels hurls.
What's sweet to do, to do will aptly find:
Each eye that saw him did enchant the mind;
For on his visage was in little drawn
What largeness thinks in Paradise was sawn.

Small show of man was yet upon his chin,
His phoenix down began but to appear
Like unshorn velvet, on that termless skin,
Whose bare out-bragg'd the web it seem'd to wear,
Yet show'd his visage by that cost more dear;
And nice affections wavering stood in doubt
If best were as it was, or best without.

His qualities were beauteous as his form,
For maiden-tongue'd he was and thereof free;

Yet if men mov'd him, was he such a storm
As oft 'twixt May and April is to see,
When winds breathe sweet, unruly though they be.
His rudeness so with his authoriz'd youth
Did livery falseness in a pride of truth.
Well could he ride, and often men would say,
'That horse his mettle from his rider takes;
Proud of subjection, noble by the sway,
What rounds, what bounds, what course, what stop he
    makes!'
And controversy hence a question takes,
Whether the horse by him became his deed,
Or he his manage by th' well-doing steed.

            ★   ★   ★

That he did in the general bosom reign
Of young, of old, and sexes both enchanted,
To dwell with him in thoughts, or to remain
In personal duty, following where he haunted,
Consents bewitch'd ere he desire have granted,
And dialogue'd for him what he would say,
Ask'd their own wills and made their wills obey.

Many there were that did his picture get
To serve their eyes, and in it put their mind;
Like fools that in th' imagination set
The goodly objects which abroad they find
Of lands and mansions, theirs in thought assign'd,
And labouring in moe pleasures to bestow them,
Than the true gouty landlord which doth owe them.

So many have, that never touched his hand,
Sweetly suppos'd them mistress of his heart.
My woeful self that did in freedom stand,
And was my own fee-simple, not in part,
What with his art in youth and youth in art,
Threw my affections in his charmed power,
Reserv'd the stalk and gave him all my flower.

            ★   ★   ★

O father, what a hell of witchcraft lies
In the small orb of one particular tear!
But with the inundation of the eyes
What rocky heart to water will not wear?
What breast so cold that is not warmed there?
O cleft effect; cold modesty, hot wrath,
Both fire from hence and chill extincture hath.

For lo, his passion, but an art of craft,
Even there resolv'd my reason into tears,
There my white stole of chastity I daff'd,
Shook off my sober guards and civil fears;
Appear to him as he to me appears,
All melting, though our drops this diff'rence bore—
His poison'd me, and mine did him restore.

In him a plenitude of subtle matter,
Applied to cautels, all strange forms receives,
Of burning blushes, or of weeping water,
Or swounding paleness; and he takes and leaves,
In either's aptness, as it best deceives,
To blush at speeches rank, to weep at woes,
Or to turn white and swound at tragic shows.

That not a heart which in his level came
Could 'scape the hail of his all-hurting aim,
Showing fair nature is both kind and tame;
And veil'd in them did win whom he would maim:
Against the thing he sought he would exclaim;
When he most burnt in heart-wish'd luxury,
He preach'd pure maid, and prais'd cold chastity.

Thus merely with the garment of a Grace
The naked and concealed fiend he cover'd;
That th' unexperient gave the tempter place,
Which like a cherubin above them hover'd.
Who young and simple would not be so lover'd?
Ay me, I fell, and yet do question make,
What I should do again for such a sake.

O that infected moisture of his eye,
O that false fire which in his cheek so glowed,
O that forc'd thunder from his heart did fly,
O that sad breath his spongy lungs bestowed,
O all that borrow'd motion seeming owed,
Would yet again betray the fore-betray'd,
And new pervert a reconciled maid!

★   ★   ★

CHRISTOPHER MARLOWE (1564–93) One of the many accusations against this great dramatist, whose private life seems to have been colourful, was that he held the opinion that 'all thei that love not tobacco and boys are fooles'. Mr. F. S. Boas inquires, in the course of his study of Marlowe, why it was that 'out of all the rich material provided by Holinshed he chose the comparatively unattractive reign of Edward II. The reason is, I believe, to be mainly found in the relation between the king and Gaveston which he brings into the forefront of the play. Homosexual affection without emphasis on its more depraved aspect, had a special attraction for Marlowe. Jove and Ganymede in *Dido*, Henry III and his "minions" in *The Massacre*, Neptune and Leander in *Hero and Leander*, are all akin, although drawn to a lighter scale, to Edward and Gaveston.' Mr. Boas points out that, although Holinshed placed the emphasis differently, Marlowe was just the man to be taken with the chronicler's opening paragraph, with its picture of the favourite 'passing his time in voluptuous pleasure, and riotous excesse . . . and other vile and naughtie ribalds, that the king might spend both daies and nights in iesting, plaieing, blanketing, and in such other filthie and dishonourable exercises'. For Marlowe has a quite different tone to Shakespeare, Michelangelo and the rest; there is a tension to him, a jeering delight and scorn, when he brings his wonderfully animal sensibility and his feeling for décor to the consideration of this subject. One thinks of the note momentarily struck in Tourneur's *Revenger's Tragedy*, when Vendice greets Spurio:

How now, sweet musk-cat, when shall we lie together?

But let us turn first to the portrait of Leander, and then to the moment when, as he swims to Hero's tower, the youth is waylaid by an amorous but surprisingly sensitive Neptune.

PORTRAIT OF LEANDER

Amorous Leander, beautiful and young,
(Whose tragedy divine Musaeus sang)
Dwelt at Abydos; since him dwelt there none
For whom succeeding times make greater moan.
His dangling tresses that were never shorn,
Had they been cut and unto Colchos borne,
Would have allured the venturous youth of Greece
To hazard more than for the Golden Fleece.
Fair Cynthia wished his arms might be her sphere;
Grief makes her pale, because she moves not there.
His body was as straight as Circe's wand;
Jove might have sipped out nectar from his hand.
Even as delicious meat is to the taste,
So was his neck in touching, and surpassed
The white of Pelop's shoulder. I could tell ye
How smooth his breast was, and how white his belly,
And whose immortal fingers did imprint
That heavenly path, with many a curious dint,
That runs along his back; but my rude pen
Can hardly blazon forth the loves of men,
Much less of powerful gods; let it suffice
That my slack muse sings of Leander's eyes,
Those orient cheeks and lips, exceeding his
That leapt into the water for a kiss
Of his own shadow, and despising many,
Died ere he could enjoy the love of any.
Had wild Hippolytus Leander seen,
Enamoured of his beauty had he been;
His presence made the rudest peasant melt,
That in the vast uplandish country dwelt;
The barbarous Thracian soldier, moved with nought,

Was moved with him, and for his favour sought.
Some swore he was a maid in man's attire,
For in his looks were all that men desire,
A pleasant smiling cheek, a speaking eye,
A brow for love to banquet royally;
And such as knew he was a man, would say,
'Leander, thou art made for amorous play;
Why art thou not in love, and loved of all?
Though thou be fair, yet be not thine own thrall.'

LOVED BY A GOD

With that he stripped him to the ivory skin,
And crying, 'Love, I come', leaped lively in.
Whereat the sapphire-visaged god grew proud,
And made his capering Triton sound aloud,
Imagining that Ganymede, displeased,
Had left the heavens; therefore on him he seized.
Leander strived; the waves about him wound,
And pulled him to the bottom, where the ground
Was strewed with pearl, and in low coral groves
Sweet singing mermaids sported with their loves
On heaps of heavy gold, and took great pleasure
To spurn in careless sort the shipwreck treasure:
For here the stately azure palace stood,
Where kingly Neptune and his train abode.
The lusty god embraced him, called him love,
And swore he never should return to Jove.
But when he knew it was not Ganymede,
For under water he was almost dead,
He heaved him up, and looking on his face,
Beat down the bold waves with his triple mace,
Which mounted up, intending to have kissed him,
And fell in drops like tears, because they missed him.
Leander, being up, began to swim,
And looking back, saw Neptune follow him;
Whereat aghast, the poor soul 'gan to cry:
'O! let me visit Hero ere I die!'
The god put Helle's bracelet on his arm,

And swore the sea should never do him harm.
He clapped his plump cheeks, with his tresses played,
And smiling wantonly, his love bewrayed.
He watched his arms, and as they opened wide,
At every stroke betwixt them would he slide,
And steal a kiss, and then run out and dance,
And as he turned, cast many a lustful glance,
And throw him gaudy toys to please his eye,
And dive into the water, and there pry
Upon his breast, his thighs, and every limb,
And up again, and close behind him swim,
And talk of love. Leander made reply:
'You are deceived, I am no woman, I.'
Thereat smiled Neptune, and then told a tale,
How that a shepherd, sitting in a vale,
Played with a boy so lovely fair and kind,
As for his love both earth and heaven pined;
That of the cooling river durst not drink
Lest water-nymphs should pull him from the brink;
And when he sported in the fragrant lawns,
Goat-footed satyrs and up-staring fauns
Would steal him thence. Ere half this tale was done,
'Ay me!' Leander cried, 'th' enamoured sun,
That now should shine on Thetis' glassy bower,
Descends upon my radiant Hero's tower.
O! that these tardy arms of mine were wings!'
And as he spake, upon the waves he springs.
Neptune was angry that he gave no ear,
And in his heart revenging malice bare;
He flung at him his mace, but as it went
He called it in, for love made him repent.
The mace returning back his own hand hit,
As meaning to be venged for darting it.
When this fresh bleeding wound Leander viewed,
His colour went and came, as if he rued
The grief which Neptune felt. In gentle breasts
Relenting thoughts, remorse, and pity rests;
And who have hard hearts and obdurate minds
But vicious, hare-brained, and illiterate hinds?

The god, seeing him with pity to be moved,
Thereon concluded that he was beloved.
(Love is too full of faith, too credulous,
With folly and false hope deluding us.)
Wherefore, Leander's fancy to surprise,
To the rich ocean for gifts he flies.
'Tis wisdom to give much; a gift prevails
When deep persuading oratory fails.
By this Leander being near the land
Cast down his weary feet, and felt the sand.

★　　★　　★

THE MINION'S STRATEGY

Gaveston:
I must have wanton poets, pleasant wits,
Musicians, that with touching of a string
May draw the pliant king which way I please.
Music and poetry is his delight;
Therefore I'll have Italian masks by night,
Sweet speeches, comedies, and pleasing shows;
And in the day, when he shall walk abroad,
Like sylvan nymphs my pages shall be clad;
My men, like satyrs grazing on the lawns,
Shall with their goat-feet dance the antic hay.
Sometime a lovely boy in Dian's shape,
With hair that gilds the water as it glides,
Crownets of pearl about his naked arms,
And in his sportful hands an olive-tree,
To hide those parts which men delight to see,
Shall bathe him in a spring; and there hard by,
One like Actaeon peeping through the grove,
Shall by the angry goddess be transformed,
And running in the likeness of an hart
By yelping hounds pulled down, shall seem to die;—
Such things as these best please his majesty.

(*Edward the Second*, Act I, Scene i)

THE QUEEN PONDERS THE SITUATION

Isabella:

O miserable and distresséd queen!
Would, when I left sweet France and was embarked,
That charming Circe walking on the waves,
Had changed my shape, or at the marriage-day
The cup of Hymen had been full of poison,
Or with those arms that twined about my neck
I had been stifled, and not lived to see
The king my lord thus to abandon me!
Like frantic Juno will I fill the earth
With ghastly murmur of my sighs and cries;
For never doated Jove on Ganymede
So much as he on curséd Gaveston:
But that will more exasperate his wrath;
I must entreat him, I must speak him fair;
And be a means to call home Gaveston:
And yet he'll ever doat on Gaveston;
And so am I for ever miserable.

(Ibid., Act I. Scene iv)

THE MORTIMERS DISCUSS IT

Elder Mortimer:

Leave now t'oppose thyself against the king.
Thou seest by nature he is mild and calm,
And, seeing his mind so doats on Gaveston,
Let him without controulment have his will.
The mightiest kings have had their minions:
Great Alexander loved Hephestion;
The conquering Hercules for Hylas wept;
And for Patroclus stern Achilles drooped
And not kings only, but the wisest men:
The Roman Tully loved Octavius;
Grave Socrates wild Alcibiades.
Then let his grace, whose youth is flexible,
And promiseth as much as we can wish,
Freely enjoy that vain, light-headed earl;
For riper years will wean him from such toys.

> *Young Mortimer:*
> Uncle, his wanton humour grieves not me;
> But this I scorn, that one so basely born
> Should by his sovereign's favour grow so pert,
> And riot it with the treasure of the realm.
> While soldiers mutiny for want of pay,
> He wears a lord's revenue on his back,
> And Midas-like, he jets it in the court,
> With base outlandish cullions at his heels,
> Whose proud fantastic liveries make such show,
> As if that Proteus, god of shapes, appeared.
> I have not seen a dapper Jack so brisk;
> He wears a short Italian hooded cloak,
> Larded with pearl, and, in his Tuscan cap,
> A jewel of more value than the crown.
> While others walk below, the king and he
> From out a window laugh at such as we,
> And flout our train, and jest at our attire.
> Uncle, 'tis this makes me impatient.
>
> (*Ibid.*, Act I, Scene iv)

★   ★   ★

IN VIEW of these quotations from dramatists, and the play that Wilde makes with the boy actors of the time in his book on Shakespeare's Sonnets – with Robin Armin, Gil. Carie attired as a mountain nymph, Nat. Field who played the 'Queen and Huntress chaste and fair', and Dicky Robinson described by Ben Jonson as 'a very pretty fellow', all of them the butt of the Puritans because the theatre was one of those

> tempting baits of hell
> Which draw more youth unto the damned cell
> Of furious lust, than all the devil could do

– in view of all this, it seems appropriate to give Jonson's epitaph to Salathiel Pavy.

EPITAPH ON SALATHIEL PAVY

Weep with me all you that read
   This little story;
And know, for whom a tear you shed,
   Death's self is sorry.
'Twas a child, that so did thrive
   In grace and feature,
As heaven and nature seemed to strive
   Which owned the creature.
Years he numbered scarce thirteen
   When fates turned cruel;
Yet three filled zodiacs had he been
   The stage's jewel;
And did act, what now we moan,
   Old men so duly;
As, sooth, the Parcae thought him one
   He played so truly.
So, by error, to his fate
   They all consented;
But viewing him since, alas, too late!
   They have repented;
And have sought, to give new birth,
   In baths to steep him;
But, being so much too good for earth,
   Heaven vows to keep him.

              (Ben Jonson, *Epigrams*)

★   ★   ★

RICHARD BARNFIELD (1574–1627) These pastorals bear an
obvious debt to Virgil. They were dedicated to Sidney's 'Stella'.

THE AFFECTIONATE SHEPHEARD

*The Teares of an Affectionate Shepheard Sicke for Love,
or the Complaint of Daphnis for the
Love of Ganimede*

[I]

Scarce had the morning starre hid from the light
Heavens crimson canopie with stars bespangled,

But I began to rue th' unhappy sight
    Of that faire boy that had my hart intangled;
Cursing the time, the place, the sense, the sin;
I came, I saw, I viewd, I slipped in.

[2]

If it be sinne to love a sweet-fac'd boy,
    Whose amber locks trust up in golden tramels
Dangle adowne his lovely cheekes with joy,
    When pearle and flowers his faire haire enamels;
If it be sinne to love a lovely lad,
Oh then sinne I, for whom my soul is sad.

[3]

His ivory-white and alabaster skin
    Is staind throughout with rare vermillion red,
Whose twinckling starrie lights doe never blin[1]
    To shine on lovely Venus, Beauties bed;
But as the lillie and the blushing rose,
So white and red on him in order growes.

[16]

Oh would to God he would but pitty mee,
    That love him more than any mortall wight!
Then he and I with love would soone agree,
    That now cannot abide his sutors sight.
O would to God, so I might have my fee,
My lips were honey, and thy mouth a bee.

[17]

Then shouldst thou sucke my sweete and my faire flower,
    That now is ripe and full of honey-berries;
Then would I leade thee to my pleasant bower,
    Fild full of grapes, of mulberries, and cherries:
Then shouldst thou be my waspe or else my bee,
I would thy hive, and thou my honey, bee.

[1] *Blin:* to cease

[19]

And every morne by dawning of the day,
   When Phoebus riseth with a blushing face,
Silvanus chappel-clarkes shall chaunt a lay,
   And play thee hunts-up in thy resting place:
My coote thy chamber, my bosome thy bed
Shall be appointed for thy sleepy head.

[20]

And when it pleaseth thee to walke abroad,
   Abroad into the fields to take fresh ayre,
The meades with Floras treasure should be strowde,
   The mantled meaddowes, and the fields so fayre.
And by a silver well with golden sands
Ile sit me downe, and wash thine ivory hands.

[21]

And in the sweltring heate of summer time,
   I would make cabinets for thee, my love;
Sweet-smelling arbours made of eglantine
   Should be thy shrine, and I would be thy dove.
Cool cabinets of fresh greene laurell boughs
Should shadow us, ore-set with thicke-set eughes.[1]

[22]

Or if thou list to bathe thy naked limbs
   Within the cristall of a pearle-bright brooke,
Paved with dainty pibbles to the brims,
   Or cleare, wherein thyselfe mayst looke;
Weele go to Ladon,[2] whose still trickling noyse
Will lull thee fast asleepe amids thy joyes.

[25]

Or if thou darst to climbe the highest trees
   For apples, cherries, medlars, peares, or plumbs,
Nuts, walnuts, filbreads, chestnuts, cervices,
   The hoary peach, when snowy winter comes;

[1] *Eughes:* yews.
[2] *Ladon:* river in Arcadia.

I have fine orchards full of mellowed fruite,
Which I will give thee to obtaine my sute.

[26]

Not proud Alcynous himselfe can vaunt
   Of goodlier orchards or of braver trees
Than I have planted; yet thou will not graunt
   My simple sute, but like the honey bees
Thou sukst the flowre till all the sweet be gone,
And loost mee for my coyne till I have none.

[28]

If thou wilt come and dwell with me at home,
   My sheepcote shall be strowed with new greene rushes;
Weele haunt the trembling prickets[1] as they rome
   About the fields, along the hauthorne bushes;
I have a pie-bald curre to hunt the hare,
So we will live with daintie forrest fare.

[29]

Nay, more than this, I have a garden plot,
   Wherein there wants nor hearbs, nor roots, nor flowers;
Flowers to smell, roots to eate, hearbs for the pot,
   And dainty shelters when the welkin lowers:
Sweet-smelling beds of lillies, and of roses,
Which rosemary banks and lavendar incloses.

[30]

There growes the gilliflower, the mynt, the dayzie
   Both red and white, the blue-veyned violet;
The purple hyacinth, the spyke[2] to please thee,
   The scarlet dyde carnation bleeding yet:
The sage, the savery, and sweet margerum,
Isop, tyme, and eye-bright, good for the blinde and dumbe.

[33]

And manie thousand moe I cannot name
   Of hearbs and flowers that in gardens grow,

---

[1] *Prickets:* bucks of the second year.
[2] *Spyke:* Lavender.

I have for thee, and coneyees that be tame,
　Young rabbits, white as swan, and blacke as crow;
Some speckled here and there with daintie spots:
　And more I have two mylch and milke-white goates.

All these and more Ile give thee for thy love,
　If these and more may tyce thy love away:
I have a pigeon-house, in it a dove,
　Which I love more than mortall tongue can say;
And last of all, I'll give thee a little lamb
To play withal, new-weanïd from his dam.

[34]

But if thou wilt not pittie my complaint,
　My teares, nor vowes, nor oathes, made to thy beautie:
What shall I do but languish, die, or faint,
　Since thou dost scorne my teares, and my soules duetie:
And teares contemned, vowes and oaths must faile,
And where teares cannot, nothing can prevaile.

[35]

Compare the love of faire Queene Guendolin[1]
　With mine, and thou shalt see how she doth love thee:
I love thee for thy qualities divine,
　But shee doth love another swaine above thee:
I love thee for thy gifts, she for hir pleasure;
I for thy vertue, she for beauties treasure.

[36]

And alwaies, I am sure, it cannot last.
　But sometime Nature will denie those dimples:
Insteed of beautie, when thy blossom's past,
　Thy face will be deformed full of wrinckles;
Then she that lov'd thee for thy beauties sake,
　When age drawes on, thy love will soone forsake.

---

[1] *Queene Guendolin:* a nymph whom the poet's Ganimede loves. He has pleaded that Guendolin and his love might forsake each other:

　　Leave Guendolen, sweet hart; though she be faire,
　　　Yet is she light; not light in verture shining . . .
　　Trust not her teares, for they can wantonnize,
　　When teares in pearle are trickling from her eyes.

[37]

But I that lov'd thee for thy gifts divine,
  In the December of thy beauties waning,
Will still admire with joy those lovely eine,
  That now behold me with their beauties baning.
Though Januarie will never come again,
Yet Aprill yeres will come in showers of raine.

[38]

When will my May come, that I may embrace thee?
  When will the hower be of my soules joying?
Why dost thou seeke in mirth still to disgrace mee?
  Whose mirth's my health, whose griefe's my hearts
                                                  annoying:
Thy bane my bale, thy blisse my blessedness,
Thy ill my hell, thy weale my welfare is.

[39]

Thus doo I honour thee that I love thee so,
  And love thee so, that so do honour thee
Much more than anie mortall man doth know,
  Or can discerne by love or jealozie:
But if that thou disdainst my loving ever,
Oh happie I, if I had loved never!

Plus fellis quam mellis amor.

(From:
The
AFFECTIONATE SHEPHEARD.
Containing the complaint of Daphnis for
the love of Ganymede.

Amor plus mellis, quam fellis, est.

London:
Printed for IOHN DANTER, for T.G. and E.N., and
are to bee sold in Saint Dunstones
Church-yeard in Fleetstreet.
1594.)

THE SECOND DAYES LAMENTATION OF
THE AFFECTIONATE SHEPHEARD

[6]

Yet if thou wilt but show me one kinde looke,
   A small reward for my so great affection,
Ile grave thy name in Beauties golden booke,
   And shrowd thee under Hellicon's protection;
Making the muses chaunt thy lovely prayse,
For they delight in shepheard's lowly layes.

[7]

And when th'art wearie of thy keeping sheepe
   Upon a lovely downe, to please thy minde,
Ile give thee fine ruffe-footed doves to keepe,
   And pretie pidgeons of another kinde:
A robbin-redbreast shall thy minstrel bee;
Chirping thee sweet and pleasant melodie.

[8]

Or if thou wilt goe shoote at little birds,
   With bow and boult, the thrustle-cocke and sparrow,
Such as our countrey hedges can afford,
   I have a fine bowe, and an yvorie arrow.
And if thou misse, yet meate thou shalt not lacke,
Ile hang a bag and bottle at thy backe.

[11]

Wilt thou set springes in a frostie night
   To catch the long-billed woodcock and the snype,
By the bright glimmering of the starrie light,
   The partridge, pheasant, or the greedie grype;
Ile lend thee lyme-twigs, and fine sparrow calls,
Wherewith the fowler silly birds inthralls.

[12]

Or with hare-pypes set in a muset hole,
   Wilt thou deceave the deep-earth-delving-coney;
Or wilt thou in a yellow boxen bole,

Taste with a wooden splent the sweet lythe honey;
Clusters of crimson grapes Ile pull thee downe,
And with vine-leaves make thee a lovely crowne.

[14]

Or wilt thou drink a cup of new-made wine,
   Froathing at top, mixt with a dish of creame
And strawberries, or bilberries, in their prime,
   Bath'd in a melting sugar-candie streame:
Bunnel and perry I have for thee alone,
When vynes are dead, and all the grapes are gone.

[15]

Then will I lay out all my lardarie
   Of cheese, of cracknells, curds and clowted-creame,
Before thy malecontent ill-pleasing eye;
   But why doo I of such great follies dreame?
Alas, he will not see my simple coate,
For all my speckled lambe, nor milk-white goate!

[25]

Against my birth-day thou shalt be my guest,
   Weele have greene-cheeses and fine silly-bubs,
And thou shalt be the chiefe of all my feast,
   And I will give thee two fine pretie cubs,
With two yong whelps, to make thee sport withall,
A golden racket, and a tennis-ball.

[70]

Oh lend thine yvorie forehead for loves booke,
Thine eyes for candles to behold the same;
That when dim-sighted ones therein shall looke,
   They may discern that proud disdainefull dame;
Yet claspe that booke, and shut that cazement light,
Lest, th'one obscured, the other shine too bright.

[71]

Behold my gray head, full of silver haires,
   My wrinckled skin, deepe furrowes in my face,

Cares bring old age, old age increaseth cares;
  My time is come, and I have run my race:
Winter hath snow'd upon my hoarie head,
And with my winter all my joyes are dead.

[72]

And thou love-hating boy, (whom once I loved),
  Farewell, a thousand-thousand times farewell;
My teares the marble-stones to ruth have moved;
  My sad complaints the babling ecchoes tell:
And yet thou wouldst take no compassion on mee,
Scorning that crosse which love hath laid upon mee.

[73]

The hardest steele with fier doth mend his misse,
  Marble is mollifyde with drops of raine;
But thou (more hard than steele or marble is),
  Doost scorne my teares, and my true love disdaine,
Which for thy sake shall everlasting bee,
Wrote in the annalls of eternitie.

*   *   *

THE SEVENTEENTH CENTURY brought the finest age of religious poetry in England as well as the complex and sophisticated explorations of changing, teasing and darkening experience undertaken by the Metaphysicals; it brought the High Renaissance of John Milton, and also the Puritan Revolution which absorbed so much of his energy and time. The new monarch, James I, to whom Donne preached like an angel out of a cloud, and who watched the exquisite *Masque of Hymen* by Ben Jonson and Inigo Jones, was himself very much of an Erotic Friend as well as an expert on tobacco and witches. He cultivated the Earls of Montgomery, Somerset and Buckingham – the egregious *Steenie* (because he possessed the angelic face of a St. Stephen). Defending his friendship in 1617 he made this remarkable pronouncement to the Council: 'I, James, am neither a god nor an angel, but a man like any other. Therefore I act like a man and confess to loving those dear to me more than other men. You may be sure that I love the Earl of Buckingham more than anyone else, and more than you who are here assembled. I wish to speak in my own behalf and not to have it thought to be a defect, for Jesus Christ did the same, and therefore I cannot be blamed. Christ had his son John, I have my George.' (Quoted in E. S. Turner, *The Court of St. James's*, Michael Joseph.) One courtier described the king as 'wondrous passionate, a lover of his favourites beyond the love of men of women'; another declared, 'The kissing them after so lascivious mode in public and upon the theatre, as it were, of the world prompted many to imagine some things done in the tyring house that exceed my expression no less than they do my experience.' With his Queen, someone has said, he shared one thing at least: 'a mutual admiration for masculine beauty'.

The greatest poem to a friend that this period provides is doubtless Milton's *Lycidas*, except that the friend turns out to be of little importance beside the themes of Fame and the corruption of the Clergy; Eros is simply not there. It has been thought best to present Francis Bacon; the grave Sir Thomas Browne, at his least baroque on this occasion; two superb religious poems – with Christ the childhood love in one, and in the other the magnanimous Host – and then a fragment from Rochester. A principal fruit of friendship is the ease and discharge of the fulness

FRANCIS BACON (1561–1626)

Of Friendship

and swellings of the heart, which passions of all kinds do cause and induce. We know diseases of stoppings and suffocations are the most dangerous in the body; and it is not much otherwise in the mind. No receipt openeth the heart, but a true friend, to whom you may impart griefs, joys, fears, hopes, suspicions, counsels, and whatsoever lieth upon the heart to oppress it, in a kind of civil shrift or confession.

It is a strange thing to observe how high a rate great kings and monarchs do set upon this fruit of friendship whereof we speak: so great, as they purchase it many times at the hazard of their own safety and greatness. For princes, in regard of the distance of their fortune from that of their subjects and servants, cannot gather this fruit except (to make themselves capable thereof) they raise some persons to be as it were companions, and almost equals to themselves, which many times sorteth to inconvenience. The modern languages give unto such persons the name of *favourites*, or *privadoes*; as if it were matter of grace, or conversation. But the Roman name attaineth the true use and cause thereof, naming them *participes curarum*;[1] for it is that which tieth the knot: and we see plainly that this hath been done, not by weak and passionate princes only, but by the wisest and most politic that ever reigned, who have oftentimes joined to themselves some of their servants, whom both themselves have called *friends*, and allowed others likewise to call them in the same manner, using the word which is received between private men.

L. Sylla, when he commanded Rome, raised Pompey (after surnamed the Great) to that height, that Pompey vaunted himself for Sylla's overmatch. For when he had carried the consulship for a friend of his, against the pursuit of Sylla, and that Sylla did a little resent thereat, and began to speak great, Pompey turned on him again, and in effect bade him be quiet; *for that more men adored the sun rising than the sun setting*. With Julius Caesar, Decimus Brutus had obtained that interest, as he set him down in his testament for heir in remainder after his nephew. And this was the man that had power with him to draw him forth to his death; for when Caesar would have discharged the senate, in regard of some ill presages, and especially a dream of Calpurnia, this man lifted him gently by the arm out of his chair, telling him he hoped he would not dismiss the senate till his wife had dreamt a better dream; and it seemeth his favour was so great, as Antonius, in a letter which is recited *verbatim* in one of Cicero's *Philippics*, calleth him *venefica*, *witch*; as if he had enchanted Caesar. Augustus raised Agrippa (though of mean birth) to that height, as, when he consulted with Maecenas about the marriage of his daughter Julia, Maecenas took the liberty to tell him, *that he must either marry his daughter to Agrippa, or take away his life*: there was no third way, he had made him so great. With Tiberius Caesar, Sejanus had ascended to that height, as they two were termed and reckoned as a pair of friends. Tiberius, in a letter to him saith, *Haec pro amicitia nostra non occultavi*;[2] and the whole senate dedicated an altar to Friendship, as to a goddess, in respect of the

---

[1] Partakers of cares.

[2] 'These things, by reason of our friendship, I have not concealed from you.'

great dearness of friendship between them two. The like, or more, was between Septimius Severus and Plautianus; for he forced his eldest son to marry the daughter of Plautianus, and would often maintain Plautianus in doing affronts to his son; and did write also, in a letter to the senate, by these words: *I love the man so well, as I wish he may over-live me.* Now, if these princes had been as a Trajan, or a Marcus Aurelius, a man might have thought that this had proceeded of an abundant goodness of nature; but being men so wise, of such strength and severity of mind, and so extreme lovers of themselves, as all these were, it proveth most plainly that they found their own felicity (though as great as ever happened to mortal men) but as an half-piece, except they might have a friend to make it entire; and yet, which is more, they were princes that had wives, sons, nephews; and yet all these could not supply the comfort of friendship.

It is not to be forgotten, what Comineus observeth of his first master, Duke Charles the Hardy, namely, that he would communicate his secrets with none; and least of all, those secrets which troubled him most. Whereupon he goeth on, and saith, that towards his latter time *that closeness did impair and a little perish his understanding.* Surely Comineus might have made the same judgement also, if it had pleased him, of his second master, Louis the Eleventh, whose closeness was indeed his tormentor. The parable of Pythagoras is dark, but true: *Cor ne edito, – eat not the heart.* Certainly if a man would give it a hard phrase, those that want friends to open themselves unto are cannibals of their own hearts: but one thing is most admirable (wherewith I will conclude this first fruit of friendship), which is, that this communicating of a man's self to his friend works two contrary effects; for it redoubleth joys, and cutteth griefs in half: for there is no man that imparteth his joys to his friend, but he joyeth the more; and no man that imparteth his griefs to his friend, but he grieveth the less . . .

The second fruit of friendship is healthful and sovereign for the understanding, as the first is for the affections; for friendship maketh indeed a fair day in the affections, from storm and tempests, but it maketh daylight in the understanding, out of darkness and confusion of thoughts. Neither is this to be understood only of faithful counsel, which a man receiveth from his friend; but before you come to that, certain it is that whosoever hath his mind fraught with many thoughts, his wits and understanding do clarify and break up in the communicating and discoursing with another: he tosseth his thoughts more easily;

he marshelleth them more orderly; he seeth how they look when they are turned into words; finally, he waxeth wiser than himself; and that more by an hour's discourse than by a day's meditation. It was well said by Themistocles to the king of Persia, *That speech was like cloth of Arras, opened and put abroad; whereby the imagery doth appear in figure; whereas in thoughts they lie but as in packs* . . .

Add now, to make this second fruit of friendship complete, that other point, which lieth more open and falleth within vulgar observation: which is faithful counsel from a friend. Heraclitus saith well in one of his enigmas, *Dry light is ever the best:* and certain it is that the light that a man receiveth by counsel from another is drier and purer than that which cometh from his own understanding and judgement; which is ever infused and drenched in his affections and customs. So as there is as much difference between the counsel that a friend giveth, and that a man giveth himself, as there is between the counsel of a friend and of a flatterer; for there is no such flatterer as is a man's self, and there is no such remedy against flattery of a man's self as the liberty of a friend. Counsel is of two sorts; the one concerning manners, the other concerning business: for the first, the best preservative to keep the mind in health is the faithful admonition of a friend . . . It is a strange thing to behold what gross errors and extreme absurdities many (especially of the greater sort) do commit for want of a friend to tell them of them, to the great damage both of their fame and fortune: for, as St. James saith, they are as men *that look sometimes into a glass, and presently forget their own shape and favour.* As for business . . . it is a rare thing, except it be from a perfect and entire friend, to have counsel given, but such as shall be bowed and crooked to some ends which he hath that giveth it . . . A friend, that is wholly acquainted with a man's estate, will beware, by furthering any present business, how he dasheth upon other inconvenience; and therefore, rest not upon scattered counsels; they will rather distract and mislead than settle and direct.

After these two noble fruits of friendship (peace in the affections, and support of the judgement), followeth the last fruit, which is like the pomegranate, full of many kernels; I mean aid, and bearing a part in all actions and occasions. Here the best way to represent to life the manifold use of friendship is to cast and see how many things there are which a man cannot do himself; and then it will appear that it was a sparing speech of the ancients to say, *that a friend is another himself*: for that a friend is far more than himself. Men have their time, and die many times in desire of some things which they principally take to heart; the bestowing of a child, the finishing of a work, or the like. If a man have a true friend, he may rest almost secure that the care of those things will continue after him ... A man hath a body, and that body is confined to a place: but where friendship is, all offices of life are. How many things are there, which a man cannot, with any face or comeliness, say or do himself! A man can scarce allege his own merits with modesty, much less extol them: a man cannot sometimes brook to supplicate or beg, and a number of the like: but all these things are graceful in a friend's mouth, which are blushing in a man's own. So again, a man's person hath many proper relations which he cannot put off. A man cannot speak to his son but as a father; to his wife but as a husband; to his enemy but upon terms: whereas a friend may speak as the case requires, and not as it sorteth with the person. But to enumerate these things were endless: I have given the rule, where a man cannot fitly play his own part: if he have not a friend, he may quit the stage.

(Essays or Counsels, Civil and Moral, 1625)

SIR THOMAS BROWNE (1605–82)

Of Sympathy and the Mystery of True Affections

There is, I think, no man that apprehends his own miseries less than my self, and no man that so neerly apprehends anothers. I could lose an arm without a tear, and with few groans, methinks, be quartered into pieces; yet can I weep most seriously at a Play, and receive with true passion the counterfeit griefs of those known and professed Impostures. It is a barbarous part of inhumanity to add unto any afflicted parties misery, or indeavour to multiply in any man a passion whose single nature is already above his patience. This was the greatest affliction of Job (Job xix), and those oblique expostulations of his Friends a deeper injury than the down-right blows of the Devil. It is not the tears of our own eyes only, but of our friends also, that do exhaust the current of our sorrows; which, falling into many streams, runs more peaceably, and is contented with a narrower channel. It is an act within the power of charity, to translate a passion out of one breast into another, and to divide a sorrow almost out of itself; for an affliction, like a dimension, may be so divided, as, if not indivisible, at least to become insensible. Now with my friend I desire not to share or participate, but to engross, his sorrows; that, by making them mine own, I may more easily discuss them; for in mine own reason, and within my self, I can command that which I cannot intreat without my self, and within the circle of another. I have often thought those noble pairs and examples of friendship not so truly Histories of what had been, as fictions of what should be; but I now perceive nothing in them but possibilities, nor any thing in the Heroick examples of Damon and Pythias, Achilles and Patroclus, which methinks upon some grounds I could not perform within the narrow compass of my self. That a man should lay down his life for his Friend, seems strange to vulgar affections, and such as confine themselves within that worldly principle, *Charity begins at home.* For mine own part I could never remember the relations that I held unto my self, nor the respect that I owe unto my own nature, in the cause of GOD, my Country, and my Friends. Next to these three, I do embrace my self. I confess I do not observe that order that the schools ordain our affections, to love our Parents, Wives, Children, and then our Friends; for, excepting the injunctions of Religion, I do not find in my self such a necessary and indissoluble Sympathy to all those of my blood. I hope I do not break the fifth Commandment, if I conceive I may love my friend before the nearest of my blood, even those to whom I owe the principles of life. I never yet cast a true affection on a woman; but I have loved my friend as I do virtue, my soul, my GOD. From hence me thinks I do conceive how GOD loves man, what happiness there is in the love of GOD. Omitting all other, there are three most mystical unions: 1. two natures in one person; 2. three persons in one nature; 3. one soul in two bodies; for though indeed they be really divided, yet are they so united, as they seem but one, and make rather a duality than two distinct souls.

There are wonders in true affection: it is a body of *Enigma's,* mysteries, and riddles; wherein two so become one, as they both become two. I love my friend before myself, and yet methinks I do not love him enough: some few months hence my multiplied affection will make me believe I have not loved him at all. When I am from him, I am dead till I be with him; when I am with him, I am not satisfied, but would still be nearer him. United souls are not satisfied with imbraces, but desire to be truly each other; which being impossible, their desires are infinite, and must proceed without a possibility of satisfaction.[1]

[1] cf. Marvell: As lines, so loves oblique may well
        Themselves in every angle greet:
    But ours, so truly parallel,
      Though infinite can never meet.

Another misery there is in affection, that whom we truly love like our own selves, we forget their looks, nor can our memory retain the Idea of their faces; and it is no wonder, for they are our selves, and our affection makes their looks our own. This noble affection falls not on vulgar and common constitutions, but on such as are mark'd for virtue: he that can love his friend with this noble ardour, will in a competent degree affect all. Now, if we can bring our affections to look beyond the body, and cast an eye upon the soul, we have found out the true object, not only of friendship, but Charity; and the greatest happiness that we can bequeath the soul, is that wherein we all do place our last felicity, Salvation; which though it be not in our power to bestow, it is in our charity and pious invocations to desire, if not procure and further. I cannot contently frame a prayer for my self in particular, without a catalogue for my friends; nor request a happiness, wherein my sociable disposition does not desire the fellowship of my neighbour . . .

(Religio Medici, Pt. 2, Sect. 5 and 6)

★　　★　　★

THE RETREAT

Happy those early days, when I
Shin'd in my Angel-infancy!
Before I understood this place
Appointed for my second race,
Or taught my soul to fancy aught
But a white celestial thought:
When yet I had not walk'd above
A mile or two from my first Love,
And looking back – at that short space –
Could see a glimpse of His bright face:
When on some gilded cloud, or flow'r,
My gazing soul would dwell an hour,
And in those weaker glories spy
Some shadows of eternity:
Before I taught my tongue to wound
My Conscience with a sinful sound,
Or had the black art to dispense
A several sin to ev'ry sense,

But felt through all this fleshly dress
Bright shoots of everlastingness.

O how I long to travel back,
And tread again that ancient track!
That I might once more reach that plain
Where first I left my glorious train;
From whence th' enlightned spirit sees
That shady City of Palm-trees.
But ah! my soul with too much stay
Is drunk, and staggers in the way!
Some men a forward motion love,
But I by backward steps would move;
And when this dust falls to the urn,
In that state I came, return.

(Henry Vaughan, 1621–95)

★　★　★

LOVE

Love bade me welcome; yet my soul drew back
    Guilty of dust and sin.
But quick-eyed Love, observing me grow slack
    From my first entrance in,
Drew nearer to me, sweetly questioning
    If I lack'd anything.

'A guest,' I answer'd, 'worthy to be here:'
    Love said, 'You shall be he.'
'I, the unkind, ungrateful? Ah, my dear
    I cannot look on thee.'
Love took my hand and smiling did reply,
    'Who made the eyes but I?'

'Truth, Lord; but I have marr'd them: let my shame
    Go where it doth deserve.'
'And know you not,' says Love, 'Who bore the blame?'
    'My dear, then I will serve.'

'You must sit down,' says Love, 'and taste my meat.'
So I did sit and eat.

(George Herbert, 1593–1632)

★　　★　　★

LYCIAS

'Tis a soft Rogue, this Lycias
And rightly understood,
He's worth a thousand Women's Nicenesses!
The Love of Women moves even with their Lust,
Who therefore still are fond, but seldom just;
Their Love is Usury, while they pretend,
To gain the Pleasure double which they lend.
But a dear Boy's disinterested Flame
Gives Pleasure, and for meer Love gathers Pain;
In him alone Fondness sincere does prove,
And the kind tender Naked Boy is Love.

(Rochester 1648–80, *Valentinian*, Act II, Sc. i)

6

Eighteenth Century and Romantics

THOMAS GRAY (1716–71) In the year 1742, after his return from Italy, and particularly in the late summer, Gray experienced a surge of creative activity he was never to know so fully again. Yet there were notes of profound melancholy even before he learned of the death of his beloved school-fellow, Benjamin West.

SONNET TO WEST

In vain to me the smiling mornings shine,
And redd'ning Phoebus lifts his golden fire:
The birds in vain their amorous descant join;
Or chearful fields resume their green attire:
These ears, alas! for other notes repine,
A different object do these eyes require.
My lonely anguish melts no heart but mine;
And in my breast the imperfect joys expire.
Yet Morning smiles the busy race to chear,
And new-born pleasure brings to happier men:
The fields to all their wonted tribute bear:

> To warm their little loves the birds complain:
> I fruitless mourn to him, that cannot hear,
> And weep the more, because I weep in vain.

★   ★   ★

'I never saw such a boy; our breed is not made on this model.'
Thus wrote Gray of Charles-Victor de Bonstetten, the gay young
Swiss to whom his friend Nicholls introduced him in December,
1769, and whom he persuaded to spend some weeks in Cambridge.
The timid don of fifty-three was enchanted, and then infatuated.
As his biographer, R. W. Ketton-Cremer, remarks: 'All his
defences were swept away – the life so carefully organised, the
formal and deliberate manner, the refuge which he had sought in
books and antiquities and the interleaved Linnaeus. He was
filled with disquiet, for he understood the secrets of his own
nature . . .' (*Life of Gray*, Cambridge University Press).

A comment to his friend, Norton Nicholls: ,

20 March, 1770

He gives me too much pleasure, and at least *an equal share* of
inquietude. You do not understand him so well as I do, but I leave my
meaning imperfect, till we meet. I have never met with so extraordinary a Person. God bless him! I am unable to talk to you about
anything else, I think.

And another:

4 April, 1770

Here I am again to pass my solitary evenings, which hung much
lighter on my hands, before I knew him. This is your fault! Pray let
the next you send me, be halt and blind, dull, unapprehensive and
wrong-headed. For this (as Lady Constance says) *Was never such a
gracious Creature born!* And yet – but no matter! burn my letter that I
wrote you, for I am very much out of humour with myself and will not
believe a word of it. You will think, I have caught madness from him
(for he is certainly mad) and perhaps you will be right. Oh! what
things are Fathers and Mothers! I thought they were to be found only
in England, but you see . . . This place never appear'd so horrible to

me, as it does now. Could not you come for a week or fortnight? It would be sunshine to me in a dark night!

Bonstetten had to leave Cambridge for the temptations of Paris, a fact which caused Gray anguish and disquietude.

TO BONSTETTEN:

12 April, 1770

Never did I feel my dear Bonstetten to what a tedious length the few short moments of our life may be extended by impatience and expectation, till you had left me: nor ever knew before with so strong a conviction how much this frail body sympathizes with the inquietude of the mind. I am grown old in the compass of less than three weeks, like the Sultan in the Turkish Tales, that did but plunge his head into a vessel of water and take it out again (as the standers-by affirm'd) at the command of a Dervish, and found he had pass'd many years in captivity and begot a large family of children. The strength and spirits that now enable me to write to you, are only owing to your last letter, a temporary gleam of sunshine. Heaven knows, when it may shine again! I did not conceive till now (I own) what it was to lose you, nor felt the solitude and insipidity of my own condition, before I possess'd the happiness of your friendship.

TO BONSTETTEN:

19 April, 1770

Alas! how do I every moment feel the truth of what I have somewhere read: *Ce n'est pas le voir que s'en souvenir*, and yet that remember- ance is the only satisfaction I have left. My life now is but a perpetual conversation with your shadow – The known sound of your voice still rings in my ears. – There, on the corner of the fender you are standing, or tinkling on the pianoforte, or stretch'd at length on the sofa. – Do you reflect, my dearest Friend, that it is a week or eight days, before I can receive a letter from you, and as much more before you can have my answer, that all that time (with more than Herculean toil) I am employ'd in pushing the tedious hours along, and wishing to annihilate them; the more I strive, the heavier they move and the longer they grow. I can not bear this place, where I have spent many tedious years within less than a month, since you left me.

This letter soon turned to anxious advice:

You do me the credit (and false or true, it goes to my heart) of ascribing to me your love for many virtues of the highest rank. Would to heaven it were so; but they are indeed the fruits of your own noble and generous understanding, that has hitherto struggled against the stream of custom, passion, and ill company, even when you were but a Child, and will you now give way to that stream, when your strength is increased? Shall the Jargon of French Sophists, the allurements of painted women *comme il faut,* or the vulgar caresses of prostitute beauty, the property of all, that can afford to purchase it, induce you to give up a mind and body by Nature distinguish'd from all others to folly, idleness, disease, and vain remorse? Have a care, my ever-amiable Friend, *of loving, what you do not approve*, and know me for your most faithful and most humble Despote.

The last of the three surviving letters was full of regret that the young man had had to go abroad:

TO BONSTETTEN:

9 May, 1770

I am return'd, my dear Bonstetten, from the little journey made into Suffolk without answering the end proposed. The thought, that you might have been with me there, has embitter'd all my hours. Your letter has made me happy; as happy as so gloomy, so solitary a Being as I am is capable of being. I know and have too often felt the disadvantages I lay myself under, how much I hurt the little interest I have in you, by this air of sadness so contrary to your nature and present enjoyments; but sure you will forgive, tho' you can not sympathize with me. It is impossible for me to dissemble with you. Such as I am, I expose my heart to your view, nor wish to conceal a single thought from your penetrating eyes. – All that you say to me, especially on the subject of Switzerland, is infinitely acceptable. It feels too pleasing ever to be fulfill'd, and as often as I read over your truly kind letter, written long since from London, I stop at these words: *La mort qui peut glacer nos bras avant qu'ils soient entrelacés.*

'Such intensity of emotion could not last for very long ... He saw the absurdity of his relationship with Bonstetten as well as its sadness; and indeed the absurdity, for all his over-mastering charm, of Bonstetten himself' (R. W. Ketton-Cremer). The letters from Paris were full of affectations and exhibitionism. Hence this comment to Nicholls:

May, 1771

I hardly know how to give you any account of it and desire you would not speak of it to any body. That he has been *le plus malheureux des hommes*, that he is *decidé à quitter son pays*, that is, to pass the next winter in England: that he cannot bear *la morgue de l'aristocratie, et l'orgueil armé des loix*, in short, strong expressions of uneasiness and confusion of mind, so much as to talk of *un pistolet et du courage*, all without the shadow of a reason assign'd, and so he leaves me. He is either disorder'd in his intellect (which is too possible) or has done some strange thing, that has exasperated his whole family and friends at home, which (I'm afraid) is at least equally possible. I am quite at a loss about it. You will see and know more: but by all means curb these vagaries and wandering imaginations, if there be any room for counsels.

The trip that Nicholls and Gray had planned to take to Switzerland (and Bonstetten) never occurred. Nicholls went alone. And in July Gray died.

★ ★ ★

WILLIAM BECKFORD (1760–1844) 'His singing, playing and mimicry, as well as his wealth, intelligence and charm, made him welcome nearly everywhere; he moved in the highest society in London and Paris, playing the fool wherever he went and inclining towards rather fast women a good deal older than himself. His censorious family became worried about him, and with good cause. He was heavily entangled with his first cousin's wife, Louisa Beckford, who was six years his senior. Worse still, in 1779 he had met at Powderham Castle the son of the house, William Courtenay, an effeminate child of ten, the spoiled darling of his parents and thirteen sisters. This became the dominating and consuming attachment of his life until it ended in his irretrievable ruin.' (Boyd Alexander, *Life at Fonthill*, Hart-Davis.)

Beckford, whose early life was much gayer than the long years of travel and semi-retirement, introduces two new notes to this collection: he was an incorrigible romantic, and the gossiping nicknaming bibelot-fondling and acridly complaining style of his letters suggests the type of witty and aesthetically minded invert with whom we are all familiar today. He was as much a martyr as Wilde, and almost certainly a more interesting and civilized man. Nobody quite knows why, after his marriage to a girl he seems to have been genuinely fond of, he should have been overwhelmed by the rumours rising from another visit to Powderham and the sixteen-year-old 'Kitty' Courtenay in 1784 except that he had enemies then staying at the Castle. The *Morning Herald* was typically ferocious: 'The rumour concerning a *Grammatical mistake of* Mr. B – and the *Hon. Mr. C –* , in regard to the genders, we hope for the honour of Nature originates in *Calumny*!' Such an attitude in the Press immediately puts one in mind of the treatment of Paul Verlaine and Arthur Rimbaud in a Paris newspaper: 'Amongst the men of letters to be seen at Coppée's first night was the poet Paul Verlaine giving his arm to a charming young person, Mademoiselle Rimbaud.' At least Beckford did not, like so many of his contemporaries in society, at once seek refuge abroad. He braved the matter out and the charges were not pressed to the point of prosecution. And later he shielded himself behind the twelve-foot wall and within the Gothic fantasies of the abbey he got Wyatt to build for him beside the family mansion at Fonthill.

Mr. Boyd Alexander points out that the average squire did not live in seclusion with a staff bearing the ambiguous nicknames of Doll, Bijou, the Monkey, Mme Bion, the Calf and the Turk – nor, in reference to a valet called Richardson (as Mme Bion was), write in a letter: 'I would not fly from a nice York patapouf if Providence sent him to me . . . What most confounds and disgusts me is a certain kind of frigidity and insipidity like Mme Bion's (the devil take you, you blonde beast).' Nor, when he delighted in a brief spell of fine weather in the climate of the 'rosbifish island' with its normally 'medicine-coloured sky', would a squire admit: 'Everything here is lovely and green; but it is not for mountains and valleys, however green and lovely, that I am looking. It is other objects, objects which I certainly do not find here and which I want to find more than ever, that are interesting and dear to me. What are forests without fauns, and thickets from which there does not emerge some gay frolicsome clown of a satyr, making his sport . . . ?'

In his vivacious letters there are references to 'purse trouble and the trouble which is a hundred times worse than all others – boy trouble', to an infatuation with a boy acrobat, 'Master Saunders, the celebrated Equestrian Infant-phenomenon', and to the savage scandals of the day, about which there is so little material extant: the raid on the White Swan in Vere Street in 1810, the execution of Eglerton for sodomy in 1816, the flight of the Marquess Townshend and of the Bishop of Clogher, caught with a private of the Foot Guard in a back room of the White Lion, St. James's. Of the Vere Street affair, where many a 'Miss Butterfly' was manhandled by the mob on leaving the police court, Beckford wrote: 'Poor sods – what a fine ordeal, what a procession, what a pilgrimage, what a song and dance, what a rosary! What a pity not to have a balcony in Bow Street to see them pass, and worse still triumph in the sorry sequence of events.' (Once again we are reminded of a literary echo: A. E. Housman's poem to the 'young sinner' – *They are taking him to prison for the colour of his hair.*) The verdict against Eglerton, reached by the jury in ten minutes, called forth the following: 'Tomorrow they are going to hang a poor honest sodomite. I should like to know what kind of deity they fancy they are placating with these shocking human sacrifices. In a numerous list of thieves, assassins, house-breakers, violators . . . he was the only one to be sent to the gallows; all the others were "respited during pleasure".'

The following extracts are from the very early Oriental romance of *Vathek*, which is certainly as decadent as *A Rebours* or Firbank, with a dappling of beauty, luxury and cruelty – but it turns out that the boys, and especially the little Kitty Courtenay of a Gulchenrouz, are rescued in the end and enjoy an existence less hypocritical and sentimental than Peter Pan's.

THE SACRIFICE OF THE BOYS

[This strategy is performed in order that Vathek may gain the favour, and secrets, of a formidable Indian Giaour]

The prevalence of this gay humour was not a little grateful to Vathek, who perceived how much it conduced to his project. He put on the appearance of affability to every one; but especially to his viziers and the grandees of his court, whom he failed not to regale with a sumptuous banquet; during which he insensibly directed the conversation to the children of his guests. Having asked, with a good-natured air, which of them were blessed with the handsomest boys, every father at once asserted the pretensions of his own; and the contest imperceptibly grew so warm, that nothing could have witholden them from coming to blows but their profound reverence for the person of the caliph. Under the pretence, therefore, of reconciling the disputants, Vathek took upon him to decide; and, with this view, commanded the boys to be brought.

It was not long before a troop of these poor children made their appearance, all equipped by their fond mothers with such ornaments as might give the greatest relief to their beauty, or most advantageously display the graces of their age. But, whilst this brilliant assemblage attracted the eyes and hearts of every one besides, the caliph scrutinized each, in his turn, with a malignant avidity that passed for attention, and selected from their number the fifty whom he judged the Giaour would prefer.

With an equal show of kindness as before, he proposed to celebrate a festival on the plain, for the entertainment of his young favourites, who, he said, ought to rejoice still more than all at the restoration of his health, on account of the favours he intended for them.

The caliph's proposal was received with the greatest delight, and soon published through Samarah. Litters, camels, and horses were prepared. Women and children, old men and young, every one placed himself as he chose. The cavalcade set forward, attended by all the confectioners in the city and its precincts; the populace, following on foot, composed an amazing crowd, and occasioned no little noise. All was joy; nor did any one call to mind what most of them had suffered when they lately travelled the road they were now passing so gaily.

The evening was serene, the air refreshing, the sky clear, and the flowers exhaled their fragrance. The beams of the declining sun, whose mild splendour reposed on the summit of the mountain, shed a glow of ruddy light over its green declivity, and the white flocks sporting upon it. No sounds were heard, save the murmurs of the four fountains, and the reeds and voices of shepherds, calling to each other from different eminences.

The lovely innocents, destined for the sacrifice, added not a little to the hilarity of the scene. They approached the plain full of sportiveness, some coursing butterflies, others culling flowers, or picking up the shining little pebbles that attracted their notice. At intervals they nimbly started from each other for the sake of being caught again and mutually imparting a thousand caresses.

The dreadful chasm, at whose bottom the portal of ebony was placed, began to appear at a distance. It looked like a black streak that divided the plain. Morakanabad and his companions took it for some work which the caliph had ordered. Unhappy men! little did they surmise for what it was destined. Vathek, unwilling that they should examine it too nearly, stopped the procession, and ordered a spacious circle to be formed on this side, at some distance from the accursed chasm. The body-guard of eunuchs was detached, to measure out the lists intended for the games, and prepare the rings for the arrows of the young archers. The fifty competitors were soon stripped, and presented to the admiration of the spectators the suppleness and grace of their delicate limbs. Their eyes sparkled with a joy, which those of their fond parents reflected. Every one offered wishes for the little candidate nearest his heart, and doubted not of his being victorious. A breathless suspense awaited the contests of these amiable and innocent victims.

The caliph, availing himself of the first moment to retire from the crowd, advanced towards the chasm; and there heard, yet not without shuddering, the voice of the Indian, who, gnashing his teeth, eagerly demanded, 'Where are they? – where are they? – perceivest thou not how my mouth waters?' – 'Relentless Giaour!' answered Vathek, with emotion; 'can nothing content thee but the massacre of these lovely victims? Ah! wert thou to behold their beauty, it must certainly move thy compassion.' – 'Perdition on thy compassion, babbler!' cried the Indian: 'give them me; instantly give them, or my portal shall be closed against thee for ever!' – 'Not so loudly,' replied the caliph, blushing. – 'I understand thee,' returned the Giaour with the grin of an ogre; 'thou wantest no presence of mind: I will for a moment forbear.'

During this exquisite dialogue, the games went forward with all alacrity, and at length concluded, just as the twilight began to overcast the mountains. Vathek, who was still standing on the edge of the chasm, called out, with all his might, 'Let my fifty little favourites approach me, separately; and let them come in the order of their success. To the first, I will give my diamond bracelet; to the second, my collar of emeralds; to the third, my aigret of rubies; to the fourth, my girdle of topazes; and to the rest, each a part of my dress, even down to my slippers.'

This declaration was received with reiterated acclamations; and all extolled the liberality of a prince who would thus strip himself for the amusement of his subjects and the encouragement of the rising genera-tion. The caliph in the meanwhile, undressed himself by degrees, and, raising his arm as high as he was able, made each of the prizes glitter in the air; but whilst he delivered it with one hand to the child who sprung forward to receive it, he with the other pushed the poor innocent into the gulf, where the Giaour, with a sullen muttering, incessantly repeated, 'More! more!'

This dreadful device was executed with so much dexterity, that the boy who was approaching him remained unconscious of the fate of his forerunner; and, as to the spectators, the shades of the evening, together with their distance, precluded them from perceiving any object distinctly. Vathek, having in this manner thrown in the last of the fifty, and, expecting that the Giaour, on receiving him, would have presented the key, already fancied himself as great as Soliman, and consequently above being amenable for what he had done; when, to his utter amazement, the chasm closed, and the ground became as entire as the rest of the plain.

★   ★   ★

THE CHARMING GULCHENROUZ

But let us leave the caliph immersed in his new passion, and attend Nouronihar beyond the rocks, where she had again joined her beloved Gulchenrouz.

This Gulchenrouz was the son of Ali Hassan, brother to the emir; and the most delicate and lovely creature in the world. Ali Hassan, who had been absent ten years on a voyage to the unknown seas, committed, at his departure, this child, the only survivor of many, to the care and protection of his brother. Gulchenrouz could write in various characters with precision, and paint upon vellum the most elegant arabesques that fancy could devise. His sweet voice accompanied the lute in the most enchanting manner; and when he sang the loves of Megnoun and Leilah, or some unfortunate lovers of ancient days, tears insensibly overflowed the cheeks of his auditors. The verses he composed (for, like Megnoun, he, too, was a poet) inspired that unresisting languor, so frequently fatal to the female heart. The women all doted upon him; and, though he had passed his thirteenth year, they still detained him in the harem. His dancing was light as the gossamer waved by the zephyrs of spring; but his arms, which twined so gracefully with those of the young girls in the dance, could neither dart the lance in the chase, nor curb the steeds that pastured in his uncle's domains. The bow, however, he drew with a certain aim, and would have excelled his competitors in the race, could he have broken the ties that bound him to Nouronihar.

The two brothers had mutually engaged their children to each other; and Nouronihar loved her cousin more than her own beautiful eyes. Both had the same tastes and amusements; the same long, languishing looks; the same tresses; the same fair complexions; and, when Gulchenrouz appeared in the dress of his cousin, he seemed to be more feminine than even herself. If, at any time, he left the harem to visit Fakreddin, it was with all the bashfulness of a fawn, that consciously ventures from the lair of its dam: he was, however, wanton enough to mock the solemn old grey-beards, though sure to be rated without mercy in return. Whenever this happened, he would hastily plunge into the recesses of the harem; and, sobbing, take refuge in the fond arms of Nouronihar, who loved even his faults beyond the virtues of others.

It fell out this evening, that, after leaving the caliph in the meadow, she ran with Gulchenrouz over the green sward of the mountain, that sheltered the vale where Fakreddin had chosen to reside. The sun was dilated on the edge of the horizon; and the young people, whose fancies were lively and inventive, imagined they beheld, in the gorgeous clouds of the west, the domes of Shaddukian and Ambreabad, where the Peries have fixed their abode. Nouronihar, sitting on the slope of the hill, supported on her knees the perfumed head of Gulchenrouz. The unexpected arrival of the caliph, and the splendour that marked his appearance, had already filled with emotion the ardent soul of Nouronihar. Her vanity irresistibly prompted her to pique the prince's attention;

and this she before took good care to effect, whilst he picked up the jasmine she had thrown upon him. But when Gulchenrouz asked after the flowers he had culled for her bosom, Nouronihar was all in confusion. She hastily kissed his forehead, arose in a flutter, and walked with unequal steps on the border of the precipice. Night advanced, and the pure gold of the setting sun had yielded to a sanguine red, the glow of which, like the reflection of a burning furnace, flushed Nouronihar's animated countenance. Gulchenrouz, alarmed at the agitation of his cousin, said to her, with a supplicating accent, 'Let us be gone; the sky looks portentous, the tamarisks tremble more than common, and the raw wind chills my very heart. Come! let us be gone; 'tis a melancholy night!' Then taking hold of her hand, he drew it towards the path he besought her to go. Nouronihar unconsciously followed the attraction; for a thousand strange imaginations occupied her spirits. She passed the large round of honeysuckles, her favourite resort, without ever vouchsafing it a glance; yet Gulchenrouz could not help snatching off a few shoots in his way, though he ran as if a wild beast were behind.

The young females seeing them approach in such haste, and, according to custom, expecting a dance, instantly assembled in a circle and took each other by the hand; but Gulchenrouz, coming up out of breath, fell down at once on the grass. This accident struck with consternation the whole of this frolicsome party; whilst Nouronihar, half distracted and overcome, both by the violence of her exercise and the tumult of her thoughts, sunk feebly down at his side, cherished his cold hands in her bosom, and chafed his temples with a fragrant perfume. At length he came to himself, and wrapping up his head in the robe of his cousin, entreated that she would not return to the harem. He was afraid of being snapped at by Shaban his tutor, a wrinkled old eunuch of a surly disposition; for, having interrupted the wonted walk of Nouronihar, he dreaded lest the churl should take it amiss. The whole of this sprightly group, sitting round upon a mossy knoll, began to entertain themselves with various pastimes, whilst their superintendents, the eunuchs, were gravely conversing at a distance. The nurse of the emir's daughter, observing her pupil sit ruminating with her eyes on the ground, endeavoured to amuse her with diverting tales; to which Gulchenrouz, who had already forgotten his inquietudes, listened with a breathless attention. He laughed, he clapped his hands, and passed a hundred little tricks on the whole of the company, without omitting the eunuchs, whom he provoked to run after him, in spite of their age and decrepitude.

During these occurrences, the moon arose, the wind subsided, and the evening became so serene and inviting, that a resolution was taken to sup on the spot. One of the eunuchs ran to fetch melons, whilst others were employed in showering down almonds from the branches that overhung this amiable party. Sutlememe, who excelled in dressing a salad, having filled large bowls of porcelain with eggs of small birds, curds turned with citron juice, slices of cucumber, and the inmost leaves of delicate herbs, handed it round from one to another, and gave each their shares with a large spoon of cocknos. Gulchenrouz, nestling, as usual, in the bosom of Nouronihar, pouted out his vermilion little lips against the offer of Sutlememe; and would take it only from the hand of his cousin, on whose mouth he hung like a bee inebriated with the nectar of flowers.

★   ★   ★

A BLISS OF CHILDHOOD

Carathis, inflated with the venom of her projects, strode hastily over the rock, and found the amiable Gulchenrouz asleep in an arbour, whilst the two dwarfs were watching at his side, and ruminating their accustomed prayers. These diminutive personages possessed the gift of divining whenever an enemy to good Mussulmans approached; thus they anticipated the arrival of Carathis, who, stopping short, said to herself, 'How placidly doth he recline his lovely little head! how pale and languishing are his looks! it is just the very child of my wishes!' The dwarfs interrupted this delectable soliloquy by leaping instantly upon her, and scratching her face with their utmost zeal. But Nerkes and Cafour, betaking themselves to the succour of their mistress, pinched the dwarfs so severely in return, that they both gave up the ghost, imploring Mahomet to inflict his sorest vengeance upon this wicked woman and all her household.

At the noise which this strange conflict occasioned in the valley, Gulchenrouz awoke, and, bewildered with terror, sprung impetuously and climbed an old fig-tree that rose against the acclivity of the rocks; from thence he gained their summits, and ran for two hours without once looking back. At last, exhausted with fatigue, he fell senseless into the arms of a good old genius, whose fondness for the company of children had made it his sole occupation to protect them. Whilst performing his wonted rounds through the air, he had pounced on the cruel Giaour, at the instant of his growling in the horrible chasm, and had rescued the fifty little victims which the impiety of Vathek had devoted to his voracity. These the genius brought up in nests still higher than the clouds, and himself fixed his abode in a nest more capacious than the rest, from which he had expelled the rocs that had built it.

These inviolable asylums were defended against the dives and the afrits by waving streamers; on which were inscribed in characters of gold, that flashed like lightning, the names of Alla and the Prophet. It was there that Gulchenrouz, who as yet remained undeceived with respect to his pretended death, thought himself in the mansions of eternal peace. He admitted without fear the congratulations of his little friends, who were all assembled in the nest of the venerable genius, and vied with each other in kissing his serene forehead and beautiful eyelids. Remote from the inquietudes of the world, the impertinence of harems, the brutality of eunuchs, and the inconstancy of women, there he found a peace truly congenial to the delights of his soul. In this peaceable society his days, months and years glided on; nor was he less happy than the rest of his companions: for the genius, instead of burdening his pupils with perishable riches and vain sciences, conferred upon them the boon of perpetual childhood.

(Beckford, Vathek)

★   ★   ★

JOHANN WINCKELMANN (1717–68) Walter Pater's essay describes how this poor German scholar gradually made his way to Italy and a discovery of the art and culture of Ancient Greece. On his way back to Germany, where the youthful Goethe eagerly awaited him, he was murdered for the medals he had won. Many Teutons were to follow him, including in the first half of the Nineteenth Century Count Platen and his circle, all men whose tastes were 'Greek'.

. . . Enthusiasm, – that, in the broad Platonic sense of the *Phaedrus*, was the secret of his divinatory power over the Hellenic world. This enthusiasm, dependent as it is to a great degree on bodily temperament, has a power of re-inforcing the purer emotions of the intellect with an almost physical excitement. That his affinity with Hellenism was not merely intellectual, that the subtler threads of temperament were inwoven in it, is proved by romantic, fervent friendships with young men. He has known, he says, many young men more beautiful than Guido's arch-angel. These friendships, bringing him into contact with the pride of human form, and staining the thoughts with its bloom, perfected his reconcilation to the spirit of Greek sculpture. A letter on taste, addressed from Rome to a young nobleman, Freidrich von Berg, is the record of such a friendship.

'I shall excuse my duty,' he begins, 'in fulfilling my promise of an essay on the taste for beauty in works of art, in the words of Pindar. He says to Agesidamus, a youth of Locri – ἰδέᾳ τε καλὸν, ὥρᾳ τε κεκραμένον – whom he had kept waiting for an intended ode, that a debt paid with usury is the end of reproach. This may win your good-nature on behalf of my present essay, which has turned out far more detailed and circumstantial than I had at first intended.

'It is from yourself that the subject is taken. Our intercourse has been short, too short both for you and me; but the first time I saw you, the affinity of our spirits was revealed to me: your culture proved that my hope was not groundless; and I found in a beautiful body a soul created for nobleness, gifted with the sense of beauty. My parting from you was therefore one of the most painful of my life; and that this feeling continuous our common friend is witness, for your separation from me leaves me no hope of seeing you again. Let this essay be a memorial of our friendship, which, on my side, is free from every selfish motive, and ever remains subject and dedicate to yourself alone.'

The following passage is characteristic—

'As it is confessedly the beauty of man which is to be conceived under one general idea, so I have noticed that those who are observant of beauty only in women, and are moved little or not at all by the beauty of men, seldom have an impartial, vital, inborn instinct for beauty in art. To such persons the beauty of Greek art will ever seem wanting, because its supreme beauty is rather male than female. But the beauty of art demands a higher sensibility than the beauty of nature, because the beauty of art, like tears shed at a play, gives no pain, is without life, and must be awakened and repaired by culture. Now, as the spirit of culture is much more ardent in youth than in manhood, the instinct of which I am speaking must be exercised and directed to what is beautiful, before that age is reached, at which one would be afraid to confess that one had no taste for it.'

Certainly, of that beauty of living form which regulated Winckelmann's friendships, it could not be said that it gave no pain. One notable friendship, the fortune of which we may trace through his letters, begins with an antique, chivalrous letter in French, and ends noisily in a burst of angry fire. Far from reaching the quietism, the bland indifference of art, such attachments are nevertheless more susceptible than any others of equal strength of a purely intellectual culture. Of passion, of physical excitement, they contain only just so must as stimulates the eye to the finest delicacies of colour and form. These friendships, often the caprices of a moment, make Winckelmann's letters, with their troubled colouring, an instructive but bizarre addition to the *History Of Art*, that shrine of grave and mellow light around the mute Olympian family. The impression which Winckelmann's literary life conveyed to those about him was that of excitement, intuition, inspiration, rather than the contemplative evolution of general principles. The quick, susceptible enthusiast, betraying his temperament even in appearance, by his olive complexion, his deepseated, piercing eyes, his rapid movements, apprehended the subtlest principles of the Hellenic manner, not through the understanding, but by instinct or touch.

(Walter Pater, *The Renaissance*)

★ ★ ★

GEORGE GORDON, LORD BYRON (1788–1824) 'My school friendships were with me passions (for I was always violent),' Byron declared in his *Detached Thoughts* and it is now quite clear that this capacity for romantic friendship lasted throughout his life; the suppressed *Memoirs* might have been able to clear up many darker questions about this side of his nature and its relation to his disastrous marriage. (Mr. G. Wilson Knight discusses the matter exhaustively in his *Lord Byron's Marriage*, Routledge and Kegan Paul.) Certainly Byron liked women – he liked most people who were affectionate to him – but his very promiscuity may be indicative; in a little over a year at Venice, which he called the Sea-Sodom, he claimed to have enjoyed 'I think at least two hundred of one sort or another' despite the fact that it was 'a hot climate where they grow relaxed and doughy, and flumpity a short time after breeding'. It was in Venice that Shelley, who saw in him the 'spirit of an angel in the mortal paradise of a decaying body', wrote anxiously to Peacock that he cultivated people 'who do not scruple to avow practices which are not only not named, but I believe seldom even conceived in England'.

Byron had left Cambridge to plunge into 'an abyss of sensuality' where he suffered from 'literally too much love'; nevertheless he delighted to dress his mistress as a page. The obverse of his promiscuity was the desire for a deeper, and almost certainly a purer love; he looked back to the protective friendships he had formed at Harrow with younger boys like Dorset, Delawarr and Clare; of the latter he remarked that 'it began one of the earliest and lasted longest . . . I never hear the word Clare without a beating of the heart even *now*' and when, years afterwards, he encountered his old friend on a highroad in Italy, 'This meeting annihilated for a moment all the years between the present time and the days of Harrow. It was a new and inexplicable feeling, like a rising from the grave, to me. Clare, too, was much agitated – *more* in appearance than even myself, for I could feel his heart beat to his fingers' ends, unless, indeed, it was the pulse of my own which made me think so . . . We were but five minutes together, and in the public road; but I hardly recollect an hour of my existence which could be weighed against them.' (*Detached Thoughts.*) There is a poem to Lord Clare in the very early *Hours of Idleness.*

Several biographers have noted the protective quality in Byron's liking for boys like Clare, the Cambridge chorister John Edleston, Nicolo Giraud who was chief of the 'sylphs' during his wonderful first visit to Greece, and 'the boy from the Morea', Loukas, whom he had with him at Messalonghion; it contrasted with that passivity towards women so beautifully expressed in Haidee's ministrations to the half-drowned Don Juan.

It now seems certain that the Thyrza poems were inspired by

John Edleston – the 'violent, though *pure*, love and passion' of his Cambridge days – and that the last poems of his life owe much to an infatuation for Loukas. He thus becomes the Platonist of his period, although Shelley had his *Epipsychidion* phase with Emilia (and also left an account of a deep schoolboy friendship) and Wordworth's 'first affections' must have been deep and tender – but of Wordsworth Coleridge is reported to have made a remark not usually elicited by a man of artistic genius: '. . . every great man he ever knew had something of the woman in him, with one exception: and the exception was Wordsworth. Now, mind! The observation was intended as no reproach to great men generally, but praise – and the subject defined had no relation to *effeminacy* (strictly speaking) but to softness, tenderness!' (Elizabeth Barrett to Miss Mitford.)

John Edleston, who had given Byron a cornelian heart, died while his friend and protector was on his Greek tour.

THE CORNELIAN

No specious splendour of this stone
    Endears it to my memory ever;
With lustre only once it shone,
    And blushes modest as the giver.

Some, who can sneer at friendship's ties,
    Have, for my weakness, oft reproved me;
Yet still the simple gift I prize,
    For I am sure the giver loved me.

He offer'd it with downcast look,
    As fearful that I might refuse it;
I told him, when the gift I took,
    My only fear should be to lose it.

This pledge attentively I view'd,
    And sparkling as I held it near,
Methought one drop the stone bedew'd,
    And ever since I've loved a tear.

Still, to adorn his humble youth,
   Nor wealth nor birth their treasures yield;
But he who seeks the flowers of truth
   Must quit the garden for the field.

'Tis not the plant uprear'd in sloth,
   Which beauty shows, and sheds perfume;
The flowers which yield the most of both
   In Nature's wild luxuriance bloom.

Had Fortune aided Nature's care,
   For once forgetting to be blind,
His would have been an ample share,
   If well proportion'd to his mind.

But had the goodness clearly seen,
   His form had fix'd her fickle breast;
Her countless hoards would his have been,
   And none remain'd to give the rest.
                       (*Hours of Idleness*)

TO THYRZA

Without a stone to mark the spot,
   And say, what Truth might well have said,
By all, save one, perchance forgot,
   Ah! wherefore art thou lowly laid?

By many a shore and many a sea
   Divided, yet beloved in vain;
The past, the future fled to thee,
   To bid us meet – no – ne'er again!

Could this have been – a word, a look,
   That softly said, 'We part in peace',
Had taught my bosom how to brook,
   With fainter sighs, thy soul's release.

And didst thou not, since Death for thee
    Prepared a light and pangless dart,
Once long for him thou ne'er shalt see,
    Who held, and holds thee in his heart?

Oh! who like him had watch'd thee here?
    Or sadly mark'd thy glazing eye,
In that dread hour ere death appear,
    When silent sorrow fears to sigh,

Till all was past? But when no more
    'Twas thine to reck of human woe,
Affection's heart-drops, gushing o'er,
    Had flow'd as fast – as now they flow.

Shall they not flow, when many a day
    In these, to me, deserted towers,
Ere call'd but for a time away,
    Affection's mingling tears were ours?

Ours too the glance none saw beside;
    The smile none else might understand;
The whisper'd thought of hearts allied,
    The pressure of the thrilling hand;

The kiss, so guiltless and refined,
    That Love each warmer wish forbore;
Those eyes proclaim'd so pure a mind,
    Even passion blush'd to plead for more.

The tone, that taught me to rejoice,
    When prone, unlike thee, to repine;
The song, celestial from thy voice,
    But sweet to me from none but thine;

The pledge we wore – I wear it still,
    But where is thine? – Ah! where art thou?
Oft have I borne the weight of ill,
    But never bent beneath till now!

Well hast thou left in life's best bloom
  The cup of woe for me to drain.
If rest alone be in the tomb,
  I would not wish thee here again.

But if in worlds more blest than this
  Thy virtues seek a fitter sphere,
Impart some portion of thy bliss,
  To wean me from mine anguish here.

Teach me – too early taught by thee!
  To bear, forgiving and forgiven:
On earth thy love was such to me;
  It fain would form my hope in heaven!
                                    (*Occasional Pieces*)

AWAY, AWAY, YE NOTES OF WOE!

Away, away, ye notes of woe!
  Be silent, thou once soothing strain,
Or I must flee from hence – for, oh!
  I dare not trust those sounds again.
To me they speak of brighter days –
  But lull the chords, for now, alas!
I must not think, I may not gaze,
  On what I am – on what I was.

The voice that made those sounds more sweet
  Is hush'd, and all their charms are fled
And now their softest notes repeat
  A dirge, an anthem o'er the dead!
Yes, Thyrza! yes, they breathe of thee,
  Beloved dust! since dust thou art;
And all that once was harmony
  Is worse than discord to my heart!

'Tis silent all! – but on my ear
  The well remember'd echoes thrill;
I hear a voice I would not hear,
  A voice that now might well be still:

Yet oft my doubting soul 'twill shake;
　Even slumber owns its gentle tone,
Till consciousness will vainly wake
　To listen, though the dream be flown.

Sweet Thyrza! waking as in sleep,
　Thou art but now a lovely dream;
A star that trembled o'er the deep,
　Then turn'd from earth its tender beam.
But he who through life's dreary way
　Must pass, when heaven is veil'd in wrath,
Will long lament the vanish'd ray
　That scatter'd gladness o'er his path.

(Ibid.)

ONE STRUGGLE MORE, AND I AM FREE

One struggle more and I am free
　From pangs that rend my heart in twain;
One last long sigh to love and thee,
　Then back to busy life again.
It suits me well to mingle now
　With things that never pleased before!
Though every joy is fled below,
　What future grief can touch me more?

Then bring me wine, the banquet bring;
　Man was not form'd to live alone:
I'll be that light, unmeaning thing
　That smiles with all, and weeps with none.
It was not thus in days more dear,
　It never would have been, but thou
Hast fled, and left me lonely here;
　Thou'rt nothing – all are nothing now.

In vain my lyre would lightly breathe!
　The smile that sorrow fain would wear
But mocks the woe that lurks beneath,
　Like roses o'er a sepulchre.

Though gay companions o'er the bowl
   Dispel awhile the sense of ill:
Though pleasure fires the maddening soul,
   The heart, – the heart is lonely still!

On many a lone and lovely night
   It sooth'd to gaze upon the sky;
For then I deem'd the heavenly light
   Shone sweetly on thy pensive eye:
And oft I thought at Cynthia's noon,
   When sailing o'er the Aegean wave,
'Now Thyrza gazes on that moon' –
   Alas, it gleam'd upon her grave!

When stretch'd on fever's sleepless bed,
   And sickness shrunk my throbbing veins,
'Tis comfort still,' I faintly said,
   'That Thyrza cannot know my pains:'
Like freedom to the time-worn slave,
   A boon 'tis idle then to give,
Relenting Nature vainly gave
   My life, when Thyrza ceased to live!

My Thyrza's pledge in better days,
   When love and life alike were new!
How different now thou meet'st my gaze!
   How tinged by time with sorrow's hue!
The heart that gave itself with thee
   Is silent – ah, were mine as still!
Though cold as e'en the dead can be,
   It feels, it sickens with the chill.

Thou bitter pledge! thou mournful token!
   Though painful, welcome to my breast!
Still, still preserve that love unbroken,
   Or break the heart to which thou'rt press'd.
Time tempers love, but not removes,
   More hallow'd when its hope is fled:
Oh! what are thousand living loves
   To that which cannot quit the dead?   *(Ibid.)*

AND THOU ART DEAD, AS YOUNG AND FAIR

'Heu, quanto minus est cum reliquis versari quam tui meminisse!'

And thou art dead, as young and fair
    As ought of mortal birth:
And form so soft, and charms so rare,
    Too soon return'd to Earth!
Though Earth received them in her bed
And o'er the spot the crowd may tread
    In carelessness of mirth,
There is an eye which could not brook
A moment on that grave to look.

I will not ask where thou liest low,
    Nor gaze upon the spot;
There flowers or weeds at will may grow,
    So I behold them not:
It is enough for me to prove
That what I loved, and long must love,
    Like common earth can rot;
To me there needs no stone to tell,
'Tis nothing that I loved so well.

Yet did I love thee to the last
    As fervently as thou,
Who didst not change through all the past,
    And canst not alter now.
The love where Death has set his seal,
Nor age can chill, nor rival steal,
    Nor falsehood disavow:
And, what were worse, thou canst not see
Or wrong, or change, or fault in me.

The better days of life were ours;
    The worst can be but mine:
The sun that cheers, the storm that lowers,
    Shall never more be thine.
The silence of that dreamless sleep
I envy now too much to weep;

Nor need I to repine,
That all those charms have pass'd away;
I might have watch'd through long decay.

The flower in ripen'd bloom unmatch'd
   Must fall the earliest prey;
Though by no hand untimely snatch'd,
   The leaves must drop away:
And yet it were a greater grief
To watch it withering, leaf by leaf,
   Than see it pluck'd today;
Since earthly eye but ill can bear
To trace the change to foul from fair.

I know not if I could have borne
   To see thy beauties fade;
The night that follow'd such a morn
   Had worn a deeper shade:
Thy day without a cloud hath pass'd,
And thou wert lovely to the last;
   Extinguish'd not decay'd;
As stars that shoot along the sky
Shine brightest as they fall from high.

As once I wept, if I could weep,
   My tears might well be shed,
To think I was not near to keep
   One vigil o'er thy bed;
To gaze, how fondly! on thy face,
To fold thee in a faint embrace,
   Uphold thy drooping head;
And show that love, however vain,
Nor thou nor I can feel again.

Yet how much less it were to gain,
   Though thou hast left me free,
The loveliest things that still remain,
   Than thus remember thee!
The all of thine that cannot die

Through dark and dread Eternity
Returns again to me,
And more thy buried love endears
Than aught except its living years.

(*Ibid.*)

IF SOMETIMES IN THE HAUNTS OF MEN

If sometimes in the haunts of men
Thine image from my breast may fade,
The lonely hour presents again
The semblance of thy gentle shade:
And now that sad and silent hour
Thus much of thee can still restore,
And sorrow unobserved may pour
The plaint she dare not speak before.

Oh, pardon that in crowds awhile
I waste one thought I owe to thee,
And self-condemn'd, appear to smile,
Unfaithful to thy memory:
Nor deem that memory less dear,
That then I seem not to repine;
I would not fools should overhear
One sigh that should be wholly *thine*.

If not the goblet pass unquaff'd,
It is not drain'd to banish care;
The cup must hold a deadlier draught,
That brings a Lethe for despair.
And could Oblivion set my soul
From all her troubled visions free,
I'd dash to earth the sweetest bowl
That drown'd a single thought of thee.

For wert thou vanish'd from my mind,
Where could my vacant bosom turn?
And who could then remain behind
To honour thine abandon'd Urn?

No, no – it is my sorrow's pride
    That last dear duty to fulfil:
Though all the world forget beside,
    'Tis meet that I remember still.

For well I know, that such had been
    Thy gentle care for him, who now
Unmourn'd shall quit this mortal scene,
    Where none regarded him, but thou:
And, oh! I feel in *that* was given
    A blessing never meant for me;
Thou wert too like a dream of Heaven
    For earthly Love to merit thee.

(Ibid.)

ON A CORNELIAN HEART WHICH WAS BROKEN

Ill-fated Heart! and can it be,
    That thou should'st thus be rent in twain?
Have years of care for thine and thee
    Alike been all employ'd in vain?

Yet precious seems each shatter'd part,
    And every fragment dearer grown,
Since he who wears thee feels thou art
    A fitter emblem of *his own*.

(Ibid.)

★   ★   ★

Byron had rescued John Edleston from drowning: he protected
the fifteen-year-old Loukas Chalandritsanos during an attack from
a Turkish battleship on the way to Messalonghion – 'I would
sooner cut him in pieces, and myself too, than have him taken
out by those barbarians' – and he is also reputed to have saved
Loukas from threatened shipwreck by diving with the boy on his
back, but the relationship was clearly a tormented one.

ON THIS DAY I COMPLETE MY THIRTY-SIXTH YEAR

'Tis time this heart should be unmoved,
　　Since others it has ceased to move:
Yet, though I cannot be beloved,
　　Still let me love!

My days are in the yellow leaf;
　　The flowers and fruits of love are gone;
The worm, the canker, and the grief
　　Are mine alone!

The fire that on my bosom preys
　　Is lone as some volcanic isle;
No torch is kindled at its blaze –
　　A funeral pile.

The hope, the fear, the jealous care,
　　The exalted portion of the pain
And power of love, I cannot share,
　　But wear the chain.

But 'tis not *thus* – and 'tis not *here* –
　　Such thoughts should shake my soul, nor *now*,
Where glory decks the hero's bier,
　　Or binds his brow.

The sword, the banner, and the field,
　　Glory and Greece, around me see!
The Spartan, borne upon his shield,
　　Was not more free.

Awake! (not Greece – she *is* awake!)
　　Awake, my spirit! Think through *whom*
Thy life-blood tracks its parent lake,
　　And then strike home!

Tread those reviving passions down,
　　Unworthy manhood! – unto thee

Indifferent should the smile or frown
    Of beauty be.

If thou regrett'st thy youth, *why live?*
    The land of honourable death
Is here: – up to the field, and give
    Away thy breath!

Seek out – less often sought than found –
    A soldier's grave, for thee the best;
Then look around, and choose thy ground,
    And take thy rest.

(Ibid.)

LOVE AND DEATH

I watched thee when the foe was at our side,
    Ready to strike at him – or thee and me,
Were safety hopless – rather than divide
    Aught with one loved, save love and liberty.

I watched thee on the breakers, when the rock
    Received our prow, and all was storm and fear,
And bade thee cling to me through every shock;
    This arm would be thy bark, or breast thy bier.

I watched thee when the fever glazed thine eyes,
    Yielding my couch, and stretched me on the ground,
When overworn with watching, ne'er to rise
    From thence, if thou an early grave hadst found.

The earthquake came, and rocked the quivering wall,
    And men and nature reeled as if with wine.
Whom did I seek around the tottering hall?
    For thee. Whose safety first provide for? Thine.

And when convulsive throes denied my breath
    The faintest utterance to my fading thought,
To thee – to thee – e'en in the gasp of death
    My spirit turned, oh! oftener than it ought.

Thus much and more; and yet thou lov'st me not,
    And never wilt! Love dwells not in our will.
Nor can I blame thee, though it be my lot
    To strongly, wrongly, vainly love thee still.

                    (Quoted G. Wilson Knight *op. cit.*)[1]

LAST WORDS ON GREECE

What are to me those honours or renown
    Past or to come, a new-born people's cry?
Albeit for such I could despise a crown
    Of aught save laurel, or for such could die.
I am a fool of passion, and a frown
    Of thine to me is as an adder's eye
To the poor bird whose pinion fluttering down
    Wafts unto death the breast it bore so high;
Such is this maddening fascination grown,
    So strong thy magic or so weak am I.

                                            (*Ibid.*)

                    ★   ★   ★

JOHN KEATS (1795–1821) Can it be denied that, for all the
normality of Keats, the spirit of Eros pervades the following
scene?

After a thousand mazes overgone,
At last, with sudden step, he came upon
A chamber, myrtle wall'd, embower'd high,
Full of light, incense, tender minstrelsy,
And more of beautiful and strange beside:
For on a silken couch of rosy pride,
In midst of all, there lay a sleeping youth
Of fondest beauty; fonder, in fair sooth,
Than sighs could fathom, or contentment reach:
And coverlids gold-tinted like the peach,
Or ripe October's faded marigolds,
Fell sleek about him in a thousand folds –
Not hiding up an Apollonian curve

---

[1] Hartley Coleridge provided the title for this poem, about which Hobhouse
commented that it was 'The last he ever wrote'. It and its companion were
omitted from the early editions, first appearing in *Murray's Magazine*, February,
1887.

Of neck and shoulder, nor the tenting swerve
Of knee from knee, nor ankles pointing light;
But rather, giving them to the fill'd sight
Officiously. Sideway his face reposed
On one white arm, and tenderly unclosed,
By tenderest pressure, a faint damask mouth
To slumbery pout; just as the morning south
Disparts a dew-lipp'd rose. Above his head,
Four lily stalks did their white honours wed
To make a coronal; and round him grew
All tendrils green, of every bloom and hue,
Together intertwined and trammell'd fresh:
The vine of glossy sprout; the ivy mesh,
Shading its Ethiop berries; and woodbine,
Of velvet leaves and bugle-blooms divine;
Convolvulus in streaked vases flush;
The creeper, mellowing for an autumn blush;
And virgin's bower, trailing airily;
With others of the sisterhood. Hard by,
Stood serene Cupids watching silently.
One, kneeling to a lyre, touch'd the strings,
Muffling to death the pathos with his wings;
And, ever and anon, uprose to look
At the youth's slumber; while another took
A willow-bough, distilling odorous dew,
And shook it on his hair; another flew
In through the woven roof, and fluttering-wise
Rain'd violets upon his sleeping eyes.

(*Endymion*, Book II)

7

The Nineteenth Century

It is perhaps a perversity of editorship which depletes this chrono-logical section of some famous names and important works through the belief that they will figure more appropriately under the general heading of Moderns. Verlaine and Rimbaud are thus relegated; less excusably Melville and Whitman join the other Americans in a sub-section of their own. The result is that Tennyson occupies almost as solitary a position in his period as does Byron among the Romantics he was so powerfully to renounce.

★   ★   ★

ALFRED, LORD TENNYSON (1809–92)   During the seventeen years that elapsed between the death of Arthur Hallam at Vienna in 1833 and the publication of *In Memoriam* in 1850 Tennyson had been writing poems about his gifted and high-minded friend, the 'Apostle' of the Cambridge days about whom, when he was nineteen, a slightly older undergraduate had remarked: 'Hallam has gone back to Cambridge. He was not well while he was in London; moreover, he was submitting himself to the influence of the outer world more than (I think) a man of his genius ought to do.' In this period of elegies (Shelley's *Adonais*, Arnold's *Thyrsis*) Tennyson's is remarkable for its frank emotionalism. The 'holy urn', the 'fair companionship', the star 'bright As our pure love', 'The man I held as half-divine', the poet's spirit languishing 'like some poor girl', these phrases serve to remind us of the power of Eros Ouranos even among the Victorians. Admittedly *The Times* criticized the poem's flavour and Tennyson confessed to having received many letters of abuse about it; it was nevertheless generally respected and admired. (Hugh Ross Williamson has pointed out that in 'Crossing The Bar', a pious and consolatory poem if ever there was one, the Pilot is not Christ but Hallam.)[1] For that matter, the dark-skinned valetudinarian poet with his endless pipe-puffing, his hydropathy and devotion to port and rice-pudding, and his habit of writing his poems in butchers' books, was no conventional figure. His friend Edward FitzGerald described *In Memoriam* as 'full of the finest things but it is monotonous, and has the air of being evolved by a Poetical Machine of the highest order'.

from IN MEMORIAM A.H.H.

[6]

One writes, that 'Other friends remain,'
    That 'Loss is common to the race' –
    And common is the commonplace,
And vacant chaff well meant for gain.

That loss is common would not make
    My own less bitter, rather more:
    Too common! Never morning wore
To evening, but some heart did break.

O father, wheresoe'er thou be,
    Who pledgest now thy gallant son;
    A shot, ere half thy draught be done,
Hath still'd the life that beat from thee.

O mother, praying God will save
    Thy sailor, – while thy head is bow'd,

[1] See *The Arrow and the Sword*, Faber & Faber, for this and other references to our subject.

His heavy-shotted hammock-shroud
Drops in his vast and wandering grave.

Ye know no more than I who wrought
  At that last hour to please him well;
  Who mused on all I had to tell,
And something written, something thought;

Expecting still his advent home;
  And ever met him on his way
  With wishes, thinking, 'here today,'
Or 'here tomorrow will he come.'

O somewhere, meek, unconscious dove,
  That sittest ranging golden hair;
  And glad to find thyself so fair,
Poor child, that waitest for thy love!

For now her father's chimney glows
  In expectation of a guest;
  And thinking 'this will please him best,'
She takes a riband or a rose;

For he will see them on tonight;
  And with the thought her colour burns;
  And, having left the glass, she turns
Once more to set a ringlet right;

And, even when she turn'd, the curse
  Had fallen, and her future Lord
  Was drown'd in passing thro' the ford,
Or kill'd in falling from his horse.

O what to her shall be the end?
  And what to me remains of good?
  To her, perpetual maidenhood,
And unto me no second friend.

[7]

Dark house, by which once more I stand
  Here in the long unlovely street,
  Doors, where my heart was used to beat
So quickly, waiting for a hand,

A hand that can be clasp'd no more –
  Behold me, for I cannot sleep,
  And like a guilty thing I creep
At earliest morning to the door.

He is not here; but far away
  The noise of life begins again,
  And ghastly thro' the drizzling rain
On the bald street breaks the blank day.

[12]

Lo, as a dove when up she springs
  To bear thro' Heaven a tale of woe,
  Some dolorous message knit below
The wild pulsation of her wings;

Like her I go; I cannot stay;
  I leave this mortal ark behind,
  A weight of nerves without a mind,
And leave the cliffs, and haste away

O'er ocean-mirrors rounded large,
  And reach the glow of southern skies,
  And see the sails at distance rise,
And linger weeping on the marge,

And saying; 'Comes he thus, my friend?
  Is this the end of all my care?'
  And circle moaning in the air:
'Is this the end? Is this the end?'

And forward dart again, and play
  About the prow, and back return

To where the body sits, and learn
That I have been an hour away.

[13]

Tears of the widower, when he sees
  A late-lost form that sleep reveals,
  And moves his doubtful arms, and feels
Her place is empty, fall like these;

Which weep a loss for ever new,
  A void where heart on heart reposed;
  And, where warm hands have prest and closed,
Silence, till I be silent too.

Which weep the comrade of my choice,
  An awful thought, a life removed,
  The human-hearted man I loved,
A Spirit, not a breathing voice.

Come Time, and teach me, many years,
  I do not suffer in a dream;
  For now so strange do these things seem,
Mine eyes have leisure for their tears;

My fancies time to rise on wing,
  And glance about the approaching sails.
  As tho' they brought but merchants' bales,
And not the burthen that they bring.

[18]

'Tis well; 'tis something; we may stand
  Where he in English earth is laid,
  And from his ashes may be made
The violet of his native land.

'Tis little; but it looks in truth
  As if the quiet bones were blest
  Among familiar names to rest
And in the places of his youth.

Come then, pure hands, and bear the head
   That sleeps or wears the mask of sleep,
   And come, whatever loves to weep,
And hear the ritual of the dead.

Ah yet, ev'n yet, if this might be,
   I, falling on his faithful heart,
   Would breathing thro' his lips impart
The life that almost dies in me;

That dies not, but endures with pain,
   And slowly forms the firmer mind,
   Treasuring the look it cannot find,
The words that are not heard again.

[22]

The path by which we twain did go,
   Which led by tracts that pleased us well,
   Thro' four sweet years arose and fell,
From flower to flower, from snow to snow:

And we with singing cheer'd the way,
   And, crown'd with all the season lent,
   From April on to April went,
And glad at heart from May to May:

But where the path we walk'd began
   To slant the fifth autumnal slope,
   As we descended following Hope,
There sat the Shadow fear'd of man;

Who broke our fair companionship,
   And spread his mantle dark and cold,
   And wrapt thee formless in the fold,
And dull'd the murmur on thy lip,

And bore thee where I could not see
   Nor follow, tho' I walk in haste,
   And think, that somewhere in the waste
The Shadow sits and waits for me.

[27]

I envy not in any moods
　　The captive void of noble rage,
　　The linnet born within the cage,
That never knew the summer woods:

I envy not the beast that takes
　　His license in the field of time,
　　Unfetter'd by the sense of crime,
To whom a conscience never wakes;

Nor, what may count itself as blest,
　　The heart that never plighted troth
　　But stagnates in the weeds of sloth;
Nor any want-begotten rest.

I hold it true, whate'er befall;
　　I feel it, when I sorrow most;
　　'Tis better to have loved and lost
Than never to have loved at all.

[49]

Be near me when my light is low,
　　When the blood creeps, and the nerves prick
　　And tingle; and the heart is sick,
And all the wheels of Being slow.

Be near me when the sensuous frame
　　Is rack'd with pangs that conquer trust;
　　And Time, a maniac scattering dust,
And Life, a Fury slinging flame.

Be near me when my faith is dry,
　　And men the flies of latter spring,
　　That lay their eggs, and sting and sing
And weave their petty cells and die.

Be near me when I fade away,
　　To point the term of human strife,
　　And on the low dark verge of life
The twilight of eternal day.

[69]

I cannot see the features right,
　　When on the gloom I strive to paint
　　The face I know; the hues are faint
And mix with hollow masks of night;

Cloud-towers by ghostly masons wrought,
　　A gulf that ever shuts and gapes,
　　A hand that points, and palled shapes
In shadowy thoroughfares of thought;

And crowds that stream from yawning doors,
　　And shoals of pucker'd faces drive;
　　Dark bulks that tumble half alive,
And lazy lengths on boundless shores;

Till all at once beyond the will
　　I hear a wizard music roll,
　　And thro' a lattice on the soul
Looks thy fair face and makes it still.

[78]

'More than my brothers are to me,' –
　　Let this not vex thee, noble heart!
　　I know thee of what force thou art
To hold the costliest love in fee.

But thou and I are one in kind,
　　As moulded like in Nature's mint;
　　And hill and wood and field did print
The same sweet forms in either mind.

For us the same cold streamlet curl'd
　　Thro' all his eddying coves; the same

All winds that roam the twilight came
In whispers of the beauteous world.

At one dear knee we proffer'd vows,
  One lesson from one book we learn'd,
  Ere childhood's flaxen ringlet turn'd
To black and brown on kindred brows.

And so my wealth resembles thine,
  But he was rich where I was poor,
  And he supplied my want the more
As his unlikeness fitted mine.

[90]

When rosy plumelets tuft the larch,
  And rarely pipes the mounted thrush;
  Or underneath the barren bush
Flits by the sea-blue bird of March;

Come, wear the form by which I know
  Thy spirit in time among thy peers;
  The hope of unaccomplish'd years
Be large and lucid round thy brow.

When summer's hourly-mellowing change
  May breathe, with many roses sweet,
  Upon the thousand waves of wheat,
That ripple round the lonely grange;

Come: not in watches of the night,
  But where the sunbeam broodeth warm,
  Come, beauteous in thine after form,
And like a finer light in light.

[125]

Love is and was my Lord and King,
  And in his presence I attend
  To hear the tidings of my friend,
Which every hour his couriers bring.

Love is and was my King and Lord,
   And will be, tho' as yet I keep
   Within his court on earth, and sleep
Encompass'd by his faithful guard,

And hear at times a sentinel
   Who moves about from place to place,
   And whispers to the worlds of space,
In the deep night, that all is well.

[128]

Dear friend, far off, my lost desire,
   So far, so near in woe and weal;
   O loved the most, when most I feel
There is a lower and a higher;

Known and unknown; human, divine;
   Sweet human hands and lips and eye;
   Dear heavenly friend that canst not die,
Mine, mine, for ever, ever mine;

Strange friend, past, present, and to be;
   Loved deeplier, darklier understood;
   Behold, I dream a dream of good,
And mingle all the world with thee.

★   ★   ★

EDWARD FITZGERALD (1809–83) Tennyson wrote of the eccentric and crotchety Fitz, 'I had no truer friend: he was one of the kindliest of men, and I have never known one of so fine and delicate a wit.' And friendship was certainly important to Fitz-Gerald, who once described himself as having something of a lady-like temperament to which friendships more resembled passions. His marriage to the uncomely, big-boned and bass-voiced Miss Burton was undertaken as a matter of duty and honour, and soon led to separation; his mournful behaviour at the wedding-breakfast is well known – the fluttery female who proffered him blancmange was repulsed with 'Ugh! Congealed bridesmaid'. In 1864 Fitz met the Lowestoft fisherman Joseph Fletcher or 'Posh', then twenty-six years old, and of the blue-eyed auburn-haired and ruddy type that Hopkins would have admired, or Melville. 'A grand fellow, like one of those first British sent over to Rome – a very humane Savage . . . I seem to have jumped back to a regard of near forty years ago; and while I am with him feel young again, and when he goes shall feel old again . . . The Man is, I do think, of a Royal Nature, I have told him he is liable to one Danger (the Hare with many Friends) – so many wanting him to *drink*.' So ran his comments at various times (see A. M. Terhune, *The Life of Edward FitzGerald*, O.U.P.). He fussed over Posh as Gray did over Bonstetten, and went into partnership with him as herring merchants, fitting out the lugger *Meum and Teum* or, as the locals called it, 'Mum and Tum'. But the partnership was uneasy and finally dissolved and, through Posh's love of the bottle, the friendship also lost its first glow. Yet in 1877 Fitz-Gerald could still write, '. . . the Man is Royal, tho' with the faults of ancient Vikings . . . His Glory is somewhat marred; but he looks every inch a King in his Lugger now. At home (when he is there and not at the Tavern) he sits among his Dogs, Cats, Birds, etc. always with a great Dog following him abroad, and aboard. This is altogether the Greatest Man I have known.'

Here is a piece of early light verse addressed to Thackeray, of whom Fitz was, as various letters show, exceedingly fond.

[1]

I cared not for life: for true friend had I none
I had heard 'twas a blessing not under the sun:
Some figures called friends, hollow, proud, or cold-hearted
Came to me like shadows – like shadows departed:
But a day came that turned all my sorrow to glee
When first I saw Willy, and Willy saw me!

[2]

The thought of my Willy is always a cheerer;
My wine has new flavour – the fire burns clearer;

The sun ever shines – I am pleased with all things; –
And this crazy old world seems to go with new springs; –
And when we're together, (oh! soon may it be!)
The world may go kissing of comets for me!

[3]

The chair that Will sat in, I sit in the best;
The tobacco is sweetest which Willy hath blest;
And I never found out that my wine tasted ill
When a tear would drop in it, for thinking of Will.

[4]

And now on my window October blows chilly,
I laugh at blue devils, and think of my Willy:
I think that our friendship will not drop away
Like the leaves from the trees, or our locks when they're
grey:
I think that old age shall not freeze us, until
He creeps with Death's warrant to me and my Will.

[5]

If I get to be fifty – may Willy get too:
And we'll laugh, Will, at all that grim sixty can do;
Old age – let him do of what poets complain,
We'll thank him for making us children again;
Let him make us grey, gouty, blind, toothless, or silly,
Still old Ned shall be Ned – and old Willy be Willy!

[6]

We may both get so old that our senses expire
And leave us to doze half-alive by the fire:
Age may chill the warm heart which I think so divine,
But what warmth it has, Willy, shall ever be thine!
And if our speech goes, we must pass the long hours
When the earth is laid bare with a Winter like ours,
Till Death finds us waiting him patiently still,
Willy looking at me, and I looking at Will!

(Quoted in A. K. Terhune, *op. cit.*)

★   ★   ★

ROBERT BROWNING (1812–89)

MAY AND DEATH

[1]

I wish that when you died last May,
   Charles, there had died along with you
Three parts of spring's delightful things;
   Ay, and, for me, the fourth part too.

[11]

A foolish thought, and worse, perhaps!
   There must be many a pair of friends
Who, arm in arm, deserve the warm
   Moon-births and the long evening-ends.

[111]

So, for their sake, be May still May!
   Let their new time, as mine of old,
Do all it did for me: I bid
   Sweet sighs and sounds throng manifold.

[1v]

Only, one little sight, one plant,
   Woods have in May, that starts up green
Save a sole streak which, so to speak,
   In spring's blood, spilt its leaves between, –

[v]

That, they might spare; a certain wood
   Might miss the plant; their loss were small:
But I, – whene'er the leaf grows there,
   Its drop comes from my heart, that's all.

                            (from *Dramatis Personae*)

★   ★   ★

WILLIAM MORRIS (1834–96)

A DREAM OF JOHN BALL

Forsooth, brethren, fellowship is heaven, and lack of fellowship is hell: fellowship is life, and lack of fellowship is death: and the deeds that ye do upon the earth, it is for fellowship's sake that ye do them, and the life that is in it, that shall live on and on for ever, and each one of you part of it, while many a man's life upon the earth from the earth shall wane. Therefore I bid you not dwell in hell but in heaven, or while ye must, upon earth, which is a part of heaven, and forsooth no foul part.

(*Reprinted from* The '*Commonweal*'.)

*   *   *

WILLIAM JOHNSON CORY (1823–92) The author of one famous poetic translation, 'They told me, Heraclitus', was for many years a schoolmaster at Eton, although from time to time he came near to receiving grander appointments. In the Introduction to the third edition of his small volume of verse, *Ionica* (1905), A. C. Benson pays him a softly and blandly revealing tribute. 'He was sensitive to the charm of eager, high-spirited, and affectionate natures . . . Yet he was apt to make favourites; and though he demanded of his chosen pupils and friends a high intellectual zeal, though he was merciless to all sloppiness and lack of interest, yet he forfeited a wider influence by his reputation for partiality, and by an obvious susceptibility to grace of manner and unaffected courtesy. Boys who did not understand him, and whom he did not care to try to understand, thought him simply fanciful and eccentric.'

Such to varying degrees might be said of many a schoolmaster and clergyman whose privately printed verses may still be picked up on second-hand stalls and whose muted sensuousness, moral, often patriotic fervour and capacity for sentimental idealization are faintly redolent of the Odes of Pindar – and even the Pipes of Pan – as though these came filtered across hundreds of cricket-pitches and through the drone of innumerable classrooms, were lent new Anglo-Saxon tones on many a parade-ground, acquired deeper shadows in many a Chapel porch, now and then to retrieve something of their pristine quality by the river bathing-pool on a July evening. A veritable Parsons' Pleasure of such versifiers could be assembled, who only rarely – and then as often as not with the ludicrous shock of the Unconscious at work – achieve the directness of Kilvert's remarks about girls, and Hopkins's celebrations of his fellow-men.

DESIDERATO

Oh, lost and unforgotten friend,
   Whose presence change and chance deny;
   If angels turn your soft proud eye
To lines your cynic playmate penned,

Look on them, as you looked on me,
   When both were young; when, as we went
   Through crowds of forest ferns, you leant
On him who loved your staff to be;

And slouch your lazy length again
   On cushions fit for aching brow
   (Yours always ached, you know), and now
As dainty languishing as then,

Give them but one fastidious look,
   And if you see a trace of him
   Who humoured you in every whim,
Seek for his heart within his book:

For though there be enough to mark
   The man's divergence from the boy,
   Yet shines my faith without alloy
For him who led me through that park;

And though a stranger throw aside
   Such grains of common sentiment,

Yet let your haughty head be bent
To take the jetsom of the tide;

Because this brackish turbid sea
　　Throws toward thee things that pleased of yore,
　　And though it wash thy feet no more,
Its murmurs mean: 'I yearn for thee.'
　　　　　　　　　　　　(*Ionica*, George Allen)

　　　　　★　　★　　★

A FOOTBALL PLAYER

If I could paint you, friend, as you stand there,
Guard of the goal, defensive, open-eyed,
Watching the tortured bladder slide and glide
Under the twinkling feet; arms bare, head bare,
The breeze a-tremble through crow-tufts of hair;
Red-brown in face, and ruddier having spied
A wily foeman breaking from the side;
Aware of him, – of all else unaware:
If I could limn you, as you leap and fling
Your weight against his passage, like a wall;
Clutch him, and collar him, and rudely cling
For one brief moment till he falls – you fall:
My sketch would have what Art can never give –
Sinew and breath and body; it would live.
　　　　　(Edward Cracroft Lefroy, *His Life and Poems*,
　　　　　　edited by Wilfred A. Gill, John Lane, 1897)

A PALAESTRAL STUDY

The curves of beauty are not softly wrought:
These quivering limbs by strong hid muscles held
In attitudes of wonder, and compelled
Through shapes more sinuous than a sculptor's thought,
Tell of dull matter splendidly distraught,
Whisper of mutinies divinely quelled, –
Weak indolence of flesh, that long rebelled,
The spirit's domination bravely taught.
And all man's loveliest works are cut with pain.

> Beneath the perfect art we know the strain,
> Intense, defined, how deep soe'er it lies.
> From each high master-piece our souls refrain,
> Not tired of gazing, but with stretched eyes
> Made hot by radiant flames of sacrifice.

(Ibid.)

★   ★   ★

THE REVEREND E. E. BRADFORD (d. 1944) wrote more than ten volumes of verse with such titles as *The Romance Of Youth*, *Passing The Love Of Women* and *Boyhood* which were often favourably reviewed, as when the *Times Literary Supplement* commented, 'Dr. Bradford's numerous books of verse have been devoted especially to hymning male friendships. He has the gift of fervent and melodious expression . . .' or *Poetry* remarked, 'A breezy, masculine, invigorating performance, full of wisdom and tolerance . . .' Inevitably several pointed out that Dr Bradford's deeply felt Christianity was tinged with a Platonism as sensuous as it was pure.

> Manhood has power, Age peace: Boyhood alone
> The joyous rainbow light around the Throne.

Some of the volumes are little novels in verse, with 'chapters' lasting only one or two pages and often prefaced with an epigrammatic couplet or a lyric; they will be about friends growing up (and vividly talking) against a background of Cornwall and church, and these friends will have names like Norman de Vere, Leslie de Lampton, Clinton Fane and Master Merivale Trelawny Bates, albeit liberally interspersed with Jims, Jacks and Joes and, much more rarely, a Joan or a Nell. Not all the boys' characters are nice, although the author has a good word to say for them sooner or later. Steve Ailwyn in *Boyhood* is described as a Fallen Angel. Hugh discovers him sketching.

> The boy came in – a fair-haired child of ten,
>   With big blue eyes, a pale, transparent face
> That any slight emotion now and then

Would flood with colour, and a form whose grace
Was marred by lack of plumpness. Quick as thought
  Steve whipped his sketch away. But Hugh had seen
And from the passing glimpse that he had caught
  He recognized the picture was obscene!
Steve popped it in his mouth, chewed it to pulp,
  And swallowed it . . .

Sometimes Bradford turns to the ideal sea-side town he calls
Belton, and which is clearly his version of the Great Good Place:
the traveller arriving there

Sees underneath the railway line, and all along the beach,
Lovely little naked fays as far as eye can reach.
Talk about the Greeks' impeccability of form!
Give to me a Belton boy whose flesh and blood are warm!

*   *   *

Here is a glimpse of Belton:

No bird or brute's more shy than the boy bather
  In Belton cove. If in a sheltered nook
He's run to earth, he eyes the bold invader
  With startled look.

Although perhaps his coat lies neatly folded
  Upon a rock, he'll promptly put it on,
Then like a timid puppy struck or scolded,
  He's up and gone.

You'd best begin by talking of the weather,
  Or asking if the water's hot or cold:
Then, when you've had a little chat together,
  He'll grow more bold.

From time to time he'll give you furtive glances,
  And if you make him laugh or even smile

The game is won. Your friendship soon advances,
   And in a while

His coat comes off again, his trousers follow,
   And by the time his sunburnt body's bare
He'll laugh and chatter, whistle, shout and holler
   As free as air.
            (*The Kingdom Within You*, Rev. E. E. Bradford,
                        Kegan Paul, Trench)

BOYISH BEAUTY

See that lad, of late a child
Irresponsible and wild
Now look up with earnest eyes
Tender, passionate and wise!
   Love has lent him for an hour
   Beauty's holy, awful power:
   When he's ripe for toil and pain,
   Love will take it back again.

Boyish beauty comes and goes,
Like a rivulet that flows:
Woman, as a placid pool,
Long is fair if clean and cool.
      Yet the running waters shine
      With a splendour more divine:
   So the fairest woman's grace
   Fades before a boyish face!
(*Boyhood*, Rev. E. E. Bradford, Kegan Paul, Trench)

PLATONIC FRIENDSHIP

Two little Loves, as baby boys,
   Are like as sheep and sheep:
But one will turn to marriage joys,
   And one to friendship keep.

In morals we have won a wide accord.
    The Sermon on the Mount, the Parables,
The blessings and the warnings of our Lord
    Appeal to all. And certain principles –
Such as the tree being best known by its fruits –
    May guide us where we differ. This is now
Not least on love; for those whom marriage suits
    Oft eye askance all such as fail to bow
Beneath its yoke. Yet Christ Himself declared
    'All men cannot receive this saying.' Some,
And surely not the worst, have never shared
    That passion for the sex which has become
To others a religion. Their desires
    Are weak and changeable. What will they do?
Seek passing unions like their savage sires?
    With women? God forbid! Nay, for these few
Platonic friendship, it must be confessed
Will prove the safest solace and the best.

                                      (*Ibid.*)

          ★   ★   ★

Alan Dave and Clinton Fane are both serious-minded but unconventional youths who plan religious careers. Their friendship is eventually sealed by a church ceremony.

MATES

    Two peers may work with one accord,
    As love-bound slave and love-crowned lord.

The bridal party left, the guests departed,
    And Clinton Fane, as Alan seemed to be
A trifle pensive, if not heavy-hearted,
    Proposed a quiet stroll to Shingle Quay
They climbed a cliff and reached an open down
    Of close-shorn turf, resilient to the feet;
And soon they saw the little fishing town,
    Whose windows shimmered through a haze of heat.

The ocean's thunder rose from far below;
   All else was still, till Alan ventured: 'Clin,
We've been acquainted for long, you know.
   I think it's time real friendship should begin.'
'True friendship neither can begin nor end.
   It is eternal,' Fane said thoughtfully.
'A friend's revealed, not made. If you're my friend,
   You always have been, and will always be.
But there's a working partnership for life
   Where one of two close comrades may agree
To serve the other something like a wife.
   Shall I do that for you, or you for me?'
Then Alan told him Herbert Eaton's scheme
   Of missionary labours. 'By and by
To come again to England is my dream,
   And live and work with you until I die.'
This speech evoked no comment. Clinton Fane
In silence lashed at thistles with his cane.
(*Strangers and Pilgrims*, Rev. E. E. Bradford, Kegan Paul, Trench)

THE WORLD WELL LOST

Lovers wise at life's beginning,
Kick the world and send it spinning.

The sun went down, and by degrees the light
   Grew dimmer in the sky, still neither spoke.
Mile after mile they walked. The moon was bright
   And they were nearing home ere Alan broke
His thoughtful silence. 'Clin,' he said at last,
   'If I give up this missionary plan,
Could we become real friends?' Fane's heart beat fast.
   'Yes,' he said simply. 'And no other man
Would ever come between us?' 'No one would
   You'd always be my first friend.' 'Pete Conway
Could you supplant me?' 'No, he never could.'
   'Then, Clin, I'll do it. But I ought to say –
I'd best be honest with you from the first –
   Of course, it isn't only for your sake.

I've felt uneasy long, and felt it worst
  When I have been with you. If you can make
Me see and say what's true, and do what's right –
  And I am sure you can – I'll be your friend,
And let you lead me, and with all my might
  I'll serve and follow you until life's end.
  That's what you call a working friendship?' 'Yes.
  A partnership for life. Our family
Have made such pacts for centuries. Unless
  You want more time to think, we'll ratify
The contract in our chapel Sunday night,
And make our vows, according to our rite.'

                                        (Ibid.)

8

The Moderns

INTRODUCTION

With modern times, here pretty arbitrarily separated from those preceding, the material becomes too rich for anything like a comprehensive treatment of British and American authors, let alone the French, Germans, Italians, Greeks, etc. This is the period of Freud and psychiatry and social research. Havelock Ellis, Edward Carpenter and John Addington Symonds are among the first to understand and explain the extremists' position: the 'ambi-dextrous' and the 'bi-metallists' are anatomized; notebooks, and then tape-recorders, and finally government committees, edge in upon the scenes where Wilde found it exciting to 'dine with panthers'. It is an age of frankness, of Gide's *Corydon* and autobiographical confessions, of Proust's discreet ambiguities counteracted by grim psychological analyses and a marvellous display of specialized sensibility, of the gentle self-revelations of a Forrest Reid or a Denton Welch, or the robust innuendoes of a Norman Douglas. One sort of 'mystery', at least, has begun to fade – that which was felt as a self-limiting belt-tightening reticence and bitterness in A. E. Housman and T. E. Lawrence. This increasing honesty is reflected in the school story where we move from the high moral tone of Tom Brown's protection of the frail and saintly George Arthur to the varied, almost startling, freedoms of the many post-Waugh books.

Only superficially, however, does Eros Ouraneios suffer. A Renaissance sensuousness is seen as part of idealizing love; Melville's Billy Budd is certainly as spiritually beautiful and significant as Tennyson's Arthur Hallam while Whitman lends to the 'animal magnetism' of comradeship the glow of the new, democratic West. In Germany Stefan George builds a mystical cult about his short-lived Maximin. Perhaps a key figure here is, as so often, D. H. Lawrence. To this pioneer of deepened consciousness, with his enormous interest in the relations of men and women, the beauty and psychic force of the male cannot be disregarded.

The passages below are grouped by countries. Concluding sections deal with Exotic Encounters (loves and friendships in unfamiliar surroundings) and the School Story.

1. IN FRANCE

PAUL VERLAINE (1844–96) and ARTHUR RIMBAUD (1854–91)
Against the rules of strict chronology one thinks of the poetry of Baudelaire and then of Verlaine and Rimbaud as being modern, in rather the same way that one finds a pioneering modernity in the work of Hopkins; we seem to be the children of Baudelaire and Rimbaud while our family relationship with Tennyson and Browning is much more distant. The same may be true of friendships. Tennyson and Arthur Hallam, FitzGerald and the fisherman 'Posh', Arnold and Clough ... these seem Victorian relationships, as indeed they are, dimly and decently manifesting themselves through mists of elegy and high thinking, while the appallingly muddled glamour and squalor of the French poets' infatuation with each other is still hot from the press. The facts themselves are, of course, extraordinary: a poet great before he was seventeen, with the face of an angel and the habits of a guttersnipe; the *Cher Maître*, ten years older, whom he seduces first from pregnant wife and genteel in-laws, and then from his literary circle in Paris, in order that they may go travelling and quarrelling and drinking and very fruitfully writing; in Soho,

in Camden Town, in Belgium, where the boy is shot and the Master imprisoned, and finally in Germany where the boy knocks the Master out in a forest before renouncing poetry for ever . . .

What was the measure of their bond? Verlaine wrote of 'passions satisfaites absolument outre mesure' and called little Arthur 'mon grand péché radieux' and 'mortel, ange et demon . . . tres beau d'une beauté paysanne et rusée'. He described their room in Paris, in the Rue Campagne-Première, like this:

> Seule, ô chambre, qui fuis en cônes affligeantes,
> Seule, tu sais! mais sans doute combien de nuits
> De noce auront dévirginé leurs nuits, depuis . . .

Rimbaud, on his side, produced the fiercely obscene *Le Bon Disciple*.

> Toi le jaloux qui m'as fait signe,
> Ah! me voici, voici tout moi!
> Vers toi je rampe, encore indigne!
> – Monte sur mes reins et trépigne.

Miss Enid Starkie has this to say of the relationship: 'It is impossible to prove conclusively whether Verlaine and Rimbaud actually practised sodomy, or whether their relationship was merely a violent form of sentimental and romantic friendship with its less extreme physical manifestations . . . Of the physical rapture felt by both the men no doubt can be entertained and Verlaine was of too simple a nature to attempt to disguise it in his writings; he wished all to know of it and to share with him his bliss. This desire was, however, coupled with the fear of consequences – a residue of his latent respectability – and he invariably gave a twist to the poems to make his intention less obvious . . . Whatever may have been the nature of their relationship, it brought them at first great joy and a sense of fulfilment, as well as literary stimulation, but it was eventually to prove for both of them the source of deep suffering, bitterness and all the devouring jealousy that such a relationship seems fated to produce. Only two members of the same sex have power to wound one another

so deeply, when things go wrong between them, and to wound
one another where hurt is most intolerable.'

(Enid Starkie, *Arthur Rimbaud*, Hamish Hamilton)

THE FOOLISH VIRGIN

The Infernal Bridegroom

Let's hear now a hell-mate's confession:

'O heavenly Bridegroom, my Lord, do not reject the confession of
the saddest of your handmaidens. I am lost. I am drunk. I am unclean.
What a life!

'Forgive me, heavenly Lord, forgive me! Ah! forgive me! How
many tears! And how many more tears later, I hope!

'Later I shall know the heavenly Bridegroom! I was born His
slave.—The other can beat me now!

'At present I am at the bottom of the world! O my friends . . .
no, not my friends . . . Never delirium and tortures like these . . . How
stupid!

'Ah! I suffer, I scream. I really suffer. Yet everything is permitted
me, burdened with the contempt of the most contemptible hearts.

'At any rate let me tell my secret, free to repeat it twenty times again
– just as dreary, just as insignificant!

'I am a slave of the infernal Bridegroom, the one who was the undoing of the foolish virgins. He is really that very demon. He is not a
ghost, he is not a phantom. But I who have lost all reason, who am
damned and dead to the world – they will not kill me! How describe
him to you! I can no longer even speak. I am in mourning. I weep. I
am afraid. A little coolness, Lord, if you will, if you only will!

'I am a widow . . . I used to be a widow . . . ah, yes, I was really
respectable once, and I was not born to be a skeleton! . . . He was
hardly more than a child. His mysterious tenderness had seduced me. I
forgot all human duty to follow him. What a life! Real life is absent.
We are not in the world. I go where he goes. I have to. And often he
flies into a rage at me, *me, the poor soul*. The Demon! He is a demon, you
know, *he is not a man.*

'He says: "I do not like women: love must be reinvented, that's obvious. A secure position is all they're capable of desiring now. Security once gained, heart and beauty are set aside: cold disdain alone is left, the food of marriage today. Or else, I see women marked with the signs of happiness, and whom I could have made my comrades, devoured first by brutes with as much feeling as a log . . ."

'I listen to him glorifying infamy, clothing cruelty with charm. "I am of a distant race: my ancestors were Norsemen; they used to pierce their sides, drink their blood. – I will cover myself with gashes, tattoo my body. I want to be as ugly as a Mongol; you'll see, I will howl through the streets. I want to become raving mad. Never show me jewels, I should grovel and writhe on the floor. My riches, I want them spattered all over with blood. Never will I work . . ." Many nights his demon would seize me and rolling on the ground I would wrestle with him.— Often at night, drunk, he lies in wait for me, in streets, in houses, to frighten me to death.—"They will really cut my throat; it will be revolting." Oh! those days when he goes wrapped in an air of crime!

'Sometimes he speaks in a kind of melting dialect, of death that brings repentance, of all the miserable wretches there must be, of painful toil, of partings that lacerate the heart. In low dives where we would get drunk, he used to weep for those around us, cattle of misery. He would lift up drunkards in the dark streets. He had the pity of a bad mother for little children.—He would depart with the graces of a little girl going to her catechism.—He pretended to have knowledge of everything, business, art, medicine.—I followed him. I had to!

'I saw the whole setting with which in his mind he surrounded himself; clothing, sheets, furniture; I lent him arms, another face. I saw everything relating to him as he would have liked to create it for himself. When his mind was absent, I followed him, yes I, in strange and complicated actions, very far, good or bad: I was certain of never entering his world. How many hours of the night, beside his dear sleeping body I kept watch, trying to understand why he so longed to escape reality. Never a man had such a wish. I realized – without any fear for him – that he could be a serious danger to society. Perhaps he had some secrets for *changing life*? No, I would say to myself he is only looking for them. In short, his charity is bewitched, and I, its prisoner. No other soul would have enough strength – strength of despair! – to endure it, and to be protected and loved by him. Moreover, I never imagined him with another soul: one sees one's own Angel, never the Angel of someone else – I believe. I was in his soul as in a palace they had emptied, so that no one should see so mean a person as oneself: that was all. Alas! I was really dependent on him. But what could he want with my dull, my craven life? He was making me no better if he wasn't driving me to death! Sometimes, chagrined and sad, I said to him: "I understand you." He would shrug his shoulders.

'Thus my sorrow always renewed, and seeming in my eyes more lost than ever – as in the eyes of all who might have watched me had I not been condemned to be forgotten by all forever! – I hungered for his kindness more and more. With his kisses and his friendly arms, it was really heaven, a sombre heaven into which I entered and where I longed to be left, poor and deaf and dumb and blind. Already he had grown into a habit. I thought of us as two good children, free to wander in the Paradise of sadness. We understood each other. Enraptured, we used to work together. But after a profound caress he would say: "How queer it will seem to you when I am no longer here – all you have gone through. When you no longer have my arm beneath your head, nor my heart for resting place, nor these lips upon your eyes. For I shall have to go away, very far away, one day. After all I must help others too: it is my duty. Not that it's very appetising . . . dear heart . . ." Right away I saw myself, with him gone, my senses reeling, hurled into the most horrible darkness: death. I used to make him promise never to leave me. He made it twenty times, that lover's promise. It was as vain as when I said to him: "I understand you."

'Ah! I have never been jealous of him. He will not leave me, I believe. What would become of him? He knows nothing; he will never work. He wants to live a sleep walker. Will his goodness and his charity alone give him the right to live in the real world? There are moments when I forget the abjection to which I have fallen; he will make me strong, we will travel, hunt in the deserts, we will sleep on the pavements of unknown cities, uncared for and without a care. Or else I shall awake, and the laws and customs will have changed – thanks to his magic power – or the world, while remaining the same, will leave me to my desires, joys, heedlessness. Oh! the life of adventure in children's books, to recompense me. I have suffered so, will you give me that? He cannot. His ideal is unknown to me. He told me he had regrets, hopes: that should be no concern of mine. Does he talk to God?

I should appeal to God, perhaps. I am in the lowest depths, and I can no longer pray.

'If he explained his sadness to me, would I understand it any more than his mockery? He assails me, he spends hours making me ashamed of everything in the world that may have touched me, and is indignant if I weep.

'You see the elegant young man going into the beautiful, calm house; his name is Smith, Miller, Maurice, John, or something or other! A woman has devoted her life to loving that wicked idiot: she is dead, she must be a saint in heaven now. You will kill me as he has killed that woman. It is our lot, the lot of us, charitable hearts . . . ! Alas! he had days when all busy men seemed to him grotesque playthings of delirium: he would laugh long and horribly. Then he would revert to his manners of a young mother, a big sister. If he were less untamed we should be saved! But his tenderness too is deadly. I am his slave.—Ah! I am mad!

'One day, perhaps, he will miraculously disappear; but I must know if he is really to ascend into some heaven again, so that I'll not miss the sight of my darling boy's assumption!'

Queer couple!

(Arthur Rimbaud. *A Season In Hell*, tr. Louise Varèse, The New Classics Series, New Directions, Norfolk, Connecticut)

★   ★   ★

And here is Verlaine, whose *Romances Sans Paroles* were a product of the affair:

GREEN

Here are fruits, flowers, leaves and boughs
And here is my heart, beating for you alone.
Do not tear it with your two white hands,
And to your eyes so beautiful let the humble gift be sweet.

I come covered still with dew
Frozen upon my brow by the morning wind.
Allow my weariness, at your feet resting,
To dream of sweet moments refreshing.

Let my head upon your young breast sink,
Ringing still with your last kisses;
Let it seek peace from the kind storm,
And let me sleep a little, since you rest.
(*Forty Poems*, tr. Roland Gant and Claude Apcher, Falcon Press)

LONDON: A LIMPING SONNET

Here all is gloom, here all things end in ill;
Fate cannot brook so much calamity,
As if some simple beast brought to the kill
Saw its blood stream before its glazing eye.

Here London smokes and roars. City of the Plain!
Gas flares and floats; the scarlet inn-signs swing;
Huddled in fright the houses shrink between,
As fearful as an old wives' gathering.

The dreadful past springs – bawl and brawl and yell –
In red and tawny fogs in foul Sohos,
With their 'indeeds', 'all rights' and Cockney 'aohs'.

Here is a martyrdom of hopeless pain;
Here all is gloom, here all things end in ill . . .
Skies, hurl your fire on this City of the Plain!
(*The Sky above the Roof*, tr. Brian Hill, Hart-Davis)

CRIMEN AMORIS

In Ecbatana a palace of gold, silk-hung,
   Shelters a demon-horde of fair young djinns;
To strains of Mohammedan music they have flung
   All five senses to the Seven Deadly Sins.

The feast of the Seven Sins is here. O fine!
   All the Desires are aflame with a brutal glow,
And the Appetites haste to bear round rosy wine
   Like beckoned Ganymedes hurrying to and fro.

To hymeneal cadences dancers throng
   As the music sweetly swoons in a sobbing key;
And voices of youths and maids in glorious song
   Rise and fall like the surging waves of the sea.

So powerful are the enchantments that repose
   In the benevolence breathed by these rites
That the countryside has blossomed with the rose
   And the night has hung herself with diamond lights.

Now, of these fallen angels the most fair
   Is scarce sixteen.[1] A garland crowns his head;
Arms crossed on garment's fringe and necklace, there
   He dreams, eyes bright with ardour and tears unshed.

Vainly the revels round him wax more mad;
   Vainly his demon kin exert their charms
To ease him of the cares that make him sad,
   Striving to cheer him with caressing arms.

But he shakes off each fond cajoling hold.
   Sorrow has painted a black butterfly
On his fair forehead hung about with gold;
   Endlessly dreadful is his misery!

He speaks to them: – 'Leave me in peace, I pray!'
   Then gently kisses each, and from their clasp
With sudden twist he tears himself away;
   Scraps of his garment flutter in their grasp.

Now see him mount the loftiest tower-keep
   Of that tall palace! In his fist he shakes
A torch, like cestus in a hero's grip;
   To those below it seems that morning breaks.

What does it say, that deep and tender voice,
   That voice to match the flame's clear trumpet-cry,

[1] It was in prison that Verlaine wrote this poem about his friend's attempt to make himself a god.

That voice to make the listening moon rejoice?
   'The man who shall be God – that man am I!

'Angels and men, in this unending war
   Of Good and Evil, we've endured till now
Too much; then let us, wretched that we are,
   Restrict our aims to one most simple vow.

'Sad sinners, joyous saints, all you, all we,
   Why do we still maintain this stubborn broil?
Why should not we, so skilled in artistry,
   Make one like virtue of our life-long toil?

'Enough – too much – of this too-equal fight!
   Now must the Seven Deadly Sins once more
With Faith and Hope and Charity unite.
   Enough – too much – of stern, grim-visaged war!

'Thus do I answer Christ who in this strife
   A constant equilibrium does approve;
"Through me shall Hell (which gives this palace life)
   Make sacrifice to universal Love!"'

The flambeau from his opened hand drops down
   And with a sudden roar the fire leaps there –
Huge battles of red eagles whose wings drown
   In whirls of blackened smoke and blasts of air.

The gold in rivers melts; the marble cracks;
   Splendour and heat, a furnace of fierce fire!
The silk like cotton wool flies off in flakes
   Of heat and splendour in the blazing pyre.

Among the flames the dying demons sing;
   They understand and they accept their fate!
Voices of youths and maids in concert ring
   Before that hurricane of savage heat.

And he, arms crossed in pride and eyes turned where
   Across the sky great tongues of flame are flung,
Murmurs beneath his breath a kind of prayer
   That dies in the glad triumph of their song.

Murmurs beneath his breath a kind of prayer,
   Eyes on the sky where tongues of flame are flung –
When bursts a dreadful thunder on the ear
   And makes an end of gladness and of song!

The sacrifice was unacceptable.
   One just and strong had knowledge to provide
A clue to all the cunning and to all
   The malice in that self-deceiving pride.

And of that palace of a hundred towers
   No trace remains after its monstrous fall;
One dreadful portent blackened its fair bowers
   And made a hollow vanished dream of all.

The blue night of a thousand stars descends;
   Fields from a Gospel scene lie spread below
Austere and smooth. Like wings, each tree extends
   Impalpable as veils its feathery bough.

The cold streams curl upon their beds of rock;
   Through air with mystery and prayer perfumed
The soft owls float on undetermined stroke;
   With light a dancing wave is sometimes plumed.

The gentle shape of distant hills displays
   Itself like love still undefined in trend;
And through the hollows drags the misty haze
   Like effort with atonement as its end.

And all this, like a heart, a soul, a word,
   In virginal adoration kneels to pray,
Expanding, thrilling, urgent to be heard
   By merciful God, against all ill our stay.

                                  (*Ibid.*)

CES PASSIONS

Ces passions qu'eux seuls nomment encore amours
Sont des amours aussi, tendres et furieuses,
Avec des particularités curieuses
Que n'ont pas les amours, certes! de tous les jours.

Même plus qu'elles et mieux qu'elles héroïques,
Elles se parent de splendeurs d'âme et de sang,
Telles qu'au prix d'elles les amours dans le rang
Ne sont que Ris et Jeux ou besoins érotiques,

Que vains proverbes, ou riens d'enfants trop gâtés,
– 'Ah! les pauvres amours banales, animales,
Normales! Gros goûts lourds ou frugales fringales,
Sans compter la sottise et des fécondités!'

Peuvent dire ceux-là que sacre le haut Rite,
Ayant conquis la plénitude du plaisir,
Et l'insatiabilité de leur désir
Bénissant la fidélité de leur mérite.

La plénitude! Ils l'ont superlativement:
Baisers repus, gorges, mains privilégiées
Dans la richesse des caresses repayées,
Et ce divin final anéantissement!

Comme ce sont les forts et les forts, l'habitude
De la force les rend invaincus au déduit.
Plantureux, savoureux, débordant le déduit!
Je le crois qu'ils l'ont, la pleine plénitude!

Et pour combler leurs vœux chacun d'eux tour à tour
Fait l'action suprême, a la parfaite extase.
– Tantôt la coupe ou la bouche, et tantôt le vase, –
Pâmé comme la nuit, fervent comme le jour.

Leurs beaux ébats sont grands et gais. Pas de crises:
Vapeurs, nerfs. Non, des jeux courageux, puis d'heureux
Bras las autour du cou, pour de moins langoureux
Qu'étroits sommeils à deux, tout coupés de reprises.

Dormez, les amoureux! tandis qu'autour de vous
Le monde inattentif aux choses délicates
Bruit ou gît en somnolences scélérates,
Sans même (il est si bête!) être de vous jaloux.

Et ces réveils francs, clairs, riants, vers l'aventure
De fiers damnés d'un plus magnifique sabbat?
Et salut, témoins purs de l'âme en ce combat
Pour l'affranchissement de la lourde nature!

(*Parallèlement*)

Finally this poem by one of the modern translators:

NO. 8 GREAT COLLEGE STREET, CAMDEN TOWN

Here in this dingy street
And squalid house Verlaine
And Rimbaud turned again
From the tumbled bed. Oh, chain
Of victory and defeat
Here in this dingy street!

How many times since then
Have couples in the gloom
Of that unfeeling room
Set moving in the womb
Uncharted lives of men?
How many times since then?

But never birth like this
Poetic fatherhood!

Beauty conceived in mud,
Unfolding branch and bud
From its strange genesis.
Oh, never birth like this!

(Brian Hill)

★   ★   ★

IN THE DECADENT NOVEL *A Rebours,* whose neurotic hero experiments with so many sensations, J. K. Huysmans (1848–1907) has the following encounter:

Des Esseintes had regretted the woman, and when he recollected her artifices, other women seemed devoid of flavour; the affected graces of depraved children even appeared insipid, and so profound became his contempt for their monotonous grimaces that he could not bring himself to put up with them any more.

Still chewing the bitter cud of his disillusionment, he was walking one day all alone in the Avenue de Latour-Maubourg when he was accosted near the Invalides by a young man, almost a boy, who begged him to tell him the shortest way to go to the Rue de Babylone. Des Esseintes indicated his road and, as he was crossing the Esplanade too, they set off together.

The lad's voice, insisting, it seemed to his companion quite needlessly, on fuller instructions as to the way: – 'Then you think, do you? that by turning left, I should be taking the longer road; but I was told that if I cut obliquely across the Avenue, I should get there all the quicker,' – was timid and appealing at the same time, very low and very gentle.

Des Esseintes looked him up and down. He seemed to have just left school, was poorly dressed in a little cheviot jacket tight round the hips and barely coming below the break of the loins, a pair of close-fitting black breeches, a turn-down collar cut low to display a puffed cravat, deep blue with white lines, La Vallière shape. In his hand he carried a class book bound in boards, and on his head was a brown, flat-brimmed bowler hat.

The face was at once pathetic and strangely attractive; pale and drawn, with regular features shaded by long black locks, it was lit up by great liquid eyes, the lids circled with blue, set near the nose, which was splashed with a few golden freckles and under which lurked a little mouth, but with fleshy lips divided by a line in the middle like a ripe cherry.

They examined each other for a moment, eye to eye; then the young man dropped his and stepped nearer; soon his arm was rubbing against Des Esseintes', who slackened his pace, gazing with a thoughtful look at the lad's swaying walk.

And lo! from this chance meeting sprang a mistrustful friendship that nevertheless was prolonged for months. To this day, Des Esseintes could not think of it without a shudder; never had he experienced a more alluring liaison or one that laid a more imperious spell on his senses; never had he run such risks, nor had he ever been so well content with such a grievous sort of satisfaction.

(*Against the Grain*, The Fortune Press, 1931)

★ ★ ★

ANDRÉ GIDE (1869–1951): Gide once described himself as 'a small boy having fun combined with a Protestant pastor who bores him'. Always the moralist and teacher, and especially in the *Journal* an acute observer and critic of the life around him, he taught the lessons of his own temperament in a subversive classroom dedicated to sunlight, the pleasures and vices of North Africa, and 'les nourritures terrestres'. Unlike Marcel Jouhandeau, who presents his 'vice' with irony and detachment, Gide made a virtue of it – and wrote the courageous but somewhat naïve *Corydon* (1924) in its defence. In this work and in the autobiography *Si Le Grain Ne Meurt* (1921) he became the first major writer to confess his deviation: what was, as he says, *normal* for him. Nevertheless some of his readers still find his treatment of a pious wife hard to stomach.

We present here first his record of meetings with Proust, the first volume of whose novel he so singularly failed to appreciate, then a major bit of honesty from the autobiography, and afterwards some passages from *Corydon* and the *Journal*.

THE ADMISSIONS OF MARCEL PROUST

14 May

Spent an hour yesterday evening with Proust. For the last four days he has been sending an auto after me every evening, but each time it missed me . . . Yesterday, as I had just happened to tell him that I did not expect to be free, he was getting ready to go out, having made an appointment outside. He says that he has not been out of bed for a long time. Although it is stifling in the room in which he receives me, he is shivering; he has just left another, much hotter room in which he was covered with perspiration; he complains that his life is nothing but a slow agony, and although having begun, as soon as I arrived, to talk of homosexuality, he interrupted himself to ask me if I can enlighten him as to the teaching of the Gospels, for someone or other has told him that I talk particularly well on the subject. He hopes to find in the Gospels some support and relief for his sufferings, which he depicts at length as atrocious. He is fat, or rather puffy; he reminds me somewhat of Jean Lorrain. I am taking him *Corydon*, of which he promises not to speak to anyone; and when I say a word or two about my memoirs:

'You can tell anything,' he exclaims, 'but on condition that you never say: I.' But that won't suit me.

Far from denying or hiding his homosexuality, he exhibits it, and I could almost say boasts of it. He claims never to have loved women save spiritually and never to have known love except with men. His conversation, ceaselessly cut by parenthetical clauses, runs on without continuity. He tells me his conviction that Baudelaire was homosexual: 'The way he speaks of Lesbos, and the mere need of speaking of it, would be enough to convince me,' and when I protest:

'In any case, if he was homosexual, it was almost without his knowing it; and you don't believe that he ever practised . . .'

'What!' he exclaims. 'I am sure of the contrary; how can you doubt that he practised? He, Baudelaire!'

And in the tone of his voice it is implied that by doubting I am insulting Baudelaire. But I am willing to believe that he is right; and that homosexuals are even a bit more numerous than I thought at first. In any case I did not think that Proust was exclusively so.

(*Journal* 1921, tr. Justin O'Brien, Secker & Warburg)

Last night I was about to go to bed when the bell rang. It was Proust's chauffeur, Celeste's husband, bringing back the copy of *Corydon* that I lent to Proust on 14 May and offering to take me back with him, for Proust is somewhat better and sends a message that he can receive me if it is not inconvenient for me to come. His sentence is much longer and more complicated than I am quoting it; I imagine he learned it on the way, for when I interrupted him at first, he began it all over again and recited it in one breath. Celeste, likewise, when she opened the door to me the other evening, after having expressed Proust's regret at not being able to receive me, added: 'Monsieur begs Monsieur Gide to have no doubt that he is thinking constantly of him.' (I noted the sentence right away.)

For a long time I wondered if Proust did not take advantage somewhat of his illness to protect his work (and this seemed quite legitimate to me); but yesterday, and already the other day, I could see that he is really seriously ill. He says he spends hours on end without being able even to move his head; he stays in bed all day long, and for days on end. At moments he rubs the side of his nose with the edge of a hand that seems dead, with its fingers oddly stiff and separated, and nothing could be more impressive than this finicky, awkward gesture, which seems the gesture of an animal or a madman.

We scarcely talked, this evening again, of anything but homosexuality. He says he blames himself for that 'indecision' which made him, in order to fill out the heterosexual part of his book, transpose '*à l'ombre des jeunes filles*' all the attractive, affectionate, and charming elements contained in his homosexual recollections, so that for *Sodome* he is left nothing but the grotesque and the abject. But he shows himself to be very much concerned when I tell him that he seems to have wanted to stigmatize homosexuality; he protests; and eventually I understand that what we consider vile, an object of laughter or disgust, does not seem so repulsive to him.

When I ask him if he will ever present that Eros in a young and beautiful guise, he replies that, to begin with, what attracts him is almost never beauty and that he considers it to have very little do do with desire – and that, as for youth, this was what he could most easily transpose (what lent itself best to a transposition).

(*Ibid.*)

*   *   *

AN EVENING WITH WILDE

Nothing betrayed the café; its door was like all the other doors, half-open, we didn't have to knock. Wilde was an habitué of this place, which I have described in *Amyntas*, because as it turned out I was to go back there often. Some old Arabs were there, squatting on straw mats and smoking *kief*, but they did not move when we took our place beside them. And at first I didn't understand what it was in this café that could attract Wilde; soon, though, I made out in the shadows, near the cinder hearth, a *caouadji*, still quite young, who prepared for us two cups of ginger tea, which Wilde preferred to coffee. I was letting myself fall into a half doze with the strange torpor of the place when, in the partly opened doorway, a marvellous youth appeared. He stood there for some time, elbow raised high and leaning on the door-frame, loosening himself from the background of night. He seemed uncertain whether he should enter and I was already scared that he might go away again when he smiled at a sign made by Wilde and came to sit down in front of us on a stool which was a bit lower than the covered platform on which we were perching in the Arab manner. He pulled out of his Tunisian waistcoat a rosewood flute, which he began to play exquisitely. A little later Wilde told me that his name was Mohammed and that he was 'Bosy's boy'; if he'd hesitated at first to come into the café it was because he didn't see Lord Alfred there. His great black eyes had that languorous expression which is given by hashish; he had an olive skin; I admired the elongation of his fingers upon the flute, the smoothness of his childish body, the grace of the naked legs which thrust from the puffed white breeches, one crossed over the knee of the other. The *caouadji* had just sat down near him and was accompanying him on a species of *darbouka*. Like a constant limpid stream the music of the flute rippled across the extraordinary silence till one forgot time and place, who one was and all the cares of the world. We stayed thus, without moving, for what seemed to me an eternity, but I would have remained very much longer if Wilde hadn't suddenly seized my arm, breaking the enchantment.

– Come, he said.

We went out. We took some paces along the alley, followed by the hideous guide, and I thought that the evening must already have achieved its purpose when, at the first turning, Wilde stopped, let his huge hand fall on my shoulder and, leaning towards me – for he was much taller – said in a low voice:

– *Dear*, do you want the little musician?

Oh, how dark the alley was! I felt my heart failing me. What a surge of courage was needed for me to reply 'Yes' and in what a strangled voice!

Wilde immediately turned towards the guide, who had rejoined us, and slipped into his ear some words I did not distinguish. The guide left us, and we returned to the place where our carriage stood.

We were no sooner seated than Wilde began to laugh, to laugh loudly, with a laugh not so much of joy as of triumph; with a laugh that was endless, masterless, insolent; and the more he saw that I was disconcerted by this laugh, the more he continued. I should add that if Wilde was beginning to reveal his own way of life to me, he still knew nothing of mine; I saw to it that nothing in my remarks or actions gave him cause for the least suspicion. The proposal he had just made me was bold; what amused him so much was that it had not been repulsed. He was as delighted as a child and as a devil. The greatest pleasure of debauchery is to lead others to debauch. Since my adventure at Susa, doubtless the Fiend could no longer score a great victory over me, but this Wilde in no way knew, nor that I was conquered in advance – or if you prefer it (for should one speak of defeat when the front-line is so well re-formed?) that I had triumphed, in imagination, in thought, over all my scruples. To tell the truth I wasn't conscious of this myself; it was only, I think, in answering 'Yes' that I realized it abruptly.

Now and then, checking his laugh, Wilde excused himself.

– Forgive me for laughing in this way, but it's stronger than I am. I can't stop myself.

He laughed again when we stopped in front of a café on the theatre square, where we took leave of our carriage.

– It's still too early, Wilde told me. And I didn't dare ask him what he had arranged with the guide, nor where, how or when the little musician would come to rejoin me; and I began to doubt whether the proposition he had made me would have a result, for I feared, by questioning him, to reveal too much the violence of my desire.

Wilde made me drink a cocktail and drank several himself. We waited patiently for about half an hour. How long the time seemed to me! Wilde laughed again, but not so convulsively, and when we

occasionally spoke it was of nothing important. At last I saw him pull
out his watch.

– It's time, he said, getting up.

We walked towards a more populous quarter . . . the ugliest in the
city, but which formerly must have been one of the most beautiful.
Wilde preceded me into a house with a double entry but we had
scarcely crossed the threshold when two enormous policemen, who
must have come in by the other door, surged towards us, positively
terrifying me. Wilde was much amused at my fear.

– *Aoh!*, dear, it's to the contrary. It proves that this hotel is very safe.
They come here to protect foreigners. I know them, they're excellent
chaps who are exceedingly fond of my cigarettes. They understand
very well.

We let these cops precede us. They went up past the second floor
where we stopped. Wilde took a key out of his pocket and introduced
me into a tiny flat of two rooms where, after a moment, the unlovely
guide rejoined us. The two youths followed him, each wrapped in a
burnous which hid his face. The guide departed. Wilde made me go
into the farther chamber with little Mohammed and shut himself
in the first room with the *darbouka* player.

Since then, every time I have sought pleasure I have turned back to
the memory of that night. After my adventure in Susa I had wretchedly
sank again into the habit of masturbation. Sexual satisfaction, if once or
twice I had succeeded in plucking it in passing, had been furtively
achieved – deliciously though, one evening, in a boat with a young
boatman of the Lake of Como while my ecstasy was surrounded by
the moonlight, the misty enchantment of the lake and the moist scents
of its shores. Then nothing: nothing but a frightful desert full of appeals
without response, exhilarations without completion, inquietudes,
struggles, disturbing dreams, imaginary joys, abominable lapses. At
La Roque, the summer of the preceding year, I had thought I was going
mad . . .

Ah, from what a hell I emerged! And not a friend to whom I could
speak, not a single adviser – having believed every solution impossible
and having wished nothing but to confess myself defeated, I felt
myself floundering . . . But need I evoke those lugubrious days?
Does their recall explain the delirium of that night? The experiment
with Meriem had been an attempt at 'normalisation' which had
remained without a future, for it in no way enlisted my senses; it was

now I found my normality. Here there was no longer any constraint, precipitousness, doubt; nothing ashen in the memory I keep; my joy was immense and such that I cannot imagine it richer if love had been part of it. How had I allowed desire to dispose of my heart? My pleasure was without afterthought and must not be followed by any remorse. But how shall I express the delights of rocking in my bare arms this perfect little body, savage, ardent, lascivious and shadowy?

I stayed there a long time afterwards, when Mohammed had left me, in a state of trembling jubilation and although I had already attained the supreme moment five times beside him I revived my ecstasy a number of times more and then, back in the hotel, prolonged its echoes until morning.

. . . In the first pale light of the dawn I got up; I ran, yes really ran, in sandals, well beyond Mustapha, feeling no tiredness from my night but rather a quickening, a sort of lightness of the spirit and the flesh, which did not leave me all the day.

(*Si Le Grain Ne Meurt*, N.R.F.)

★   ★   ★

A SCIENTIFIC APPROACH

. . . The giant of science is just as rare as any other man of genius; demi-scientists abound who will accept a traditional theory to guide or mislead them, who rely on it alone for all their 'observations'. For ages, everything confirmed Nature's abhorrence of a vacuum; yes, all *observations*. Everything still confirms, at the present time, this theory of *sexual instinct* – so much so that the astonishment of some breeders is really comic when they notice homosexual habits prevalent among the species with which they are concerned; and each of these modest 'observers', limiting his observation to the species in which he is interested, notes down these habits, believing them to be a monstrous exception. 'Pigeons appear to be especially (!) prone to sexual perversion, if we believe M. J. Bailly, the competent master breeder and *astute observer*,' writes Havelock Ellis, and Mucciolo, 'The Italian scientist, *who is an authority on pigeons* (!) affirms that practices of inversion are testified to amongst Belgian carrier pigeons (!) *even in the presence of many females.*'

'Oh, come now – *The Two Pigeons* of La Fontaine?'

'They were French pigeons, so set your mind at rest. Another man observes the same behaviour in ducks, since he breeds ducks. Lacassagne, being interested in chickens, finds the same behaviour in chickens. Was it not in partridges that Bouvard or Pecuchet claimed to come across such habits? Yes, nothing could be more comic than these timid observations unless it be the conclusion they draw from them or the explanation they give them. Dr. X, having noted the great frequency of copulation between male cockchafers, argues to excuse their naughtiness.'

'Yes. That's what I was saying just now: only the male, fresh from copulation, and still reeking of the female, can offer any pretext for assault.'

'Is Dr. X really certain of what he says? Was it in fact only after mating that the males were assaulted? Did he scrupulously *observe* it, or did he not rather *assume* it for convenience' sake? I suggest this experiment – I would like to know whether a dog, deprived of all sense of smell, would not in consequence be condemned to . . .'

'To homosexuality pure and simple?'

'Or at least to celibacy, to a complete lack of heterosexual desires. But, because the dog only craves the bitch when she is in good odour, it does not, for that reason, follow that for the rest of the time his desire is dormant. And that is how the great frequency of their homosexual games comes about.

'You could easily notice it for yourself; but I know that most of the time passers-by, who see from a distance two dogs mounting each other, infer the sex of each from the position it occupies. May I take the liberty of telling you a story? It happened in one of the boulevards of Paris. Two dogs had got coupled in the pitiful manner you know well enough; each of them, completely satiated, dragged itself to get free; their opposing efforts caused considerable embarrassment to some and considerable amusement to others. I approached. Three male dogs were prowling round the group, attracted no doubt by the smell. One of them, either bolder or more excited, unable to hold back any longer, attempted to assault the couple. I saw him achieve, several times, the most difficult acrobatics in order to mount one of the coupled pair. There were quite a number of us there, as I say, watching the scene from more or less virtuous motives; but I'll wager that I was the only one to notice this fact; it was the male, and the male only, that the other dog wanted to mount. He wilfully disregarded the female; he continually exerted himself and, as the other was attached and could hardly resist, he was not far off attaining his object – when a policeman appeared and at one stroke dispersed both actors and audience.'

(*Corydon*, Second Dialogue, Secker & Warburg)

SAVAGE NUDITY

'I must admit that, in fact, so much artifice, so constantly called in as aid to nature, distresses me. I remember a passage in Montaigne: *It is not so much modesty as guile and wisdom, that makes our ladies so circumspect in denying us entry to their boudoirs before they are prinked and painted for the public gaze.* And I feel a bit doubtful whether, as conceived by Pierre Louys in *Trypheme*, an ordinary and open exposure of the favours of the fair sex, the custom of displaying oneself stark naked in both town and country, would not lead to a very different result from that which he predicts: Whether, indeed, man's desire for the other sex would not cool off somewhat. *It remains to be seen*, said Mademoiselle Guinault, *whether all the objects which excite in us so many charming and naughty feelings because they are hidden from sight, would not leave us cold and lethargic if exposed to perpetual contemplation; for there are instances of this sort of thing.* Indeed there are peoples, and the most beautiful in fact, in whom *Trypheme* achieves reality (or did, at any rate, fifty years ago, before the missionaries got to work), Tahiti, for example, when Darwin landed there in 1835. For several moving pages he describes the splendour of the natives, then he adds: *I admit that I was a trifle disillusioned by the women; they are far from being as handsome as the men* . . . Then, having proved the need for them to compensate for this lack of beauty by finery, he goes on: *It seemed to me that the women, far more than the men, greatly gained by wearing some form of garment.*'[1]

'I never realized that Darwin was a pederast!'

'Who said so?'

'Doesn't that sentence make it clear?'

'What! Are you forcing me to take M. de Courmont seriously when he writes: *It is a woman who represents Beauty. All divergent opinion will*

---

[1] See 'Exotic Encounters' below for Darwin's description – rather less than the 'several moving pages' recalled by Gide.

eternally be looked upon as a paradox or as the product of the most regrettable of sexual aberrations.'

'Eternally' seems to you a little strong?'

'Don't get excited! Darwin, as far as I know, was no more homosexual than many other explorers who, travelling among naked peoples, have marvelled at the beauty of the young men – no more homosexual than Stevenson, for instance, who, in speaking about the Polynesians, recognised that the beauty of the young men greatly surpassed that of the women. And that is precisely where their opinion is so important to me and why I agree with them, not as a Puritan, but as an artist, that modesty becomes a woman and concealment is most fitting for her – "quod decet".'

(*Ibid.*, Third Dialogue)

★   ★   ★

FROM THE JOURNALS

Emile X used to work in his father's tailoring shop. But for the last two months the fact that they are working on half-time leaves him free almost every day. And every day he spends his whole afternoon at the baths. He gets there at one and stays there until seven. Is that why he is as beautiful as a Greek statue? He swims remarkably well; and nothing so much as swimming imposes a rhythm, a harmony on one's muscles, or so hardens and strengthens them. Naked he is perfectly at ease; it is when clothed that he seems awkward. In his workman's clothes I hardly recognised him. Most likely he also owes to the habit of nudity the dull and even lustre of his flesh. Everywhere his skin is blond and downy; on the hollows of his sacrum, exactly on the spot where ancient statuary puts the little tufts on fauns, this slight down becomes darker. And indeed yesterday afternoon, in the Praxiteles pose, his shoulder leaning against the wall of the pool, firmly and most naturally planted like the Apollo Saurochtonus, with his slightly snub-nosed and mocking face, he looked like a latterday faun.

He is fifteen, one sister and one brother; all the remains of eleven children.

(*Journal* 1902, tr. Justin O'Brien)

My most recent adventures have left me an inexpressible disgust.

(*Journal* 1910)

Feel voluptuously that it is more natural to go to bed naked than in a nightshirt. My window is wide open and the moon shone directly on my bed. I remembered with anguish the beautiful night of the Rathan; but I felt no desire, either in my heart or in my mind any more than in my flesh. With what stiflings would I have heard last year Armand's flute, this evening calling me doubtfully in the darkness, O stammering melody, how I loved you on the edge of the desert! . . . But this was not even a regret; I was calm.

(Ibid.)

Saturday, 17 February
I can only note in haste the rather whirlwind life of the last few days. I am writing seated on a bench in the Bois; the weather was radiant this morning; this is the secret of my happiness. But already the sky is clouding over again; I need Apollo; I must set out.

(Journal 1912)

It has been said that I am chasing after my youth. This is true. And not only after my own. Even more than beauty, youth attracts me, and with an irresistible appeal. I believe the truth lies in youth; I believe it is always right against us. I believe that, far from trying to teach it, it is from youth that we, the elders, must seek our lessons. And I am well aware that youth is capable of errors; I know that our role is to forewarn youth as best we can; but I believe that often, when trying to protect youth, we impede it. I believe that each new generation arrives bearing a message that it must deliver; our role is to help that delivery. I believe that what is called 'experience' is often but an unavowed fatigue, resignation, blighted hope. I believe to be true, tragically true, this remark of Alfred de Vigny, often quoted, which seems simple only to those who quote it without understanding it: 'A fine life is a thought conceived in youth and realized in maturity.' It matters little to me, besides, that Vigny himself perhaps did not see all the meaning I put into it; I make that remark mine.

There are very few of my contemporaries who have remained faithful to their youth. They have almost all compromised. That is what they call 'learning from life'. They have denied the truth that was in them. The borrowed truths are the ones to which one clings most tenaciously, and all the more so since they remain foreign to our intimate self. It takes much more precaution to deliver one's own message, much more boldness and prudence, than to sign up with and add one's voice to an already existing party. Whence that accusation of indecision and uncertainty that some hurl at me, precisely because I believe that it is above all to oneself that it is important to remain faithful.

(Journal 1921)

Had Socrates and Plato not loved young men, what a pity for Greece, what a pity for the whole world!

Had Socrates and Plato not loved young men and aimed to please them, each one of us would be a little less sensible.

(Journal 1918)

★ ★ ★

MARCEL PROUST (1871–1922) That the author of *A La Recherche Du Temps Perdu* was primarily devoted to men is now admitted, although his affection for women was also genuine and there is no reason to suppose that the great novel's transposition of sexes applies, say, to the 'young girls in flower' despite their tomboy antics and Gide's opinion of them. On the other hand, the achingly meticulous and neurotic analysis of the affair with Albertine owes much to Proust's experiences with Reynaldo Hahn, Lucien Daudet and such simple people as his chauffeur-secretary, Alfred Agostinelli.

Proust knew Society homosexuals like Baron Doason and Comte Robert de Montesquiou well and doubtless drew on them for his M. de Quercy, a preliminary sketch for the formidable Baron de Charlus whose portly shadow falls across so many of the book's later pages, in which a number of characters the reader had taken for normal reveal themselves as sulphurously involved. For, as Gide pointed out, the inverts are scrutinized with a merciless eye; it is in the general sensibility of the book, the poetry of childhood and youth, and the aesthetic reveries, that their charm and romance may be felt.

M. DE QUERCY

But even as I said this to myself, I seemed to see a magical reversal taking place in M. de Quercy. He had not moved, but all of a sudden he was illuminated by a light from within, in which everything about him that I had found startling, perplexing, contradictory, had been harmoniously resolved as soon as I said those words to myself: 'One would take him for a woman'. I had understood, he *was* one. He was one of them. He belonged to that race of beings who are in effect, since it is precisely because their temperament is feminine that they worship manliness, at cross-purposes with themselves, who go through life apparently in step with other men, but bearing about with them on that little disk of the eye's pupil, through which we look at the world and on which our desire is engraved, the body, not of a nymph but of a youth, who casts his shadow, virile and erect, over all they see and all they do. A race accursed, since the thing which is for it the ideal of beauty and the food of love is also the embodiment of shame and the dread of punishment, a race compelled to live in falsehood and perjury, even when it comes to defend itself before the seat of justice and in the sight of Christ; since its desire, if it knew how to comprehend it, would be in some way unadmittable, because loving only those men who are completely manly, men who are single-sexed, it is only with such a man that it can appease a desire it ought not to feel for him, and which he ought not to feel in return – if the need for love were not an arch-cheat, and did not make it see in the most ignominious pansy the likeness of a man, of a real man like other men, who by a miracle would feel love for it, or stoop to it; since like criminals it must perforce hide its secret from those it holds dearest, dreading the grief of a family, the scorn of friends, the criminal code of a country; a race accursed, persecuted like Israel, and finally, like Israel, under a mass opprobrium of undeserved abhorrence, taking on mass characteristics, the physiognomy of a nation; all with certain characteristic features, physical features that are often repulsive, that sometimes are beautiful, all with a woman's loving, breakable heart, but with a woman's suspicions, her wilful, coquettish, tale-bearing nature, a woman's knack for being clever at everything, a woman's incapacity to do anything supremely well; cut off from family life, where they can never be quite open, from national life, where they would be regarded as undisclosed criminals, cut off even from their fellows, in whom they

inspire the chagrin of discovering in their own bosoms the warning
that the thing that they believe to be a natural love is a sickly madness –
as well as that womanliness which offends them; yet for all that, loving
hearts, cut off from friendship because when a simple friendliness is all
they feel, their friends may suspect an intention of something other
than friendship and, if they should own to feeling something else,
would not understand it; now the object of a blind incomprehension
which can only love them by not understanding them, now of an
aversion which condemns them for what is purest in them, now of a
curiosity which wants to account for them and sees them all askew,
working out a barrack-room broadmindedness towards them which
even when it supposes itself impartial is still biased and admits *a priori*
– like those judges for whom to be a Jew is to be a traitor – that
homosexuality can easily lead to murder; like Israel, still aspiring
towards what they are not, what they never could be, and yet feeling
for one another, under a show of slander and rivalry, and a contempt of
the least perverted for the most perverted like that of the most desemi-
tised Jew for the little Jew in the slop-shop, a profound solidarity – a
kind of freemasonry which is wider than that of the ghetto because
nothing is known about it and no bounds can be set to it, and inherently
more powerful than real freemasonry because it rests on a natural
conformity, on identity of taste, of need, of theory and practice, so to
speak, between the man in the cab and the guttersnipe who opens the
cab-door, or sometimes more painfully between him and his daughter's
suitor, or again with bitter irony between him and the doctor to whom
he goes to be cured of his perversion, or the man of the world who
blackballs him at the club, or the priest who hears his confession, or
the advocate who cross-examines him in a court or court-martial,
or the sovereign in whose name he is prosecuted; endlessly harping
with persevering (or exasperating) satisfaction on the theme that Cato
was a homosexual, as Jews harp on the theme that Christ was a Jew,
never understanding that just as there were no Jews before the death of
Christ there was no such thing as homosexuality in an epoch when it
was as customary and befitting to live with a young man as nowadays
it is to keep a ballet-dancer, when Socrates, the most virtuous man
there ever was, cracked jokes about two youths sitting side by side, as
we might do about a nephew and niece who make eyes at each other,
jokes that come quite naturally and which are clearer evidence of a
way of society than opinions, which might have been merely personal

to him – so that, original as it may be, the sin of homosexuality dates its historical origin from when, having lost its good name, it did not conform; but thenceforward by its resistance to exhortation, example, contempt, the sentence of the law, giving proof of a disposition that other men know to be so strong and so ingrained that they are more repelled by it than by crimes which drive a coach and horses through the ten commandments – for a crime can be a momentary thing, and theft or murder everyone can understand, but not homosexuality; the reprobate tribe of humankind, yes, but for all that, essentially, invisibly, innumerably, a branch of the human family, suspected where it does not exist, flaunting insolent and unpunished where it is not recognised, and everywhere, in the streets, in the ranks, in the house of God, at the theatre, in the prison, on the throne, mutually rending and supporting itself, unwilling to recognise itself yet recognising itself, and divining a fellow in one whom it would be most loth to admit to itself – still less have others know – it is in fellowship with; living on terms of household intimacy with those who at the sight of its offence, should a scandal break out, would turn savage as do wild animals at the sight of blood, but accustomed, seeing them at peace with it in daily life, to play with them like a lion-tamer, to talk homosexuality, to provoke their growls (so that nowhere does one talk homosexuality so freely as before a homosexual) till that day comes, as soon or late it must, when it will be torn to pieces – like the poet to whom every London drawing-room was open – it and its works prosecuted, it not able to find a roof to shelter it, nor they, a theatre to perform them, and after expiation and death seeing its statue put up above its grave; compelled to travesty its feelings, to alter its words, to put she for he, to find pretexts in its own eyes for its friendships and its angers, more hampered by compliance with the inner need, and the imperious command of its vice that it should not believe itself a prey to vice, than by the social obligation to keep its inclinations out of sight; a race whose pride is set on not being a race, or not differing from the rest of the world, lest its desires should seem like a sickness and their very fulfilment like an impossibility, its pleasures like illusions, its characteristics like blemishes, so that the first pages, (so I believe) since there have been men and men have written, that have been dedicated to it in a spirit of justice towards its virtues of soul and mind – which are not disfigured by it, as people say – and in a spirit of pity for its innate ill-starredness and its undeserved sufferings, will be those that will make it angriest to hear, and most reluctant to read, because if in the depth of almost every Jew there is an anti-Semite whom we best flatter when we attribute every kind of fault to him but treat him as a Christian, so in the depth of every homosexual there is an anti-homosexual to whom we cannot offer a greater insult than by acknowledging that he has talents, virtues, intellect, heart, and in sum, like all human characters, the right to enjoy love in the form that nature allows us to conceive of it, though respect for truth meanwhile compels us to confess that this form of love is strange, and that these men are not like other men.

· · · · ·

Some of them, taciturn and marvellously handsome, beautiful Andromedas chained to a sex that vows them to solitude, have eyes where the anguish of unattainable Paradise is reflected with a splendour to which the women who die for love of them flutter like moths killing themselves for love; hateful to those whose love they seek, they cannot satisfy the love their beauty awakens. And in others again, the woman is almost half-declared. Her breasts emerge from them, they seize every opportunity of fancy dress to show them off, they are as fond of dancing and dress and cosmetics as girls are, and at the most sedate gatherings break into giggling fits, or start singing.

I remember seeing at Querqueville a young man, much laughed at by his brothers and friends, who used to take solitary walks on the beach; he had a charming, thoughtful, melancholy face, and long black hair, whose raven hue he burnished in secret by dusting a sort of blue powder over it. He reddened his lips a little, though he pretended their colour was natural. He spent hours alone on the beach, walking or sitting on the rocks, searching the blue horizon with sad eyes, anxious and insistent even then, asking himself if this expanse of sea and pale blue sky, the same bright sky that looked down on Marathon and Salamis, would not show him, borne on the swiftly advancing boat and coming to carry him away, that Antinous of whom he dreamed all day and every night, sitting at the window of the holiday villa, where the belated passer-by saw him in the light of the moon, staring out at the night, and quickly moving back when someone noticed him. Still too innocent to suppose that such a desire as his could exist elsewhere than in books, never thinking that it could have any sort of bearing on the scenes of debauchery we associate it with, putting them on the same level as theft or murder, always going back to his rock to look at the sky and the sea, and ignoring the port where the seamen ask no better than to pick up a wage, however they may earn it. But his unacknow-ledged desire was plainly to be seen in his aloofness from his friends, or in the oddity of his talk and behaviour when he was with them. They sampled his rouge, laughed at his blue powder and his melan-choly; and wearing blue trousers and a sailor's cap, he went for his sad, solitary walks, consumed by weariness and self-reproach.

.   .   .   .   .

[When M. de Quercy was] a little boy, when his playmates told him about the pleasures of going with a woman, he pressed up against them, supposing he only partook in a common wish for the same excitements. Later on, he felt that they would not be the same; he felt it, but did not say so, nor say so to himself. On moonless nights he went out of his castle in Poitou and followed the lane into the road that goes to the castle of his cousin, Guy de Gressac. Here, at the cross-roads, they met, and on the grass bank they renewed what had been the games of their childhood, and parted from each other without having spoken a word, nor ever spoke a word about it during the day-time when they met and talked, maintaining rather a sort of enmity against each other, but from time to time meeting again in darkness, silently, as if it were an encounter between the ghosts of their childish selves. But his cousin who had become Prince de Guermantes took mistresses, and was only occasionally re-assailed by the fantastic recollection. And after waiting for hours on the grass bank at the crossroad, M. de Quercy often went home heavy-hearted. Then his cousin married, and from that time forward he only saw him as a laughing talking man, on rather cool terms with him, for all that, and never felt the ghost's embrace again.

Meanwhile, Hubert de Quercy lived on in his castle, lonelier than any medieval lady in her bower. When he went to catch the train at the railway station, for all that he had never spoken to the man, he regretted that the queerness of the legal code did not allow him to make the station-master his bride; infatuated though he was about noble lineage, perhaps he could have put up with the disparity in rank. And when the lieutenant-colonel whom he had eyed during the manœuvres went off to another garrison town, he would have liked to be able to move house. His pleasures consisted of coming down from time to time from the tower-room, where he grew as bored as Patient Grizel, and, after innumerable falterings, going into the kitchen to tell the butcher that the last leg of mutton was rather tough, or to collect his letters from the postman. Then he went up into his tower again, and studied his ancestors' pedigrees. One evening, he went so far as to put a drunk man back on the right road; on another occasion, meeting a blind man whose shirt was undone, he buttoned it up for him.

He went to Paris. He was in his twenty-fifth year, extremely good-looking and, for a man of fashion, witty, while his peculiar tastes had not as yet encompassed his person with that vexed aura which later would mark it out. But an Andromeda fettered to a sex he was in no way designed for, his eyes were filled with a nostalgia that made women fall in love with him, and while he was a thing of loathing to those he was attracted to, he could not wholeheartedly share the passions he inspired. He had mistresses. A woman killed herself for him. He began to go about with various young men of the aristocracy whose tastes were the same as his.

Who, seeing those elegant young people grouped round a table, and knowing them to be loved by women, could suspect that they were talking of pleasures incomprehensible to the rest of mankind. They hate and pour scorn on others of their race, and never go near them. They snobbishly cultivate the society of men who love only women, and go nowhere else. But they like to make merry with one or two others as well-whitened as themselves, and to feel a racial bond. Sometimes, when no one else is there, a tribal word or a ritual gesture escapes them, launched on an impulse of deliberate mockery, but from an unconscious solidarity and a deep-lying pleasure.

(*By Way of Sainte-Beuve*, tr. Sylvia Townsend Warner,
Chatto & Windus)

★　★　★

DE CHARLUS AND JUPIEN: BEE AND ORCHID

. . . I had felt it to be more convenient, when I thought that the Duke and Duchess were on the point of returning, to post myself on the staircase . . . [There I had the opportunity of] peering through the shutters of the staircase window at the Duchess's little tree and at the precious plant, exposed in the courtyard with that insistence with which mothers 'bring out' their marriageable offspring, and asking myself whether the unlikely insect would come, by a providential hazard, to visit the offered and neglected pistil. My curiosity emboldening me by degrees, I went down to the ground-floor window, which also stood open with its shutters ajar. I could hear distinctly, as he got ready to go out, Jupien[1] who could not detect me behind my blind, where I stood perfectly still until the moment when I drew quickly aside in order not to be seen by M. de Charlus, who, on his way to call upon Mme de Villeparisis, was slowly crossing the courtyard, a pursy figure, aged by the strong light, his hair visibly grey. Nothing short of an indisposition of Mme de Villeparisis . . . could have made M. de Charlus pay a call, perhaps for the first time in his life, at that hour of the day. For with that eccentricity of the Guermantes, who, instead of conforming to the ways of society, used to modify them to suit their own personal habits (habits not, they thought, social, and deserving in consequence the abasement before them of that thing of no value, Society – thus it was that Mme de Marsantes had no regular 'day', but was at home to her friends every morning between ten o'clock and noon), the Baron, reserving those hours for reading, hunting for old curiosities and so forth, paid calls only between four and six in the afternoon. At six o' clock he went to the Jockey Club, or took a stroll in the Bois. A moment later, I again recoiled, in order not to be seen by Jupien. It was nearly time for him to start for the office, from which he would return only for dinner, and not even then always during the last week, his niece and her apprentices having gone to the country to finish a dress there for a customer. Then, realising that no one could see me, I decided not to let myself be disturbed again, for fear of missing, should the miracle be fated to occur, the arrival, almost beyond the possibility of hope (across so many obstacles of distance, of adverse risks, of dangers), of the insect sent from so far as ambassador to the virgin who had so long been waiting for him to appear. I knew that this expectancy was no more passive than in the male flower, whose stamens had spontaneously curved so that the insect might more easily receive their offering; similarly the female flower that stood here, if the insect came, would coquettishly arch her styles, and, to be more effectively penetrated by him, would imperceptibly advance, like a hypocritical but ardent damsel, to meet

[1] The Guermantes' tailor.

him half-way. The laws of the vegetable kingdom are themselves governed by other laws, increasingly exalted . . . My reflexions had followed a tendency which I shall describe in due course, and I had already drawn from the visible stratagems of flowers a conclusion that bore upon a whole unconscious element of literary work, when I saw M. de Charlus coming away from the Marquise. Perhaps he had learned from his elderly relative herself, or merely from a servant, the great improvement, or rather her complete recovery from what had been nothing more than a slight indisposition. At this moment, when he did not suspect that anyone was watching him, his eyelids lowered as a screen against the sun, M. de Charlus had relaxed that tension in his face, deadened that artificial vitality, which the animation of his talk and the force of his will kept in evidence there as a rule. Pale as marble, his nose stood out firmly, his fine features no longer received from an expression deliberately assumed a different meaning which altered the beauty of their modelling; nothing more now than a Guermantes, he seemed already carved in stone, he Palamède the Fifteenth, in their chapel at Combray. These general features of a whole family took on, however, in the face of M. de Charlus a fineness more spiritualised, above all more gentle. I regretted for his sake that he should habitually adulterate with so many acts of violence, offensive oddities, tale-bearings, with such harshness, susceptibility and arrogance, that he should conceal beneath a false brutality the amenity, the kindness which, at the moment of his emerging from Mme de Villeparisis's, I could see displayed so innocently upon his face. Blinking his eyes in the sunlight, he seemed almost to be smiling, I found in his face seen thus in repose and, so to speak, in its natural state something so affectionate, so disarmed, that I could not help thinking how angry M. de Charlus would have been could he have known that he was being watched; for what was suggested to me by the sight of this man who was so insistent, who prided himself so upon his virility, to whom all other men seemed odiously effeminate, what he made me suddenly think of, so far had he momentarily assumed her features, expression, smile, was a woman.

I was about to change my position again, so that he should not catch sight of me; I had neither the time nor the need to do so. What did I see? Face to face, in that courtyard where certainly they had never met before (M. de Charlus coming to the Hôtel de Guermantes only in the afternoon, during the time when Jupien was at his office), the Baron, having suddenly opened wide his half-shut eyes, was studying with unusual attention the ex-tailor poised on the threshold of his shop, while the latter, fastened suddenly to the ground before M. de Charlus, taking root in it like a plant, was contemplating with a look of amazement the plump form of the middle-aged Baron. But, more astounding still, M. de Charlus's attitude having changed, Jupien's, as though in obedience to the laws of an occult art, at once brought itself into harmony with it. The Baron, who was now seeking to conceal the impression that had been made on him, and yet, in spite of his affectation of indifference, seemed unable to move away without regret, went, came, looked vaguely into the distance in the way which, he felt, most enhanced the beauty of his eyes, assumed a complacent, careless, fatuous air. Meanwhile Jupien, shedding at once the humble, honest expression which I had always associated with him, had – in perfect symmetry with the Baron – thrown up his head, given a becoming tilt to his body, placed his hand with a grotesque impertinence on his hip, stuck out his behind, posed himself with the coquetry that the orchid might have adopted on the providential arrival of the bee. I had not supposed that he could appear so repellent. But I was equally unaware that he was capable of improvising his part in this sort of dumb charade, which (albeit he found himself for the first time in the presence of M. de Charlus) seemed to have been long and carefully rehearsed; one does not arrive spontaneously at that pitch of perfection except when one meets in a foreign country a compatriot with whom an understanding then grows up of itself, both parties speaking the same language, even although they have never seen one another before.

This scene was not, however, positively comic, it was stamped with a strangeness, or if you like a naturalness, the beauty of which steadily increased. M. de Charlus might indeed assume a detached air, indifferently let his eyelids droop; every now and then he raised them, and at such moments turned on Jupien an attentive gaze. But (doubtless because he felt that such a scene could not be prolonged indefinitely in this place, whether for reasons which we shall learn later on, or possibly from that feeling of the brevity of all things which makes us determine that every blow must strike home, and renders so moving the spectacle of every kind of love), each time that M. de Charlus looked at Jupien, he took care that his glance should be accompanied by a spoken word, which made it infinitely unlike the glances we usually direct at a person whom we do or do not know; he stared at

Jupien with the peculiar fixity of the person who is about to say to us:
'Excuse my taking the liberty, but you have a long white thread hanging down your back,' or else: 'Surely I can't be mistaken, you come
from Zürich too; I'm certain I must have seen you there often in the
curiosity shop.' Thus, every other minute, the same question seemed to
be being intensely put to Jupien in the stare of M. de Charlus, like those
questioning phrases of Beethoven indefinitely repeated at regular
intervals, and intended – with an exaggerated lavishness of prepara-
tion – to introduce a new theme, a change of tone, a 're-entry'. On
the other hand, the beauty of the reciprocal glances of M. de Charlus
and Jupien arose precisely from the fact that they did not, for the
moment at least, seem to be intended to lead to anything further. This
beauty, it was the first time that I had seen the Baron and Jupien display
it. In the eyes of both of them, it was the sky not of Zürich but of
some Oriental city, the name of which I had not yet divined, that I
saw reflected. Whatever the point might be that held M. de Charlus
and the ex-tailor thus arrested, their pact seemed concluded and these
superfluous glances to be but ritual preliminaries, like the parties that
people give before a marriage which has been definitely 'arranged'.
Nearer still to nature – and the multiplicity of these analogies is itself
all the more natural in that the same man, if we examine him for a
few minutes, appears in turn as a man, a man-bird or man-insect, and
so forth – one would have called them a pair of birds, the male and the
female, the male seeking to make advances, the female – Jupien – no
longer giving any sign of response to these overtures, but regarding
her new friend without surprise, with an inattentive fixity of gaze,
which she doubtless felt to be more disturbing and the only effective
method, once the male had taken the first steps, and had fallen back
upon preening his feathers. At length Jupien's indifference seemed to
suffice him no longer; from this certainty of having conquered, to
making himself be pursued and desired was but the next stage, and
Jupien, deciding to go off to his work, passed through the carriage gate.
It was only, however, after turning his head two or three times that he
escaped into the street towards which the Baron, trembling lest he
should lose the trail (boldly humming a tune, not forgetting to fling
a 'Good day' to the porter, who, half-tipsy himself and engaged in
treating a few friends in his back kitchen, did not even hear him),
hurried briskly to overtake him. At the same instant, just as M. de
Charlus disappeared through the gate humming like a great bumble-

bee, another, a real bee this time, came into the courtyard. For all I knew this might be the one so long awaited by the orchid, which was coming to bring it that rare pollen without which it must die a virgin. But I was distracted from following the gyrations of the insect for, a few minutes later, engaging my attention afresh, Jupien (perhaps to pick up a parcel which he did take away with him ultimately and so, presumably, in the emotion aroused by the apparition of M. de Charlus, had forgotten, perhaps simply for a more natural reason) returned, followed by the Baron. The latter, deciding to cut short the preliminaries, asked the tailor for a light, but at once observed: 'I ask you for a light, but I find that I have left my cigars at home.' The laws of hospitality prevailed over those of coquetry. 'Come inside, you shall have everything you require,' said the tailor, on whose features disdain now gave place to joy. The door of the shop closed behind them and I could hear no more. I had lost sight of the bee. I did not know whether he was the insect that the orchid needed, but I had no longer any doubt, in the case of an extremely rare insect and a captive flower, of the miraculous possibility of their conjunction when M. de Charlus (this is simply a comparison of providential hazards, whatever they may be, without the slightest scientific claim to establish a relation between certain botanical laws and what is sometimes, most ineptly, termed homosexuality), who for years past had never come to the house except at hours when Jupien was not there, by the mere accident of Mme de Villeparisis's illness had encountered the tailor, and with him the good fortune reserved for men of the type of the Baron by one of those fellow-creatures who may indeed be, as we shall see, infinitely younger than Jupien and better looking, the man predestined to exist in order that they may have their share of sensual pleasure on this earth; the man who cares only for elderly gentlemen.

All that I have just said, however, I was not to understand until several minutes had elapsed; so much is reality encumbered by those properties of invisibility until a chance occurrence has divested it of them. Anyhow, for the moment I was greatly annoyed at not being able to hear any more of the conversation between the ex-tailor and the Baron. I then bethought myself of the vacant shop, separated from Jupien's only by a partition that was extremely slender . . .

When I was inside the shop, taking care not to let any plank in the floor make the slightest creak, as I found that the least sound in Jupien's shop could be heard from the other, I thought to myself how rash

Jupien and M. de Charlus had been, and how wonderfully fortune had favoured them. I did not dare move. The Guermantes groom, taking advantage no doubt of his master's absence, had, as it happened, transferred to the shop in which I now stood a ladder which hitherto had been kept in the coach-house, and if I had climbed this I could have opened the ventilator above and heard as well as if I had been in Jupien's shop itself. But I was afraid of making a noise. Besides, it was unnecessary. I had not even cause to regret my not having arrived in the shop until several minutes had elapsed. For from what I heard at first in Jupien's shop, which was only a series of inarticulate sounds, I imagine that few words had been exchanged. It is true that these sounds were so violent that, if one set had not always been taken up an octave higher by a parallel plaint, I might have thought that one person was strangling another within a few feet of me, and that subsequently the murderer and his resuscitated victim were taking a bath to wash away the traces of the crime. I concluded from this later on that there is another thing as vociferous as pain, namely pleasure, especially when there is added to it – failing the fear of an eventual parturition, which could not be present in this case, despite the hardly convincing example in the *Golden Legend* – an immediate afterthought of cleanliness. Finally, after about half an hour (during which time I had climbed on tip-toe on my ladder so as to peep through the ventilator which I did not open), a conversation began.

.   .   .   .   .

From the beginning of this scene a revolution, in my unsealed eyes, had occurred in M. de Charlus, as complete, as immediate as if he had been touched by a magician's wand. Until then, because I had not understood, I had not seen. The vice (we use the word for convenience only), the vice of each of us accompanies him through life after the manner of the familiar genius who was invisible to men so long as they were unaware of his presence . . . Our goodness, our meanness, our name, our social relations do not disclose themselves to the eye, we carry them hidden within us. Even Ulysses did not at once recognize Athena. But the gods are immediately perceptible to one another, as quickly like to like, and so too had M. de Charlus been to Jupien.

.   .   .   .   .

. . . Like so many creatures of the animal and vegetable kingdoms, like the plant which would produce vanilla but, because in its structure the male organ is divided by a partition from the female, remains sterile unless the humming-birds or certain tiny bees convey the pollen from one to the other, or man fertilises them by artificial means, M. de Charlus (and here the word fertilise must be understood in a moral sense, since in the physical sense the union of male with male is and must be sterile, but it is no small matter that a person may encounter the sole pleasure which he is capable of enjoying, and that every 'creature here below' can impart to some other 'his music, or his fragrance or his flame'), M. de Charlus was one of those men who may be called exceptional, because however many they may be, the satisfaction, so easy in others, of their sexual requirements depends upon the coincidence of too many conditions, and of conditions too difficult to ensure. For men like M. de Charlus (leaving out of account the compromises which will appear in the course of this story and which the reader may already have foreseen, enforced by the need of pleasure which resigns itself to partial acceptations), mutual love, apart from the difficulties, so great as to be almost insurmountable, which it meets in the ordinary man, adds to these others so exceptional that what is always extremely rare for everyone becomes in their case well nigh impossible, and, if there should befall them an encounter which is really fortunate, or which nature makes appear so to them, their good fortune, far more than that of the normal lover, has about it something extraordinary, selective, profoundly necessary . . .

.   .   .   .   .

However, I greatly exaggerated at the time, on the strength of this first revelation, the elective character of so carefully selected a combination . . . Admittedly, every man of the kind of M. de Charlus is an extraordinary creature since, if he does not make concessions to the possibilities of life, he seeks out essentially the love of a man of the other race, that is to say a man who is a lover of women (and incapable consequently of loving him); in contradiction of what I had imagined in the courtyard, where I had seen Jupien turning towards M. de Charlus like the orchid making overtures to the bee, those exceptional creatures whom we commiserate are a vast crowd, as we shall see in the course of this work, for a reason which will be disclosed only at the end of it, and commiserate themselves for being too many rather than too few. For the two angels who were posted at the gates of Sodom to learn whether its inhabitants (according to Genesis) had indeed done all the things the report of which had ascended to the Eternal Throne must have been, and of this one can only be glad, exceedingly ill chosen by the Lord, Who ought not to have entrusted the task to any but a Sodomite. Such a one the excuses: 'Father of six children – I keep two mistresses,' and so forth could never have persuaded benevolently to lower his flaming sword and to mitigate the punishment; he would have answered: 'Yes, and your wife lives in a torment of jealousy. But even when these women have not been chosen by you from Gomorrah, you spend your nights with a watcher of flocks upon Hebron.' And he would at once have made him retrace his steps to the city which the rain of fire and brimstone was to destroy. On the contrary, they allowed to escape all the shame-faced Sodomites, even if these, on catching sight of a boy, turned their heads, like Lot's wife, though without being on that account changed like her into pillars of salt. With the result that they engendered a numerous posterity with whom this gesture has continued to be habitual, like that of the dissolute women who, while apparently studying a row of shoes displayed in a shop window, turn their heads to keep track of a passing student. These descendants of the Sodomites, so numerous that we may apply to them that other verse of Genesis: 'If a man can number the dust of the earth, then shall thy seed also be numbered,' have established themselves throughout the entire world; they have had access to every profession and pass so easily into the most exclusive clubs that, whenever a Sodomite fails to secure election, the black balls are, for the most part, cast by other Sodomites, who are anxious to penalise sodomy, having inherited the falsehood that enabled their ancestors to escape from the accursed city. It is possible that they may return there one day. Certainly they form in every land an Oriental colony, cultured, musical, malicious, which has certain charming qualities and intolerable defects. We shall study them with greater thoroughness in the course of the following pages; but I have thought it as well to utter here a provisional warning against the lamentable error of proposing (just as people have encouraged a Zionist movement) to create a Sodomist movement and to rebuild Sodom. For, no sooner had they arrived there than the Sodomites would leave the town so as not to have the appearance of belonging to it, would take wives, keep mistresses in other cities where they would find, incidentally, every diversion that appealed to them. They would repair to Sodom only on days of supreme necessity, when their own town was empty, at those seasons when hunger drives the wolf from the woods; in other words, everything would go on very much as it does today in London, Berlin, Rome, Petrograd or Paris.

Anyhow, on the day in question, before paying my call on the Duchess, I did not look so far ahead, and I was distressed to find that I had, by my engrossment in the Jupien-Charlus conjunction, missed perhaps an opportunity of witnessing the fertilisation of the blossom by the bee.

(*Cities of the Plain*, Vol. 7 of *Remembrance of Things Past*, tr.
C. K. Scott Moncrieff)

2. *IN THE UNITED STATES*

WALT WHITMAN (1819–92)   In the summer of 1870 certain mysterious entries appeared in Whitman's notebooks: 'It is IMPERATIVE that I obviate and remove myself (and my orbit) *at all hazards* from this *incessant enormous* and PERTURBATION' read one, while another decided 'TO GIVE UP ABSOLUTELY & *for good, from this present hour*, this FEVERISH, FLUCTUATING, *useless undignified pursuit of 164 – too long, (much too long)* persevered in – so humiliating – *It must come at last* & had better come now – (*It cannot possibly be a success*) LET THERE FROM THIS HOUR BE NO FALTERING, NO GETTING – *at all henceforth*, (NOT ONCE, *under any circumstances*) – *avoid seeing her, or meeting her, or any talk or explanations – or* ANY MEETING WHATEVER, FROM THIS HOUR FORTH, FOR LIFE.'

Who or what was 164? One critic has referred it to a number on a phrenological chart, where it stood for Hope, personified by a woman. Some have thought that an actual woman was involved. But a long-time friend of the poet declared many years later, 'I never knew a case of Walt's being bothered by a woman'. It seems more likely that the code derived from a children's game, in which the letters of the alphabet are numbered, that 16 stood for P, and 4 for D; and that it was Peter Doyle, the same friend, who was referred to under the disguise of a feminine pronoun. Whitman did not in fact break off his friendship with Doyle, because a few days later he found that his strong feelings were reciprocated: ' – I never dreamed that you made so much of having me with you, nor that you could feel so downcast at losing me. I foolishly thought that it was all on the other side.' (See G. W. Allen, *The Solitary Singer*, Macmillan, pp. 421–4.) This is not to suggest a physical relationship. We know that at the time Whitman was worried by his 'adhesive nature' (he contrasted adhesiveness, or manly affection, with heterosexual 'amativeness') and that he wished to 'depress' it since he then found it 'in excess' – 'All this diseased, feverish disproportionate *adhesiveness.*' Indeed it was out of the struggle to control his emotions that much of his best poetry sprang, together with his concept of love as the solution to the evils of society. However, towards the end of his life, when J. A. Symonds was pressing him for the precise meaning of the Calamus Poems he made a number of misleading declarations, expressing himself 'dazed' at the 'terrible' construction Symonds put on the poems – 'morbid inferences which are disavowed by me and seem damnable' – and announcing that he had had, though unmarried, no less than six children. Yet no child, or 'fine boy' of a 'Southern grandchild', has even been discovered.

The Calamus theme itself developed from the animal magnetism of the 'great companions' in the 1856 edition of *Leaves of Grass* through the increasing preoccupation with homoeroticism in 1857 and the emotional and intellectual crisis of 1858–9, which produced twelve 'Calamus-Leaves' of a far more personal nature, to the forty-five poems printed as Calamus in 1860.

IN PATHS UNTRODDEN

In paths untrodden,
In the growth by margins of pond-waters,
Escaped from the life that exhibits itself,
From all the standards hitherto publish'd, from the pleasures,
    profits, conformities,
Which too long I was offering to feed my soul,

Clear to me now standards not yet publish'd, clear to me that
  my soul,
That the soul of the man I speak for rejoices in comrades,
Here by myself away from the clank of the world,
Tallying and talk'd to here by tongues aromatic,
No longer abash'd, (for in this secluded spot I can respond as
  I would not dare elsewhere,)
Strong upon me the life that does not exhibit itself, yet
  contains all the rest,
Resolv'd to sing no songs to-day but those of manly
  attachment,
Projecting them along that substantial life,
Bequeathing hence types of athletic love,
Afternoon this delicious Ninth-month in my forty-first year,
I proceed for all who are or have been young men,
To tell the secret of my nights and days,
To celebrate the need of comrades.

FOR YOU O DEMOCRACY

Come, I will make the continent indissoluble,
I will make the most splendid race the sun ever shone upon,
I will make divine magnetic lands,
       With the love of comrades,
           With the life-long love of comrades.

I will plant companionship thick as trees along all the rivers of America,
  and along the shores of the great lakes, and all over the prairies,
I will make inseparable cities with their arms about each other's necks,
       By the love of comrades,
           By the manly love of comrades.

For you these from me, O Democracy, to serve you ma femme!
For you, for you I am trilling these songs.

THE BASE OF ALL METAPHYSICS

And now gentlemen,
A word I give to remain in your memories and minds,
As base and finale too for all metaphysics.

(So to the students the old professor,
At the close of his crowded course.)

Having studied the new and antique, the Greek and Germanic systems,
Kant having studied and stated, Fichte and Schelling and Hegel,
Stated the lore of Plato, and Socrates greater than Plato,
And greater than Socrates sought and stated, Christ divine having
    studied long,
I see reminiscent to-day those Greek and Germanic systems,
See the philosophies all, Christian churches and tenets see,
Yet underneath Socrates clearly see, and underneath Christ the divine
    I see,
The dear love of man for his comrade, the attraction of friend to friend,
Of the well-married husband and wife, of children and parents,
Of city for city and land for land.

RECORDERS AGES HENCE

Recorders ages hence,
Come, I will take you down underneath this impassive exterior, I
    will tell you what to say of me,
Publish my name and hang up my picture as that of the tenderest lover,
The friend the lover's portrait, of whom his friend his lover was
    fondest,
Who was not proud of his songs, but of the measureless ocean of love
    within him, and freely pour'd it forth,
Who often walk'd lonesome walks thinking of his dear friends, his
    lovers,
Who pensive away from one he lov'd often lay sleepless and dissatisfied
    at night,
Who knew too well the sick, sick dread lest the one he lov'd might
    secretly be indifferent to him,
Whose happiest days were far away through fields, in woods, on hills,
    he and another wandering hand in hand, they twain apart from
    other men,
Who oft as he saunter'd the streets curv'd with his arm the shoulder of
    his friend, while the arm of his friend rested upon him also.

WHEN I HEARD AT THE CLOSE OF DAY

When I heard at the close of the day how my name had been receiv'd
   with plaudits in the capitol, still it was not a happy night for me that
   follow'd,
And else when I carous'd, or when my plans were accomplish'd, still
   I was not happy,
But the day when I rose at dawn from the bed of perfect health,
   refresh'd, singing, inhaling the ripe breath of autumn,
When I saw the full moon in the west grow pale and disappear in the
   morning light,
When I wander'd alone over the beach, and undressing bathed,
   laughing with the cool waters, and saw the sun rise,
And when I thought how my dear friend my lover was on his way
   coming, O then I was happy,
O then each breath tasted sweeter, and all that day my food nourish'd
   me more, and the beautiful day pass'd well,
And the next came with equal joy, and with the next at evening came
   my friend,
And that night while all was still I heard the waters roll slowly continually up the shores,
I heard the hissing rustle of the liquid and sands as directed to me
   whispering to congratulate me,
For the one I love most lay sleeping by me under the same cover in the
   cool night,
In the stillness in the autumn moonbeams his face was inclined toward
   me,
And his arm lay lightly around my breast – and that night I was happy.

BEHOLD THIS SWARTHY FACE

Behold this swarthy face, these gray eyes,
This beard, the white wool unclipt upon my neck,
My brown hands and the silent manner of me without charm;
Yet comes one a Manhattanese and ever at parting kisses me
   lightly on the lips with robust love,
And I on the crossing of the street or on the ship's deck give a kiss
   in return,
We observe that salute of American comrades land and sea,
We are those two natural and nonchalant persons.

I SAW IN LOUISIANA A LIVE-OAK GROWING

I saw in Louisiana a live-oak growing,
All alone stood it and the moss hung down from the branches,
Without any companion it grew there uttering joyous leaves of dark
    green,
And its look, rude, unbending, lusty, made me think of myself,
But I wonder'd how it could utter joyous leaves standing alone there
    without its friend near, for I knew I could not,
And I broke off a twig with a certain number of leaves upon it, and
    twined around it a little moss,
And brought it away, and I have placed it in sight in my room,
It is not needed to remind me as of my own dear friends,
(For I believe lately I think of little else than of them,)
Yet it remains to me a curious token, it makes me think of manly
    love;
For all that, and though the live-oak glistens there in Louisiana
    solitary in a wide flat space,
Uttering joyous leaves all its life without a friend a lover near,
I know very well I could not.

WE TWO BOYS TOGETHER CLINGING

We two boys together clinging,
One the other never leaving,
Up and down the roads going, North and South excursions
    making,
Power enjoying, elbows stretching, fingers clutching,
Arm'd and fearless, eating, drinking, sleeping, loving,
No law less than ourselves owning, sailing, soldiering, thieving,
    threatening,
Misers, menials, priests alarming, air breathing, water drinking,
    on the turf or the sea-beach dancing,
Cities wrenching, ease scorning, statues mocking, feebleness
    chasing,
Fulfilling our foray.

HERE THE FRAILEST LEAVES OF ME

Here the frailest leaves of me and yet my strongest lasting,
Here I shade and hide my thoughts, I myself do not expose them,
And yet they expose me more than all my other poems.

A GLIMPSE

A glimpse through an interstice caught,
Of a crowd of workmen and drivers in a bar-room around the stove
late of a winter night, and I unremark'd seated in a corner,
Of a youth who loves me and whom I love, silently approaching and
seating himself near, that he may hold me by the hand,
A long while amid the noises of coming and going, of drinking and
oath and smutty jest,
There we two, content, happy in being together, speaking little,
perhaps not a word.

WHAT THINK YOU I TAKE MY PEN IN HAND

What think you I take my pen in hand to record?
The battle-ship, perfect-model'd, majestic, that I saw pass the offing
to-day under full sail?
The splendours of the past day? or the splendour of the night that
envelops me?
Or the vaunted glory and growth of the great city spread around me?
— no;
But merely of two simple men I saw to-day on the pier in the midst of
the crowd, parting the parting of dear friends,
The one to remain hung on the other's neck and passionately kiss'd
him,
While the one to depart tightly prest the one to remain in his arms.

O YOU WHOM I OFTEN AND SILENTLY COME

O you whom I often and silently come where you are that I may be
with you,
As I walk by your side or sit near, or remain in the same room with
you,
Little you know the subtle electric fire that for your sake is playing
within me.

★   ★   ★

ADHESIVENESS

Intense and loving comradeship, the personal and passionate attachment of man to man – which, hard to define, underlies the lessons and

ideals of the profound saviours of every land and age, and which seems to promise, when thoroughly develop'd, cultivated and recognized in manners and literature, the most substantial hope and safety of the future of these States, will then be fully express'd.

It is to the development, identification, and general prevalence of that fervid comradeship, (the adhesive love, at least rivaling the amative love hitherto possessing imaginative literature, if not going beyond it,) that I look for the counter-balance and offset of our materialistic and vulgar American democracy, and for the spiritualization thereof. Many will say it is a dream, and will not follow my inferences: but I confidently expect a time when there will be seen, running like a half-hid warp through all the myriad audible and visible worldly interests of America, threads of manly friendships, fond and loving, pure and sweet, strong and life-long, carried to degrees hitherto unknown – not only giving tone to individual character, and making it unprecedently emotional, muscular, heroic, and refined, but having the deepest relations to general politics. I say democracy infers such loving comradeship, as its most inevitable twin or counterpart, without which it will be incomplete, in vain, and incapable of perpetuating itself.

(Democratic Vistas)

⋆   ⋆   ⋆

HERMAN MELVILLE (1819–91) The grandeur, complexity and sadness of this poet-novelist's vision included a moral and aesthetic appreciation of his fellow men. There are the portraits of Pacific savages in *Omoo* and *Typee*. And there is Jack Chase, 'Captain of the Maintop in the year 1843 in the U.S. Frigate *United States*', to whom the great short novel *Billy Budd* was to be dedicated. In his introduction to the early sailing story, *White Jacket* (John Lehmann), William Plomer has this to say of Melville's hero: 'In a book full of strange persons and happenings, nothing is stranger than the portrait of Jack Chase. It is a rhapsodic portrait, an effusion of hero-worship and personal devotion. A reader of the present day must surely not brush aside the more gushing and rhetorical passages devoted to this character as mere Melvillean rantings, even if they seem enthusiastic and, in an age where mediocrity is so much admired, a trifle embarrassing. If Jack

297

Chase seems like a dream-hero, that does not mean that there has never been any such person, for others besides Melville remembered him in the flesh. What seems highly probable is that Jack Chase was a supreme example of a kind of man sometimes to be found at sea in the eighteenth or nineteenth centuries, but now extinct.

'. . . In Melville's "poetry of ocean" Jack Chase is the ideal man, sailor, and father-image; and as dedicatee he is found presiding, years later, over the tremendous legend of Billy Budd, where another form of the manliest beauty falls a sacrifice to the appalling machinery of destiny – and of naval discipline. It was Jack Chase who won Melville's "best love", and I do not remember any evidence that anybody else ever did so. He need not be represented as the Beatrice to Melville's Dante, or as the only begetter of the whole Melvillean legend of the sea, yet he certainly seems to have been the captain, not only of the main-top in the U.S. frigate *United States* in the year 1843, but of Melville's soul.'

JACK CHASE

The first night out of port was a clear, moonlight one; the frigate gliding through the water with all her batteries.

It was my quarter-watch in the top, and there I reclined on the best possible terms with my topmates. Whatever the other seamen might have been, these were a noble set of tars, and well worthy an introduction to the reader.

First and foremost was Jack Chase, our noble first captain of the top. He was a Briton, and a true-blue; tall and well-knit, with a clear open eye, a fine broad brow, and an abounding nut-brown beard. No man ever had a better heart or a bolder. He was loved by the seamen, and admired by the officers; and even when the captain spoke to him, it was with a slight air of respect. Jack was a frank and charming man.

No one could be better company in forecastle or saloon; no man told such stories, sang such songs, or with greater alacrity sprang to his duty. Indeed, there was only one thing wanting about him, and that was a finger of his left hand, which finger he had lost at the great battle of Navarino.

He had a high conceit of his profession as a seaman; and being deeply versed in all things pertaining to a man-of-war, was universally regarded as an oracle. The main-top, over which he presided, was a sort of oracle of Delphi, to which many pilgrims ascended to have their perplexities or differences settled.

There was such an abounding air of good sense and good feeling about the man, that he who could not love him would thereby · pronounce himself a knave. I thanked my sweet stars that kind fortune had placed me near him, though under him, in the frigate; and from the outset Jack and I were fast friends.

Wherever you may be now rolling over the blue billows, dear Jack! take my best love along with you; and God bless you, wherever you are!

Jack was a gentleman. What though his hand were hard, so was not his heart, too often the case with soft palms. His manners were easy and free; none of the boisterousness, so common to tars; and he had a polite, courteous way of saluting you, if it were only to borrow your knife. Jack had read all the verses of Byron, and all the romances of Scott. He talked of Rob Roy, Don Juan, and Pelham; Macbeth and Ulysses; but, above all things, was an ardent admirer of Camoens. Parts of the *Lusiad* he could recite in the original. Where he had obtained his wonderful accomplishments is not for me, his humble subordinate, to say. Enough, that these accomplishments were so various; the languages he could converse in so numerous; that he more than furnished an example of that saying of Charles the Fifth – *he who speaks five languages is as good as five men*. But Jack, he was better than a hundred common mortals; Jack was a whole phalanx, an entire army; Jack was a thousand strong; Jack would have done honour to the Queen of England's drawing-room; Jack must have been a by-blow of some British Admiral of the Blue. A finer specimen of the island race of Englishmen could not have been picked out of Westminster Abbey of a coronation day.

His whole demeanour was in strong contrast to that of one of the captains of the fore-top. This man, though a good seaman, furnished an example of those insufferable Britons, who, while preferring other countries to their own as places of residence, still overflow with all the pompousness of national and individual vanity combined. 'When I was on board the *Audacious*' – for a long time was almost the invariable exordium to the fore-top captain's cursory remarks. It is often the custom of men-of-war's men, when they deem anything to be going on wrong aboard ship, to refer to *last cruise*, when of course everything was done *ship-shape and Bristol fashion*. And by referring to the *Audacious* – an expressive name, by the way – the fore-top captain meant a ship in the English Navy, in which he had had the honour of serving. So continual were his allusions to this craft with the amiable name that, at last, the *Audacious* was voted a bore by his shipmates. And one hot afternoon, during a calm, when the fore-top captain, like many others, was standing still and yawning on the spar-deck, Jack Chase, his own countryman, came up to him, and pointing at his open mouth, politely inquired whether that was the way they caught *flies* in Her Britannic Majesty's ship the *Audacious*? After that, we heard no more of the craft.

Now, the tops of a frigate are quite cosy and spacious. They are railed in behind so as to form a kind of balcony, very pleasant of a tropical night. From twenty to thirty loungers may agreeably recline there, cushioning themselves on old sails and jackets. We had rare times in that top. We accounted ourselves the best seamen in the ship and from our airy perch literally looked down upon the land-lopers below, sneaking about the deck, among the guns. In a large degree we nourished that feeling of *esprit de corps*, always pervading, more or less, the various sections of a man-of-war's crew. We maintop men were brothers, one and all; and we leaned ourselves to each other with all the freedom in the world.

Nevertheless, I had not long been a member of this fraternity of fine fellows ere I discovered that Jack Chase, our captain, was – like all prime favourites and oracles among men – a little bit of a dictator; not peremptorily, or annoyingly so, but amusingly intent on egotistically mending our manners and improving our taste, so that we might reflect credit upon our tutor.

He made us all wear our hats at a particular angle, instructed us in the tie of our neck-handkerchiefs, and protested against our wearing vulgar *dungaree* trowsers, besides giving us lessons in seamanship, and solemnly conjuring us forever to eschew the company of any sailor we suspected of having served in a whaler. Against all whalers, indeed, he cherished the unmitigated detestation of a true man-of-war's man. Poor Tubbs can testify to that.

Tubbs was in the after-guard; a long, lank Vineyarder, eternally talking of line-tubs, Nantucket, sperm-oil, stove boats, and Japan. Nothing could silence him, and his comparisons were ever invidious.

Now, with all his soul, Jack abominated this Tubbs. He said he was vulgar, an upstart – Devil take him, he's been in a whaler. But, like many men who have been where *you* haven't been, or seen what *you* haven't seen, Tubbs, on account of his whaling experiences, absolutely affected to look down upon Jack, even as Jack did upon him; and this it was that so enraged our noble captain.

One night, with a peculiar meaning in his eye, he sent me down on deck to invite Tubbs up aloft for a chat. Flattered by so marked an honour – for we were somewhat fastidious, and did not extend invitations to everybody – Tubbs quickly mounted the rigging, looking rather abashed at finding himself in the august presence of the assembled quarter-watch of main-top men. Jack's courteous manner, however, very soon relieved his embarrassment; but it was no use to be courteous to *some* men in this world. Tubbs belonged to that category. No sooner did the bumpkin feel himself at ease than he launched out, as usual, into tremendous laudations of whalemen; declaring that whalemen alone deserved the name of sailors. Jack stood it some time; but when Tubbs came down upon men-of-war, and particularly upon main-top men, his sense of propriety was so outraged that he launched into Tubbs like a forty-two-pounder.

'Why, you limb of Nantucket! you train-oil man! you sea-tallow strainer! you bobber after carrion! do *you* pretend to vilify a man-of-war? Why, you lean rogue you, a man-of-war is to whalemen as a metropolis to shire towns and sequestered hamlets. *Here's* the place for life and commotion; *here's* the place to be gentlemanly and jolly. And what did you know, you bumpkin! before you came on board this *Andrew Miller*? What knew you of gun-deck, or orlop, mustering round the capstan, beating to quarters, and piping to dinner? Did you ever roll to *grog* on board your greasy ballyhoo of blazes? Did you ever winter at Mahon? Did you ever '*lash and carry*'? Why, what are even a merchant seaman's sorry yarns of voyages to China after tea-caddies, and voyages to the West Indies after sugar puncheons, and voyages to the Shetlands after sealskins – what are even these yarns, you Tubbs you! to high life in a man-of-war? Why, you dead-eye! I have sailed with lords and marquises for captains; and the King of the Two Sicilies has passed me, as I here stood up at my gun. Bah! you are full of the fore-peak and the forecastle; you are only familiar with Burtons and Billy-tackles; your ambition never mounted above pig-killing! which, in my poor opinion, is the proper phrase for whaling! Topmates!

has not this Tubbs here been a misuser of good deal planks, and a vile desecrator of the thrice holy sea? turning his ship, my hearties! into a fat-kettle, and the ocean into a whale-pen? Begone, you graceless, godless knave! pitch him over the top there, White Jacket!'

But there was no necessity for my exertions. Poor Tubbs, astounded at these fulminations, was already rapidly descending by the rigging.

This outburst on the part of my noble friend, Jack, made me shake all over, spite of my padded surtout; and caused me to offer up devout thanksgiving that in no evil hour had I divulged the fact of having myself served in a whaler; for having previously marked the prevailing prejudice of man-of-war's men to that much-maligned class of mariners, I had wisely held my peace concerning stove boats on the coast of Japan.

(*White Jacket*)

*   *   *

Billy Budd was the last thing that Melville wrote; it came after the long years of silence in the Customs House and preceded its author's death by only a few months. Whatever its symbolic or allegorical significance, about which there has been much argument, it is in one sense a triangle situation of male love: 'Baby' Billy, the upright barbarian, whose only but fatal fault is a slight stutter, evokes the emotions of the two men who can understand his beauty and innocence – the evil Claggart, whom he accidentally kills when falsely accused, and the noble Captain 'Starry' Vere who both loves and kills him. Claggart's is love in reverse, soured to 'pale ire, envy and despair'; Vere's is love tempered by duty and made (perhaps in a repressed or sublimating way) morally Olympian. Yet 'the austere devotee of military duty, letting himself melt back into what remains primeval in our formalised humanity, may in the end have caught Billy to his heart, even as Abraham may have caught young Isaac on the brink of resolutely offering him up in obedience to the exacting behest'.

THE HANDSOME SAILOR

If in some cases a bit of a nautical Murat in setting forth his person ashore, the Handsome Sailor of the period in question evinced nothing of the dandified Billy-be-Damn, an amusing character all but extinct now, but occasionally to be encountered, and in a form yet more amusing than the original, at the tiller of the boats on the tempestuous Erie Canal or, more likely, vapouring in the groggeries along the tow-path. Invariably a proficient in his perilous calling, he was also more or less of a mighty boxer or wrestler. He was strength and beauty. Tales of his prowess were recited. Ashore he was the champion, afloat the spokesman; on every suitable occasion always foremost. Close-reefing topsails in a gale, there he was, astride the weather yard-arm-end, foot in 'stirrup', both hands tugging at the 'ear-ring' as at a bridle, in very much the attitude of young Alexander curbing the fiery Bucephalus. A superb figure, tossed up as by the horns of Taurus against the thunderous sky, cheerily ballooning to the strenuous file along the spar.

The moral nature was seldom out of keeping with the physical make. Indeed, except as toned by the former, the comeliness and power, always attractive in masculine conjunction, hardly could have drawn the sort of homage the Handsome Sailor in some examples received from his less gifted associates.

Such a cynosure, at least in aspect, and something such too in nature, though with important variations made apparent as the story proceeds, was welkin-eyed Billy Budd – or Baby Budd, as more familiarly, under circumstances hereafter to be given, he at last came to be called – aged twenty-one, a foretopman of the fleet toward the close of the last decade of the eighteenth century.

(*Billy Budd*)

BILLY'S NOBILITY

He was young; and despite his all but fully developed frame, in aspect looked even younger than he really was. This was owing to a lingering adolescent expression in the as yet smooth face, all but feminine in purity of natural complexion, but where, thanks to his sea-going, the lily was quite suppressed, and the rose had some ado visibly to flush through the tan . . .

As the *Handsome Sailor* Billy Budd's position aboard the seventy-four was something analogous to that of a rustic beauty transplanted from the provinces and brought into competition with the high-born dames of the court. But this change of circumstances he scarce noted.

As little did he observe that something about him provoked an ambiguous smile in one or two harder faces among the blue-jackets. Nor less unaware was he of the peculiar favourable effect his person and demeanour had upon the more intelligent gentlemen of the quarter-deck. Nor could this well have been otherwise. Cast in a mould peculiar to the finest physical examples of those Englishmen in whom the Saxon strain would seem not at all to partake of any Norman or other admixture, he showed in face that humane look of reposeful good-nature which the Greek sculptor in some instances gave to his heroic strong man, Hercules. But this again was subtly modified by another and pervasive quality. The ear, small and shapely, the arch of the foot, the curve in mouth and nostril, even the indurated hand dyed to the orange-tawny of the toucan's bill, a hand telling of the halyards and tar-buckets; but, above all, something in the mobile expression, and every chance attitude and movement, something suggestive of a mother eminently favoured by Love and the Graces; all this strangely indicated a lineage in direct contradiction to his lot. The mysteriousness here, became less mysterious through a matter of fact elicited when Billy at the capstan was being formally mustered into the service. Asked by the officer, a small, brisk little gentleman as it chanced, among other questions, his place of birth, he replied, 'Please, sir, I don't know.'

'Don't you know where you were born? Who was your father?'

'God knows, sir.'

Struck by the straightforward simplicity of these replies, the officer next asked, 'Do you know anything about your beginning?'

'No, sir. But I have heard that I was found in a pretty silk-lined basket hanging one morning from the knocker of a good man's door in Bristol.'

'*Found*, say you? Well,' throwing back his head, and looking up and down the new recruit – 'well, it turns out to have been a pretty good find. Hope they'll find some more like you, my man; the fleet sadly needs them.'

Yes, Billy Budd was a foundling, a presumable by-blow, and, evidently, no ignoble one. Noble descent was as evident in him as in a blood horse.

For the rest, with little or no sharpness of faculty or any trace of the wisdom of the serpent, nor yet quite a dove, he possessed a certain degree of intelligence along with the unconventional rectitude of a sound human creature – one to whom not yet has been proffered the questionable apple of knowledge. He was illiterate; he could not read, but he could sing, and like the illiterate nightingale was sometimes the composer of his own song.

Of self-consciousness he seemed to have little or none, or about as much as we may reasonably impute to a dog of St. Bernard's breed.

Habitually being with the elements and knowing little more of the land than as a beach, or, rather, that portion of the terraqueous globe providentially set apart for dance-houses, doxies and tapsters, in short, what sailors call a 'fiddlers' green', his simple nature remained unsophisticated by those moral obliquities which are not in every case incomparable with that manufacturable thing known as respectability. But are sailor frequenters of fiddlers' greens without vices? No; but less often than with landsmen do their vices, so-called, partake of crookedness of heart, seeming less to proceed from viciousness than exuberance of vitality after long restraint, frank manifestations in accordance with natural law. By his original constitution, aided by the co-operating influences of his lot, Billy in many respects was little more than a sort of upright barbarian, much such perhaps as Adam presumably might have been ere the urbane Serpent wriggled himself into his company.

(Ibid.)

CLAGGART

Claggart was a man of about five-and-thirty, somewhat spare and tall, yet of no ill figure upon the whole. His hand was too small and shapely to have been accustomed to hard toil. The face was a notable one; the features, all except the chin, cleanly cut as those on a Greek medallion; yet the chin, beardless as Tecumseh's, had something of the strange protuberant heaviness in its make that recalled the prints of the Rev. Dr. Titus Oates . . . It served Claggart in his office that his eye could cast a tutoring glance. His brow was of the sort phrenologically associated with more than average intellect; silken jet curls, partly clustering over it, making a foil to the pallor below, a pallor tinged with a faint shade of amber akin to the hue of time-tinted marbles of old.

This complexion singularly contrasting with the red or deeply bronzed visages of the sailors, and in part the result of his official seclusion from the sunlight, though it was not exactly displeasing, nevertheless seemed to hint of something defective or abnormal in the constitution and blood. But his general aspect and manner were so suggestive of an education and career incongruous with his naval function, that when not actively engaged in it he looked like a man of high quality, social and moral, who for reasons of his own was keeping incognito.

(*Ibid.*)

HIS ATTITUDE

That Claggart's figure was not amiss, and his face, save the chin, well moulded, has already been said. Of these favourable points he seemed not insensible, for he was not only neat but careful in his dress. But the form of Billy Budd was heroic; and if his face was without the intellectual look of the pallid Claggart's, not the less was it lit, like his, from within, though from a different source. The bonfire in his heart made luminous the rose-tan in his cheek.

In view of the marked contrast between the persons of the twain, it is more than probable that when the master-at-arms in the scene last given applied to the sailor the proverb 'Handsome is as handsome does', he there let escape an ironic inkling, not caught by the young sailors who heard it, as to what it was that had first moved him against Billy, namely, his significant personal beauty.

Now envy and antipathy, passions irreconcilable in reason, nevertheless in fact may spring conjoined like Chang and Eng in one birth. Is envy then such a monster? Well, though many an arraigned mortal has in hopes of mitigated penalty pleaded guilty to horrible actions, did ever anybody seriously confess to envy? Something there is in it universally felt to be more shameful than even felonious crime. And not only does everybody disown it, but the better sort are inclined to incredulity when it is in earnest imputed to an intelligent man. But since its lodgment is in the heart, not the brain, no degree of intellect supplies a guarantee against it. But Claggart's was no vulgar form of the passion. Nor, as directed toward Billy Budd, did it partake of that streak of apprehensive jealousy that marred Saul's visage perturbedly brooding on the comely young David. Claggart's envy struck deeper. If askance he eyed the good looks, cheery health, and frank enjoyment of young life in Billy Budd, it was because these happened to go along with a nature that, as Claggart magnetically felt, had in its simplicity never willed malice, or experienced the reactionary bite of that serpent.

To him, the spirit lodged within Billy and looking out from his welkin eyes as from windows, that ineffability which made the dimple in his dyed cheek, suppled his joints, and danced in his yellow curls, made him pre-eminently the Handsome Sailor. One person excepted, the master-at-arms was perhaps the only man in the ship intellectually capable of adequately appreciating the moral phenomenon presented in Billy Budd, and the insight but intensified his passion, which assuming various secret forms within him, at times assumed that of cynic disdain – disdain of innocence. To be nothing more than innocent! Yet in an aesthetic way he saw the charm of it, the courageous free-and-easy temper of it, and fain would have shared it, but he despaired of it.

(*Ibid.*)

PALE IRE, ENVY AND DESPAIR

. . . When Claggart's unobserved glance happened to light on belted Billy rolling along the upper gun-deck in the leisure of the second dog-watch, exchanging passing broadsides of fun with other young promenaders in the crowd, that glance would follow the cheerful sea-Hyperion with a settled meditative and melancholy expression, his eyes strangely suffused with incipient feverish tears. Then would Claggart look like the man of sorrows. Yes, and sometimes the melancholy expression would have in it a touch of soft yearning, as if Claggart could even have loved Billy but for fate and ban. But this was an evanescence, and quickly repented of, as it were, by an immitigable look, pinching and shrivelling the visage into the momentary semblance of a wrinkled walnut. But sometimes catching sight in advance of the foretopman coming in his direction, he would, upon their nearing, step aside a little to let him pass, dwelling upon Billy for the moment with the glittering dental satire of a guise. But upon any abrupt unforeseen encounter a red light would flash forth from his eye, like a spark from an anvil in a dusk smithy. That quick fierce light was a strange one, darted from orbs which in repose were of a colour nearest approaching a deeper violet, the softest of shades.

Though some of these caprices of the pit could not but be observed by their object, yet were they beyond the construing of such a nature. And the thews of Billy were hardly comparable with that sort of spiritual organisation which in some cases instinctively conveys to ignorant innocence an admonition of the proximity of the malign. He thought the master-at-arms acted in a manner rather queer at times.

That was all. But the occasional frank air and pleasant word went for what they purported to be, the young sailor never having heard as yet of the 'too fair-spoken man.'

(Ibid.)

★   ★   ★

HENRY DAVID THOREAU (1817–62):
What is commonly honoured with the name of Friendship is no very profound or powerful instinct . . . Most contemplate only what would be the accidental and trifling advantages of Friendship, as that the Friend can assist in time of need by his substance, or his influence, or his counsel; but he who foresees such advantages in this relation proves himself blind to its real advantage, or indeed wholly inexperienced in the relation itself. Such services are particular and menial compared with the perpetual and all-embracing service which it is. Even the utmost good-will and harmony and practical kindness are not sufficient for Friendship, for Friends do not live in harmony merely, as some say, but in melody. We do not wish for Friends to feed and clothe our bodies – neighbours are kind enough for that – but to do the like office for our spirits.

(A Week on the Concord and Merrimac Rivers)

★   ★   ★

SHERWOOD ANDERSON (1876–1941)

From

HANDS

. . . The story of Wing Biddlebaum's hands is worth a book in itself. Sympathetically set forth it would tap many strange, beautiful qualities in obscure men. It is a job for a poet. In Winesburg the hands had attracted attention merely because of their activity. With them Wing Biddlebaum had picked as high as a hundred and forty quarts of straw-berries in a day. They became his distinguishing feature, the source of his fame. Also they made more grotesque an already grotesque and elusive individuality. Winesburg was proud of the hands of Wing Biddlebaum in the same spirit in which it was proud of Banker White's new stone house and Wesley Moyer's bay stallion, Tony Tip, that had won the two-fifteen trot at the fall races in Cleveland.

As for George Willard, he had many times wanted to ask about the hands. At times an almost overwhelming curiosity had taken hold of him. He felt that there must be a reason for their strange activity and their inclination to keep hidden away and only a growing respect for Wing Biddlebaum kept him from blurting out the questions that were often in his mind.

Once he had been on the point of asking. The two were walking in the fields on a summer afternoon and had stopped to sit upon a grassy bank. All afternoon Wing Biddlebaum had talked as one inspired. By a fence he had stopped and beating like a giant woodpecker upon the top board had shouted at George Willard, condemning his tendency to be too much influenced by the people about him. 'You are destroying yourself,' he cried. 'You have the inclination to be alone and to dream and you are afraid of your dreams. You want to be like others in town here. You hear them talk and you try to imitate them.'

On the grassy bank Wing Biddlebaum had tried again to drive his point home. His voice became soft and reminiscent, and with a sigh of contentment he launched into a long rambling talk, speaking as one lost in a dream.

Out of the dream Wing Biddlebaum made a picture of George Willard. In the picture men lived again in a kind of pastoral golden age. Across a green open country came clean-limbed young men, some afoot, some mounted upon horses. In crowds the young men came to gather about the feet of an old man who sat beneath a tree in a tiny garden and who talked to them.

Wing Biddlebaum became wholly inspired. For once he forgot the hands. Slowly they stole forth and lay upon George Willard's shoulders. Something new and bold came into the voice that talked. 'You must try to forget all you have learned,' said the old man. 'You must begin to dream. From this time on you must shut your ears to the roaring of the voices.'

Pausing in his speech, Wing Biddlebaum looked long and earnestly at George Willard. His eyes glowed. Again he raised his hands to caress the boy and then a look of horror swept over his face.

With a convulsive movement of his body, Wing Biddlebaum sprang to his feet and thrust his hands deep into his trousers pockets. Tears came to his eyes. 'I must be getting along home. I can talk no more with you,' he said nervously.

Without looking back, the old man had hurried down the hillside and across a meadow, leaving George Willard perplexed and frightened upon the grassy slope. With a shiver of dread the boy arose and went along the road toward town. 'I'll not ask him about his hands,' he thought, touched by the memory of the terror he had seen in the man's eyes. 'There's something wrong, but I don't want to know what it is. His hands have something to do with his fear of me and of everyone.'

And George Willard was right. Let us look briefly into the story of the hands. Perhaps our talking of them will arouse the poet who will tell the hidden wonder story of the influence for which the hands were but fluttering pennants of promise.

In his youth Wing Biddlebaum had been a school teacher in a town in Pennsylvania. He went by the less euphonic name of Adolph Myers. As Adolph Myers he was much loved by the boys of his school.

Adolph Myers was meant by nature to be a teacher of youth. He was one of those rare, little-understood men who rule by a power so gentle that it passes as a lovable weakness. In their feeling for the boys under their charge such men are not unlike the finer sort of women in their love of men.

And yet that is but crudely stated. It needs the poet there. With the boys of his school, Adolph Myers had walked in the evening or had sat talking until dusk upon the schoolhouse steps in a kind of dream. Here and there went his hands, caressing the shoulders of the boys, playing about the tousled heads. As he talked his voice became soft and musical. There was a caress in that also. In a way the voice and the hands, the stroking of the shoulders and the touching of the hair was a part of the schoolmaster's effort to carry a dream into the young minds. By the caress that was in his fingers he expressed himself. He was one of those men in whom the force that creates life is diffused, not centralized. Under the caress of his hands doubt and disbelief went out of the minds of the boys and they began also to dream.

And then the tragedy. A half-witted boy of the school became enamored of the young master. In his bed at night he imagined unspeakable things and in the morning went forth to tell his dreams as facts. Strange, hideous accusations fell from his loose-hung lips. Through the Pennsylvania town went a shiver. Hidden, shadowy doubts that had been in men's minds concerning Adolph Myers were galvanized into beliefs.

The tragedy did not linger. Trembling lads were jerked out of bed and questioned. 'He put his arms about me,' said one. 'His fingers were always playing in my hair,' said another.

One afternoon a man of the town, Henry Bradford, who kept a saloon, came to the schoolhouse door. Calling Adolph Myers into the school yard he began to beat him with his fists. As his hard knuckles beat down into the frightened face of the schoolmaster, his wrath became more and more terrible. Screaming with dismay, the children ran here and there like disturbed insects. 'I'll teach you to put your hands on my boy, you beast,' roared the saloon keeper, who, tired of beating the master, had begun to kick him about the yard.

Adolph Myers was driven from the Pennsylvania town in the night. With lanterns in their hands a dozen men came to the door of the house where he lived alone and commanded that he dress and come forth. It was raining and one of the men had a rope in his hands. They had intended to hang the schoolmaster, but something in his figure, so small, white, and pitiful, touched their hearts and they let him escape. As he ran away into the darkness they repented of their weakness and ran after him, swearing and throwing sticks and great balls of soft mud at the figure that screamed and ran faster and faster into the darkness.

For twenty years Adolph Myers had lived alone in Winesburg. He was but forty but looked sixty-five. The name of Biddlebaum he got from a box of goods seen at a freight station as he hurried through an eastern Ohio town. He had an aunt in Winesburg, a black-toothed old woman who raised chickens, and with her he lived until she died. He had been ill for a year after the experience in Pennsylvania, and after his recovery worked as a day laborer in the fields, going timidly about and striving to conceal his hands. Although he did not understand what had happened he felt that the hands must be to blame. Again and again the fathers of the boys had talked of the hands. 'Keep your hands to yourself,' the saloon keeper had roared, dancing with fury in the schoolhouse yard.

Upon the verandah of his house by the ravine, Wing Biddlebaum continued to walk up and down until the sun had disappeared and the road beyond the field was lost in the grey shadows. Going into his house he cut slices of bread and spread honey upon them. When the rumble of the evening train that took away the express cars loaded with the day's harvest of berries had passed and restored the silence of the summer night, he went again to walk upon the verandah. In the darkness he could not see the hands and they became quiet. Although he still hungered for the presence of the boy, who was the medium through which he expressed his love of man, the hunger became again a part of his loneliness and his waiting. Lighting a lamp, Wing Biddle-baum washed the few dishes soiled by his simple meal and, setting up a folding cot by the screen door that led to the porch, prepared to undress for the night. A few stray white bread crumbs lay on the cleanly washed floor by the table; putting the lamp upon a low stool he began to pick up the crumbs, carrying them to his mouth one by one with unbelievable rapidity. In the dense blotch of light beneath the table, the kneeling figure looked like a priest engaged in some service of his church. The nervous expressive fingers, flashing in and out of the light, might well have been mistaken for the fingers of the devotee going swiftly through decade after decade of his rosary.

('Hands', *Winesburg, Ohio*, Boni and Liveright)

★   ★   ★

HART CRANE (1899–1932) His American editor describes Crane as one who, suffering the curse of sundered parentage, sought the tangent release of alcohol and of tender friendships with boys who followed the sea. From time to time, to quote a favourite phrase from Crane's letters, the Word became Flesh. Amongst the brilliant and powerful lyrics he beat out of himself before his early suicide, the following represents one of his deepest friendships; it took place in the shadow of that Brooklyn Bridge which provided the theme for his longest, but not greatest, poem.

VOYAGES: II

– And yet this great wing of eternity,
Of rimless floods, unfettered leewardings,
Samite sheeted and processioned where
Her undinal vast belly moonward bends,
Laughing the wrapt inflections of our love;

Take this Sea, whose diapason knells
On scrolls of silver snowy sentences,
The sceptred terror of whose sessions rends
As her demeanors motion well or ill,
All but the pieties of lovers' hands.

And onward, as bells of San Salvador
Salute the crocus lustres of the stars,
In these poinsettia meadows of her tides, –

Adagios of islands, O my Prodigal,
Complete the dark confessions her veins spell.

Mark how her turning shoulders wind the hours,
And hasten while her penniless rich palms
Pass superscription of bent foam and wave, –
Hasten, while they are true, – sleep, death, desire,
Close round one instant in one floating flower.

Bind us in time, O seasons clear, and awe.
O minstrel galleons of Carib fire,
Bequeath us to no earthly shore until
Is answered in the vortex of our grave
The seal's wide spindrift gaze toward paradise.

★   ★   ★

3. *IN GERMANY*

STEFAN GEORGE (1868–1933) Less familiar to readers of English than his contemporary, Rilke, this reserved, aristocratic, but none the less passionate poet deserves to be better known. Writing for an intimate circle, to whom he was the Master, he sought to keep alive the cult of his ideal Maximin.

This sixteen-year-old youth did not live long but he crystallized the poet's feelings once and for all and was not only the great friendship of George's life but also the focus of his mission and message, already hinted at by the Angel of *Der Teppich des Lebens* (1899) and by George's agreement with his predecessor, Hölderlin: 'The Greeks are indispensable to us' – *Hellas ewig unsre liebe*. The deification of Maximin is a matter of difficulty to many readers, for the boy is not only, like Dante's Beatrice, a symbol of the Divine but the Divine itself. (See E. K. Bennett, *Stefan George*, Bowes and Bowes.)

> Dem bist du kind, dem freund.
> Ich seh in dir den Gott
> Den schauernd ich erkannt
> Dem meine andacht gilt.

'To one you are a child, to another a friend. I see in you the God whom I recognized with awe, to whom I owe my devotion.'

To understand this it is necessary to bear in mind the emphasis that George laid upon the body:

. . . of all the utterances of the thousands of years which are known to us, the Greek idea that the body is God – the body which is the symbol of transitoriness – was by far the most creative . . . by far the boldest and the most worthy of mankind, and surpasses in sublimity every other, including the Christian one.'

These ideas seem close to the advice given by the Faun in the extract below.

BOY AND GOD

When we first met Maximin in our city, he was still in his boyhood. He came toward us from under a stone arch with the unerring certainty of a young fencer, and with a look of leadership and power, softened by the mobility and vague sadness that centuries of Christian civilization have wrought in the faces of the people. In him we recognized the representative of sovereign youth, such as we had dreamed of, youth in that unbroken fullness and purity that can still move mountains and walk on dry land through the midst of the sea, youth fitted to receive our heritage and to conquer new domains. We had heard too much of the wisdom that thinks to solve the final enigma, had savoured too much of the motley in the rush of impressions. The overwhelming freight of external possibilities had added nothing to the content, but the shimmering play of light that dulled the senses and slackened tensions. What we had need of was One who was moved by plain and simple things and could show them to us, as they are beheld by the eyes of the gods.

. . . Those of our contemporaries who did not see him, those who came later, will not understand how such a revelation could come from one so young. For although the sensitiveness and the prophetic splendour of the poems he left – mere fragments of a work in its beginnings – surpasses every valid standard known to us, he himself ascribed no particular importance to them, and the core of his influence will be apparent only from that which may be vouchsafed us to produce through the communion with his spirit. But we know that only sapless eras see in youth a preliminary stage and a promise, never the peak and perfection, that more in their contours than in their words and deeds, lies the lasting power of all the heroes and the mighty and those who in the grace of their spring walk the fields of summer for but a brief space, who bleed to death at the forest's verge or sink into dark waters, to be transported to heaven and to rule with deathless names over all the generations of men. We know that the great expeditions that changed the face of our world, were planned by the schoolboy Alexander, that the twelve-year-old son of Galilee instructed the scribes in the capital, that the Lord of the longest world rule we know of, did not die in his thirties, but as a youth found the eternal symbols on his bloomy path, and that he died as a youth.

. . . Maximin lived among us for only a short time. In accordance with a covenant that he had made in his early years, he was raised to another star before he became less like gods and more like men. To the colourful and diverse destiny of a splendid mortal, he preferred the calm and quiet reign of the celestials. Even his childhood had been filled with seething divinations of the Beyond, and the struggle with One Unnamed. To Him he turned as to the only one against whom he would measure himself. Him he implored for tasks and tests and, in his yearning nights pleaded that in reward he might see the holy face. When he had learned that God could not reveal Himself in this way, he offered Him this covenant: Then let me behold you in the best of your visible creations! Give me Leda, the beloved, give me the great man, the Master! And if it is true that here every structure falls, every flame is extinguished, every flower fades, let me stand upon your summit once and then be snatched away swiftly by your eagle. After these days of transport, he passed from a fevered dream to death – so quickly that we could only stare at a grave like other graves, and not believe that it contained him.

(Quoted in *Stefan George, Poems*, Pantheon Books, Inc.)

ON THE LIFE AND DEATH OF MAXIMIN

Your eyes were dim with distant dreams, you tended
No more with care the holy fief and knew
In every space the breath of living ended –
Now lift your head with joy has come to you.

The cold and dragging year that was your share,
A vernal tide of dawning wonders bore,
With bloomy hand, with shimmers in his hair
A god appeared and stepped within your door.

Unite in gladness, now no longer darkened
And flushing for an age whose gold is flown:
The calling of a god you too have hearkened,
It was a god whose mouth has kissed your own.

You also were elect – no longer mourn
For all your days in unfulfillment sheathed . . .
Praise to your city where a god was born!
Praise to your age in which a god has breathed!
    (*Ibid.*, tr. Carol North Valhope and Ernst Morwitz)

    My child came home
The sea-wind tangled in his hair,
      His gait still rocks
With conquered fears and young desire for quest.

    The salty spray
Still tans and burns the bloom upon his cheek:
      Fruit swiftly ripe
In savage scent and flame of alien suns.

    His eyes are grave
With secrets now, that I shall never learn,
      And faintly veiled,
Since from a spring he came into our frost.

    So wide the bud
That almost shyly I withdrew my gaze,
      And I abstained
From lips that had already chosen lips.

    My arm enclasps
One who unmoved by me, grew up and bloomed
      To other worlds –
My own and yet, how very far from me!
            (*Ibid.*)

So lovely a poem deserves to be read in its original tongue.

Mein kind kam heim.
Ihm wehtden seewind noch im haar.
Noch wiegt sein tritt
Bestandne furcht und junge lust der fahrt.

Vom salzigen sprühn
Entflammt noch seiner wange brauner schmelz:
Frucht schnell gereift
In fremder sonnen wildem duft und brand.

Sein blick ist schwer
Schon vom geheimnis das ich niemals weiss
Und leicht umflort
Da er vom lenz in unsern winter traf.

So offen quoll
Die knospe auf dass ich fast scheu sie sah
Und mir verbot
Den mund der einen mund zum kuss schon kor.

Mein arm umschliesst
Was unbewegt von mir zu andrer welt
Erblüht und wuchs –
Mein eigentum und mir unendlich fern.
(*Ibid.*, Verlag Helmut Küpper, Düsseldorf)

THE DANCER

Through gardens rocks the children's roundelay,
Their song the gentle air of evening grooves,
In pairs they sally, dance in circles swinging,
And hop in rhythm to the selfsame singing,
How glad, each little hand in hand, they sway!
But One there is who marks the beats and moves.

How soft and lithe his hip in bending seems,
With turn and stop his nimble foot beguiles!

317

His hair in darkness sheds a trembling shimmer,
He is the lodestar in the midst of glimmer,
He is the whole of youth with all its dreams,
He is the whole of youth with all its smiles.

(Ibid.)

ENCOMIUM

You are my lord! When on my path you loom
In many changing shapes and yet familiar
And beautiful, I bend my neck before you.
No longer have you garments, wings or weapons,
You wear but one adornment: in your hair
The clustered wreath. You touch – a fragrant draught
Of frenzy sways the mind that feels your breath,
And every fibre quivers from your blow.
Who called you The Assuager in the past,
He never fancied that your slender finger
Your rosy heel could shatter so completely.
I fling my body back in patient pain,
Yes, even when you come with your battalions
Of beasts that brand a mark with pointed talons
And tear with fangs, extorting sighs and anguish
Unutterable. As from you is breathed
The scent of mellow fruit and sappy green,
From them the fetid odour of the jungle,
The wet and dust they reek does not repel us:
No thing that in your circle weaves is foul.
You cleanse the taint, you heal the gash and banish
All weeping with the sweetness you exhale.
In threat or thrall, if only we are steadfast
Each day shall have in victory its ending –
Your service also: homage done again,
Oblivious smile into the starry blue.

(Ibid.)

DIALOGUE BETWEEN FAUN AND MAN

The Faun

You are but man, and where your wisdom ends
Our own begins, you only see the brink

When you have suffered for the step beyond.
When ripe your grain has grown, your cattle thrive,
The sacred trees their oil and wine surrender,
You think this only comes through ruse of yours.
The earths that breathe in stolid nights primeval
Do not decay, if ever they were joined
They sunder when a link escapes the ring.
Your rule is right for your appointed time.
Now hasten back! You have beheld the faun.
The worst, you do not know, is that your mind
Which can do much, in clouds may be enmeshed,
May rend apart the bond with clod and creature –
Loathing and lust, monotony and flux,
And dust and light and death and being born,
No more will grasp within the course of things.

Man

Who tells you so? For this the gods be sponsors.

The Faun

We never speak of them, but in your folly
You think they help you; without go-betweens
They never came to you: you dawn, you die –
Whose thing you are in truth, you never learn.

Man

Soon you will have no space for shameless sport.

The Faun

Soon whom you spurn without, you call within.

Man

You poisonous monster with the crooked mouth,
Despite your twisted shape, you are too kindred
To ours, or else my dart would strike you now.

The Faun

The beast is void of shame, the man of thanks.
With all contrivances you never learn

What most you need . . . but we in silence serve.
This only: slaying us, you slay yourselves.
Where we have trailed our shag, there spurts the milk,
Where we withheld our hooves, there grows no grass.
Your mind alone at work – and long ago
Your kind had been destroyed and all it does.
Your field would lie unsown and dry your brake . . .
Only by magic, Life is kept awake.

(Ibid. An extract only)

SEASONG

When on the verge with gentle fall
Down dips the fire-reddened ball,
Then on the dunes I pause to rest
That I may see a cherished guest.

This time of day is dull at home,
The flower wilts in salty foam,
And in a house so far away
With alien woman, none will stay.

With naked limbs, with cloudless eye
A goldhaired child now passes by,
It sings and dances as it nears,
Behind the boat it disappears.

I watch it come, I watch it go,
Though never words for it I know,
And never speech for me it had,
The brief beholding makes me glad.

My hearth is good, my roof is tight,
But bare it is of all delight.
The rents in every net I sewed,
And room and kitchen are bestowed.

So then I sit and wait astrand,
My temple pulses in my hand:
What use the day from dawn to dawn
If now the blondehaired child is gone!

(*Ibid.*)

★   ★   ★

You who are as pure as flame and slender,
You shoot from fine strain flowering,
You like the dawn serene and tender,
You like a simple, secret spring,

My fellow through the sunlit meadows,
Thrill round me when eve darkeneth,
Lighting my path among the shadows,
You cooling wind, you fiery breath.

You are my longing and my thinking,
I breathe you in all air that is,
I sip you when my lips are drinking,
In every fragrance find your kiss.

You like the dawn serene and tender,
You like a simple, secret spring,
You who are as pure as flame and slender,
You shoot from fine strain flowering.
(*Heritage of Symbolism*, tr. C. M. Bowra, Macmillan)

4. *IN GREECE*

CONSTANTINE CAVAFY, or KABÁFES (1863–1933) was an
Alexandrian Greek who stood apart from the lyrical revolution
and the experiments with language associated with Palamas,
Sikelianos and Kazantsakis. He preferred his wry and jewelled re-
constructions of the Hellenistic world of Alexandria and Antioch,
of Sidon and Kommagênê, to which were added accounts of his
'lawless' pleasures and regrets in the Egypt of his day, where
debauchery fired and tempered his verse. Thus the poem about

Myres shows what it felt like to be the pagan friend of a Christian in A.D. 340 while 'To Remain' and 'The Mirror in the Hall' are reminders, the one savage, the other tender, of a sensibility that lit a candle whenever a beautiful boy entered his small house.

DESIRES

Like beautiful bodies dead that had not grown old
And they shut them up, with tears in a splendid tomb adorning
With roses at their heads and jasmine at their feet –
Desires are like that, desires that have grown cold
And not been satisfied; never vouchsafed one sweet
Night time of pleasure or one gleam of morning.
  (*The Poems of C. P. Cavafy*, tr. John Mavrogordato, Hogarth)

THE WINDOWS

In these dark chambers here what weary days
I spend, walk up and down as in a maze
To find the windows. – Only to unclose
One of these windows will be some relief. –
But somehow windows this room hasn't got,
Or I can't find them. Perhaps I'd better not.
Perhaps the light would be another grief.
What fresh surprises there might be, who knows?

(*Ibid.*)

I WENT

I was not bound. I let myself go completely, went
To those indulgences, half actual,
And half were turned about in my own brain;
Went into the illuminated night;
And drank strong wines, as when
The champions of pleasure drink strong wine.

(*Ibid.*)

AT THE CAFÉ ENTRANCE

My attention something they said beside me
Turned towards the entrance of the café.

And I saw the beautiful body which looked
As if Eros himself had made it with his extreme skill –
Modelling with delight the symmetry of his limbs;
Lifting up the sculpture of his figure;
Modelling the face with affection
And leaving from the touch of his own fingers
A feeling on the forehead, on the eyes and on the lips.

(Ibid.)

IN THE STREET

His quite attractive face a little pale;
His brown eyes as if dazzled;
Twenty-five years old, but looks more like twenty;
With something rather artistic in his dress,
Some colour of his tie, and shape of collar –
Aimlessly he walks along the street,
Still as if hypnotised by the lawless pleasure,
The very lawless pleasure has been his.

(Ibid.)

ONE OF THEIR GODS

When one of them was passing through the market
Of Seleukeia, about the hour of evenfall,
Like a tall, a beautiful, a perfect youth,
With the joy of incorruptibility in his eyes,
With his black and perfumed hair,
The passers-by would look at him,
And one would ask another if he knew him,
And if he was a Greek of Syria, or a stranger. But a few
Who observed with greater attention
Would understand and draw aside;
And while he disappeared under the arcades,
In the shadows and in the lights of evening,
Going towards the quarter which at night only
Lives, with orgies and debauchery,
And every kind of drunkenness and lust,
They would wonder which it could be of Them,

323

And for what disreputable sensuality
He had come down into the streets of Seleukeia
From those Majestical, All-holy Mansions.

(Ibid.)

TO REMAIN

It must have been one o'clock at night,
Or half past one.

                In a corner of the wine shop;
Behind the wooden partition.
Except the two of us the shop quite empty.
A paraffin lamp hardly lighted it.
The waiter who had to sit up was asleep at the door.

No one would have seen us. But anyhow
We had become so excited
We were incapable of precautions.
Our clothes had been half opened – they were not many
For a divine month of July was blazing.

Enjoyment of the flesh in the middle
Of our half-opened clothes;
Quick baring of the flesh – and the vision of it
Has passed over twenty-six years; and now has come
Here in these verses to remain.

(Ibid.)

MÝRÊS: ALEXANDRIA
A.D. 340

When I heard of the disaster, that Mýrês was dead,
I went to his house, although I avoid
Going into the houses of the Christians,
Especially when they have mournings or holidays.

I stood in a passage, I did not want
To go farther inside, because I noticed
That the relations of the dead boy were looking at me
With evident perplexity and with displeasure.

They had him in a large room
Of which from the end where I stood
I could see something; all valuable carpets,
And vessels of silver and gold.

I was standing and weeping at one end of the passage.
And I was thinking that our gatherings and our excursions
Would not be worth while any more without Mýrês;
And I was thinking I should not see him any more
At our lovely and disorderly nights-out,
Enjoying himself, and laughing, and reciting verses
With his perfect sense of Greek rhythm;
And I was thinking that I had lost for ever
His beauty, that I had lost for ever
The youth whom I adored passionately.

Some old women, near me, were speaking quietly about
The last day he was alive –
On his lips continually the name of Christ,
In his hands he was holding a cross. –
Afterwards there came into the room
Four Christian priests, and began to say prayers
Fervently and supplications to Jesus,
Or to Mary (I don't know their religion well).

We knew, of course, that Mýrês was a Christian.
From the first hour we knew it, when
The year before last he joined our gang.
But he lived absolutely like us.
More given to our pleasures than any of us;
Scattering his money unsparingly in our amusements.
About the world's esteem regardless,
He would throw himself gladly into rows at night

When our gang happened
To meet an opposing gang in the street.
He never spoke about his religion.
In fact once we told him
That we would take him with us to the Serapion.

But he seemed to dislike
That joke of ours; I remember now.
O and two other times come into my mind now.
When we were making libations to Poseidon,
He withdrew from our circle, and turned his looks away.
And when enthusiastically one of us
Said, 'Let our company be under
The favour and protection of the great
The all-beautiful Apollo' – Mýrês whispered
(The others did not hear) 'Excepting me'.

The Christian priests in loud voices
Were praying for the young man's soul. –
I noticed with how much diligence,
With what strained attention
To the formalities of their religion, they were preparing
Everything for the Christian funeral.
And suddenly there mastered me a strange
Impression. Indefinitely, I felt
As if Mýrês was going from my side;
I felt that he was made one, a Christian,
With his own people; and that I was becoming
A stranger, quite a stranger; I noticed besides
A doubt coming over me: perhaps I had even been tricked
By my own passion, and had always been a stranger to him. –
I rushed out of their dreadful house,
I fled quickly before it should be seized, before it should be
    changed
By their Christianity, my memory of Mýrês.

(*Ibid.*)

THE MIRROR IN THE HALL

The rich house had in the hall
An enormous mirror, very old;
Bought at least eighty years ago.

A very handsome boy, assistant at a tailor's
(On Sundays an amateur athlete),

Was standing there with a parcel. He handed it
To someone of the house, and he took it inside
To fetch the receipt. The tailor's assistant
Was left alone, and waited.
He went up to the mirror and began to look at himself
And put his tie straight. After five minutes
They brought him the receipt. He took it and went away.

But the old mirror which had seen, and seen,
In the many years it had been
In existence, thousands of things and faces;
The old mirror was glad now
And was proud to have received upon itself
That entire beauty for a few minutes.

(*Ibid.*)

5. IN BRITAIN

EDWARD CARPENTER (1844–1929): Carpenter is best remembered as a leading literary figure in English socialism in the
later part of the nineteenth century. Though in his early life a
clergyman, and always retaining in his writing a moral fervour
and concern – coloured by more pagan feeling than orthodox
Christianity allowed – his ideas are a reaction against the con-
ventions and restrictive ethos of Victorian society towards a
simpler, more permissive ethic. His effusive socialist idealism,
centring on large emotional conceptions of democracy, freedom,
love, lent itself to giving a prominent place to a passionate and
all-but explicitly erotic relationship of male friendship.

Carpenter's large volume of poetry, collected under the title
of *Towards Democracy*, was obviously – too obviously – written
under the intoxication of Whitman. In his book, *The Intermediate
Sex*, he concerned himself directly with part of the subject of
this anthology, and a quotation from that work may serve to
introduce the extracts that follow it from *Towards Democracy*.

The homogenic attachment left unrecognised, easily loses some of its best quality and becomes an ephemeral or corrupt thing. Yet, as we have seen, it may, when occurring between an elder and younger, prove to be an immense educational force; while, as between equals, it may be turned to social and heroic uses, such as can hardly be demanded or expected from the ordinary marriage. It would seem high time, I say, that public opinion should recognise these facts; and so give to this attachment the sanction and dignity which arise from public recognition, as well as the definite form and outline which would flow from the existence of an accepted ideal or standard in the matter. It is often said how necessary for the ordinary marriage is some public recognition of the relation, and some accepted standard of conduct in it. May not, to a lesser degree, something of the same kind be true of the homogenic attachment? It has had its place as a recognised and guarded institution in the elder and more primitive societies; and it seems quite probable that a similar place will be accorded to it in the societies of the future.

★　★　★

THROUGH THE LONG NIGHT

You, proud curve-lipped youth, with brown sensitive face,
Why, suddenly, as you sat there on the grass, did you turn
    full upon me those twin black eyes of yours,
With gaze so absorbing so intense, I a strong man trembled and
    was faint?
Why in a moment between me and you in the full summer
    afternoon
        did Love sweep – leading it after in procession across the lawn
        and the flowers and under the waving trees huge dusky shadows
        of Death and the other world?

I know not.
Solemn and dewy-passionate, yet burning clear and stedfast at
    the last,

Through the long night those eyes of yours, dear, remain to me –
And I remain gazing into them.

(From Towards Democracy.)

WHEN I AM NEAR TO YOU

Now when I am near to you, dear friend,
   Passing out of myself, being delivered –
Through those eyes and lips and hands, so loved, so
ardently loved,
   I am become free;
In the sound of your voice I dwell
As in a world defended from evil.

   What I am accounted by the world to be – all that
I leave behind:
   It is nothing to me any longer.
Like one who leaves a house with all its mouldy old
furniture and pitches his camp under heaven's blue,
   So I take up my abode in your presence –
I find my deliverance in you.

(Ibid.)

PARTED LIPS

Parted lips, between which love dwells—
   Only a little space of breath and shadow,
Yet here the gate of all the world to me.

(Ibid.)

SUMMER HEAT

Sun burning down on back and loins, penetrating the
skin, bathing their flanks in sweat,
   Where they lie naked on the warm ground, and the
ferns arch over them,
   Out in the woods, and the sweet scent of fir-needles
Blends with the fragrant nearness of their bodies;

329

In-armed together, murmuring, talking,
Drunk with wine of Eros' lips,
Hourlong, while the great wind rushes in the branches,
And the blue above lies deep beyond the fern-fronds
and fir-tips;

Till, with the midday sun, fierce scorching, smiting,
Up from their woodland lair they leap, and smite,
And strike with wands, and wrestle, and bruise each other,
In savage play and amorous despite.

(Ibid.)

SPENDING THE NIGHT ALONE

To lie all night beside the loved one – how lovely!
To hold in one's arms something so precious, so
beautiful,
Dear head and hair and lips and limbs that shrine eternity,
Through scent and sense and breath and touch and love –
Forgetting all but this one – all but this one.

And then again to spend the night alone, to resume
oneself –
To sail out in the silent watches over the sleeping world,
and drink of the intoxication of space,
Calm, self-centred, to the great first One united;
Over-looking the wide sleeping-grounds of Time – forms
of the past, the future – comrades, innumerable,
Lovers possible, all safely eternally embosomed;
Kissing them lightly on the lips, the forehead,
Leaving them sleeping,
Spending the night alone.

(Ibid.)

JOHN ADDINGTON SYMONDS (1840–93): Symonds, like Carpenter, was consciously concerned with the subject of this anthology. He was a literary critic of great distinction, and a student of Greek literature and Renaissance literature and art (extracts from his classic biography of Michelangelo and of his translations of Michelangelo's sonnets are represented elsewhere in this anthology); his verse is occasional and greatly inferior to his prose writings. Throughout his work he returns to the question of male friendship; his most extensive single exploration of the subject is his study, *A Problem in Greek Ethics*.

Keenly conscious of his own personal need and lack, and faced by the taboos of society and of his conscience in his own erotic relationships, Symonds, like so many others during this period, tended to transpose his desires into more generalized social and political and philanthropic channels. But even so, writing before and concurrently with the 'aesthetes' yet not one of them, and for that matter writing before Havelock Ellis, it took some courage and integrity on Symonds' part to write as openly and extensively as he did on the question. Finally, as his verse indicates (e.g. *Clifton and a Lad's Love*), the problem remained for him still rather tormenting and unresolved.

CLIFTON AND A LAD'S LOVE

This time it is no dream that stirs
    The ancient fever of my brain:
The burning pulses throb again,
    The thirst I may not quench recurs.

In vain I tell my beating heart
    How poor and worthless were the prize:
The stifled wish within me dies,
    But leaves me unextinguished smart.

It is not for the love of God
    That I have done my soul this wrong;
'Tis not to make my reason strong
    Or curb the currents of my blood.

> But sloth, and fear of men, and shame
> Impose their limit on my bliss:
> Else had I laid my lips to his,
> And called him by love's dearest name.
> (From *In the Key of Blue* by J. A. Symonds.)

OSCAR WILDE (1856–1900) and LORD ALFRED DOUGLAS (1870–1945)

MY OWN BOY,—

Your sonnet is quite lovely, and it is a marvel that those red rose-leaf lips of yours should be made no less for the madness of music and song than for the madness of kissing. Your slim-gilt soul walks between passion and poetry. I am sure Hyacinthus whom Apollo loved so madly was you in Greek days. Why are you alone in London, and when do you go to Salisbury? Do go there and cool your hands in the grey twilight of Gothic things. Come here whenever you like. It is a lovely place and lacks only you. Do go to Salisbury first. Always with undying love,

Yours,

OSCAR.

★   ★   ★

Savoy Hotel,
Victoria Embankment, London

DEAREST OF ALL BOYS,—

Your letter was delightful, red and yellow wine to me, but I am sad and out of sorts. Bosie, you must not make scenes with me. They kill me, they wreck the loveliness of life. I cannot see you, so Greek and gracious, distorted with passion. I cannot listen to your curved lips saying hideous things to me. I would sooner [indecipherable] than have you bitter, unjust, hating. . . . I must see you soon. You are the divine thing I want, the thing of genius and beauty; but I don't know how to do it. Shall I come to Salisbury? My bill here is £49 a week, I have also got a new sitting-room . . . Why are you not here, my dear, my wonderful boy? I fear I must leave – no money, no credit, and a heart of lead.

YOUR OWN OSCAR.

★   ★   ★

THE DEAD POET

I dreamed of him last night, I saw his face
All radiant and unshadowed of distress,
And as of old, in music measureless,
I heard his golden voice and marked him trace
Under the common thing the hidden grace,
And conjure wonder out of emptiness,
Till mean things put on beauty like a dress
And all the world was an enchanted place.

And then me thought outside a fast locked gate
I mourned the loss of unrecorded words,
Forgotten tales and mysteries half said,
Wonders that might have been articulate,
And voiceless thoughts like murdered singing birds.
And so I woke and knew that he was dead.
                    (Lord Alfred Douglas, *Complete Poems*, Secker)

TWO LOVES

Two loves I have of comfort and despair
    Which like two spirits do suggest me still,
The better angel is a man right fair,
    The worser spirit a woman coloured ill.

                                        –Shakespeare.

I dreamed I stood upon a little hill,
And at my feet there lay a ground, that seemed
Like a waste garden, flowering at its will
With flowers and blossoms. There were pools that dreamed
Black and unruffled; there were white lilies
A few, and crocuses, and violets
Purple or pale, snake-like fritillaries
Scarce seen for the rank grass, and through green nets
Blue eyes of shy pervenche winked in the sun.
And there were curious flowers, before unknown,
Flowers that were stained with moonlight, or with shades
Of Nature's wilful moods; and here a one
That had drunk in the transitory tone
Of one brief moment in a sunset; blades

Of grass that in an hundred springs had been
Slowly but exquisitely nurtured by the stars,
And watered with the scented dew long cupped
In lilies, that for rays of sun had seen
Only God's glory, for never a sunrise mars
The luminous air of heaven. Beyond, abrupt,
A gray stone wall, o'ergrown with velvet moss,
Uprose. And gazing I stood long, all mazed
To see a place so strange, so sweet, so fair.
And as I stood and marvelled, lo! across
The garden came a youth, one hand he raised
To shield him from the sun, his wind-tossed hair
Was twined with flowers, and in his hand he bore
A purple bunch of bursting grapes, his eyes
Were clear as crystal, naked all was he,
White as the snow on pathless mountains frore,
Red were his lips as red wine-spilth that dyes
A marble floor, his brow chalcedony.
And he came near me, with his lips uncurled
And kind, and caught my hand and kissed my mouth,
And gave me grapes to eat, and said 'Sweet friend,
Come, I will shew thee shadows of the world
And images of life. See, from the south
Comes the pale pageant that hath never an end.'
And lo! within the garden of my dream
I saw two walking on a shining plain
Of golden light. The one did joyous seem
And fair and blooming, and a sweet refrain
Came from his lips; he sang of pretty maids
And joyous love of comely girl and boy,
His eyes were bright, and 'mid the dancing blades
Of golden grass his feet did trip for joy.
And in his hands he held an ivory lute,
With strings of gold that were as maiden's hair,
And sang with voice as tuneful as a flute,
And round his neck three chains of roses were.
But he that was his comrade walked aside;
He was full sad and sweet, and his large eyes
Were strange with wondrous brightness, staring wide

With gazing; and he sighed with many sighs
That moved me, and his cheeks were wan and white
Like pallid lilies, and his lips were red
Like poppies, and his hands he clenchèd tight,
And yet again unclenchèd, and his head
Was wreathed with moon-flowers pale as lips of death.
A purple robe he wore, o'erwrought in gold
With the device of a great snake, whose breath
Was fiery flame: which when I did behold
I fell a-weeping and I cried 'Sweet youth,
Tell me why, sad and sighing, thou dost rove
These pleasant realms? I pray thee speak me sooth
What is thy name?' He said, 'My name is Love.'
Then straight the first did turn himself to me
And cried, 'He lieth, for his name is Shame,
But I am Love, and I was wont to be
Alone in this fair garden, till he came
Unasked by night; I am true Love, I fill
The hearts of boy and girl with mutual flame.'
Then sighing said the other, 'Have thy will,
I am the Love that dare not speak its name.'

(*Lyrics*, Rich and Cowan 1935)

★　★　★

A. E. HOUSMAN (1859–1936)   It is now generally understood
that the stoical Professor of Classics at Cambridge, who chose
the dull Manilius for his texual expertise and who worked off
his spleen by bitter invectives on shoddy scholars, concealed the
friend that a certain Jackson, the hero of his young manhood,
abandoned or denied. The resulting 'mystery', the complex of
frustrated emotions singing briefly and rarely after walks and
beer, peopled the Shropshire in which he had never lived with
ageing youths, pessimistic soldiers and rascals doomed to be
hanged. W. H. Auden's famous sonnet has a savage truth:

A. E. HOUSMAN

No one, not even Cambridge, was to blame;
– Blame if you like the human situation –

Heart-injured in North London, he became
The leading classic of his generation.

Deliberately he chose the dry-as-dust,
Kept tears like dirty postcards in a drawer;
Food was his public love, his private lust
Something to do with violence and the poor.

In savage footnotes on unjust editions
He timidly attacked the life he led.
And put the money of his feelings on

The uncritical relations of the dead,
Where purely geographical divisions
Parted the coarse hanged soldier from the don.

(*Another Time*, Random House)

*   *   *

TO AN ATHLETE DYING YOUNG

The time you won your town the race
We chaired you through the market-place;
Man and boy stood cheering by,
And home we brought you shoulder-high.

To-day, the road all runners come,
Shoulder-high we bring you home,
And set you at your threshold down,
Townsman of a stiller town.

Smart lad, to slip betimes away
From fields where glory does not stay
And early though the laurel grows
It withers quicker than the rose.

Eyes the shady night has shut
Cannot see the record cut,
And silence sounds no worse than cheers
After earth has stopped the ears:

Now you will not swell the rout
Of lads that wore their honours out,

Runners whom renown outran
And the name died before the man.

So set, before its echoes fade,
The fleet foot on the sill of shade,
And hold to the low lintel up
The still-defended challenge-cup.

And round that early-laurelled head
Will flock to gaze the strengthless dead,
And find unwithered on its curls
The garland briefer than a girl's.

(A Shropshire Lad, XIX)

Loitering with a vacant eye
Along the Grecian gallery,
And brooding on my heavy ill,
I met a statue standing still.
Still in marble stone stood he,
And steadfastly he looked at me.
'Well met,' I thought the look would say,
'We both were fashioned far away;
We neither knew, when we were young,
These Londoners we live among.'

Still he stood and eyed me hard,
An earnest and a grave regard:
'What, lad, drooping with your lot?
I too would be where I am not.
I too survey that endless line
Of men whose thoughts are not as mine.
Years, ere you stood up from the rest,
On my neck the collar prest;
Years, when you lay down your ill,
I shall stand and bear it still.
Courage, lad, 'tis not for long:
Stand, quit you like stone, be strong.'
So I thought his look would say;

And light on me my trouble lay,
And I stept out in flesh and bone
Manful like the man of stone.

(A Shropshire Lad, LI)

★　　★　　★

Because I liked you better
　　Than suits a man to say,
It irked you, and I promised
　　To throw the thought away.

To put the world between us
　　We parted, stiff and dry;
'Good-bye,' said you, 'forget me.'
　　'I will, no fear,' said I.

If here, where clover whitens
　　The dead man's knoll, you pass,
And no tall flower to meet you
　　Starts in the trefoiled grass,

Halt by the headstone naming
　　The heart no longer stirred,
And say the lad that loved you
　　Was one that kept his word.

(More Poems, XXXI)

A.J.J.

When he's returned I'll tell him – oh,
　　Dear fellow, I forgot:
Time was you would have cared to know,
　　But now it matters not.

I mourn you, and you heed not how;
　　Unsaid the word must stay;
Last month was time enough, but now
　　The news must keep for aye.

Oh, many a month before I learn
　　Will find me starting still
And listening, as the days return,
　　For him that never will.

Strange, strange to think his blood is cold
　　And mine flows easy on,
And that straight look, that heart of gold,
　　That grace, that manhood gone.

The word unsaid will stay unsaid
　　Though there was much to say;
Last month was time enough: he's dead,
　　The news must keep for aye.
(More Poems, XLII)

★　　★　　★

He would not stay for me; and who can wonder?
　　He would not stay for me to stand and gaze.
I shook his hand and tore my heart in sunder
　　And went with half my life about my ways.
(Additional Poems, VII)

★　　★　　★

Ask me no more, for fear I should reply;
　　Others have held their tongues, and so can I;
Hundreds have died, and told no tale before:
　　Ask me no more, for fear I should reply –

How one was true and one was clean of stain
　　And one was braver than the heavens are high,
And one was fond of me: and all are slain.
　　Ask me no more, for fear I should reply.
(Additional Poems, VI)

Oh who is that young sinner with the handcuffs on his wrists?
And what has he been after that they groan and shake their fists?
And wherefore is he wearing such a conscience-stricken air?
Oh they're taking him to prison for the colour of his hair.

339

'Tis a shame to human nature, such a head of hair as his;
In the good old time 'twas hanging for the colour that it is;
Though hanging isn't bad enough and flaying would be fair
For the nameless and abominable colour of his hair.

Oh a deal of pains he's taken and a pretty price he's paid
To hide his poll or dye it of a mentionable shade;
But they've pulled the beggar's hat off for the world to see and stare,
And they're haling him to justice for the colour of his hair.

Now 'tis oakum for his fingers and the treadmill for his feet
And the quarry-gang on Portland in the cold and in the heat,
And between his spells of labour in the time he has to spare
He can curse the God that made him for the colour of his hair.

(*Ibid.*, xviii)

★ ★ ★

FREDERICK ROLFE, 'BARON CORVO' (1860-1913)   'Selfish?
Yes, selfish. The selfishness of a square peg in a round hole,'
this writer once explained himself, between the habitual invective
and compensatory fantasy, for he was a 'haggard shabby shy
priestly-visaged individual' who always failed to find 'the divine
friend much-desired'. Sexual, temperamental, spiritual abnor-
mality – a sort of genius – was at the back of it all; he failed as
schoolmaster and candidate for the priesthood, but in *Hadrian
the Seventh* triumphed as Pope. 'I believe that somebody carelessly lied, that someone clumsily blundered, and that all concerned were determined not to own themselves, or anyone else
but me, in the wrong. A mistake – a justifiable mistake seeing
that I am an abnormal creature and my superiors about as
commonplace a gaggle of fatwitted geese as this hemisphere
produces – was made; and, by quibbles, intimidations, every
hole and corner means conceivable, it has been perpetuated.'

Towards the very end of his life, in Venice, he shed his inhibitions and began to follow his desires. *The Desire and Pursuit of
the Whole* dates from this period.

NICHOLAS AND ZILDO

Suddenly the boy stepped down from the poop, trailing his oar to rest, and came close to Nicholas. His face had whitened and his great eyes strained open wide. 'Sior, with permission, has the earthquake done ill to you? Don't you know? Has it broken your hotel? Like La Tasca? O, Sior, are you wounded? Why, my master, are you here, like this, at this hour? Sa?'

'No one is wounded; and nothing is broken. But foolish people are mad with fear. Therefore, I came that you might take the news from me. You must not be frightened, Zildo.'

'Sior, I have no fear.'

'Bravo! Then give me the oar and let me row, for I am cold.'

Zildo changed places in silence; and Nicholas mounted and rowed viciously toward the club. He wanted coffee and a razor.

As they slipped by the Istrian firewood boats moored off Daganole, the boy softly said: 'Sior, I understand that you have waited, during several hours, in the cold, at Santrovaso, so that I might not be frightened.'

'It is nothing,' Nicholas repeated, rowing on.

They both became mute and rigid as they crossed the Grand Canal: for the most usual unusual thing had happened. They have told me of it separately and together: so I know. I will try to explain. So far, Nicholas had known himself for Nicholas. He was himself; and his body was his own habitation – his own. Other people's were theirs. One could deal with other people's, take them, use them, given or by force: but they remained other people's: they never became one's own. They never could become one's own. One was not the person who owned them, any more than one was the person who inhabited them. Just that. Zildo, on his part, had never examined the problem: never had been conscious of it, so far. He says that he made a certain discovery, on the topo, at the moment when Nicholas told him that he was absolutely alone in the world. For the rest, he was called Zildo; and that was all about it. And then, all of a sudden, on this iridescent morning of opals in January, when the lips of Zildo touched the hand of Nicholas, owner of lips and owner of hands experienced a single definite shock: an electric shiver tingled through their veins: hot blood went surging and romping through their hearts: a blast, as of rams' horns, sang in their ears and rang in their beings, and down went all sorts of separations. They were bewitched. They were startled beyond measure. Of course we others are well aware that this was merely the commonplace casting of the commonplace spell by their millions of dead ancestors recognising (in these two) the possessors by inheritance of the multitudinous charm of all other own dead loves – that it was nothing more than the quickening in these separated entities of the dormant prenatal knowledge of homogeneity. At the moment of recognition, Zildo says that he felt only satisfaction. He had faith from that moment the day after La Tasca: now he had the evidence which he had hoped for. Then, he attained knowledge of something unseen: now, he gained the substance of it. For him, fact had replaced theory. But Nicholas only knew that something had happened to him, something liable to appal him unless he was careful, something absolutely antecedent to any previous experiment of his. It was far more awful than an earthquake. It was the dragging of all anchors. It was the breaching of innermost bulwarks. He had nothing to hold on by. He was naked and unarmed to all the world. His citadel was open. Crab-like, he instantly shut himself up in his shell, throwing up ramparts and earthworks to conceal and protect his individuality. So, while Nicholas landed at the club, wearing an aspect rather more stark (not to say forbidding) than usual, Zildo (simple also, but firmer and not in the very least dependent on external fortifications) was sensible of no fear, of no abashment, of no revolt; and sedately performed his duties with the bark, fetching up the leathern bag of books, and following his master to the hotel as docilely as ever. For Nicholas, the experience was a revelation. For Zildo, it had been a confirmation. That was all the difference.

(Baron Corvo, *The Desire and Pursuit of the Whole*, pp. 117–8, Cassell, 1953)

. . . [Nicholas] sank into the cane arm-chair amidships, and began to roll a cigarette.

A hand curved from the poop behind him, laying four notes of ten lire each with three silver lire and five pajanche in copper on his lap.

'Còssa xe?' he blankly demanded.

'Sior', answered a voice of infinite young jubilation, 'that is the price of three collars of pomegranates, in silver beads on pearls, in pearl beads on silver, and in silver beads on gold, which I wove for my young-lady American. And here, also, is a design' (shewing a paper) 'for a new collar of tiny feathers of peacocks, which tomorrow I shall weave in gold beads with green and blue, for sending to America to the same.'

'Benissimo.' He folded the coins in the notes, and, turning round, placed them in the boy's hands.

'But – Sior—'

'Put your deniers in your pocket.'

'Nòssior.'

'I am not disputing. I am telling you.'

'Sior, listen' (gabbling hurriedly), 'I wove the collars with beads which I bought with your deniers which I took from Sior Caloprin of the Cassa di Risparmio—'

'Zildo, listen. There are no deniers of mine in the Cassa di Risparmio. – The deniers which you take from Sior Caloprin are your earned wages. – You have woven collars of beads bought with your own deniers, not mine. Bravo, my Zildo. Do it again. I am very contented with you. Make some more, and yet some more. Fill your pockets with deniers while you can. Good auguries to you. That is all. Understand? Good. And, now, do me the pleasure of rowing me to Burano: for I wish to repose myself with my thoughts—'

Tears welled in unchecked flood from the boy's frank wistful innocent eyes. Nicholas felt like a perfect beast: but he set his teeth against any sort of putrid foolery. Better feel like one than be one; and he shuddered to think how near to the verge of an embrace his heart had so suddenly thrust him. He hardened, and struck a match for his cigarette.

Zildo blinked a bit, without wile, that he might see his way to cast off; and his ripe young lips closed courageously against so ruthlessly bitter and cruel a disappointment. But he obeyed his master implicitly, saying not another word. In half a minute the bark was flying on, driven by the long regular sweeps of his oar. He says that this was when he first knew that he must wait and wait.

Nicholas remained rigid, facing prow-ward, thankful that only his back was visible to his servant: for certain emotions were beginning to play a fierce game with him. The love and the lealty, the gently delicate honour, the unswerving faith and trust, the grave deliberate singleness of purpose, of the exquisite soul which inhabited that splendidly young and vigorous and alluring form behind him, rang echoing through every secret cavern of his being. Zildo was minded to give. For his own part, he also yearned to give. But he yearned to take as well. And Zildo! Light of light! What would be the unravelling of this tangle, in which he had involved himself with Zildo? Why had Zildo so conclusively refused to leave him? Why had he, with such unusual weakness, acquiesced in that refusal? What portended this content with the position – this content – this – no, not content – this suppressed consuming longing to take and to give, to give and to take all, all, to mingle and dissolve in as one? What was this hunger, this thirst, this ravenous sense of desire for the Χτῆμα ἐς ἀεί of that soul and body? It was not mere everyday lust: his admiration was as great for the naïve spring-like soul, for the mind as gently and firmly bright as a star, as for the long lithe limbs, the soft firm fragrant flesh, the noble features, the stalwart grace, the virginal freshness (all once seen, and never for a moment forgotten); and his admiration (for beauty pure and simple) was refrained by impregnable virtue proclaiming its object sacrosanct and inviolable. Nor was it mere vulgar recognition, in the humble manner of Christians (that latebrosa et lucifuga, natio, as Minucius Felix calls them) of any inferiority in his own soul or in his own body. He was aware of his own distinction and force and untainted excellence of form and feature, of his inexhaustible youth and strength. He knew himself to be capable of thoughts and deeds as worthy as Zildo's, fine and rare and cardinal as those undoubtedly were. Was it, then, only the effect of the shock, the appulse, the thunderclap of joy, at the knowledge that he had (actually in his hand and devoted to him) one so completely sympathetic, so precisely resembling the majestic eternal primaveral ideal which he formed for his own attainment? His friends – never, in all his life, had he had such a friend – never had he even seen anyone capable of being such a friend as Zildo seemed to wish to be, and might be – one and all of them had taken the most hideous and egregious tosses at the very first approach to his ideal. Sympathy – oh yes, they said that they sympathised with him. They roared it. But they knew no Greek: they hadn't the faintest notion of what they were saying. Asked to define, they whimpered that they felt for him. Felt for him – yes, they felt feelings of their own; and expected him to feel them too. The idea of feeling his feelings never entered their fat heads. They felt for, not with, him; and, what they thought was sym-pathy, was actually dys-pathy. No one had ever felt with him. No one had ever been able to take his part. What heaps of miawling minnocks thought themselves so beastly virtuose for taking –

and one admits that they took it with both hands – was, not his part
but, that which they thought ought to be his part; and their precious
taking of it was their gain and his loss.

(Ibid.)

★ ★ ★

D. H. LAWRENCE (1885–1930) In the spring of 1916 John
Middleton Murry was living next door to the Lawrences in
Cornwall, and became worried about his friend's proposal of
Blutbrüderschaft with its accompanying ritual. 'If I love you, and
you know I love you, isn't that enough?' he would say, while
Lawrence was likely to reply, 'I hate your love, I *hate* it. You're
an obscene bug, sucking my life away.' Murry was to explain
much later that 'what is generally understood by the word homosexuality' could not be applied to Lawrence. Yet from the towel-
rubbing incident in *The White Peacock* (1911) to the oath scene in
The Plumed Serpent (1926) Lawrence was clearly interested in
states of deep feeling between men, as one might add was
demanded by his 'dark' philosophy (it was all part of deepened
consciousness.) The Gladiatorial Scene in *Women in Love* suggests
'a compensatory urge, an identification of a frail body with a
strong, through a vicarious athleticism'. (See Harry T. Moore,
The Intelligent Heart, Heinemann.) During the Cornish period
there was also the intense friendship with the young farmer,
William Henry Hocking, and the 'mateship' in the fields.

A PASTORAL BATHE

At the end of June the weather became fine again. Hay harvest was to
begin as soon as it settled. There were only two fields to be mown this
year, to provide just enough stuff to last until the spring. As my vaca-
tion had begun I decided I would help, and that we three, the father,
George and I, would get in the hay without hired assistance.

I rose the first morning very early, before the sun was well up. The
clear sound of challenging cocks could be heard along the valley. In
the bottoms, over the water and over the lush wet grass, the night

mist still stood white and substantial. As I passed along the edge of the meadow the cow-parsnip was as tall as I, frothing up to the top of the hedge, putting the faded hawthorn to a wan blush. Little, early birds – I had not heard the lark – fluttered in and out of the foaming meadow-sea, plunging under the surf of flowers washed high in one corner, swinging out again, dashing past the crimson sorrel cresset. Under the froth of flowers were the purple vetch-clumps, yellow milk vetches, and the scattered pink of the wood-betony, and the floating stars of marguerites. There was a weight of honeysuckle on the hedges, where pink roses were waking up for their broad-spread flight through the day.

Morning silvered the swaths of the far meadow, and swept in smooth, brilliant curves round the stones of the brook; morning ran in my veins; morning chased the silver, darting fish out of the depth, and I, who saw them, snapped my fingers at them, driving them back.

I heard Trip barking, so I ran towards the pond. The punt was at the island, where from behind the bushes I could hear George whistling. I called to him, and he came to the water's edge half dressed.

'Fetch a towel,' he called, 'and come on.'

I was back in a few moments, and there stood my Charon fluttering in the cool air. One good push sent us to the islet. I made haste to undress, for he was ready for the water, Trip dancing around, barking with excitement at his new appearance.

'He wonders what's happened to me,' he said, laughing, pushing the dog playfully away with his bare foot. Trip bounded back, and came leaping up, licking him with little caressing licks. He began to play with the dog, and directly they were rolling on the fine turf, the laughing, expostulating, naked man, and the excited dog, who thrust his great head on to the man's face, licking, and, when flung away, rushed forward again, snapping playfully at the naked arms and breasts. At last George lay back, laughing and panting, holding Trip by the two forefeet which were planted on his breast, while the dog, also panting, reached forward his head for a flickering lick at the throat pressed back on the grass, and the mouth thrown back out of reach. When the man had thus lain still for a few moments, and the dog was just laying his head against his master's neck to rest too, I called, and George jumped up, and plunged into the pond with me, Trip after us.

The water was icily cold, and for a moment deprived me of my senses. When I began to swim, soon the water was buoyant, and I was sensible of nothing but the vigorous poetry of action. I saw George swimming on his back laughing at me, and in an instant I flung myself like an impulse after him. The laughing face vanished as he swung over and fled, and I pursued the dark head and the ruddy neck. Trip, the wretch, came paddling towards me, interrupting me; then all bewildered with excitement, he scudded to the bank. I chuckled to myself as I saw him run along, then plunge in and go plodding to George. I was gaining. He tried to drive off the dog, and I gained rapidly. As I came up to him and caught him, with my hand on his shoulder, there came a laughter from the bank. It was Emily.

I trod the water, and threw handfuls of spray at her. She laughed and blushed. Then Trip waded out to her and she fled swiftly from his shower-bath. George was floating beside me, looking up and laughing.

We stood and looked at each other as we rubbed ourselves dry. He was well proportioned, and naturally of handsome physique, heavily limbed. He laughed at me, telling me I was like one of Aubrey Beardsley's long, lean, ugly fellows. I referred him to many classic examples of slenderness, declaring myself more exquisite than his grossness, which amused him.

But I had to give in, and bow to him, and he took on an indulgent, gentle manner. I laughed and submitted. For he knew how much I admired the noble, white fruitfulness of his form. As I watched him, he stood in white relief against the mass of green. He polished his arm, holding it out straight and solid; he rubbed his hair into curls, while I watched the deep muscles of his shoulders, and the bands stand out in his neck as he held it firm; I remembered the story of Annable.

He saw I had forgotten to continue my rubbing, and laughing he took hold of me and began to rub me briskly, as if I were a child, or rather, a woman he loved and did not fear. I left myself quite limply in his hands, and, to get a better grip of me, he put his arm round me and pressed me against him, and the sweetness of the touch of our naked bodies one against the other was superb. It satisfied in some measure the vague, indecipherable yearning of my soul; and it was the same with him. When he had rubbed me all warm, he let me go, and we looked at each other with eyes of still laughter, and our love was perfect for a moment, more perfect than any love I have known since, either for man or woman.

(D. H. Lawrence, *The White Peacock*)

*　*　*

GERALD AND BIRKIN

There was a pause of strange enmity between the two men, that was very near to love. It was always the same between them; always their talk brought them into a deadly nearness of contact, a strange, perilous intimacy which was either hate or love, or both. They parted with apparent unconcern, as if their going apart were a trivial occurrence. And they really kept it to the level of trivial occurrence. Yet the heart of each one burned from the other. They burned with each other, inwardly. This they would never admit. They intended to keep their relationship a casual free-and-easy friendship, they were not going to be so unmanly and unnatural as to allow any heart-burning between them. They had not the faintest belief in deep relationship between men and men, and their disbelief prevented any development of their powerful but suppressed friendliness.

(*Women in Love*, Ch. II)

MAN TO MAN

Whilst he was laid up, Gerald came to see him. The two men had a deep, uneasy feeling for each other. Gerald's eyes were quick and restless, his whole manner tense and impatient, he seemed strung up to some activity. According to conventionality, he wore black clothes, he looked formal, handsome and *comme il faut*. His hair was fair almost to whiteness, sharp like splinters of light, his face was keen and ruddy, his body seemed full of northern energy.

Gerald really loved Birkin, though he never quite believed in him. Birkin was too unreal; Gerald felt that his own understanding was much sounder and safer. Birkin was delightful, a wonderful spirit, but after all, not to be taken seriously, not quite to be counted as a man among men.

.   .   .   .   .   .

He knew Birkin could do without him – could forget, and not suffer. This was always present in Gerald's consciousness, filling him with bitter unbelief: this consciousness of the young, animal-like spontaneity of detachment . . .

Quite other things were going through Birkin's mind. Suddenly he saw himself confronted with another problem – the problem of love

and eternal conjunction between two men. Of course this was necessary
– it had been a necessity inside himself all his life – to love a man
purely and fully. Of course he had been loving Gerald all along, and all
along denying it.

He lay in the bed and wondered, whilst his friend sat beside him,
lost in brooding. Each man was gone in his own thoughts.

'You know how the old German knights used to swear a *Blutbrüderschaft*,' he said to Gerald, with quite a new happy activity in his eyes.

'Make a little wound in their arms, and rub each other's blood into
the cut?' said Gerald.

'Yes – and swear to be true to each other, of one blood, all their
lives. That is what we ought to do. No wounds, that is obsolete. But
we ought to swear to love each other, you and I, implicitly, and
perfectly, and finally, without any possibility of going back on it.'

He looked at Gerald with clear, happy eyes of discovery. Gerald
looked down at him, attracted, so deeply bondaged in fascinated
attraction, that he was mistrustful, resenting the bondage, hating the
attraction.

'We will swear to each other, one day, shall we?' pleaded Birkin.
'We will swear to stand by each other – be true to each other –
ultimately – infallibly – given to each other, organically – without
possibility of taking back.'

Birkin sought hard to express himself. But Gerald hardly listened.
His face shone with a certain luminous pleasure. He was pleased. But he
kept his reserve. He held himself back.

'Shall we swear to each other, one day?' said Birkin, putting out his
hand towards Gerald.

Gerald just touched the extended fine, living hand, as if withheld
and afraid.

'We'll leave it till I understand it better,' he said, in a voice of excuse.

Birkin watched him. A little sharp disappointment, perhaps a touch
of contempt came into his heart.

'Yes,' he said. 'You must tell me what you think, later. You know
what I mean? Not sloppy emotionalism. An impersonal union that
leaves one free.'

They lapsed both into silence. Birkin was looking at Gerald all the
time. He seemed now to see, not the physical, animal man, which he
usually saw in Gerald, and which usually he liked so much, but the
man himself, complete, and as if fated, doomed, limited. This strange

sense of fatality in Gerald, as if he were limited to one form of existence, one knowledge, one activity, a sort of fatal halfness, which to himself seemed wholeness, always overcame Birkin after their moments of passionate approach, and filled him with a sort of contempt, or boredom. It was the insistence on the limitation which so bored Birkin in Gerald. Gerald could never fly away from himself, in real indifferent gaiety. He had a clog, a sort of monomania.

There was silence for a time. Then Birkin said, in a lighter tone, letting the stress of the contact pass:

'Can't you get a good governess for Winifred? – somebody exceptional?' . . .

. . . 'Good-bye,' said Gerald, taking the warm hand of his friend in a firm grasp. 'I shall come again. I miss you down at the mill.'

'I'll be there in a few days,' said Birkin.

The eyes of the two men met again. Gerald's, that were keen as a hawk's, were suffused now with warm light and with unadmitted love, Birkin looked back as out of a darkness, unsounded and unknown, yet with a kind of warmth, that seemed to flow over Gerald's brain like a fertile sleep.

'Good-bye then. There's nothing I can do for you?'

'Nothing, thanks.'

Birkin watched the black-clothed form of the other man move out of the door, the bright head was gone, he turned over to sleep.

(*Women in Love*, Ch. xvi)

GLADIATORIAL

After the fiasco of the proposal, Birkin had hurried blindly away from Beldover, in a whirl of fury. He felt he had been a complete fool, that the whole scene had been a farce of the first water. But that did not trouble him at all. He was deeply, mockingly angry that Ursula persisted always in this old cry: 'Why do you want to bully me?' and in her bright, insolent abstraction.

He went straight to Shortlands. There he found Gerald standing with his back to the fire, in the library, as motionless as a man is, who is completely and emptily restless, utterly hollow. He had done all the work he wanted to do – and now there was nothing. He could go out in the car, he could run to town. But he did not want to go out in the car, he did not want to run to town, he did not want to call on the Thirlbys. He was suspended motionless, in an agony of inertia, like a machine that is without power.

This was very bitter to Gerald, who had never known what boredom was, who had gone from activity to activity, never at a loss. Now, gradually, everything seemed to be stopping in him. He did not want any more to do the things that offered. Something dead within him just refused to respond to any suggestion. He cast over in his mind, what it would be possible to do, to save himself from this misery of nothingness, relieve the stress of this hollowness. And there were only three things left, that would rouse him, make him live. One was to drink or smoke hashish, the other was to be soothed by Birkin, and the third was women. And there was no-one for the moment to drink with. Nor was there a woman. And he knew Birkin was out. So there was nothing to do but to bear the stress of his own emptiness.

When he saw Birkin his face lit up in a sudden, wonderful smile.

'By God, Rupert,' he said, 'I'd just come to the conclusion that nothing in the world mattered except somebody to take the edge off one's being alone: the right somebody.'

The smile in his eyes was very astonishing, as he looked at the other man. It was the pure gleam of relief. His face was pallid and even haggard.

'The right woman, I suppose you mean,' said Birkin spitefully.

'Of course, for choice. Failing that, an amusing man.'

He laughed as he said it. Birkin sat down near the fire.

'What were you doing?' he asked.

'I? Nothing. I'm in a bad way just now, everything's on edge, and I can neither work nor play. I don't know whether it's a sign of old age, I'm sure.'

'You mean you are bored?'

'Bored, I don't know. I can't apply myself. And I feel the devil is either very present inside me, or dead.'

Birkin glanced up and looked in his eyes.

'You should try hitting something,' he said.

Gerald smiled.

'Perhaps,' he said. 'So long as it was something worth hitting.'

'Quite!' said Birkin, in his soft voice. There was a long pause during which each could feel the presence of the other.

'One has to wait,' said Birkin.

'Ah God! Waiting! What are we waiting for?'

'Some old Johnny says there are three cures for *ennui*, sleep, drink, and travel,' said Birkin.

'All cold eggs,' said Gerald. 'In sleep, you dream, in drink you curse, and in travel you yell at a porter. No, work and love are the two. When you're not at work you should be in love.'

'Be it then,' said Birkin.

'Give me the object,' said Gerald. 'The possibilities of love exhaust themselves.'

'Do they? And then what?'

'Then you die,' said Gerald.

'So you ought,' said Birkin.

'I don't see it,' replied Gerald. He took his hands out of his trousers pockets, and reached for a cigarette. He was tense and nervous. He lit the cigarette over a lamp, reaching forward and drawing steadily. He was dressed for dinner, as usual in the evening, although he was alone.

'There's a third one even to your two,' said Birkin. 'Work, love, and fighting. You forget the fight.'

'I suppose I do,' said Gerald. 'Did you ever do any boxing—?'

'No, I don't think I did,' said Birkin.

'Ay—' Gerald lifted his head and blew the smoke slowly into the air. 'Why?' said Birkin.

'Nothing. I thought we might have a round. It is perhaps true, that I want something to hit. It's a suggestion.'

'So you think you might as well hit me?' said Birkin.

'You? Well—! Perhaps—! In a friendly kind of way, of course.'

'Quite!' said Birkin, bitingly.

Gerald stood leaning back against the mantel-piece. He looked down at Birkin, and his eyes flashed with a sort of terror like the eyes of a stallion, that are blood-shot and overwrought, turned glancing backwards in a stiff terror.

'I feel that if I don't watch myself, I shall find myself doing something silly,' he said.

'Why not do it?' said Birkin coldly.

Gerald listened with quick impatience. He kept glancing down at Birkin, as if looking for something from the other man.

'I used to do some Japanese wrestling,' said Birkin. 'A Jap lived in the same house with me in Heidelberg, and he taught me a little. But I was never much good at it.'

'You did!' exclaimed Gerald. 'That's one of the things I've never ever seen done. You mean jiu-jitsu, I suppose?'

'Yes. But I am no good at those things – they don't interest me.'

'They don't? They do me. What's the start?'

'I'll show you what I can, if you like,' said Birkin.

'You will?' A queer, smiling look tightened Gerald's face for a moment, as he said, 'Well, I'd like it very much.'

'Then we'll try jiu-jitsu. Only you can't do much in a starched shirt.'

'Then let us strip, and do it properly. Hold on a minute—' He rang the bell, and waited for the butler.

'Bring a couple of sandwiches and a syphon,' he said to the man, 'and then don't trouble me any more to-night – or let anybody else.'

The man went. Gerald turned to Birkin with his eyes lighted.

'And you used to wrestle with a Jap?' he said. 'Did you strip?'

'Sometimes.'

'You did! What was he like then, as a wrestler?'

'Good, I believe. I am no judge. He was very quick and slippery and full of electric fire. It is a remarkable thing, what a curious sort of fluid force they seem to have in them, those people – not like a human grip – like a polyp—'

Gerald nodded.

'I should imagine so,' he said, 'to look at them. They repel me, rather.'

'Repel and attract, both. They are very repulsive when they are cold, and they look grey. But when they are hot and roused, there is a definite attraction – a curious kind of full electric fluid – like eels.'

'Well—, yes—, probably.'

The man brought in the tray and set it down.

'Don't come in any more,' said Gerald.

The door closed.

'Well then,' said Gerald; 'shall we strip and begin? Will you have a drink first?'

'No, I don't want one.'

'Neither do I.'

Gerald fastened the door and pushed the furniture aside.

The room was large, there was plenty of space, it was thickly carpeted. Then he quickly threw off his clothes, and waited for

Birkin. The latter, white and thin, came over to him. Birkin was more a presence than a visible object; Gerald was aware of him completely, but not really visually. Whereas Gerald himself was concrete and noticeable, a piece of pure final substance.

'Now,' said Birkin, 'I will show you what I learned, and what I remember. You let me take you so—' And his hands closed on the naked body of the other man. In another moment, he had Gerald swung over lightly and balanced against his knee, head downwards. Relaxed, Gerald sprang to his feet with eyes glittering.

'That's smart,' he said. 'Now try again.'

So the two men began to struggle together. They were very dissimilar. Birkin was tall and narrow, his bones were very thin and fine. Gerald was much heavier and more plastic. His bones were strong and round, his limbs were rounded, all his contours were beautifully and fully moulded. He seemed to stand with a proper, rich weight on the face of the earth, whilst Birkin seemed to have the centre of gravitation in his own middle. And Gerald had a rich, frictional kind of strength, rather mechanical, but sudden and invincible, whereas Birkin was abstract as to be almost intangible. He impinged invisibly upon the other man, scarcely seeming to touch him, like a garment, and then suddenly piercing in a tense fine grip that seemed to penetrate into the very quick of Gerald's being.

They stopped, they discussed methods, they practised grips and throws, they became accustomed to each other, to each other's rhythm, they got a kind of mutual physical understanding. And then again they had a real struggle. They seemed to drive their white flesh deeper and deeper against each other, as if they would break into a oneness. Birkin had a great subtle energy, that would press upon the other man with an uncanny force, weigh him like a spell put upon him. Then it would pass, and Gerald would heave free, with white, heaving, dazzling movements.

So the two men entwined and wrestled with each other, working nearer and nearer. Both were white and clear, but Gerald flushed smart red where he was touched, and Birkin remained white and tense. He seemed to penetrate into Gerald's more solid, more diffuse bulk, to interfuse his body through the body of the other, as if to bring it subtly into subjection, always seizing with some rapid necromantic foreknowledge every motion of the other flesh, converting and counteracting it, playing upon the limbs and trunk of Gerald like some hard wind. It was as if Birkin's whole physical intelligence inter-penetrated into Gerald's body, as if his fine, sublimated energy entered into the flesh of the fuller man, like some potency, casting a fine net, a prison, through the muscles into the very depths of Gerald's physical being.

So they wrestled swiftly, rapturously, intent and mindless at last, two essential white figures working into a tighter closer oneness of struggle, with a strange, octopus-like knotting and flashing of limbs in the subdued light of the room; a tense white knot of flesh gripped in silence between the walls of old brown books. Now and again came a sharp gasp of breath, or a sound like a sigh, then the rapid thudding of movement on the thickly-carpeted floor, then the strange sound of flesh escaping under flesh. Often, in the white interlaced knot of violent living being that swayed silently, there was no head to be seen, only the swift, tight limbs, the solid white backs, the physical junction of two bodies clinched into oneness. Then would appear the gleaming, ruffled head of Gerald, as the struggle changed, then for a moment the dun-coloured, shadow-like head of the other man would lift up from the conflict, the eyes wide and dreadful and sightless.

At length Gerald lay back inert on the carpet, his breast rising in great slow panting, whilst Birkin kneeled over him, almost uncon-scious. Birkin was much more exhausted. He caught little, short breaths, he could scarcely breathe any more. The earth seemed to tilt and sway, and a complete darkness was coming over his mind. He did not know what happened. He slid forward quite unconscious, over Gerald, and Gerald did not notice. Then he was half-conscious again, aware only of the strange tilting and sliding of the world. The world was sliding, everything was sliding off into the darkness. And he was sliding, endlessly, endlessly away.

He came to consciousness again, hearing an immense knocking out-side. What could be happening, what was it, the great hammer-stroke resounding through the house? He did not know. And then it came to him that it was his own heart beating. But that seemed impossible, the noise was outside. No, it was inside himself, it was his own heart. And the beating was painful, so strained, surcharged. He wondered if Gerald heard it. He did not know whether he were standing or lying or falling.

When he realised that he had fallen prostrate upon Gerald's body he wondered, he was surprised. But he sat up, steadying himself with his hand and waiting for his heart to become stiller and less painful. It hurt very much, and took away his consciousness.

Gerald however was still less conscious than Birkin. They waited dimly, in a sort of not-being, for many uncounted, unknown minutes.

'Of course—' panted Gerald, 'I didn't have to be rough – with you – I had to keep back – my force—'

Birkin heard the sound as if his own spirit stood behind him, outside him, and listened to it. His body was in a trance of exhaustion, his spirit heard thinly. His body could not answer. Only he knew his heart was getting quieter. He was divided entirely between his spirit, which stood outside, and knew, and his body, that was a plunging, unconscious stroke of blood.

'I could have thrown you – using violence—' panted Gerald. 'But you beat me right enough.'

'Yes,' said Birkin, hardening his throat and producing the words in the tension there, 'you're much stronger than I – you could beat me – easily.'

Then he relaxed again to the terrible plunging of his heart and his blood.

'It surprised me,' panted Gerald, 'what strength you've got. Almost supernatural.'

'For a moment,' said Birkin.

He still heard as if it were his own disembodied spirit hearing, standing at some distance behind him. It drew nearer however, his spirit. And the violent striking of blood in his chest was sinking quieter, allowing his mind to come back. He realised that he was leaning with all his weight on the soft body of the other man. It startled him, because he thought he had withdrawn. He recovered himself, and sat up. But he was still vague and unestablished. He put out his hand to steady himself. It touched the hand of Gerald, that was lying out on the floor. And Gerald's hand closed warm and sudden over Birkin's, they remained exhausted and breathless, the one hand clasped closely over the other. It was Birkin whose hand, in swift response, had closed in a strong, warm clasp over the hand of the other. Gerald's clasp had been sudden and momentaneous.

The normal consciousness however was returning, ebbing back. Birkin could breathe almost naturally again. Gerald's hand slowly withdrew, Birkin slowly, dazedly rose to his feet and went towards the table. He poured out a whiskey and soda. Gerald also came for a drink.

'It was a real set-to, wasn't it?' said Birkin, looking at Gerald with darkened eyes.

'God, yes,' said Gerald. He looked at the delicate body of the other man, and added: 'It wasn't too much for you, was it?'

'No. One ought to wrestle and strive and be physically close. It makes one sane.'

'You do think so?'

'I do. Don't you?'

'Yes,' said Gerald.

There were long spaces of silence between their words. The wrestling had some deep meaning to them – an unfinished meaning.

'We are mentally, spiritually intimate, therefore we should be more or less physically intimate too – it is more whole.'

'Certainly it is,' said Gerald. Then he laughed pleasantly, adding: 'It's rather wonderful to me.' He stretched out his arms handsomely.

'Yes,' said Birkin. 'I don't know why one should have to justify oneself.'

'No.'

The two men began to dress.

'I think also that you are beautiful,' said Birkin to Gerald, 'and that is enjoyable too. One should enjoy what is given.'

'You think I am beautiful – how do you mean, physically?' asked Gerald, his eyes glistening.

'Yes. You have a northern kind of beauty, like light refracted from snow – and a beautiful, plastic form. Yes, that is there to enjoy as well. We should enjoy everything.'

Gerald laughed in his throat, and said:

'That's certainly one way of looking at it. I can say this much, I feel better. It has certainly helped me. Is this the Brüderschaft you wanted?'

'Perhaps. Do you think this pledges anything?'

'I don't know,' laughed Gerald.

'At any rate, one feels freer and more open now – and that is what we want.'

'Certainly,' said Gerald.

They drew to the fire, with the decanters and the glasses and the food.

'I always eat a little before I go to bed,' said Gerald. 'I sleep better.'

'I should not sleep so well,' said Birkin.

'No? There you are, we are not alike. I'll put a dressing-gown on.' Birkin remained alone, looking at the fire. His mind had reverted to Ursula. She seemed to return again into his consciousness. Gerald came down wearing a gown of broad-barred, thick black-and-green silk, brilliant and striking.

'You are very fine,' said Birkin, looking at the full robe.

'It was a caftan in Bokhara,' said Gerald. 'I like it.'

'I like it too.'

Birkin was silent, thinking how scrupulous Gerald was in his attire, how expensive too. He wore silk socks, and studs of fine workmanship, and silk underclothing, and silk braces. Curious! This was another of the differences between them. Birkin was careless and unimaginative about his own appearance.

'Of course you,' said Gerald, as if he had been thinking; 'there's something curious about you. You're curiously strong. One doesn't expect it, it is rather surprising.'

Birkin laughed. He was looking at the handsome figure of the other man, blond and comely in the rich robe, and he was half thinking of the difference between it and himself – so different; as far, perhaps, apart as man from woman, yet in another direction. But really it was Ursula, it was the woman who was gaining ascendance over Birkin's being, at this moment. Gerald was becoming dim again, lapsing out of him.

'Do you know,' he said suddenly, 'I went and proposed to Ursula Brangwen to-night, that she should marry me.'

He saw the blank shining wonder come over Gerald's face.

'You did?'

'Yes. Almost formally – speaking first to her father, as it should be, in the world – though that was accident – or mischief.'

Gerald only stared in wonder, as if he did not grasp.

'You don't mean to say that you seriously went and asked her father to let you marry her?'

'Yes,' said Birkin, 'I did.'

'What, had you spoken to her before about it, then?'

'No, not a word. I suddenly thought I would go there and ask her – and her father happened to come instead of her – so I asked him first.'

'If you could have her?' concluded Gerald.

'Ye-es, that.'

'And you didn't speak to her?'

'Yes. She came in afterwards. So it was put to her as well.'

'It was! And what did she say then? You're an engaged man?'

'No, – she only said she didn't want to be bullied into answering.'

'She what?'

'Said she didn't want to be bullied into answering.'

' "Said she didn't want to be bullied into answering!" Why, what did she mean by that?'

Birkin raised his shoulders. 'Can't say,' he answered. 'Didn't want to be bothered just then, I suppose.'

'But is this really so? And what did you do then?'

'I walked out of the house and came here.'

'You came straight here?'

'Yes.'

Gerald stared in amazement and amusement. He could not take it in.

'But is this really true, as you say it now?'

'Word for word.'

'It is?'

He leaned back in his chair, filled with delight and amusement.

'Well, that's good,' he said. 'And so you came here to wrestle with your good angel, did you?'

'Did I?' said Birkin.

'Well, it looks like it. Isn't that what you did?'

Now Birkin could not follow Gerald's meaning.

'And what's going to happen?' said Gerald. 'You're going to keep open the proposition, so to speak?'

'I suppose so. I vowed to myself I would see them all to the devil. But I suppose I shall ask her again, in a little while.'

Gerald watched him steadily.

'So you're fond of her then?' he asked.

'I think – I love her,' said Birkin, his face going very still and fixed.

Gerald glistened for a moment with pleasure, as if it were something done specially to please him. Then his face assumed a fitting gravity, and he nodded his head slowly.

'You know,' he said, 'I always believed in love – true love. But where does one find it nowadays?'

'I don't know,' said Birkin.

'Very rarely,' said Gerald. Then, after a pause, 'I've never felt it myself – not what I should call love. I've gone after women – and been keen enough over some of them. But I've never felt *love*. I don't believe

I've ever felt as much *love* for a woman, as I have for you – not *love*. You understand what I mean?'

'Yes. I'm sure you've never loved a woman.'

'You feel that, do you? And do you think I ever shall? You understand what I mean?' He put his hand to his breast, closing his fist there, as if he would draw something out. 'I mean that–that— I can't express what it is, but I know it.'

'What is it, then?' asked Birkin.

'You see, I can't put it into words. I mean, at any rate, something abiding, something that can't change—'

His eyes were bright and puzzled.

'Now do you think I shall ever feel that for a woman?' he said, anxiously.

Birkin looked at him, and shook his head.

'I don't know,' he said. 'I could not say.'

Gerald had been on the *qui vive*, as awaiting his fate. Now he drew back in his chair.

'No,' he said, 'and neither do I, and neither do I.'

'We are different, you and I,' said Birkin. 'I can't tell your life.'

'No,' said Gerald, 'no more can I. But I tell you – I begin to doubt it!'

'That you will ever love a woman?'

'Well – yes – what you would truly call love—'

'You doubt it?'

'Well – I begin to.'

There was a long pause.

'Life has all kinds of things,' said Birkin. 'There isn't only one road.'

'Yes, I believe that too. I believe it. And mind you, I don't care how it is with me – I don't care how it is – so long as I don't feel—' he paused, and a blank, barren look passed over his face, to express his feeling – 'so long as I feel I've *lived*, somehow – and I don't care how it is – but I want to feel that—'

'Fulfilled,' said Birkin.

'We-ell, perhaps it is, fulfilled; I don't use the same words as you.'

'It is the same.'

(Ibid., Chap. xx)

★   ★   ★

FORREST REID (1876–1947) This Ulster novelist has been described as incapable of creating a major character of the female sex or over the age of about sixteen. His understanding of small boys is unquestioned; he liked them and they liked him; and despite the strong element of fantasy and Greek symbolism revealed in his personal confessions, the stories are usually unpretentious and earthy mixtures of boyish expeditions and hobbies, friendships with animals, school problems and an occasional bit of black, or more likely white, magic. Nevertheless, beneath the very normal grubby-kneed and doggy surface, the robustness and common sense, there exists a prevailing current in favour of male love. The trilogy *Young Tom* was in fact composed in the reverse order, with *Uncle Stephen* written first – and it is this book, found embarrassing by many critics after the excellencies of its companion volumes, which Reid was himself most excited about. Tom has run away to his Uncle Stephen, who turns out to be a magician, with a statue of Hermes in his room; the friend of his own age whom Tom goes about with is Uncle Stephen metamorphosed into youth; and uncle and boy finally go off travelling together in a Socratic relationship whose terms are sensuous but imprecise.

Forrest Reid is represented here by the conclusion to the sensitive account of his childhood and youth, *Apostate*, where he prepares to tell a new friend the secrets of his heart; a note on *Uncle Stephen* from the later reminiscences, *Private Road*; and some of the climactic pages from that novel.

THE NEW APPRENTICE

I had been at work for only a very few months when a new apprentice came. It was my business to teach him his duties, and on a cold bright winter morning, when the ground was white with frost and a thin powder of snow, we set off for the docks. In the still, grey water the boats, looking strangely naked and black, were reflected as in a glass. Gulls wheeled restlessly about the masts and funnels; the wintry sun shone on frozen ropes and slippery decks; the ground rang with a hard metallic sound. Crates and bales, boxes and sacks were being piled on the wharves; iron trucks were busy, for the dock-labourers were working hard to keep themselves warm, their faces, ears, and hands scarlet, their breath turning to vapour the moment it passed their lips.

I had always found the scene attractive, and, though it was by now familiar enough, and I knew these boats were, with one or two rare exceptions, merely cross-channel steamers and coasters, it still continued to suggest romance, the great unexplored world that lay beyond my experience, glimmering with a mysterious fascination. Today there was added to this the pleasure of acting as guide to my companion, of showing him *our* boats, *our* sheds, of telling him what he must do, of introducing him to the different shipping clerks. And through it all I was becoming more and more conscious of something pleasanter still, of an uplifting of the spirit that turned everything to beauty and filled my mind with sunlight. I knew this sunlight well, because it was the sunlight of my dream world. A long time had gone by since it had last shone for me, but with its first rays it burned up the intervening period like a thin sheet of paper, and filled me with a peculiar exultation. I seemed to be approaching a point; we both seemed, actually, physically, with every step we took, to be drawing nearer to a point where the wide sea flowing between my two worlds was narrowed to a stream one might pass dry-shod: my conduct of the business we were engaged on grew more and more mechanical.

Meanwhile the new boy walked beside me, rather shy, and with a simple, unconscious charm about him that I had felt from the moment (an hour or two back) when he had been introduced to me by his father. I prolonged our walk unnecessarily: I did not want to go back at all . . .

And thus began a friendship which as the days passed, and then the weeks and the months, grew ever closer and deeper, till at last it seemed to draw into itself the two divergent streams of my life, so that for the first time, in dreaming and waking, they found a single channel. Somehow, somewhere, I felt that a shadow had been lifted. It was as if in my spirit a new day were breaking, transforming everything in the world around me, because I saw everything now in its fresh clear light.

When I was with this boy I was happy, and I could conceive of no greater happiness than to be with him always. He was an odd enough youngster in his ways, not a bit like any other boy I had known; but he was extraordinarily lovable. Sometimes, indeed, the sunshine, filled with little dancing golden dust specks, touching his hair or his cheek, would set me dreaming of him as a kind of angel who had strayed into this world by chance, or perhaps not quite by chance. The pleasantness of his manner, of his temper; his kindness, his intelligence, a sort of childish quality there was in his gaiety – all helped to deepen the affection I had for him. The future lay before us like a wide green plain. There were plans and day-dreams – plans that involved leaving our present employment and going to a university. Life in this humdrum old warehouse, amid its simple daily tasks, amid its comings and goings, its working hours and hours of leisure, became a wonderful voyage of discovery to be undertaken no longer alone.

Both here, and at home after the day's work was finished, we were constantly together. I showed him my writings, I got him to read poetry, to listen to music; I poured out all my enthusiasms, and in return became absorbed in his. That they took me into the unfamiliar paths of scientific theory and experiment did not matter. I read books on astronomy, and geology, and physics; he tried to interest me in mathematics, and of all our studies this was the only one I was obliged to abandon. But if I could make no headway here, we splashed happily enough in the shallows of philosophy, and it was while we were reading Caird's *Evolution of Religion* that between his father and mother a momentous discussion took place (of which I heard nothing until years later) as to whether this friendship should be discouraged or allowed to continue. They had been extremely kind to me, asking me frequently to the house; but they were very strict in their attitude to religion, and it was because of the Caird book and of Spencer's *First Principles*, which were supposed to have been my choice, that the discussion arose. In the end (I cannot help thinking it was his mother's council that prevailed) they decided not to interfere, but to let things take their course . . .

I have wandered too far into the future in all this – farther than the scheme of these pages really carries me. For I see them, somehow, as embracing a definite period, which began in dreamland and ended with the winter morning of this chapter's opening. Or perhaps I should say that it ends on an evening some five or six months later.

I had never spoken of the affection which now filled my life: I had never alluded to it, though I had often longed to do so, though I had even once or twice tried to do so, though I knew it must for ever

remain incomplete unless I did do so. Incomplete, that is, for me: for
the rest I did not, could not know. And thus it went on, until I thought
of a way by which I might surmount my shyness, or at least circumvent
it – a way which would at any rate be easier than speech.

For some months back I had been keeping a diary, or journal,
writing in it not regularly, but still fairly frequently. I wrote just
before going to bed, and I poured out everything I felt, for I intended to
destroy it (and did do so) when the book should be filled. What I
wrote was not meant to be read. I wrote as the servant of King Midas
whispered into the hollow earth. Yet now I wanted him to read it. I
knew it contained pages he might find bewildering, extravagant, and
perhaps distasteful: but I also knew that if I looked back over it with a
view to tearing out such pages I should never show it at all.

And the desire to take him completely into my confidence had begun
to haunt me. It was what filled my mind as we walked home together
one day some five or six months after our first meeting, and what
kept me silent when, later on, we went out for a ramble through the
fields and woods by the Lagan. Yet, though I was silent, I was intensely
excited, for I had made up my mind to conquer my cowardice. Already
I had had an opportunity to do so, and had put it off by coming out
here. I would put it off no longer.

'There is something I have at home which I want to show you –
something I have written. Do you mind turning back?'

Without questioning me he did what I asked.

And when once more we had reached the house in Mount Charles I
took him upstairs to the room I now used as a study, and where I knew
we should not be disturbed. It was growing dusk, but I welcomed the
minutes I could employ on busying myself with the lamp, and fumbled
longer than was necessary as I unlocked the desk where was my
manuscript book. I gave him the book, moved the lamp over near to an
arm-chair, and myself sat down at the table, some distance off, and
facing the window. For the first time I had admitted someone to my
secret world, to my innermost thoughts . . .

Already he must have crossed the threshold. In the quiet of the room
I could hear no sound but now and then the rustle of a page when he
turned it. For an instant I glanced at him. His face was a little flushed,
his dark hair tumbled down over his forehead. But I turned away
quickly and did not look back. I sat waiting, trying now to shut out
every thought from my mind . . .

The time slowly drew on: half an hour, nearly an hour must have gone by. The window grew darker and darker, and presently I knew that in a little, a very little while, the reading must come to an end. Then the silence seemed all at once to grow so intense that I felt nothing could ever again break it.

(*Apostate*, Ch. XXII, Constable)

* * *

A DREAM STORY

Uncle Stephen in its first form was really and completely a dream story. That is to say, from beginning to end, it was composed in sleep – or perhaps I should say 'lived', for I undoubtedly was Tom. Of the exact date of this dream I have no note, but next morning I wrote it all out and sent a summary of it, in the form of a letter, to Walter de la Mare. The first date I have is attached to *his* letter – 16th November, 1928 – but it is unlikely that more than a few days separated our communications. 'Has the magician come on any further?' he asks. 'What you said in your letter should be a vivifying nucleus; and though a wicked magician would be easier, a good one would be far more original, and offer a more delicate scope. Have you put anything on paper yet?'

.   .   .   .   .

I loved writing this book, and I wrote it slowly – I might almost say luxuriously. During the two years spent on it Tom grew to be extraordinarily real to me – real, I think, in a way none of my other characters has ever been, so that sometimes for a few minutes I would stop writing because he seemed to be actually there in the room. I knew the tones of his voice, I caught glimpses of him in the street, and one evening, after finishing a chapter, I put down my work to go out for a walk with him.

(*Private Road*)

* * *

From

UNCLE STEPHEN

He remembered Uncle Stephen's words – that in approaching the God in a spirit of love and worship he became a priest. He remembered that in ancient Greece there had been boy priests. He remembered the beautiful opening of Euripides' play, where, after the speech of Hermes, the young boy Ion decorates the porch of Apollo's temple with laurel branches, drops the lustral water on the ground, and chases the birds away. The scene was infinitely lovely as it floated before him now. It was as if the sunlight of that morning long ago had been caught and imprisoned in the words, to burst out with renewed glory when their spell was whispered. And all this loveliness was eternal. It could never fade until the earth grew cold and dead, or some cloud descended on the world, darkening men's minds until nobody was left who sought for and loved it . . .

His troubles dropped from him. He believed that the God had welcomed him, and was his lover, his friend. This was Hermes the shepherd, Hermes who, Uncle Stephen had said, guarded young boys, and would guard him. His eyes half shut, and on his face was a strange dreamy expression, gentle and happy. Nobody had ever seen him quite like this, and nobody ever would, for he was more than half out of his body, on the confines of another world. The whole house, he now knew, was the spiritual creation of Uncle Stephen and this God; and here, in this room, he was in its very heart, which was beating in tune with his own.

When he rose at last, his knees were stiff and sore and for a moment he staggered, but it was as if his mind had been bathed in some fresh mountain stream, and he knew that he could sleep. Putting the candle on the table by the bed, he looked down again at the slumbering Stephen. To Tom the whole room was still humming and vibrating with a secret life. This impression was so vivid, indeed, as to produce in him the strange feeling that merely by stretching out his hands he could make the surrounding air break into a flame. But Stephen slept on. Nothing that had taken place had disturbed him. It had passed over him and round him, leaving him untouched, as the fire had played harmlessly over the wise men in their burning fiery furnace. And gradually for Tom too its waves began to subside. His mind grew quiet, and he became all at once aware that his God was pouring sleep upon him – softly, ceaselessly, compellingly. Tom's eyes slid round to him, liquid and dark. The pale, honey-coloured marble was still warm and breathing, but the spirit was only lingering there till Tom himself should be safely tucked in and his eyes sealed. 'Sleep – sleep,' a faint voice whispered. 'Sleep—'

Tom smiled drowsily. He must go back to his own room; but

somehow his own room seemed miles and miles away, and to leave his present sanctuary would be like going out into a cold, wet, winter's night.

There was no longer anything but silence. The whisper had died away, but its command was overwhelming. Tom's chin sank forward on his breast. He blinked and opened his eyes; he was dropping asleep on his feet. Stephen had pushed aside one of the pillows, which had fallen to the floor. Tom replaced it: then crept under the clothes and blew out the candle.

.　　.　　.　　.　　.

The miracle had not happened:[1] Tom seemed to know that even in his dreams, for he heaved a deep sigh before his eyes opened. Instinctively he clung to the sleepiness that prevented complete realization. He put his arms round Stephen's neck and wriggled himself closer till their heads lay on one pillow. He hoped it was very early, and that they need not get up for a long time. He did not want to awake; the day before him, he knew, was going to be full of trouble; he put his other arm round Stephen and buried his nose in the short crisp hair above his ear. He listened to twittering bird notes, he felt rather than saw the drowsy sunlight floating through the open window.

But Stephen would not let him stay like this. Tom might snuggle up against him and murmur that he wanted to go to sleep again, but Stephen was wide awake. He proposed getting up and going for a swim. 'I had the rummiest dream,' he declared. 'At least, it seems so now.' He gave Tom a little shake. 'Are you listening? Wake up!'

'I'm not asleep,' said Tom. But a warm delightful languor was diffused through his body, and he nestled closer.

'You're next door to it. Remember, I don't intend to tell you this twice . . . You'll be sorry, too, because it's very much in your line: in fact you were in it . . . All right, I'll not tell you. And please don't breathe into my ear.'

Tom slightly altered his position. 'Is that better?' he asked.

'Not very much, and I don't see why you aren't in your own bed. You certainly weren't here when I went to sleep last night. . . It was

[1] Tom has realized his friend Philip Coombe is in fact 'Stephen' – a creation of his uncle, who has disappeared. He is hoping that the boy will turn back into the man.

about your uncle – my dream. I dreamt I was in the room downstairs
– the room with all the books – and you were there too.'

'Yes?' Tom still kept his eyes tight shut.

'Don't you see?' said Stephen, giving him another shake. 'Don't you
see how queer it was? Of course it must have been the result of what
you told me yesterday, but it was queer all the same.'

'Why?' Tom whispered. 'I don't see anything queer about it.'

'Well it was: you'll understand why presently. Do lie over a bit:
I'm far too hot: besides, you're choking me.'

Tom moved grudgingly. 'You might be more comfortable,' he
mumbled. But Stephen had spoiled his own drowsy sensations, and he
lay on his back blinking up at the ceiling. 'What happened?' he asked.

Stephen stretched out his arms and sat up. He looked down at Tom.
'Nothing happened. I was just there: it's not that that was queer.'

'Was I in the room?'

'Yes; I've said so already: I knew you weren't listening.'

'What was I doing?'

'You were sitting on the hearthrug untangling a heap of string and
winding it round a stick.'

'I did do that once.'

'Very likely. Most people have wound a ball of string.'

'What was queer then?' said Tom, with a shade of impatience.
'Was Uncle Stephen there?'

'I'm coming to that . . . Uncle Stephen was there in one sense.' He
paused deliberately, but Tom would ask no further questions. 'He was
there in the sense that you called *me* Uncle Stephen . . . But what really
was queer was the way I thought of you.'

'Thought of me?'

'Yes. Though I don't mean "thought" exactly. It was really the way I
felt about you. I was frightfully fond of you. I didn't know anybody
could care for another person so much.'

To this Tom made no answer, and Stephen after a moment went on.
'You see, I've always liked you quite well; but this was a good deal
more. In fact, it strikes me now as rather absurd.'

'Yes, it would,' said Tom.

'Well, hang it all, you're not an angel! You're a pretty averagely
bad boy – with faint streaks of a better nature.'

Tom buried his face in the pillow. 'Is that all?' he asked in a muffled
voice.

'Yes, I think so.' Stephen kicked aside the clothes and swung his legs over the edge of the bed. He took off his pyjamas – Uncle Stephen's they were – and proceeded to test the muscles of his arms. Tom, peeping out at him, watched this latter performance moodily. Somehow it had the effect of making the return of Uncle Stephen seem infinitely improbable, though last night it had seemed imminent. But nothing could be more remote from Uncle Stephen than this boy light-heartedly parading his nakedness and rejoicing in the strength of his body.

Stephen stood beside the bed, looking down at him and smiling. 'Well?' he said.

'Well what?' muttered Tom. 'Aren't you going to put some clothes on?'

Stephen smiled more broadly. 'Not at present. Aren't you going to get up?'

Tom slowly assumed a sitting posture, and still more slowly put his feet to the ground. Stephen bent down and, half lifting him, pulled him out into the middle of the floor. 'Look here,' he said, 'don't be so frightfully dumpy about it.'

'I can't help it,' Tom muttered. The pleasanter Stephen was to him, the more difficult everything became. He half wished he would be *un*pleasant – or at any rate that he didn't look so nice. He wouldn't look at him. He put his hand against Stephen's breast and pushed him back almost roughly. 'I'm going to my own room. *Your* bathroom is the first door on the left.'

'Come and take your bath with me.'

'No . . . Leave me *alone*, Stephen! You're a bully – that's what you are.'

'Well, I like that! When a minute ago you were hugging me.'

'Yes, and you wouldn't let me.' He struggled free, and picking up his dressing-gown, ran along the passage back to his own room.

(*Uncle Stephen*, Faber)

★　★　★

THE 'THIRTIES

This period of social comment and commitment, when many young writers deserted their middle-class background to take sides with the Popular Front and the beleaguered liberal government of Spain, nevertheless tended to link revolutionary comradeship with Eros. Early poems by Auden and Day Lewis were saturated with the atmosphere of the public school; although their subject-matter was of course subversive, their tone was often that of the Head of the House, hearty, self-righteous, didactic and hectoring. Boy Scout buglings, the *Kameradschaft* of the German *Wandervogel* and obscure references to guerrilla warfare and military manœuvres occurred against a rugged northern landscape of kestrels, hawks, glaciers, tarns, mine-workings, rail-heads and the ever-present frontier. The essentially lyrical and indeed traditional Day Lewis was capable of writing a line to Auden such as this: 'Look west, Wystan, lone flyer, birdman, my bully boy!' and describing his associates in these terms: 'We are going about together, we've mingled blood.' Meanwhile the poets' friend, Christopher Isherwood, exploring pre-Hitler Berlin, drew the portrait of the paederastic Baron von Pregnitz, who nourished his imagination on British publications such as the *Boy's Own Paper*, together with descriptions of various bi-sexual or 'available' youths. Here is the picture of a somewhat heterodox youth club:

This morning I went to see Rudi's club-house, which is also the office of a pathfinders' magazine. The editor and scoutmaster, Uncle Peter, is a haggard, youngish man, with a parchment-coloured face and deeply sunken eyes, dressed in corduroy jacket and shorts. He is evidently Rudi's idol. The only time Rudi will stop talking is when Uncle Peter has something to say. They showed me dozens of photographs of boys, all taken with the camera tilted upwards, from beneath, so that they look like epic giants, in profile against enormous clouds. The magazine itself has articles on hunting, tracking, and preparing food – all written in super-enthusiastic style, with a curious underlying note of hysteria, as though the actions described were part of a religious or erotic ritual. There were half-a-dozen other boys in the room with us: all of them in a state of heroic semi-nudity, wearing the shortest of shorts and the thinnest of shirts or singlets, although the weather is so cold.

When I had finished looking at the photographs, Rudi took me into the club meeting-room. Long coloured banners hung down the walls,

embroidered with initials and mysterious totem devices. At one end of
the room was a low table covered with a crimson embroidered cloth –
a kind of altar. On the table were candles in brass candlesticks.

'We light them on Thursdays,' Rudi explained, 'when we have our
camp-fire palaver. Then we sit round in a ring on the floor, and sing
songs and tell stories.'

Above the table with the candlesticks was a sort of icon – the framed
drawing of a young pathfinder of unearthly beauty, gazing sternly
into the far distance, a banner in his hand. The whole place made me
feel profoundly uncomfortable. I excused myself and got away as soon
as I could.

(*The Berlin Stories*, New Directions)

* * *

STEPHEN SPENDER (1909–) Of these writers it is Stephen
Spender who has chosen to reveal a personal experience of the
male Eros during the days of his youth. (See his excellent autobiography, *World Within World*, with its descriptions of youth
circles in Hamburg in 1928.) Like Auden and Isherwood, though,
he was aware of neurosis and its *Angst*.

For the uncreating chaos descends
And claims you in marriage: though a man, you were ever a bride:
Ever beneath the supple surface of summer muscle,
The evening talk like fountains cupping the summer stars,
The friend who chucked back the lock from his brow in front of a glass,
You were only anxious that all these loves would last.
Your primal mover anxiety
Was a grave lecher, a globe-trotter, one
Whose moods were straws, the winds that puffed them, aeroplanes.
'Whatever happens, I shall never be alone
I shall always have a boy, a railway fare, or a revolution.'

It is significant that, no doubt in order to approach a note of
universality, the middle-aged Spender has changed the final
line, substituting 'an affair' for the suspect and restrictive 'boy'.
(Compare early editions of *The Faber Book of Modern Verse*
with the *Collected Poems*.)

* * *

How strangely this sun reminds me of my love!
Of my walk alone at evening, when like the cottage smoke
Hope vanished into the red fading of the sky.
I remember my strained listening to his voice
My staring at his face and taking the photograph
With the river behind, and the woods touched by Spring:
Till the identification of a morning –
Expansive sheets of blue rising from fields
Roaring movements of light discerned under shadow –
With his figure leaning over a map, is now complete.

What is left of that smoke which the wind blew away?
I corrupted his confidence and his sun-like happiness
So that even now in his turning of bolts or driving a machine
His hand will show error. That is for him.
For me this memory which now I behold,
When, from the pasturage, azure rounds me in rings,
And the lark ascends, and his voice still rings, still rings.

(Collected Poems, Faber)

★　★　★

Oh young men oh young comrades
it is too late now to stay in those houses
your fathers built where they built you to breed
money on money it is too late
to make or even to count what has been made
Count rather those fabulous possessions
which begin with your body and your fiery soul:
the hairs on your head the muscles extending
in ranges with lakes across your limbs
Count your eyes as jewels and your valued sex
then count the sun and the innumerable coined light
sparkling on waves and spangling under trees
It is too late now to stay in great houses where the ghosts
　　are prisoned
– those ladies like flies perfect in amber
those financiers like fossils of bones in coal.
Oh comrades, step beautifully from the solid wall

advance to rebuild and sleep with friend on hill
advance to rebel and remember what you have
no ghost ever had, immured in his hall.

(*Ibid.*)

*　　*　　*

Abrupt and charming mover,
Your pointed eyes under lit leaves,
Your light hair, your smile,
I watch burn in a foreign land
Bright through my dark night
And sheltered by my hand.

My ribs are like a Jonah's whale
In which I dream you: from day
I have recalled your play
Disturbing as birds flying
And with the Spring's infection
And denial of satisfaction.

You dance, forgetting all: in joy
Sustaining that instant of the eye
Which like a Catherine wheel spins free.
Your games of cards, hockey with toughs,
Winking at girls, shoes cribbed from toffs,
Like the encircling summer dew
Glaze me from head to toe.

By night I hold you, and by day
I watch you weave the silk cocoon
Of a son's or a skater's play.
We have no meeting place
Beneath the brilliantine-bright surface.
The outward figure of delight
Creates your image that's no image
Dark in my dark language.

(*Ibid.*)

*　　*　　*

TO T.A.R.H.

Even whilst I watch him I am remembering
The quick laugh of the wasp-gold eyes.
The column turning from the staring window
Even while I see I remember, for love
Dips what it sees into a flood of memory
Vaster than itself, and makes the seen
Be drowned in all that past and future seeing
Of the once seen. Thus what I wore I wear
And shall wear always – the glint of the quick lids
And the body's axle turning: these shall be
    What they are now within the might of Ever.
Night when my life lies with no past or future
But only endless space. It wakes and watches
Hope and despair and the small vivid longings
Gnaw the flesh, like minnows. Where it drank love
It breathes in sameness. Here are
The signs indelible. The wiry copper hair,
And the notched mothlike lips, and that after all human
Glance, which makes all else forgiven.

                                         (Ibid.)

★   ★   ★

GEORGE BARKER (1912–   )

THE SEAL BOY

See he slips like insinuations
Into the waves and sidles
Across breakers, diving under
The greater tidals,

Plunging, a small plane
Down dark altitudes,
Trailing bubbles like aerial bombs
Or a balloon's broods.

O moving ecstatic boy
Sliding through the gloomy seas

Who brings me pearls to enjoy
Rarer than to be found in these seas—

Between the fixed bars of your lips
Darts the kiss like silver
Fish, and in my wild grip
You harbour, for ever.

(Selected Poems, Faber & Faber)

★   ★   ★

A LOVE POEM

My joy, my jockey, my Gabriel
Who bares his horns above my sleep
Is sleeping now. And I shall keep him
In valley and on pinnacle
And marvellous in my tabernacle.

My peace is where his shoulder holds
My clouds among his skies of face;
His plenty is my peace, my peace:
And like a serpent by a boulder
His shade I rest in glory coiled.

Time will divide us, and the sea
Wring its sad hands all day between;
The autumn bring a change of scene.
But always and for ever he
At night will sleep and keep by me.

(Eros in Dogma, Faber)

★   ★   ★

A MEMORIAL SONNET

*(For two young seamen lost overboard in a storm
in Mid-Pacific, January, 1940)*

The seagull, spreadeagled, splayed on the wind,
Span backwards shrieking, belly facing upward,

375

Fled backwards with a gimlet in its heart
To see the two youths swimming hand in hand
Through green eternity. O swept overboard
Not could the thirty-foot jaws them part,
Or the flouncing skirts that swept them over
Separate what death pronounced was love.

I saw them, the hand flapping like a flag,
And another like a dolphin with a child
Supporting him. Was I the shape of Jesus
When to me hopeward their eyeballs swivelled,
Saw I was standing in the posture of vague
Horror, oh paralyzed with mere pity's peace?

(Collected Poems, Faber)

*   *   *

DENTON WELCH (1915–48) During the War years this young writer and artist, already fighting a succession of illnesses, sprang into prominence and bravely and doggedly poured himself into autobiographical novels and stories, until he grew so ill that he could only write for a few moments at a time. Rarely has so specialized a sensibility been displayed with such simplicity and force. Welch is both childlike and feminine, but unlike other admirers of virility he is never mannered, gossipy or arch; his style is as crisp as the Ryvita he enjoyed on his bicycle trips to churches and antique shops, and equally slimming where emotional flatulence and flabbiness are concerned; his observation of others, and himself, has always a cool accuracy. Readers may wish to refer to the novel *Maiden Voyage*, and to stories such as '*When I Was Thirteen*'.

FROM THE JOURNALS

26 September, Saturday

That portrait of Gerard Hopkins in the Lit. Sup., so quiet, so thoughtful, so almost prettily devout. Strange to think that many many years ago he actually sat exactly in that position, with folded hands (although they are not there), with secret, slightly hooded eyes, with gentle, posed mouth and soft tongues of hair lying on his forehead, licking sleekly down beside his ear.

Then the verbose article that tells one nothing – nothing of the secret from which his genius sprung. It is an insult to hide his secret – to pretend he was 'normal', in other words ordinary.

(*The Denton Welch Journals*, 1942, Hamish Hamilton)

14 December, Monday

Suddenly I remember that afternoon by the river near Henfield. It must have been in the summer of 1933 when I was in a sort of disgrace with my aunt and grandfather because I had left China to go to an art school and *would not* 'settle down'. My aunt had said, 'If you want to study art, why don't you do some work? You should be sketching every day; instead of that, you wander in the fields doing nothing at all from morning till night.'

I left the house and wandered again as she had described, only this time I wandered on my bicycle and got as far as the river. It is a forgotten place, because the road-bridge was washed away a hundred years ago and now there is only a footbridge and a track across the fields.

I threw my bicycle into the hedge and started off across the tufty grass. In the winter, I thought, this will be all flooded. Now it was hot and heavenly with the scented, dried-up grass and a loneliness almost piercing.

I sat down on the bank where I had sometimes seen small boys bathing. The river was wider and deeper there and one could dive from the bridge.

I sat there nursing my solitude yet longing for somebody to talk to. And as I longed, I saw approaching from the old farmhouse on the opposite bank, a brown figure – almost the colour of the landscape – that sort of worn, lichen, olive green-brown.

It crossed the bridge and walked along the bank in my direction. While he was still some way off I saw that his hair was of that pale 'washed' gold, because it suddenly glinted in the sun as if it were metal.

He came up to me coolly, with the loose, bent-kneed stride of someone used to walking over rough fields.

'Thinking of going in?' he said pleasantly and in an unexpectedly 'educated' voice.

I was so pleased at his sudden appearance and so curious that I looked him straight in the face and smiled. He smiled back.

I saw the gold hair, untidy and rough, gold eyebrows too, sunburnt chestnut skin and the vivid brick-dust cheeks and lips which framed the almond-white teeth. Not distinguished or handsome – the ears were thick, the nose was short and thick, the lips were thick, all the details unfinished, yet the skin, the teeth, the eyes, the hair had that wonderful, shorter-than-springtime, polished, shining look as of some liquid or varnish of life spread over the whole body. The shirt and the breeches were the colour of mud and the cow-dung caked on them. By their dullness and drabness they stimulated one's imagination so that one could almost feel the tingling fire and coolness of the body they sheathed.

'Lusty' and 'rough' were the words that flooded through me as I looked at him. In their right sense they fitted him perfectly. As you can see I was extremely impressed by him. He must have been a few years older than I was and my capacity for hero-worship was enormous at that time. It still is. He was all that I was not – stalwart, confident and settled into a 'manly' life.

The only thing I could not quite understand was the 'educated' voice. It struck a slightly jarring note, yet made communication much easier and more 'natural'. I started the eternal game of placing people and fitting them into their right pigeon-holes. He could not be ordinary 'gentry'. Nobody would wear quite such dirty clothes or such hob-nailed boots unless they were *really* working. Besides, he had come, as if from home, from that ancient farmhouse, which, by its untouched appearance where no single beam was exposed, proved that no 'improver' had been near it since the eighteenth century.

On the other hand he could not be an ordinary farm hand. I was just deciding that perhaps he was the farmer's ambitiously educated son, when he stopped all my dreary surmises by saying that he was down here learning farming – at least I think he said this, but I am not absolutely sure for at that moment he started undressing.

With the words 'If there are any women round here they'll get an eyeful!' he started to pull his shirt over his head. I was shocked at the whiteness of the skin on his chest and upper arms when he stood up in only his trousers. They were junket-white, but matt, as if powdered with oatmeal. The long gloves of his burnt arms and hands and the bronze helmet of his face and neck joining this whiteness, did something curious to me. I could only gape and wonder as he stripped his wonderful body. He unlaced the boots and kicked them off, then peeled down his thick and sweat-sticky stockings. The breeches he pulled off roughly, and stood revealed with the gold hair glinting on his body as well as on his head.

As I say, I could only watch. This was not just an ordinary man taking off his clothes for a swim – and yet it was. It was this prosaic, mundane quality and the bubbling-up spring of some poetry which held me enthralled.

He flung back his hair with the gesture which is considered girlish when used by effeminate men. (When used by others it has, of course, a quite different effect.) Then he dived into the muddy water and came up spitting and laughing. 'Bloody filthy water,' he shouted, and spluttered, 'bloody filthy water but it's lovely.'

He stood up near the bank, so that the water gartered his legs round the middle of his calves. The hairs on his body and legs dripped like sparkles of water. He looked like a truncated statue fixed to a base in the bowl of a fountain.

He whirled his arms round, dived, and swam about for some time; then he crawled up the bank and lay down beside me on the grass. As he lay with his face to the sky and his eyes shut I watched the rivulets coursing off his body. The main stream flowed down his chest, between the hard pectorals, over the mushroom-smooth belly, to be lost in curly gold hair. I could just descry the quicksilver drops weaving a painful way through the golden bush.

He opened his eyes and saw me staring at him; he didn't seem to mind. He sat up and started to rub his arms and chest brutally with a dirty towel.

'I'm working down here at the moment. What do you do?' he asked, abruptly but without giving offence.

'I, I'm at an art school,' I got out with difficulty. The shame and fear of sinking in his estimation were very real.

'Oh – my sister's a very clever artist, too,' he said confidently. 'She's been studying for some time and has got a scholarship. She's going abroad.'

He continued talking about his sister and his family. I got the impression, perhaps wrongly, that he was a little in disgrace too. This thrilled me. I felt I had found a brother. When he talked of being drunk and brawling, I was tremendously impressed and horrified – to be so cool and casual about it all! Then I had the fear that the beer would decay his teeth or that they would be knocked out in the fights. This caused me the sort of pain one feels when some beautifully-made and intricate thing is threatened.

(Ibid., 1942)

⋆   ⋆   ⋆

Further on I came to two people cutting the hedge, one old, one young. The young one, with coarse nose and big leathery lips, held a billhook on a long handle. As I passed close to him, I had the feeling that he looked unreliable, almost simple, and that he might easily attack me with his weapon. A cart with a barrel on it passed me at the same time, the barrel seemed full of some curious wash to put on trees or plants.

From a treetop nearby I heard whistling. I looked up and saw a faded blue shirt and a slouch cap pulled smartly over one eye. Some rakish youth was picking the cherries there. You could tell how cocksure and brutal he was, by the whistle, the cap, and the way he looked down from his high perch.

Earlier, in a field of hay which had just been mown, I saw another youth of the same sort, but this one was in a white shirt and a heavy leather belt plastered with brass badges of all sorts; they looked exactly like horse brasses only smaller. I could not tell if they were regimental badges. I wanted to go up and examine it. He was using their favourite word '—ing' just as I passed. It rang out cheerfully, cruelly. One sees and knows how hard they all are in these sudden sights and sounds.

.   .   .   .   .

Last Monday I went to supper with Noel Adeney. We had cold soup flavoured with claret, and fennel in long green shreds; then a sort of pilau of rice, onions fried, pimento excitingly scarlet like dogs' tools, and grated cheese. The tiniest new potatoes and salad. Afterwards plums, and creamy mild tomato cocktail to drink. A charming meal.

We sat and talked a long time and then went looking for a pair of fisherman's red trousers which she said she wanted to give me. We turned a whole trunk out, but could not find them. There was printed velvet, linen, a Jane Austen period dress of Indian chintz with a waist under the arm-pits. (The arm-pits were padded with white cotton, against sweat.)

In the cupboard was a tin of 'Earl Grey' tea which she threw at me and told me to take home.

You see this is what goes on in nineteen forty-three, the year of the greatest war to stop all wars, if I have the quotation right.

(*Ibid.*, 1943)

*　*　*

Beyond, by the powerful, massive new locks, where water gushes perpetually from many square mouths and there are little iron platforms and bridges, I saw a naked youth of about sixteen with very square shoulders and head, sitting on a piece of round black machinery. One could tell he worked in the fields, for there was a sunburnt V on his chest where his shirt opened, and an arresting change of colour on his upper arms where his sleeves were rolled. The rest of his body was rather swarthy white, and when I came nearer I saw some reddish spots.

He shook all the dark wet hair off his face, and said the water was lovely. I sat down on the grass and watched him dive. He did it specially for me. 'Do you ever go off there?' I asked him, pointing to one of the little platforms quite high in the air. 'I did once, but I hit my head,' he said shyly. We went on talking. He told me how last year some of the hop-pickers rushed down to the river, all lit up from the nearby pub, and how they began to rock the old high footbridge which used to be near here until at last the whole thing crashed into the water with two men of nineteen or twenty on it. He mentioned their age for some reason. They managed to scramble out all right but that was the end of the bridge.

He lay back in the sun and said, 'My mate ought to be down soon. He'll dive off the high platform, you wait for him.' I said I would.

We were joined at this point by a small gold-brown-haired girl who was wheeling in a pram a still small boy in a cotton sun hat whose left leg was completely encased in plaster of paris. Under the instep was a shiny metal support.

'Has he broken his leg?' I asked obviously. 'Yes,' she murmured, too quietly to hear.

Suddenly there was a whoop from the boy on the bank. 'Here's my mate,' he yelled to me. I looked up and saw a very light-sandy-haired boy on a bike dashing towards the weir. He leapt off and darted

381

across the bridge, a tremendous sense of urgency about him. 'Quick, Ginger,' his friend yelled unnecessarily to him, 'get your clothes off and come and dive off the high platform.'

Ginger disappeared into the long grass by a mound, and I caught glimpses of clothes being pulled into the air, and the sudden dead whiteness of his shoulders.

He rushed out of the grass, dead pearly white except for his freckled face, with a little, lumpy, rather over-developed stomach and pectoral muscles. A rather broken up, not pretty, surface fussiness. Different from his friend's smooth lazy-looking body.

Pulling his mouth back and showing his teeth in a wild, mad, excited gesture he rushed at the water and dived, going so deep and straight down that his legs almost turned a somersault.

'He dives too deep,' I said to the friend.

'Yes,' he said indulgently, then when Ginger came up spitting and gurgling. 'Get up on the board and do your dive!'

'I can't,' Ginger said with assumed babyishness, quavering, making his limbs tremble.

'You're a bleedin' liar,' the friend said.

'You got to come too,' Ginger insisted.

'I'll go off the lower one; I hit my head last time,' said the first boy.

Ginger got on to the top board, about eight or ten feet up, and dived again very deeply. The other boy shouted, 'Coo, you've hit the bottom, look at the mud.'

Ginger swore and said he hadn't. The other boy dived off the lower board quickly to get the ordeal over. Then they both swam about, talking and spitting and dragging their hair back. Ginger's hair now looked metallically shiny and yet dead at the same time.

At last they both came out of the water and sat down on the grass beside me. The first boy lay flat on his back and half shut his eyes. He looked charmingly coarse and young-animalish now, with thick brown neck, smooth arms and hairs round each brown-red nipple. Ginger turned his extremely white and nobbly back to me and almost bent over his friend, talking to him about his work, and how he had been late because he had been staying at home, pressing his trousers for the dance that night.

'Aren't you going?' he asked.

'No,' the other said scornfully.

'I thought you was.'

'Well, maybe I will, I don't know yet.'

They went on talking about work. There was something about a saw breaking, and the work being all right but—

At last Ginger turned to me and said with exquisite politeness.

'Well, is it warm enough for you?' He evidently felt that I had been neglected.

'It's wonderful, isn't it,' I said, then I asked him if my clock was right. It said a quarter to six.

'It's more than that,' he said. 'It's more like six.' I got up.

'Then I must get on, good-bye.'

'Cheerio,' they called together.

I hated to leave the happiness there. It made me think of Dorian Gray. (I suppose the youth-age business.) I thought of the boys in years to come. They would not be nearly so nice, quite horrible in fact. They had both talked about going into the services; one plumped for the R.A.F., the other for the Navy. All the happiness would melt away. I began to think of Oscar Wilde and Lord Ronald Leveson-Gower and all the people who have longed to become young again.

(*Ibid.*, 1943)

*   *   *

8 January, Monday, 5.20 p.m. Grey half-light.

. . . My life is a great unfoldment with many marvellous things about it. I would not have thought that I would be damaged and ill so soon (twenty) or that so comparatively late (twenty-eight and a half) I should find someone with whom I could live in almost complete peace. All of life before that had seemed quite necessarily a solitary affair – and so it still is, but with an utterly different quality of solitude.

In my heart are hung two extraordinary pictures: one is called 'Accident and Illness' and the other, exactly opposite, tilted forward as if to meet it, is called 'Love and Friendship'.

Now they play Bach concerto (for harpsichord, but on a piano wonderfully) on the wireless, and the gas fire, with steel blue and orange flame, roars. Down the windows dribble long tears of condensation. The birds are snapping and creaking out their calls before bed.

(*Ibid.*, 1945)

*   *   *

We conclude this section with a brief miscellany of pieces by contemporary authors.

SOLDIERS BATHING

The sea at evening moves across the sand.
Under a reddening sky I watch the freedom of a band
Of soldiers who belong to me. Stripped bare
For bathing in the sea, they shout and run in the warm air;
Their flesh, worn by the trade of war, revives
And my mind towards the meaning of it strives.
All's pathos now. The body that was gross,
Rank, ravenous, disgusting in the act or in repose,
All fever, filth and sweat, its bestial strength
And bestial decay, by pain and labour grows at length
Fragile and luminous. 'Poor bare forked animal,'
Conscious of his desires and needs and flesh that rise and fall,
Stands in the soft air, tasting after toil
The sweetness of his nakedness: letting the sea-waves coil
Their frothy tongues about his feet, forgets
His hatred of the war, its terrible pressure that begets
A machinery of death and slavery,
Each being a slave and making slaves of others: finds that he
Remembers lovely freedom in a game,
Mocking himself, and comically mimics fear and shame.

He plays with death and animality.
And reading in the shadows of his pallid flesh, I see
The idea of Michelangelo's cartoon
Of soldiers bathing, breaking off before they were half done
At some sortie of the enemy, an episode
Of the Pisan wars with Florence. I remember how he showed
Their muscular limbs that clamber from the water,
And heads that turn across the shoulder, eager for the slaughter,
Forgetful of their bodies that are bare,
And hot to buckle on and use the weapons that are lying there.
– And I think too of the theme another found
When, shadowing men's bodies on a sinister red ground,

Another Florentine, Pollaiuolo,
Painted a naked battle: warriors straddled, hacked the foe,
Dug their bare toes into the ground and slew
The brother-naked man who lay between their feet and drew
His lips back from his teeth in a grimace.

They were Italians who knew war's sorrow and disgrace
And showed the thing suspended, stripped: a theme
Born out of the experience of war's horrible extreme
Beneath a sky where even the air flows
With *lacrimae Christi*. For that rage, that bitterness, those blows,
That hatred of the slain, what could it be
But indirectly or directly a commentary
On the Crucifixion? And the picture burns
With indignation and pity and despair by turns,
Because it is the obverse of the scene
Where Christ hangs murdered, stripped upon the Cross. I mean,
That is the explanation of its rage.

And we too have our bitterness and pity that engage
Blood, spirit in this war. But night begins
Night of the mind: who nowadays is conscious of our sins?
Though every human deed concerns our blood,
And even we must know, what nobody has understood,
That some great love is over all we do,
And that is what has driven us to this fury, for so few
Can suffer all the terror of that love:
The terror of that love has set us spinning in this groove
Greased with our blood.
                    These dry themselves and dress,
Combing their hair, forget the fear and shame of nakedness.
Because to love is frightening we prefer
The freedom of our crimes. Yet, as I drink the dusky air,
I feel a strange delight that fills me full,
Strange gratitude, as if evil itself were beautiful,
And kiss the wound in thought, while in the west
I watch a streak of red that might have issued from Christ's breast.
(F. T. Prince, *Soldiers Bathing and Other Poems*, Fortune Press)

★   ★   ★

ARCHAIC APOLLO

Dredged in a net the slender god
Lies on deck and dries in the sun,
His head set proudly on his neck
Like a runner's whose race is won.

On his breast the Aegean lay
While the whole of history was made;
That long caress could not warm the flesh
Nor the antique smile abrade.

He is as he was, inert, alert,,
The one hand open, the other lightly shut,
His nostrils clean as holes in a flute,
The nipples and navel delicately cut.

The formal eyes are calm and sly,
Of knowledge and joy a perfect token –
The world being caught in the net of the sky
No hush can drown a word once spoken.

(William Plomer, *Visiting the Caves*, Cape)

*   *   *

SPIV SONG

Where are you going, my spiv, my wide boy
down what grey streets will you shake your hair,
what gutters shall know the flap of your trousers
and your loud checked coat, O my young despair?

Have you been in a blind pig over whiskey
where bedbugs spot the discoloured walls,
did you play *barbotte* and lose all your money
or backroom billiards with yellowed balls?

It's midnight now and the sky is dusty,
the police are going their rounds in the square,
the coffee is cold and the chromium greasy
and the last bus leaves, O my young despair.

Don't you just hate our personal questions
with your 'Take me easy and leave me light,'
with your meeting your friends in every direction
– and sucking in private the thumb of guilt.

There are plenty of friends, my man, my monster,
for a Ganymede kid and a Housman lad
and plenty more you would hate to discover
what you do for a living, my spiv, my id.

And isn't it awkward, their smiles so friendly,
their voices so bright as they ask where you work:
a job in a store, or driving a taxi,
or baseball still in the sunlit park?

O why do you sit in the nightclub so sulky,
why so dramatic breaking the glass:
you've heard again that your mother is dying?
You think that you've caught a social disease?

Your looks are black, my spiv, my wide boy,
will you jump from the bridge to the end of the world
and break on the ice, my pleasure, my puppy,
your forehead so hot and your kisses so cold?

What desperate plan is this job that you talk of –
we'll read tomorrow what happens tonight . . . ?
and where you are off to, my son, my shadow,
with the bill unpaid, as the door swings shut?
(Patrick Anderson, *The Colour as Naked*, McClelland & Stewart)

NOT THOSE LONG VISTAS

Not those long vistas through the mountain pass,
The panoramas wheeling from the train,
New lands, new lakes you loved, but lawns and trees
Electric with habitual charge of life,
Dangerous to see, to touch, they could release
Such high-powered current through the veins, recalling
Voices at nightfall coming from the river,
Tom Tiddler's ground, and hands caressing hair,
Trees climbed, tears wept and dried; not that friend there
Known for a fortnight, nor those others found
To make a circle broken as by rain
Light spider-rings, but those who shapes are seen
Childish against an urn or by a raft
knotting wet ropes before, in countless scenes
Turned in deep workings of the mind that grope
To finds defaced and rare; not the diffused
White light of midday on the meadow slopes
Under unshapen cloud, but rays direct
Burning shut eyelids from an August sun
While peaches on the bricks grow sweet and fall
And all loved lawns and trees and friends return.

(J. Lehmann, *The Age of the Dragon*, Longmans, Green & Co.)

9

Exotic Encounters

INTRODUCTION

Travel to foreign places may lead not only to new friendships, but to friendships of a different order, habits or inhibitions dissolving among unfamiliar customs or under a different sun. An example of this occurs in Thomas Mann's *Death In Venice* when the austere self-disciplined German author becomes enchanted by the Rumanian child, Tadzio. In a wider, less morbid context it is the theme of Henry James's *The Ambassadors*. Sometimes the emphasis will lie more on new scenes and customs than on the observing, and perhaps resisting, heart. Colonel T. E. Lawrence does not approve of the extremes to which his Arabs went, but his disavowal has emotional undertones. Many native peoples put, or used to put, a delightful trust in their white visitors: thus Melville and Thoreau. The field must be enormous and we cross it briefly with references to Rome, Athens, Arabia, India, Ceylon, Malaya, the South Seas, North America and the Arctic; prison is the last stop.

ROME

In Rome women do not appear upon the stage; there are castrati dressed as women. This has an exceedingly bad effect upon morality, for nothing, that I know of, does more to encourage the growth of platonic love among the Romans ... There were when I was in Rome, at the Theatre of Capranica, two little eunuchs, Mariotti and Chiostra, dressed as women, who were the most ravishing creatures I ever saw

389

in my life, and who would have inspired the tastes of Gomorrah in men who had the least depraved of tastes in this respect.

A young Englishman, believing one of them to be a woman, became wildly enamoured of him and he continued in this state of infatuation for upwards of a month.

(Montesquieu, *Voyages I*)

★   ★   ★

ATHENS

The pseudonymous novel, *The Firewalkers*, gives an amusing and extremely accurate picture of one small part of the life of contemporary Athens. Those who have had the privilege of meeting the original of Colonel Theo Grecos will recognize at once both the man and the astonishing house he has now had to relinquish, but will certainly feel some qualms at the frankness of the portrayal, which borders on cruelty, and at the propriety of killing off a man who in real life is so much alive.

The following passage, necessarily somewhat cut, concerns Theo, the huge ugly German of whom he is so fond, and the narrator, Frank.

'So you've found your way to our Zappeion, have you?' Theo said in a tone of playful insinuation. 'Ah, but it's not what it used to be! We've *la sottise* Peyrefitte and "Les Ambassades" to thank for that. The moment that book appeared, they began to talk about putting these wretched lights here. And the absurd thing is that we have power cuts in Athens! . . . Excuse me a moment.' He slipped off into the darkness under the trees in pursuit of some shadowy figure which might either be male or female.

'How are you enjoying life in Athens?' I asked Götz, whose face gleamed greyish green above me in a transverse beam of moonlight.

Götz sighed. 'There is so much,' he said, 'so much that is vonderful . . . But the one thing . . .' Again he sighed. Reaching up with his long arms he grasped the branch of a tree and swung himself back and forth. 'Have you a woman, Frank?'

Fortunately I was saved from having to answer this question by the return of Theo. He whispered something in Götz's ear and Götz at once brightened; again they whispered and I saw Theo pass Götz a note – it seemed to be for ten or twenty drachmae – which Götz first refused energetically and then at last accepted. 'All right – be off!' Theo gave him a push and Götz, his shadow leaping behind him, disappeared from sight.

Theo linked his arm in mine again; 'It's sad that these traces of Europeanism should cling to our friend. In so many ways he is *Greek* – I am sure that at heart he is *Greek* – but on this particular subject he's so far from finding his true self.' He pressed my arm: 'And what is your true self? That is something we'd all like to discover.' I said nothing and he went on: 'Imagine that I'm your fairy god-mother. What would you like me to give you – here, now, in the Zappeion at this moment?'

'A nice strong cup of tea. I'm really quite exhausted.'

Theo looked momentarily put out; then he said: 'Come, let's take a taxi. But you'll have to pay for it. I gave my last scrap of money to Götz. I shall make you some tea at home. I think you will enjoy it. Usually I drink Earl Grey, but I'm now trying a new blend: I believe it is called' – he thought for a moment – 'Lyons. Yes, Lyons. I like that name. It sounds grand and regal and utterly British . . .'

Some rickety outside stairs led up to the front door which was on the first floor, and I had just begun to climb when I halted astonished. Standing in the doorway I could dimly see the enormous figure of a military policeman. He was wearing shorts, and his naked thighs and knees gleamed through the darkness. As I paused I heard Theo chuckle again beside me. 'Go on!' he said. 'He's not real!'

I then realized that this superhuman figure had been painted on the doorway.

'Tsarouchis did it for me. I particularly like the position of the knocker. That seems to me a good joke.' He gave a smart rat-tat, and then giggled. We both looked up at the square-jawed face, with the horizontal black line of its moustache, its eyes set close together and its high peasant cheek-bones; the same kind of stylisation had been achieved with the male Greek face as is achieved on the cover of *Esquire* with the American female one. On the bare forearms and thighs black hairs sprouted like the prickles on a cactus. In a corner was the single Greek word: Ela!

'You know what that means?' Theo asked. 'It's pleasantly ambiguous. It can be a challenge; it can be an invitation. "Come and get it" was Maurice Bowra's translation.' Theo sighed, and again banged the knocker. 'I feel he's an appropriate guardian to my shrine . . . Enter, please!'

I accepted the invitation, but having once stepped into the hall, I looked about me in amazement. On one wall there was suspended an aeroplane propeller surmounted by two archaic Greek helmets and a straw boater which, Theo told me, had belonged to a young Etonian, the son of a former British Ambassador. On the other wall there was a long string of masks which Greeks wear during the Carnival period, a picture by Zographos of the War of Independence, a photograph of Theo in a sailor suit at the age of eight, and a glass-covered case in which a number of regimental badges and buttons rested on red velvet. Everywhere there was dust and a strange sweet-sour odour.

'Go through to the sitting-room, my dear, and make yourself comfortable.'

But to make oneself comfortable in a room that is half a museum and half a junk-shop is not an easy task . . .

At last he chuckled and said: 'This is my art.' He added as my bewilderment remained: 'This is my fantasiometry. . . . Here, for example, is the Baroness Shutz.' The face had been constructed with a brilliant economy out of a potato, now black with age, into which two jet hat-pins had been thrust to make eyes glittering malevolently on the end of their antennae. 'The hat-pins were, of course, her own. I purloined them when I went to tea at the German Embassy – entirely in the interest of my art, of course.' His blue eyes twinkled. 'The ribbon round the throat is also hers; I snipped it from one of her evening dresses – fortunately she did not notice . . . Oh, and her hair is also hers – I got it from her hairdresser. Here she has only one breast, as you see' – he indicated a sea-shell – 'in fact, she had two. But I wanted to symbolise her Amazonian nature . . . This, next to her' – he pointed to a dried frog from the head of which the main spring of a watch curled quivering upwards – 'is Bakolas, the famous banker. You will see that I have had to mutilate this creature' – he turned the frog upside down – 'as poor Bakolas, who was in love with the Baroness, suffered from a psychological impotence . . . Ah, you're looking at the watch spring. That, of course, symbolises his fanatical precision – and it enters into his brain as, in the end, it drove the poor man mad . . . Now who else would interest you? That is one of those muddled, and not even always well-intentioned young Britishers who were dropped into this country by your Government in the war. The body, as you see, is made from a Gordon's gin bottle, and the face is a piece of what I believe you call "Lifebuoy" soap. There used to be a halo which was made of one of those gold sovereigns which you used to scatter with such generosity – thus permanently dislocating the whole economy of Greece – but alas, at an hour of need I had to go and sell it . . . Yes, that's a German swastika on one cheek and a Communist hammer and sickle on the other – your policy here was always two-faced, if you will forgive my saying so. The blood-stained bit of rag lying at his feet I cut from a young man whom I found dead outside my house in the civil war . . . The whole thing is, as proper, surmounted by a Union Jack. . . .'

Theo returned with a tray on which there were two chipped Crown Derby tea-cups, resting on white utility saucers, a battered tin tea-pot and what looked like a tea-cosy, made to resemble a thatched cottage out of coloured silks and raffia, standing not over the tea-pot but apparently on its own. He rummaged in a cupboard, scattering old magazines and letters to the floor, and at last produced a tin, with a Scottie painted on the lid, that contained petit-beurre biscuits, moist and crumbling with age.

'Milk?'

'Yes, please.' Then I realised that there was no milk jug on the tray. 'Oh, don't bother. I'd just as soon have it without.'

Theo gave a smirk. 'No. You shall have milk. I was hoping you would ask for it.' Deliberately he poured the tea, and then, with the theatrical assurance of a conjuror revealing some surprise, he plucked the tea-cosy off the tray between thumb and forefinger.

Next to the tea-pot there now stood a large and realistic phallus which Theo raised, in a pretence of nonchalance, and inclined towards my tea-cup. The milk trickled out, and as it did so, he glanced up at me mischievously from under his bushy eyebrows to see how I was taking the joke.

'But, Theo, where on earth did you get that object?'

'Peasant art, my dear. There was a man, in Peiraeus, who used to make them – alas, he's had a stroke, and his son, who has taken over from him, refuses to continue with that – er – line. It's charming, don't you think? And extremely practical. It unscrews here – rather like a cocktail shaker. Of course, the Greeks wouldn't use it for milk, but for ouzo.' Ruminatively he ran the knobbly fingers of one hand over the gold fronds; then he said: 'I used to have three. I gave one to the wife of the former French Ambassador, and one I sold to an insufferable American who said he wanted it for the Anthropological Museum at Mexico City – I never really believed him. But this is the biggest, so of course I kept it for myself . . . Do have another biscuit.'

'No, really, thank you.' One had been enough.

Theo sighed. 'That's a change I've noticed in the English. They used to eat tea; but now, when I have guests here, they never seem to want anything . . . I wonder how Götz is doing? Poor boy!'

As he began to speak of the German with a kind of paternal sorrow – of his ugliness, and goodness, and of the women who repaid his devotion with jeers or demands for cash or merely indifference – I realised, for the first time, the extent of Theo's affection for the other man. He liked Cecil, he liked me, I could see; but this was something different – obsessive, all-embracing, unremitting in its ardour.

'He has made a great difference to my life,' Theo said, 'I don't like being alone – I never have. When my wife first left me, I almost went mad.' I was startled; I had never guessed that Theo had been married. 'Cecil has, of course, been here off and on these last two months, but that is another thing. He lives his own life and leaves me to live mine. He's generous to me, so I really shouldn't object if he regards my home as a maison de passe. But Götz – Götz is different, quite different. You see, he *relies* on me: that is the important point. And I – I have come to rely on him. I don't simply mean, of course, that he does so much about the house or even that he's been such a help to me with my work. It's more than just that. We really understand each other.' He got up. 'Now let me play you the ninth movement of the Athens Concerto.' He opened the piano and, putting his left hand on his knee, began to rub it with his right. 'It was Götz who suggested this movement to me. Originally there were to be ten movements; now there will be eleven. This is to be called "The Tavern Dancers" and in the course of nineteen minutes you will hear – if you are clever – no less than sixty-nine popular tunes. Quite a tour de force, eh?' He continued to rub his hands gleefully as he spun round on the piano stool to face me. 'You may not believe this, but I never had a music lesson in my whole life. I'm entirely self-taught . . . Well, *andiamoe.*' He spun back on the stool and scrabbled some arpeggios. Then, breaking off: 'You must understand, firstly, that the work is still in a fluid state, and secondly, that I shall have to try to suggest to you the various instrumental parts. My scoring is most elaborate,' he added with a certain self-satisfaction. 'Ready – steady – go!'

(Frank Cauldwell, *The Firewalkers*, Murray)

★   ★   ★

ARABIA

The everlasting battle stripped from us care of our own lives or of others'. We had ropes about our necks, and on our heads prices which showed that the enemy intended hideous tortures for us if we were caught. Each day some of us passed; and the living knew themselves just sentient puppets on God's stage: indeed, our taskmaster was merciless, merciless, so long as our bruised feet could stagger forward on the road. The weak envied those tired enough to die; for success looked so remote, and failure a near and certain, if sharp, release from toil. We lived always in the stretch or sag of nerves, either on the crest or in the trough of waves of feeling. This impotency was bitter to us, and made us live only for the seen horizon, reckless what spite we inflicted or endured, since physical sensation showed itself meanly transient. Gusts of cruelty, perversions, lusts ran lightly over the surface without troubling us; for the moral laws which had seemed to hedge about these silly accidents must be yet fainter words. We had learned that there were pangs too sharp, griefs too deep, ecstasies too high for our finite selves to register. When emotion reached this pitch the mind choked; and memory went white till the circumstances were humdrum once more.

Such exaltation of thought, while it let adrift the spirit, and gave it licence in strange airs, lost it the old patient rule over the body. The body was too coarse to feel the utmost of our sorrows and our joys. Therefore, we abandoned it as rubbish: we left it below us to march forward, a breathing simulacrum, on its own unaided level, subject to influences from which in normal times our instincts would have shrunk. The men were young and sturdy; and hot flesh and blood unconsciously claimed a right in them and tormented their bellies with strange longings. Our privations and dangers fanned this virile heat, in

395

a climate as racking as can be conceived. We had no shut places to be alone in, no thick clothes to hide our nature. Man in all things lived candidly with man.

The Arab was by nature continent; and the use of universal marriage had nearly abolished irregular courses in his tribes. The public women of the rare settlements we encountered in our months of wandering would have been nothing to our numbers, even had their raddled meat been palatable to a man of healthy parts. In horror of such sordid commerce our youths began indifferently to slake one another's few needs in their own clean bodies – a cold convenience that, by comparison, seemed sexless and even pure. Later, some began to justify this sterile process, and swore that friends quivering together in the yielding sand with intimate hot limbs in supreme embrace, found there hidden in the darkness a sensual co-efficient of the mental passion which was welding our souls and spirits in one flaming effort. Several, thirsting to punish appetites they could not wholly prevent, took a savage pride in degrading the body, and offered themselves fiercely in any habit which promised physical pain or filth.

(T. E. Lawrence [1888–1935], *Seven Pillars of Wisdom*, Cape)

★   ★   ★

INDIA

J. R. ACKERLEY (1896–   ) This author's *Hindoo Holiday* is remembered by many as a little classic. It tells how the narrator spent some months as a young man acting as a sort of resident conversationalist and entertainer to the ruler of a small native state. The following extracts show His Highness's Greek proclivities.

'You know, Mr. Ackerley, I like the old times. I like the Greeks and Romans. I think of them always, always. I would like to have all my people dressed like Greeks and Romans. In my palace I keep a Greek toga, and when my friends in England used to come to stay with me and talk about those times, I would put on my toga and recline on my couch like this.' He laid the palm of one hand against his cheek, setting the other on his hip, and sank sideways into the corner of the car, which

pushed his hat rather tipsily to one side. 'And my friends would clap
their hands and say "The Greeks have been born again in Chhokrapur".'

.   .   .   .   .

'One day you shall come to my palace,' he said, 'and I will show the
Gods to you.'

I had heard of this entertainment from other sources, and had been
anxiously hoping for an invitation rarely extended to Europeans.

'I should like that very much,' I said.

'And you shall tell me which of the boys you like best.'

I readily agreed; and he was very pleased.

'Will you come the day after tomorrow?'

'Yes, whenever you like.'

'Or perhaps tomorrow late I could arrange something. If I can, I will
send a carriage for you.'

'That will be very nice,' I said. 'And will there be dancing?'

'Yes, yes. Music and dancing. And the boys will be dressed like the
Gods.'

'Will they paint their faces?'

'No, no paint. I have done away with paint. I don't like all this . . .
tattooing. But you must tell me which you like best.'

'Of course I will,' I said. 'Are they very beautiful?'

'Very beautiful. But you will see.'

'It will be good to see a beautiful face,' I said; 'for I haven't yet seen
one in Chhokrapur, and I've been looking about for a bearer for
myself. In fact, only yesterday, I was saying to your Tahsildar, "I want
a bearer, please, but he must be young and beautiful." '

'I have the son of my barber,' said His Highness. 'He works for me.
I will show him to you. He is very beautiful . . . fair but unreadable. I
call him the White Sphinx. He is sixteen, and has been with me for
two years; but he does nothing, nothing, but look at motors and go to
sleep.'

For some time after this he was thoughtful; then he asked: 'Haven't
you a saying in England, "No man can be a hero to his valet"?'

'Yes. Why?'

'I will tell you tomorrow,' he said mysteriously, and called for a
cigarette.

.   .   .   .   .

'Now the Gods are coming,' he said; 'and you must tell me which you like best.'

Immediately some servants came forward from the back and held outstretched between us and the scene a pretty blue velvet cloth, bordered with silver thread. The music began, a strange thrilling sound, accompanied by chanting; then the cloth was dropped, and Rama, one of the earthly manifestations of the God Vishnu, was revealed seated upon his throne with his wife Sita beside him. A maidservant stood on each side of the dais. All were boys. Rama was splendidly dressed in bright colours, a rose-coloured coat and gold silk trousers fastened round the ankles. He wore an enormous headdress and ropes of artificial pearls, and had a line of red and yellow paint down the bridge of his nose. Sita was also gilded, but not so gay, and wore a coronet. She sat in a heap with her chin on her chest, and looked very peevish. Both of them wore a single pearl suspended from the tips of their noses. The maidservants were also dressed in gold; they were very young, about twelve years old, and blinked self-consciously.

'What do you think of him? What do you think of him?' His Highness kept repeating.

'I don't think I'm very impressed by his personal appearance,' I said.

'No?' said His Highness, astonished.

'Will he dance?'

'No, he cannot dance.'

'May I go out and have a closer look?' – It was difficult to get a comprehensive view through the holes in the wall.

'Of course. But you must not smoke in front of the God, or tread on his carpet.'

The music still continued, repeating a perpetual phrase, but the Gods sat immovable. Then an elderly man dressed in female attire appeared upon the carpet in front of Rama. He wore a long heavy dark-blue silk shirt, a pink veil over his head and bells round his ankles. Addressing himself to the God, he performed a heel-and-toe dance, gyrating slowly with outstretched arms, and chanting.

I returned to ask the King who this personage was, but he gave me no opportunity.

'What do you think of him?' he at once asked, still referring to Rama.

I said I thought he had good physique but that he looked stupid, and I didn't think him very nice.

His Highness seemed very surprised at this, and rather pained.

could not have been more finely made, or have had limbs more beautifully proportioned and moulded. As Gamameda also displayed a peculiar talent as butler, and never allowed anyone else to open me a cocoa-nut or offer me a glass of palm-wine, it was no more than right that I should dub him Ganymede.

Among the many beautiful figures which move in the foreground of my memories of the paradise of Ceylon, Ganymede remains one of my dearest favourites. The poor boy, as a miserable outcast of the Rodiya caste, had been from his birth the object of the deepest contempt of his fellowmen, and subjected to every sort of brutality and ill-treatment. He was evidently as much surprised as delighted to find me willing to be kind to him from the first. . . . Not only did he fulfil his duties with the greatest attention and conscientiousness, but he developed a personal attachment and devotion to me which touched me deeply. . . . Hardly was I out of bed in the morning when he was standing before me with a freshly opened cocoa-nut, out of which he poured and offered me a cool morning draught of the milk. At dinner he never took his eyes off me, and always knew beforehand what I should want. When I was at work he cleaned my dissecting instruments and the lenses of the microscope. But Ganymede was never so happy as when I took him out in the cocoa-nut grove, or on the sea-shore, to paint and collect, shoot and fish. When I allowed him to carry my paint-box or photographic camera, my gun or a tin for botanical specimens, he would walk behind me radiant with satisfaction, and glancing proudly round him at the astonished Cinghalese, who looked upon him as an outcast Rodiya, and could not understand his having attained to such honour. My interpreter William was especially jealous and indignant; he took every opportunity of blackening Ganymede's character, but soon arrived at the conclusion that I would allow my favourite to come to no harm. I owe many beautiful and valuable contributions to my museum to Ganymede's unfailing zeal and dexterity. With the keen eye, the neat hand, and the supple agility of the Cinghalese youth, he could catch a fluttering moth or a gliding fish with equal promptitude; and his nimbleness was really amazing when, out hunting, he climbed the tall trees like a cat, or scrambled through the densest jungle to recover the prize I had killed.

. . . When eventually the time came for me to leave Belligam, my hardest duty of all was the parting from my faithful Ganymede; the poor lad wept bitterly, and implored me to take him with me to

'And you do not think he is beautiful?' he asked.
'No, I don't. Do you?'
'Of course; I think he is very beautiful.'
'How old is he?' I asked.
'Sixteen.'
'And what else does he do besides being a God?'
'Nothing. The Gods are not allowed to do any other work. And when they are seventeen years old they cannot be Gods any more.'
'What happens to them then?'
'They are all fools,' was all he said.

Meanwhile the dance had ended, the cloth was spread again, and when it was removed Rama had retired to be replaced by Krishna, with his favourite Gopi maiden, Radha, who was impersonated by the same boy who had played Sita. Krishna was a much nicer-looking boy than Rama, and I said so at once to His Highness's prompt and inevitable question . . . a reply which seemed to intensify his astonishment. Krishna was dressed in bright green and wore bells round his ankles, which indicated that he was not a lily of the field like Rama, but was able, at any rate, to spin; but he began his performance by singing from his throne in a pleasant, rather monotonous voice, gesticulating awkwardly from side to side with stiff brown hands. Then he rose to his feet and performed a fine exhilarating dance (in which the elderly 'lady', who was now seated in the 'wings' eventually joined), beginning with heel taps and slow, stiff, dignified gyrations, which got faster and faster until he sank to the carpet and whirled like a top on his knees. This excited me to applaud, until I remembered Rama, and stopped for fear of causing jealousy. This boy was replaced by another, also impersonating Krishna, while Radha still occupied the other chair and took no part, and apparently little interest, in the proceedings.

This third boy was dressed in dark-blue silk and was not at all attractive. He was stunted and had a tendency to spinal curvature; but he was said to act well in the play about to be performed.

.   .   .   .   .

'Did you like it?' asked His Highness.
'Yes, indeed! I thought it was all—'
'And which of the Gods did you like the best?'

'Krishna.'

'Hookah!' remarked the King.

'I beg your pardon?' I said.

But the remark was not addressed to me. From the shadows behind the *charpai*, where, unnoticed by me, he had been squatting, a white-turbaned servant rose and left the chamber by the other door, returning in a few moments with a hookah pipe, ready lighted, which he set on the ground by the spittoon, laying the stem upon the table.

I looked at him with interest.

He was young and tall, with big bony hands and feet, but his face was strikingly handsome – fairer than usual and lighted by large glowing eyes, which every now and then rested curiously upon me.

He returned to the shadows, moving silently; and then I noticed that the King was watching me. He had uncurled, and his little thin legs were dangling over the edge of the *charpai* above the brazier.

'That is the barber's son I spoke of,' he said, removing the stem of the hookah from his mouth. 'He is my personal servant – my valet. Do you like him?'

'Well, I've hardly seen him,' I said, 'but he seemed very handsome indeed.'

He opened wide his eyes, as though surprised.

'I will show him to you,' he said, and with a slight movement of his hand he brought the magnificent boy out of the shadows again into the patch of light which filtered through the reed blind. He moved noise-lessly into it and stood there facing me, motionless, expressionless, awaiting my inspection.

But I couldn't manage that – sitting there studying him as though he were a slave; so I hurriedly murmured my satisfaction, and another motion of the royal hand restored him to his shadows.

'Would you call him beautiful?' asked the King at once.

'Very beautiful,' I answered. 'More beautiful than any of your Gods.'

'Oh—h!' The filmy eyes widened again, 'More beautiful than Rama?'

'Yes, more beautiful than Rama.'

'Oh—h!'

(*Hindoo Holiday*, Chatto & Windus)

*   *   *

CEYLON

A SERVANT IN CEYLON

Of course I had acquired the best information procurable in Galle and Colombo as to the resources of Belligam, when once I had decided on fixing my zoological quarters there for a few months. But in spite of all my inquiries, I could learn very little beyond the facts that the village was very beautiful, situated in the midst of Cocos woods, that the sheltered bay was rich in corals, and that the government rest-house was tolerably good; on the negative side I was told that neither a single European nor any trace of European comfort or civilization was to be found there . . . So it was with excited anticipations that, on the morning of December 12th [1881], I mounted the light carriage which was to carry me along the south coast as far as Belligam.

. . . Charmed at first sight with the situation and idyllic surroundings of the rest-house, I eagerly proceeded up the side steps on the east-front to go inside. Here, at the bottom of the steps, I was met with another address, half in English and half in Pali, from the steward of my new quarters, the old rest-house keeper. . . . I was reminded of the well-known bust of Socrates, which in so many details resembles the head of a satyr; and as I could never remember my philosophical host's long Cinghalese name, I named him Socrates out of hand.

It really seemed as though I should be pursued by the familiar aspects of classical antiquity from the first moment of my arrival at my idyllic home. For, as Socrates led me up the steps into the open central hall of the rest-house, I saw before me, with uplifted arms in an attitude of prayer, a beautiful naked, brown figure, which could be nothing else than the famous statue of the 'Youth adoring'. How surprised I was when the graceful bronze statue suddenly came to life, and dropping his arms fell on his knees, and after raising his black eyes imploringly to my face bowed his handsome face so low at my feet that his long black hair fell on the floor! Socrates informed me that this boy was a Pariah, a member of the lowest caste, the Rodiyas, who had lost his parents at an early age, so he had taken pity on him. He was told off to my exclusive service. . . . In answer to the question what I was to call my new body-servant, the old man informed me that his name was Gamameda (from Gama, a village, and Meda, the middle). Of course, I immediately thought of Ganymede, for the favourite of Jove himself

Europe. In vain had I assured him many times before that it was
impossible, and told him of our chill climate and dull skies. He clung
to my knees and declared that he would follow me unhesitatingly
wherever I might take him. I was at last almost obliged to use force
to free myself from his embrace. I got into the carriage which was
waiting, and as I waved a last farewell to my friends I almost felt as if
I had been expelled from paradise.

(Ernst Haeckel [Professor of Zoology, University of Jena]
A Visit to Ceylon, tr. Clara Bell:
Kegan Paul, Trench & Co., 1883)

★ ★ ★

MALAYA

A SINGAPORE BAR

The bar is quiet enough for Terence to ask one of the soldiers if he
would like to see his photographs. These he produces from the large
drawer under the counter in which he seems to keep most of his
belongings. Terence as a sailor-boy, delicately tinted. Terence as
Carmen Miranda. Terence as a young man about town. Terence
simpering . . . He hands them over with a smile of extraordinary
sweetness which quickly fades as he waits for the expected compliment,
his eyes twitching nervously. Meanwhile the other soldier is trying to
bargain with Mrs. Lee for one of the pink plaster nudes 'draped' in a
swirl of silver paint which stand on the dusty top shelf. She isn't in
the least surprised that he wants to have it, reaches it down and places
it in front of him, naming a high price and never for one moment
relaxing her firm grip on its ornamental base. There it stands in all its
hideous insouciance: an odd rival to the various manifestations of
Terence nearby. Both in a sense represent art, but, while Terence's
soldier treats the big photographs in their gold frames with a great deal
of respect, his mate tries to grab the statuette, wheedling and jeering.
If it were later at night he would obviously regard it as something to
steal, not to buy, and I think he already feels conscious of this. After
Terence has shown both the portrait studies and a great many snapshots
(and some of the recent letters he has received from P. and O. liners
on their way home), he announces rather primly that it is time for

403

him 'to take his bath' and disappears, with a new set of clothes over his arm, to a mysterious cubbyhole beside the lavatory. I can't imagine what kind of bath is possible in so restricted a space and I have never heard the sound of a shower. However he certainly looks very fresh on his return. His trousers are spotlessly white and he wears a singlet of blue and white stripes which, although his chest is quite well developed, shows a rather too indolent line in front. His first job is to rectify this by much fussing with straps and buckles. He tightens himself into a wasp-waist and then, reassured about his figure, his arms come to life again and his hands flutter, as though he wished to gain security from the atmosphere around him, as though he wandered through petals and gossamer with admirers' glances made tangible, and flattery possessing the air like a south wind, and it is now that a great deal of hair-combing takes place, and an enormous bottle of eau-de-cologne is produced from the same drawer which contains the photographs. With this he perfumes his handkerchief and coquettishly dabs himself behind the ears.

(Patrick Anderson, *Snake Wine*, Chatto and Windus.)

★　　★　　★

THE SOUTH SEAS

The really curious way in which all the Polynesians are in the habit of making bosom friends at the shortest possible notice is deserving of remark. Although, among a people like the Tahitians, vitiated as they are by sophisticating influences, this custom has in most cases degenerated into a mere mercenary relation, it nevertheless had its origin in a fine, and in some instances, heroic sentiment, formerly entertained by their fathers.

In the annals of the island are examples of extravagant friendships, unsurpassed by the story of Damon and Pythias: in truth, much more wonderful; for, notwithstanding the devotion – even of life in some cases – to which they led, they were frequently entertained at first sight for some stranger from another island.

Filled with love and admiration for the first whites who came among them, the Polynesians could not testify the warmth of their emotions more strongly than by instantaneously making their abrupt proffer of friendship. Hence, in all old voyages we read of chiefs coming off from the shore in their canoes, and going through with strange antics, expressive of the desire. In the same way, their inferiors accosted the seamen; and thus the practice has continued in some islands down to the present day.

There is a small place, not many days' sail from Tahiti, and seldom visited by shipping, where the vessel touched to which I then happened to belong.

Of course, among the simple-hearted natives, we had a friend all round. Mine was Poky, a handsome youth, who never could do enough for me. Every morning at sunrise, his canoe came alongside loaded with fruits of all kinds; upon being emptied, it was secured by a line to the bowsprit, under which it lay all day long, ready at any time to carry its owner ashore on an errand.

Seeing him so indefatigable, I told Poky one day that I was a virtuoso in shells and curiosities of all kinds. That was enough; away he paddled for the head of the bay, and I never saw him again for twenty-four hours. The next morning, his canoe came gliding slowly along the shore with the full-leaved bough of a tree for a sail. For the purpose of keeping the things dry, he had also built a sort of platform just behind the prow, railed in with green wicker-work; and here was a heap of yellow bananas and cowree shells; young cocoa-nuts and antlers of red coral; two or three pieces of carved wood; a little pocket idol, black as jet, and rolls of printed tappa.

We were given a holiday; and upon going ashore, Poky, of course, was my companion and guide. For this, no mortal could be better qualified; his native country was not large, and he knew every inch of it. Gallanting me about, everyone was stopped and ceremoniously introduced to Poky's 'tayo karhowree nuee' or his particular white friend.

He showed me all the lions; but more than all, he took me to see a charming lioness – a young damsel – the daughter of a chief – the reputation of whose charm had spread to the neighbouring islands, and even brought suitors therefrom. . . .

Though there was no end to Poky's attentions, not a syllable did he ever breathe of reward; but sometimes he looked very knowing. At last the day came for sailing, and with it, also his canoe, loaded down to the gunwale with a sea stock of fruits. Giving him all I could spare from my chest, I went on deck to take my place at the windlass; for the anchor was weighing. Poky followed, and heaved with me at the same handspike.

The anchor was soon up; and away we went out of the bay with more than twenty shallops towing astern. At last they left us; but long as I could see him at all, there was Poky, standing alone and motionless in the bow of his canoe.

(Herman Melville [1819–1891], *Omoo*)

* * *

TAHITI

I was pleased with nothing so much as with the inhabitants. There is a mildness in the expression of their countenances which at once banishes the idea of a savage, and an intelligence which shows that they are advancing in civilization. The common people, when working, keep the upper part of their bodies quite naked; and it is then that the Tahitians are seen to advantage. They are very tall, broad-shouldered, athletic, and well-proportioned. It has been remarked that it requires little habit to make a dark skin more pleasing and natural to the eye of a European than his own colour. A white man bathing by the side of a Tahitian, was like a plant bleached by the gardener's art, compared with a fine dark green one growing vigorously in the open fields. Most of the men are tattooed, and the ornaments follow the curvature of the body so gracefully that they have a very elegant effect. One common pattern, varying in its details, is somewhat like the crown of a palm-tree. It springs from the central line of the back, and gracefully curls round both sides. The simile may be a fanciful one, but I thought the body of a man thus ornamented was like the trunk of a noble tree embraced by a delicate creeper.

. . . I was much disappointed in the personal appearance of the women. They are far inferior in every respect to the men.

(Charles Darwin, *Naturalist's Voyage Round The World*)

* * *

NORTH AMERICA

The Friendship which Wawatam testified for Henry the fur-trader, as described in the latter's *Adventures* so almost bare and leafless, yet not blossomless nor fruitless, is remembered with satisfaction and security.

The stern, imperturbable warrior, after fasting, solitude, and mortification of the body, comes to the white man's lodge and affirms that he is the white brother whom he saw in his dream, and adopts him henceforth. He buries the hatchet as it regards his Friend, and they hunt and feast and make maple-sugar together. 'Metals unite from fluxility; birds and beasts from motives of convenience; fools from fear and stupidity; and just men at sight.' If Wawatam would taste the 'white man's milk' with his tribe, or take his bowl of human broth made of the trader's fellow-countrymen, he first finds a place of safety for his Friend, whom he has rescued from a similar fate. At length, after a long winter of undisturbed and happy intercourse, in the family of the chieftain in the wilderness, hunting and fishing, they return in the spring to Michilimackinac to dispose of their furs; and it becomes necessary for Wawatam to take leave of his Friend at the Isle aux Outardes, when the latter, to avoid his enemies, proceeded to the Sault de Sainte Marie, supposing that they were to be separated for a short time only. 'We now exchanged farewells,' says Henry, 'with an emotion entirely reciprocal. I did not quit the lodge without the most grateful sense of the many acts of goodness which I had experienced in it, nor without the sincerest respect for the virtues which I had witnessed among its members. All the family accompanied me to the beach, and the canoe had no sooner put off than Wawatam commenced an address to the Kichi Manito, beseeching him to take care of me, his brother, till we should meet next. We had proceeded to too great a distance to allow of our hearing his voice before Wawatam had ceased to offer up his prayers.' We never hear of him again.

(H. D. Thoreau [1817–62]: *A Week On The Concord And Merrimac Rivers*)

*   *   *

THE ARCTIC

An apparition at the Post pulled me up one day with a shock of amazement. I am as well aware as the next man that sexual aberration knows no geography and no chronology, that inversion is a phenomenon observable in ancient as in modern times, in primitive as in civilized societies. Yet it was not in my thoughts that I should one day see a homosexual Eskimo; and if I put this man in my notebooks, and write about him now, it is not because of his aberration but because he was, in his repellent way, a singularly comic and glittering figure, at once loathsome and fascinating.

There was never such a master of pantomime as this infinitely strange, perpetually agitated, and yet extraordinarily self-possessed rogue who dropped in one afternoon from Back's River and was off again the next day. He seemed to take it for granted that neither Gibson nor I would understand his speech, for immediately on coming in he began to display his talent as mime, and he did it with obvious relish. He had no need of words: his face and hands sufficed him to paint for us his four days on the trail. He had run out of tea on the second day, and he wrote in sign language a poem of the brewing and drinking of his last cup. He had started with only a little coal-oil; and in a moment he was coaxing the last drop of oil out of an invisible tin, aping marvellously – how he did it I do not know – the very tin itself, showing us with his hands what emptiness was. He simulated the mangy dogs trotting with lowered heads and flopping ears, their rumps convulsed and tense with fear of the whip. He acted out for us the sled bumping and scraping over the pack ice for want of mud on its runners. Forgetting himself momentarily, he would speak rapid words, but his pantomime went faster than his words, and he would fasten his eyes on your face with the shrewdness and the childish self-satisfaction of an old actor, as if saying, 'Don't you admire the way I am doing this?'

Another thing: he looked exactly like portraits of Louis XIII; and not only did I sketch him, but fearing that my drawing might be the fruit of my imagination, I photographed him; and it was Louis XIII to the life who stared at me from the negative. A narrow strip of beard that looked half natural and half make-up, ran down his chin, and he was either all courtesies and scrapings, bowing forward with rounded back to leer at you while his hands went dismayingly over your person and he murmured over the beauty of your clothes, or he would straighten up abruptly, stick out his chest, and posture stiffly as if posing for his portrait.

In the South Seas I had come upon a Cannibal who was the spit and image of Robespierre. Here, at the other end of the earth, I saw before me a rakish Louis XIII who fumbled disgustingly with your clothes, paid you a thousand compliments accompanied by a thousand bows, and then let you know without a change of voice or visage that a little tin of solidified alcohol for his Primus stove was exactly what he

needed. Each broadside of compliments was so much artillery pre-
paration before the real attack, which spoke of three planks for his
sled, a plug of tobacco, another mug of tea. The Kabloona seems not to
be ripe. Let us try again. 'How warm your house is, how solidly built
this bench!' He aimed at random in every direction, and soon he ceased
to take pains with his discourse of seduction. The window was *na-mak-
to*, was very fine; everything became *na-mak-to*, as if the word must
make wonderful music in the white man's ear.

And then he would sit stiffly down, motionless in a sort of comical
dignity, while he watched you out of the corner of his eye. But his
hands never ceased from fluttering, and even in the air they did not
draw forms, they caressed them. His eyelids fell into folds when he
shut his eyes, and there was something about them both pink and
obscene. From where I sat, his eyes appeared to me like the eyes in a
primitive drawing – one staring straight ahead and the other seen only
in part, as in a face drawn in profile. It was absurd, grotesque: the
crow's feet at the eyes, the sly little goat's beard, the hands fluttering
at the end of arms too short; plump tiny hands that twitched, expressed
impatience, were reaching out for you and trying to cajole you, and
that in a skilfully graphic gesture were describing just what they
wanted – a package of cigarette paper. Thank you! He would put the
paper right into his pocket. There! And the man would sit down again,
and again he would fix you with those eyes, decide that you were
growing cool towards him, and start up his pantomime. What a
magnificent pipe that is you are smoking! What a pity that he had lost
his own pipe some weeks ago. (His pipe was most certainly in his
pocket.) Ah, how he loved to smoke a pipe!

To heighten the impression of inversion the man dragged along
with him, behind him, a child whose features were no less astonishing
than his own – a little Aiglon with romantic locks brushed across his
forehead and immense, incredibly ringed eyes that were a little
melancholy and rather protuberant. What was this? Was it a girl, a
boy? A boy, yes, said our Louis XIII, turning round to stroke the
passive forehead; and a very good trapper. He got two foxes the other
day. The word 'trapper' went very ill with the look of the boy, and I
was sure that the man was lying about his minion. As the evening wore
on, and the child began to droop with sleep, he refused to allow the
boy to go off to the igloo alone, explaining with inconceivable
gestures that they always slept together (gesture of rocking the child

N*–E

to sleep in his arms) and saying that the boy was never able to go to sleep without him.

Of what strange elements this scene was composed! Thirty below in a Post banked with six feet of snow; Louis XIII; l'Aiglon; the weaving of those lewd hands; the tin of alochol on the table; the child's astonishing eyes and girlish face contrasting so strangely with the rough clothes; Gibson's manifest and uneasy disgust. The whole thing was beyond words disconcerting, and I said to myself that next day, when this man and the child had moved off over the sea, had vanished into the infinity of the North, I should be perfectly right to believe that the whole thing had been a dream.

(Gontran de Poncins, *Kabloona*, Cape)

★   ★   ★

LOVE'S PRISON FLOWER

. . . In the large cage at the centre of the block, the men employed about the cell-house congregate in their idle moments. The shadows steal silently in and out of the inclosure, watchful of the approach of a guard. Within sounds the hum of subdued conversation. . . .

. . . In detail, my friend traces the various phases of his psychic development since his imprisonment (he is a qualified medical man). . . . For two years the very thought of such matters filled him with disgust.

For a moment George pauses. Presently he says: 'Aleck, I'm going to speak very frankly to you. I'm much interested in the subject. . . .

'As the months and years passed, my emotions manifested themselves . . . I wanted something to love. Somehow the thought of woman gradually faded from my mind. When I saw my wife, it was just like a dear friend. But I didn't feel toward her sexually. One day, as I was passing in the hall, I noticed a young boy. He had been in only a short time, and he was rosy-cheeked, with a smooth little face and sweet lips – he reminded me of a girl I used to court before I married. After that I frequently surprised myself thinking of the lad. I felt no desire toward him, except just to know him and get friendly. I became acquainted with him, and when he heard I was a medical man, he would often call to consult me about the stomach trouble he suffered.

Well, Aleck, I could hardly believe it myself, but I grew so fond of the boy, I was miserable when a day passed without my seeing him. I would take big chances to get near him. I was rangeman then, and he was assistant on a top tier. We often had opportunities to talk. I got him interested in literature, and advised him what to read, for he didn't know what to do with his time. He had a fine character, that boy, and he was bright and intelligent. At first it was only a liking for him, but it increased all the time, till I couldn't think of any woman. But don't misunderstand me, Aleck; it wasn't that I wanted a "kid". I swear to you, the other youths had no attraction for me whatever; but this boy – his name was Floyd – he became so dear to me, why, I used to give him everything I could get. I had a friendly guard, and he'd bring me fruit and things. Sometimes I'd just die to eat it, but I always gave it to Floyd. And, Aleck – you remember when I was down in the dungeon six days? Well, it was for the sake of that boy. He did something, and I took the blame on myself. And the last time – they kept me nine days chained up – I hit a fellow for abusing Floyd: he was small and couldn't defend himself. I did not realize it at the time, Aleck, but I know now that I was simply in love with the boy; wildly, madly in love. It came very gradually. For two years I loved him without the least taint of sex desire. It was the purest affection I ever felt in my life. It was all-absorbing, and I would have sacrificed my life for him if he had asked it. But by degrees the psychic stage began to manifest all the expressions of love between the opposite sexes. I remember the first time he kissed me. It was early in the morning; only the rangemen were out, and I stole up to his cell to give him a delicacy. He put both hands between the bars, and pressed his lips to mine. Aleck, I tell you, never in my life had I experienced such bliss as at that moment. It's five years ago, but it thrills me every time I think of it. It came suddenly; I didn't expect it. It was entirely spontaneous: our eyes met, and it seemed as if something drew us together. He told me he was very fond of me. From then on we became lovers. I used to neglect my work, and risk great danger to get a chance to kiss and embrace him. I grew terribly jealous, too, though I had no cause. I passed through every phase of a passionate love. With this difference, though – I felt a touch of the old disgust at the thought of actual sex contact. That I didn't do. It seemed to me a desecration of the boy, and of my love for him. But after a while that feeling also wore off, and I desired sexual relation with him. He said he loved me enough to do even that for me, though

411

he had never done it before. And yet, somehow I couldn't bring myself to do it; I loved the lad too much for it. Perhaps you will smile, Aleck, but it was real, true love. When Floyd was unexpectedly transferred to the other block, I felt that I would be the happiest man if I could only touch his hand again, or get one more kiss. You – you're laughing?' he asks abruptly, a touch of anxiety in his voice.

'No, George. I am grateful for your confidence. I think it is a wonderful thing; and, George – I had felt the same horror and disgust at these things, as you did. But now I think quite differently about them.'

'Really, Aleck? I'm glad you say so. Often I was troubled – is it viciousness or what, I wondered; but I could never talk to anyone about it. Yet I knew in my heart that it was a true, honest emotion.'

(Alexander Berkman: *Prison Memoirs of an Anarchist*, Mother Earth
Pub. Assn., New York, 1912)

IO

The School Story

Maxima debetur puero reverentia - certainly the boys' school makes a fascinating study, whether it be Arnold's Rugby or the Prep. from which Holden Caulfield is flunking out in *The Catcher in the Rye*. We have already quoted C. K. Scott Moncrieff's witticism: 'Like the pagan deities who have shrunk in peasant mythology to be elves and pooks and suchlike mannikins, these creatures, banished from the polite reading of the Victorians, reappeared instantly in that grotesque microcosm of life which the Victorians invented as an outlet for one of their tightest repressions, the School Story.' Such tales are usually regarded as being either pre- or post- Alec Waugh, whose *Loom of Youth*, written at the early age of seventeen, cast a critical but by no means savage eye on Sherborne, the school that as a monastic establishment prides itself on having trained King Alfred the Great. The friends of Mr. Green's beautifully written prep-school novel and of M. Peyrefitte's erudite and witty account of a college saturated with religion are all under fifteen, despite their independence and sophistication. To some readers this air of gem-like integrity will ring truer than the more conventional emotions of the older Maddox and David Blaize (or of the friends in the equally typical *Tell England*, not represented here); perhaps the more middle-class public schools, such as Mr. E. M. Forster's Sawston, tend to inhibit and sentimentalize, making innocence self-conscious and youth callow; both Mr. Cyril Connolly[1] and

[1] See *Enemies of Promise* (Penguin), both for an account of a platonic friendship and for a discussion of the Pre-Raphaelitism pervading Greek studies at Eton. Sex was 'the forbidden tree round which our little Eden dizzily revolved'.

Sir Lawrence Jones have different stories to tell of a freer school like Eton. Not that many boys, either young or old, meet anyone quite so formidably ambiguous as Father de Trennes. As two of M. Peyrefitte's characters put it, after the Father's expulsion: 'It was something to be woken up in the middle of the night to hear someone deliver a talk, incongruously, about beauty . . .' '. . . and, impurely, about purity'.

We start off with part of a wise essay by Waugh, then cast a look back at Shelley, Leigh Hunt and Disraeli, and forthwith proceed with a number of key passages (public and prep.) from the ever-increasing literature.

THE ROMANTIC FRIENDSHIP

A boy of seventeen is passing through a highly romantic period. His emotions are searching for a focus. He is filled with wild, impossible loyalties. He longs to surrender himself to some lost cause. He hungers for adventures. On occasions he even goes so far as to express himself in verse, an indiscretion that he will never subsequently commit. And what focus does a Public School provide for this eager emotionalism? There are the fierce contests of the football field, but they are, when all is said and done, the business of life, the cause for his existence. They are an enthusiasm he shares with three hundred others. He longs for something more intimate, more personal; he is, in fact, in love with love; he does not see a girl of his own age, of his own class, from one end of the term to the other; it is in human nature to accept the second best.

In this environment there is nothing unnatural about the attraction exercised by a small boy over an elder one. A small boy is the nearest approach possible to the feminine ideal. Indeed a small boy at a Public School has many of the characteristics that a man would hope and expect to find in a woman. He is small, weak, and stands in need of protection. He is remote as a woman is, in that he moves in a different circle of school life, with different friends, different troubles, different ambitions. He is an undiscovered country. The emotion experienced is genuine, and usually takes the elder boy by surprise. In a man's love for a woman there is often a degree of premeditation. A man looks at a woman and wonders if he could ever come to fall in love with her. As he walks homewards from her drawing-room he asks himself whether or not he is in love with her. He analyses his emotions; very often he persuades himself he is in love with her when in reality he is not. Either way he is prepared.

But the schoolboy is taken off his guard. He has not realised it is possible that he should fall in love with another boy. He has no previous experience which will enable him to recognise the symptoms. He has heard older boys spoken of as being 'keen' on someone or other, but he has associated such an assertion with the references in sermons to the corruption of a young mind. He does not, therefore, know what is happening when he finds himself becoming increasingly interested in some quite small boy. He has noticed him playing a plucky game on the Lower and has congratulated him. They have happened to meet on the way up from hall and have walked across together to the studies. They have smiled when they passed each other as they changed from one class-room to another in break. The elder boy is surprised: he is still more surprised when he finds himself frequently walking into the smaller boy's study on no very necessary errand, to borrow a book he does not want or to return a book he has borrowed; and that he should stop there to talk for an indefinite period. The day on which he has not seen or spoken to his small friend is empty for him. He does not understand his increasing wish for the company of an admittedly inferior person. But it is all very delightful. He is desperately anxious to appear in his best light. He makes strenuous, and often successful, efforts to abandon certain habits he has contracted. He may even work harder in form, and certainly he will make superhuman efforts on the football field, feeling that success will render him more attractive. He wonders what the small boy thinks of him, and persuades one whose social position lies midway between the two of them to make inquiries. The growing intimacy is a rich enchantment. He becomes curious, and, in a way, jealous of the life that his friend is leading; their standards, their environment, their friends are so different. He knows instinctively that one has more in common with one's contemporaries than with those who lie outside the circle of one's immediate interests, and this knowledge distresses him. There are times when he feels intensely miserable, others when he feels radiantly happy. At any rate he is living more intensely and less selfishly than he did before. He is on a distinctly higher plane of emotional tension.

(Alec Waugh, *Public School Life*, Collins, 1922)

SHELLEY'S CHILDHOOD FRIEND

I once had a friend whom an inextricable multitude of circumstances has forced me to treat with apparent neglect. To him I dedicate this essay. If he finds my own words condemn me, will he not forgive?

The nature of love and friendship is very little understood, and the distinction between them ill-established. This latter feeling – at least, a profound and sentimental attachment to one of the same sex, often precedes the former. It is not right to say, merely, that friendship is exempt from the smallest alloy of sensuality. It rejects, with disdain, all thoughts but those of an elevated and imaginative character. I remember forming an attachment of this kind at school. I cannot recall to my memory the precise epoch at which this took place, but I imagine it must have been at the age of eleven or twelve.

The object of these sentiments was a boy about my own age, of a character eminently generous, brave and gentle; and the elements of human feeling seemed to have been, from his birth, genially compounded within him. There was a delicacy and simplicity in his manners, inexpressibly attractive. It has never been my fortune to meet with him since schoolboy days; but either I confound my present recollections with the delusions of past feelings, or he is now a source of honour and utility to every one around him. The tones of his voice were so soft and winning, that every word pierced into my heart; and their pathos was so deep, that in listening to him the tears have involuntarily gushed from my eyes. Such was the being for whom I first experienced the sacred sentiments of friendship. I remember in my simplicity writing to my mother a long account of his admirable qualities and my own devoted attachment. I suppose she thought me out of wits, for she returned no answer to my letter. I remember we used to walk the whole play-hours up and down by some moss-covered palings, pouring out our hearts in youthful talk. We used to speak of the ladies, with whom we were in love, and I remember that our usual practice was to confirm each other in the everlasting fidelity, in which we had bound ourselves towards them, and towards each other. I recollect thinking my friend exquisitely beautiful. Every night, when we parted to go to bed, we kissed each other like children, as we still were.

(From a paper found after Shelley's death)

LEIGH HUNT AT CHRIST'S HOSPITAL

If I had reaped no other benefit from Christ's Hospital, the school would be ever dear to me from the recollection of the friendships I formed in it, and of the first heavenly taste it gave me of that most spiritual of the affections. I use the word 'heavenly' advisedly; and I call friendship the most spiritual of the affections, because even one's kindred, in partaking of our flesh and blood, become, in a manner, mixed up with our entire being. Not that I would disparage any other form of affection, worshipping, as I do, all forms of it, love in particular, which, in its highest state, is friendship and something more. But if ever I tasted a disembodied transport on earth it was in those friendships which I entertained at school, before I dreamt of any maturer feeling. I shall never forget the impression it first made on me. I loved my friend for his gentleness, his candour, his truth, his good repute, his freedom even from my own livelier manner, his calm and reasonable kindness. It was not any particular talent that attracted me to him, or anything striking whatsoever. I should say, in one word, it was his goodness. I doubt whether he ever had a conception of a tithe of the regard and respect I entertained for him; and I smile to think of the perplexity (though he never showed it) which he probably felt sometimes at my enthusiastic expressions; for I thought him a kind of angel. It is no exaggeration to say, that, take away the unspiritual part of it – the genius and the knowledge – and there is no height of conceit indulged in by the most romantic character in Shakespeare, which surpassed what I felt towards the merits I ascribed to him, and the delight which I took in his society. With the other boys I played antics, and rioted in fantastic jests; but in his society, or whenever I thought of him, I fell into a kind of Sabbath state of bliss; and I am sure I could have died for him.

I experienced this delightful affection towards three successive schoolfellows, till two of them had for some time gone out into the world and forgotten me; but it grew less with each, and in more than one instance became rivalled by a new set of emotions, especially in regard to the last, for I fell in love with his sister.

(Autobiography, The Cresset Press)

MILLBANK AND CONINGSBY

The influence of the individual is nowhere so sensible as at school. There the personal qualities strike without any intervening and counteracting causes. A gracious presence, noble sentiments, or a happy talent, make their way there at once, without preliminary enquiries as to what set they are in, or what family they are of, how much they have a year, or where they live. Now, on no spirit had the influence of Coningsby, already the favourite, and soon probably to become the idol, of the school, fallen more effectually than on that of Millbank, though it was an influence that no one could suspect except its votary or victim.

At school, friendship is a passion. It entrances the being; it tears the soul. All loves of after-life can never bring its rapture, or its wretchedness; no bliss so absorbing, no pangs of jealousy or despair so crushing and so keen! What tenderness and what devotion; what illimitable confidence; infinite revelations of inmost thoughts; what ecstatic present and romantic future; what bitter estrangements and what melting reconciliations; what scenes of wild recrimination, agitating explanations, passionate correspondence; what insane sensitiveness, and what frantic sensibility; what earthquakes of the heart and whirlwinds of the soul are confined in that simple phrase, a schoolboy's friendship! 'Tis some indefinite recollection of these mystic passages of their young emotion that makes grey-haired men mourn over the memory of their schoolboy days. It is a spell that can soften the acerbity of political warfare, and with its witchery can call forth a sigh even amid the callous bustle of fashionable saloons.

The secret of Millbank's life was a passionate admiration and affection for Coningsby. Pride, his natural reserve, and his father's injunctions [against courting the society of the aristocracy] had, however, hitherto successfully combined to restrain the slightest demonstration of these sentiments. Indeed, Coningsby and himself were never companions, except in school, or in some public game. The demeanour of Coningsby gave no encouragement to one, who, under any circumstances, would have required considerable invitation to open himself. So Millbank fed in silence on a cherished idea. It was his happiness to be in the same form, to join in the same sport, with Coningsby; occasionally to be thrown in unusual contact with him, to exchange slight and not unkind words. In their division they were rivals; Millbank sometimes triumphed, but to be vanquished by Coningsby was for him not without a degree of wild satisfaction. Not a gesture, not a phrase from Coningsby, that he did not watch and ponder over and treasure up. Coningsby was his model, alike in studies, in manners, or in pastimes; the aptest scholar, the gayest wit, the most graceful associate, the most accomplished playmate: his standard of the excellent.

(Disraeli, *Coningsby*, 1844)

TOM BRANGWEN

He was glad to leave school. It had not been unpleasant, he had enjoyed the companionship of the other youths, or had thought he enjoyed it, the time had passed very quickly, in endless activity. But he knew all the time that he was in an ignominious position, in this place of learning. He was aware of failure all the while, of incapacity. But he was too healthy and sanguine to be wretched, he was too much alive. Yet his soul was wretched almost to hopelessness.

He had loved one warm, clever boy who was frail in body, a consumptive type. The two had had an almost classic friendship, David and Jonathan, wherein Brangwen was the Jonathan, the server. But he had never felt equal with his friend, because the other's mind outpaced his, and left him ashamed, far in the rear. So the two boys went at once apart on leaving school. But Brangwen always remembered his friend that had been, kept him as a sort of light, a fine experience to remember.

(D. H. Lawrence, *The Rainbow*)

★ ★ ★

PRETTY WHITE-HANDED CURLY-HEADED BOYS

Tom took one hand out of his breeches-pocket and stuck it in his back hair for a scratch, giving his hat a tilt over his nose, his one method of invoking wisdom. He stared at the ground with a ludicrously puzzled look, and presently looked up and met East's eyes. That young gentleman slapped him on the back, and then put his arm round his shoulder as they strolled through the quadrangle together. 'Tom,' said he, 'blest if you ain't the best old fellow ever was – I do like to see you go into a thing. Hang it, I wish I could take things as you do – but I never can get higher than a joke. Everything's a joke. If I was going to be flogged next minute, I should be in a blue funk, but I couldn't help laughing at it for the life of me.'

'Brown and East, you go and fag for Jones on the great fives-court.'

'Hullo, tho', that's past a joke,' broke out East, springing at the young gentleman who addressed them and catching him by the collar. 'Here, Tommy, catch hold of him t'other side before he can holla.'

The youth was seized, and dragged struggling out of the quadrangle into the School-house Hall. He was one of the miserable little pretty white-handed curly-headed boys, petted and pampered by some of the big fellows, who wrote their verses for them, taught them to drink and use bad language, and did all they could to spoil them for everything[1] in this world and the next. One of the avocations in which these young gentlemen took particular delight, was in going about and getting fags for their protectors, when those heroes were playing any game. They carried about pencil and paper with them, putting down the names of all the boys they sent, always sending five times as many as were wanted, and getting all those thrashed who didn't go. The present youth belonged to a house which was very jealous of the School-house, and always picked out School-house fags when he could find them. However, this time he'd got the wrong sow by the ear. His captors slammed the great door of the Hall, and East put his back against it, while Tom gave the prisoner a shake-up, took away his list, and stood him up on the floor, while he proceeded leisurely to examine that document.

'Let me out, let me go!' screamed the boy in a furious passion. 'I'll go and tell Jones this minute, and he'll give you both the — thrashing you ever had.'

'Pretty little dear,' said East, patting the top of his hat; 'hark how he swears, Tom. Nicely brought-up young man, ain't he, I don't think.'

'Let me alone, — you!' roared the boy, foaming with rage and kicking at East, who quietly tripped him up, and deposited him on the floor in a place of safety.

'Gently, young fellow,' said he; ''taint improving for little whipper-snappers like you to be indulging in blasphemy; so you stop that, or you'll get something you won't like.'

'I'll have you both licked when I get out, that I will,' rejoined the boy, beginning to snivel.

[1] A kind and wise critic, and old Rugboean, notes here in the margin: 'The small friend system was not so utterly bad from 1841–47.' Before that, too, there were many noble friendships between big and little boys, but I can't strike out the passage; many boys will know why it is left in.

'Two can play at that game, mind you,' said Tom, who had finished his examination of the list. 'Now you just listen here. We've just come across the fives'-court, and Jones has four fags there already, two more than he wants. If he'd wanted us to change, he'd have stopped us himself. And here, you little blackguard, you've got seven names down on your list besides ours, and five of them School-house.' Tom walked up to him and jerked him on to his legs; he was by this time whining like a whipped puppy.

'Now just listen to me. We ain't going to fag for Jones. If you tell him you've sent us, we'll each of us give you such a thrashing as you'll remember.' And Tom tore up the list and threw the pieces into the fire.

(Thomas Hughes, *Tom Brown's Schooldays*, Dent)

THE FRIEND RESTORED

It was evening when the housekeeper summoned him to the sick-room. Arthur was lying on the sofa by the open window, through which the rays of the western sun stole gently, lighting up his white face and golden hair. Tom remembered a German picture of an angel which he knew; often had he thought how transparent and golden and spirit-like it was; and he shuddered to think how like it Arthur looked, and felt a shock as if his blood had all stopped short, as he realized how near the other world his friend must have been to look like that. Never till that moment had he felt how his little chum had twined himself round his heart-strings; and as he stole gently across the room, and knelt down, and put his arm round Arthur's head on the pillow, he felt ashamed and half angry at his own red and brown face, and the bounding sense of health and power which filled every fibre of his body, and made every movement of mere living a joy to him. He needn't have troubled himself, it was this very strength and power so different from his own which drew Arthur so to him.

Arthur laid his thin white hand, on which the blue veins stood out so plainly, on Tom's great brown fist, and smiled at him; and then looked out of the window again, as if he couldn't bear to lose a moment of the sunshine, into the tops of the great feathery elms, round which the rooks were circling and clanging, returned in flocks from their evening's foraging parties. The elms rustled, the sparrows in the ivy just outside the window chirped and fluttered about, quarrelling and making it up again; the rooks young and old talked in chorus, and the merry shouts of the boys, and the sweet click of the cricket-bats, came up cheerfully from below.

(Ibid.)

. . . . .

Tom was rattling on, half in joke, half in earnest, for he wanted to get Arthur out of his serious vein, thinking it would do him harm: but Arthur broke in:

'Oh, please, Tom, stop, or you'll drive all I had to say out of my head. And I'm already horribly afraid I'm going to make you angry.'

'Don't gammon, young 'un,' rejoined Tom (the use of the old name, dear to him from old recollections, made Arthur start and smile, and feel quite happy); you know you ain't afraid, and you've never made me angry since the first month we chummed together. Now I'm going to be quite sober for a quarter of an hour, which is more than I am once in a year, so make the most of it; heave ahead, and pitch into me right and left.'

'Dear Tom, I ain't going to pitch into you,' said Arthur piteously; 'and it seems so cocky in me to be advising you, who've been my backbone ever since I've been at Rugby, and have made the school a paradise to me. Ah, I see I shall never do it, unless I go head-over-heels at once, as you said when you taught me to swim. Tom, I want you to give up using vulgus-books and cribs.'

(Ibid)

★　　★　　★

WINTER PLAY

They walked farther into the hills, crossing a summit and down a valley and over the next hill. They met no one from the school, but at times they came upon a stray village boy with a desolate home-made sledge. They had been gone for more than an hour, trying their toboggan down slopes that were too uneven or slow or ended in stones where a wall had collapsed under drifts, and were following the top of a ridge. Randal felt hot under his sweater. They stopped and breathing hard looked down into a steep clough, which neither of them recognised. At the foot of its long slope, broken by a dip about half-way, was a rut of turbulent snow, the watercourse which had filled the combe. Bounding both sides on their right and damming the combe was a black beech wood.

'This should do. All right, Greco?'

'Yes.'

He looked down, where the air from below struck icily at his face as if it moved past them, then back at the empty wastes stretching on every side. The place was big and soundless. Their voices were lost in it.

'It's too far for the others,' he said.

He was alone with Felton on that wide platform where only the two tracks of their sledge marked the glittering expanse which filled their eyes. Randal wanted in all his actions to equal Felton so that he would not regret that he had brought him here instead of taking his sledge to Trelawney Hill. But Felton showed a disengaged friendliness towards him. As he bent to shorten the cords of the sledge, his quiet, even movements seemed unconscious of any time apart from Randal, of any place away from this combe and beech wood. Felton's life amid the school in which Randal believed he could never share, belonged now to another age. They seemed bound more closely by the absence of the others, and every gesture they made was for each other. Felton stood lifting the rope to him in his hand and looked down near him at the unpredictable descent into the hollow shade of the combe.

They had lost all count of their falls past the black edge of the wood, Felton grasping Randal's arms, with one hand tight on the cords, and steering in some wonderful way behind him. The wry jerk in the blood as they ricocheted across the dip, the solemnity of their entry into the shade, were now anticipated by them, infallible as forest trackers. The pause when the sledge lay dead by the frozen stream was longer. When Randal leaned across Felton to gather the cords he saw again the thick sweater which covered him. He saw the knitted wool, the pattern of close-packed ears of corn. His arm as he stretched for the ropes was heavy, for he could have touched and held the shoulders where the wool was reefed like corn.

They were slower as they dragged up the sledge, their feet trudging through the drifts of snow and leaves near the wood. The shade from the combe had spread its deepening grey over the hills and a pink glow showed where the sun had set. They reached the top of the slope where the snow was powdery under the sledge. Against the faintly cracking trees and the shrubs hung with the frosted scarfs of Old Man's Beard, Felton stood and listened, as if the freezing air tinkled whilst it narrowed its darkening snow-wrack unrecognisably round them. On that high plateau, decked with its motionless white wreaths and garlands, nothing was in sight but the snow and the long wood.

'It's begun to freeze,' Felton said. 'One last run, Greco. Then we'll turn back.'

Randal had felt no dread in the lateness gathering in these hills, farther than he had ever been from the school, nor in the speed of the sledge, for he had lodged all fear in Felton's safe confidence. But when they turned back, this day with Felton which had seemed a world, endless and without beginning, would be lost unless he could keep some part, a secret talisman, for ever.

'Jump on, Greco.'

He climbed on the sledge. Felton held him, and pushed gradually forward by his heels making purple gashes in the snow. Randal felt wholly aware of this last ride. He willed that it might never end.

'All set – we're off.'

The sledge fell towards the dusk far below. The swiftness quickened his veins, making his eyes shine like a gazelle's in danger as he glanced back at Felton whirling past the unending barrier of the wood. The threat to their day slid like a weight to the edge of his mind. He closed his eyes and felt against his head the warm firm sweater covering Felton's body. The weight which he had been forced to hold revolved and fell. He released his grip against the speed and was held by Felton entirely, alone with him, Felton, alone on the falling sledge. He seemed to fall into sleep against his body, holding him safe, flying with him as on a swan's back through a world of space. Once long ago he had slept in Kit's arms on a drive through the night. He was drawn by Felton's arm tightly back to him and with one lift of the sledge they were across the dip. He laid his head against the wool of Felton's shoulder. The cool of the valley closed over them. With the thought 'This is the end' came a longing to die there.

The sledge lay still. Randal could feel himself heavy in Felton's arms. He turned, his feet dropping from the sledge. His hand closed over Felton's fingers crooked round the cord on the boards, and he pressed his face into the thick collar of the sweater. His breath made the wool damp. He raised his head and gazed into Felton's face, beautiful and firm in the strange reflection of the snow. It was terribly close to him under the short bright hair. The snow was chill in his shoes. Time was endless where he gazed at Felton and was held by him in his arms. He need never move. The darkening and glistening snow lay round them for a still instant in the silent combe. Felton rose. He steadied Randal, pressing his hands on his shoulders, and kept him on the sledge.

'Stay there, Greco,' he said, 'I'll pull you back. It won't be long.'

He pulled Randal on the sledge along the combe. As it grew dark he became a vague figure coming into consciousness and away like an animal suddenly near and lost again on the hillside. The steep hills held back the sky and the first stars over their slow progress. Randal finally lost the figure but his eyes rimmed with tiredness followed the feet heavy with snow and the now known and half-clenched hands which were drawing the twisted ropes. All the way back to the school, moving on the sledge through the night of snow, Randal watched the hands. He watched them as a duty and a right, thinking of nothing else.

They came to the terrace. They stood together in the night and saw the massed fanfare of lights which blazed from all the windows, and heard behind it the echoing stampede down the corridors and stairs.

'We're late,' Felton said. 'You can sit by me.'

Randal felt no embarrassment as he sat by Felton at the prefects' table, seeing for the first time whilst he ate his tea the lit length of the bright and noisy hall. . . . Across the table Harding recounted the excitements of Trelawney Hill as if they had been exempt from some affair in which the whole school had been involved. Felton seemed to hear these accidents against an alien impression which he shared only with Randal. They seemed like two boys who had descended from an alpine mission, keeping in their eyes and gestures the echo of a solitude which none in the populous valleys could have known. Before Felton answered them he glanced at Randal, and together they laughed.

(G. F. Green, *In The Making*, Peter Davies, 1952)

DORMITORY

. . . Then he went to the door, opened it and closed it softly behind him. He groped his way down the passage. His eyes were full of darkness and he moved purposefully like a sleep-walker. He went down the narrow stairs. From the end of the dormitory corridor the gas jet flickered along the beeswaxed floor. He walked toward it. He saw his striped flannel pyjamas and his bare feet in the stream of light.

. . . He pushed open the door and went into the dormitory.

A faint light fell from the open windows on the two rows of beds. He went to the prefect's bed at the far end of the room where Felton slept. He stood beside him. Felton was turned away and his fair hair was brushed from the cold light of a window. His throat was bare. His lips were parted in his sleep and his smooth and even face was fresh with the cool breeze, which did not stir the lashes of his closed eyelids. Shadow lay under his eyes and at the corners of his mouth and in the dent of the pillow beneath his head. A hand held the sheet against his bared chest through the unbuttoned jacket of his pyjamas, and the creases of his loosely curved fingers showed minutely with the marks of dirt in his small square finger-nails. He had only the sheet over him because of the warmth and his straight and relaxed body showed in the half light as if he were naked. Randal gazed at Felton, where he had never before seen him, with an intensity and for so long that he seemed to dream of him. His eyes hurt with the desire to end Felton and at the same time wholly to possess him, until at last they drew him to where he lay. He sank on the bed with his arms on either side of Felton. He laid his hand across the mouth for silence, and the lips were full and soft against his palm. He slid his hands over the flutter of the eyelids to cover the eyes. The nose and mouth were clear under his mask of hands. Felton gripped his wrists and drew back his fingers into the thick hair. He thus pulled Randal on to him, and he lay over Felton's firm body and felt his warmth beat upwards to him. His hands were clenched in the ruffled hair and he gazed absorbed into Felton's eyes. The blood knocked through his body and blinded him. He pressed his lips on Felton's mouth. Felton stirred, and Randal remained motionless. His search and his desire were for the instant forgotten for they had momentarily become that action.

(*Ibid.*)

* * *

HAPPY THOSE EARLY DAYS WHEN I
SHIN'D IN MY ANGEL INFANCY

'I know boys,' the Father continued. 'And that knowledge has made me understand a Greek sophism – that snow is black. What an illusion is their candour! Some of them will accuse themselves, at the tribunal of penitence, of nothing worse than being too fond of jam, while practising sins without name – such sins as St. Paul would not – and how rightly – have so much as mentioned among Christians. It is, perhaps, only to prove that St. Paul was right that the boys in question, while practising these very sins, prefer not to mention them, at least to their director of conscience.

'I was exasperated, on Saturday, as I watched your schoolfellows coming back from confession, all perfectly cool and collected. What I saw in their faces was not the soul's peace, but the triumph of perversity. And indeed the hour of confession, when the whole secret life of this college should be laid bare, is, instead, the hour of utter fraud. My colleagues are not altogether to blame: how can a man who has never been a boy himself, not a real one, a man who has crushed the boy in himself by force of will and prayer, know how to question a boy? Occasions for sinning are so numerous – seven times a day for the righteous, according to scripture. And boys are so very unlike the righteous! They sin in their thoughts even more often than men, for they have more leisure and are more observant – yes, in their thoughts, by sight, hearing, when they cannot sin *de facto*.

'You have probably read neither the *Confessions* of St. Augustine, nor those of St. Peter Canisius, nor, certainly the *Benedictine Customs* of Bec and Cluny.

'St. Augustine, having given us some indications of the misdemeanours he committed with his playmates as a boy, adds the following, which reveals a great deal more: "Is this the supposed innocence of children? There is none such in them, Lord; my God" – he repeats himself – "there is none, and even today I ask Your forgiveness for having been one of those innocents." He concludes with a passage which is still stronger, although somewhat strange: it is to the effect that, in his opinion, when Our Lord declares that the Kingdom of Heaven shall belong to those who are like little children, he is not putting forward their supposed innocence as a model of virtue, but only their small size as a symbol of humility.

'That, then, is what the Father of the Latin Church has to say about it. St. Peter Canisius, who, in the sixteenth century, was one of the reformers of Catholic education, is even more shattering in his admission of the errors and evil communications of his childhood; but it is perhaps as well to make some allowance of the holy exaggerations of humility. I confine myself to quoting his pertinent conclusion: "Lord, open the eyes of the teachers of our youth, that they may cease to be blind guides."

'In the Middle Ages the monks of St. Benedict had meditated St. Augustine's remarks and forestalled the prayer of St. Peter Canisius. This is proved by the rules in their schools. There is, for example, the following: "Wherever the boys may be, they are forbidden to draw too near to each other . . ." "In class, each boy must be given a separate seat, instead of a bench in common for all." Each pupil was never out of sight of his pedagogue, who slept in a bed beside the boy, at night.

'Nowadays, childish innocence is fashionable. Here, as elsewhere, this prejudice, favourable to every charming hypocrite, reigns supreme. The rules, like the laws, are unanimous in drawing their inspiration, in this article, from the celebrated *Maxima debetur puero reverentia*. This formula, which we owe to Juvenal, as you know, sums up the moral doctrine which Christendom inherited from the pagan world on the problem of childhood. Perhaps you have read Greek and Latin authors elsewhere than at St. Claude's. If you have not you will be apt to believe, following the worthy Juvenal, that children, in antiquity, were so respectable that they were notably worthy of respect. Yet, though I have been able to hint to you, without excessive shame, what the childhood of two great saints was like, I should hesitate to speak of the childhood of the greatest men of antiquity. And let us not blame nature for all these miseries: for all this is the fault of original sin.

'All of which, my dear Georges, will serve to show you how fragile a virtue is chastity. In the Life of St. Bernardin of Siena, we read that "nobody, to whom God has not granted the gift of chastity, could be chaste". But he says, also, that before He favours us with that gift, He requires that we ask it of Him. And even to that end we have to be able to ask it and to know how to ask it.

'Such thoroughness is rather beyond the strength of a boy of your age. If you remain alone, I mean without help against either yourself or others, you will succumb. It is necessary that an attentive and friendly eye keep watch over your heart. I will provide that eye.'

He smiled at his own words, and rose.

'Good night,' he said, pressing Georges' hand. 'Naturally, the offer I have just made you applies equally to your friend. Let us be three friends together.'

(Roger Peyrefitte, *Special Friendships*, tr. Edward Hyams, Secker & Warburg)

ASSIGNATION

Alexander arrived at the conservatory still animated by the pleasure of the afternoon's expedition. His hair was rather untidy. Followed the pleasure of combing it – an operation which was now a permanent feature of their meetings.

His class had gone botanising in the woods. To Georges he said, 'The flowers I gathered were for you. As I picked them I was saying. "These violets are for him, and these lilies of the valley and this red squill – for him." And here they are!'

He pulled a small bouquet from his pocket.

'It's a pity,' he went on, 'that it's wilted a bit. There's a spray of wistaria, too. I picked it on the way back, near a house.'

Hyacinth and wistaria were truly *ben trovato*; it was as if the boy had guessed what flowers in another conservatory had been put into the envelope of his letter. Georges told him of it and, since it came aptly, recounted the legend of the beautiful Hyacinth from which came Apollo's name of Hyacinthian.

Laughing, Alexander said, 'We will call the red squill *Hyacinthus Georgianus*. I am very good at botany; as good as you in mythology. You've told me what a hyacinth is, but do you know what *Taraxacum* is? What, has the cat got your tongue? It's a dandelion. In my botany book I write the Latin names in red ink, so as to remember them better.'

'Red is certainly our colour. By the way, I almost forgot my good wishes for your day – it's May 3rd, which, according to the *Martyrology*, is St. Alexander's. I should have brought *you* a bouquet. You will have to make do with flowers of rhetoric. Oh, and incidentally, I discovered from my prayer-book that September 11th, your birthday, is the feast of St. Hyacinth, Martyr. You are hyacinth in both our religions.'

'Yes, but in both cases my blood gets spilt. Perhaps that's why red is my colour? I should have thought twice before adopting your tie.'

Georges smiled.

'The colour has another meaning – in fact, two. I made a kind of allusion to the fact at our first meeting. The *Song of Songs* – I'm always talking to you about it! – teaches us that "love has lamps of fire and flames" – that is, it is red. Besides which, in the Bible, sins are always scarlet – remember that preacher quoting the passage? Love, or sin – that was the choice confronting us; we made the better choice.'

'But we didn't choose either. We chose friendship.'

'What does the word matter? It means being fond of each other. In your notes, your canticle, and your letter, you said you loved me.'

'I write it. I don't say it.'

'But you do – in despite of yourself, for you're blushing. Another red – the red of admission. But I hadn't finished with St. Alexander.

'At meditation yesterday I was pleased when the Superior spoke of "that great Pope, St. Alexander, who governed the Church in the reign of the emperor Hadrian". Well, that Sunday when you sensed me I remember thinking that you might become Pope if you wanted to, I had no idea that you *had* been already. In the *Roman History* which the Superior lent me, I read that the emperor Hadrian had a young favourite called Antinous, whose beauty became famous – like Alexander himself – Alexander the Great, not the great Pope. And temples were erected to Antinous, after his death, as to Hyacinthus. I thought that had I been a Roman emperor and you my friend, I would have built temples for you, but during your lifetime, so that you would have been a god on earth. That would have been better than being Pope. These were the things I was thinking of during meditation: Antinous made me love St. Alexander, as Alexander had made me love Alexis, in one of Virgil's eclogues.'

'Juventius, Antinous, Alexis, Hyacinthus,' said Alexander, counting on his fingers. 'There are four of us.'

(*Ibid.*)

BATHE

The boys scattered among the trees to change into bathing-slips, clad in which they shortly began to reappear. Georges looked at them in surprise. He hardly recognised them, never having seen them in this guise before; for showers were taken in single cubicles, and dormitory behaviour was extremely modest. But now even the physically ill-endowed were not wanting in grace: it was as if they were trying to bear themselves more handsomely in honour of the sun and their companions. One, usually so hideously awkward, was now trans-figured; another, as a rule so clumsy in his clothes, yet trod the grass with style. And all the boys came running up at last, happy at being out of their clothes, free, proud, and almost insolent. And they seemed to take pleasure in putting off the moment when the water would hide their bodies. They leaped, turned somersaults, barged and wrestled each other on the improvised palestra provided by the turf. Until, at last, in one leap, they were all in the water, sending up a great spout of spray. Lucien went with them, but Georges sat down on the bank, his legs crossed under him: he was the scribe, about to observe and note their games. Here, at last, were Gymnopaediae.

The Supervisor, moreover, seemed equally unable to recognise his charges in these wild and naked young creatures, so that he considered himself deprived of authority over them. He went off gathering flowers and pretended to be seeing nothing. Then putting, no doubt, his faith in God, he sat down at the foot of a tree. He crossed himself and began to read his prayers, like some saint set down by devils in the very midst of a bacchanalia.

Yet what was going forward beside him was an eternal rite, the rite of the bath. This rite had not, like the processions, the object of ensur-ing the fruits of the earth, but that, rather, of exposing the fruits of young bodies. The boys of St. Claude's had returned as one to nature, their element.

The divers, gathered together upon a rock, raised their arms in an invocation, and then dived, each, religiously, in his proper order. Some swam as they listed; others raced. A few glided just below the surface, or swam under water, only their glistening behinds breaking surface. There were others who let themselves sink, supine, only to emerge suddenly and violently, like young tritons, spouting water. Others, to tease the Father – but he was as devoid of eyes as of ears – pulled off their slips and then shouted that they had lost them. Lucien, a prey to the general madness, gambolled in the stream, beat its surface with his hands, turned somersaults in the water, drunk with the joy simply of being. And even Georges, for a while, loved his college, since it could yield such moments . . .

.   .   .   .   .

With what feverish haste, inspired by the spectacle of their elders, did the new arrival of bathers pull off their clothes! The first to be ready were already running up, yet their ardour was checked by hesitation: they shivered a little in the breeze, tested the water with their toes, crouched to wet hands and arms and even torsos. Others came up, bolder spirits, and plunged in without hesitating, splashing the timid. Then, like their elders, they became possessed of a sort of delirium; playing and fighting, they moved farther away.

Georges had not been less surprised by this spectacle than by the first one. He would never have believed that life radiated from every one of these puny schoolboys with such sweetness and such strength. But he was, likewise, aware that their nudity was misleading: these boys, the oldest as well as the youngest, had not put off all their veils. Those bodies, which they flaunted so shamelessly, yet remained their own private mysteries. In this college, where priestly masters never ceased from talking to them of God, each boy was his own priest, if not, indeed, his own god, sowing his own religion: each, then, a worthy continuator of those sacerdotal roles which the Greeks entrusted to boys.

But suddenly there were no more sights to observe, and no more thoughts: only a person. Crossing the meadow, among the willows, Alexander was drawing near, wearing a blue bathing-slip. He had picked a red gladiolus and was amusing himself, as he walked, by trying to balance it upright on the palm of his hand. The thin gold chain danced about his neck. He was borne up by the sun's rays, for the grass-blades barely bent beneath his feet. Georges had never dreamed of a more exquisite vision, and he whispered to himself, 'All my life, I shall remember that I have seen this, that this happened.'

Alexander, who was alone, had drawn near to the trees, facing those which concealed Georges. It was almost as if they had chosen the place for a meeting. They could not help but meet. Now Alexander was staring towards the senior boys, no doubt hoping to see Georges. But Georges, eager to go on feasting his eyes, preferred not to show himself yet. The idea that his own image was, at the moment, filling the mind's eye in that fair head across the river was intoxicating; as was the realisation that, in a moment, when he chose, they would be revealed to each other. Today was a feast-day in very truth, making up for the imaginary quality of the one which, on the second day of Rogations, Georges had conjured into existence and set under the skies which had looked down upon Hyacinthus.

Now, Alexander was looking the other way, towards his own division of the school. He stood with his right arm raised and pressing against the inclined trunk of a tree, while from his other hand the gladiolus hung down to his feet. *In thy splendour and thy beauty, come, triumph and reign.* Surely the liturgical text had been written in anticipation of this moment of glory. But what Georges was admiring was not only, as in other boys – a thousand times more than in other boys – an enchanting outward seeming; it was not, now, simply the Thespis Cupid. It was the divine incarnation of a soul divine, a mind altogether above the boy's age, and a heart full of strength, honesty and friendship.

(*Ibid.*)